# #48 Chaos & Netherworld I

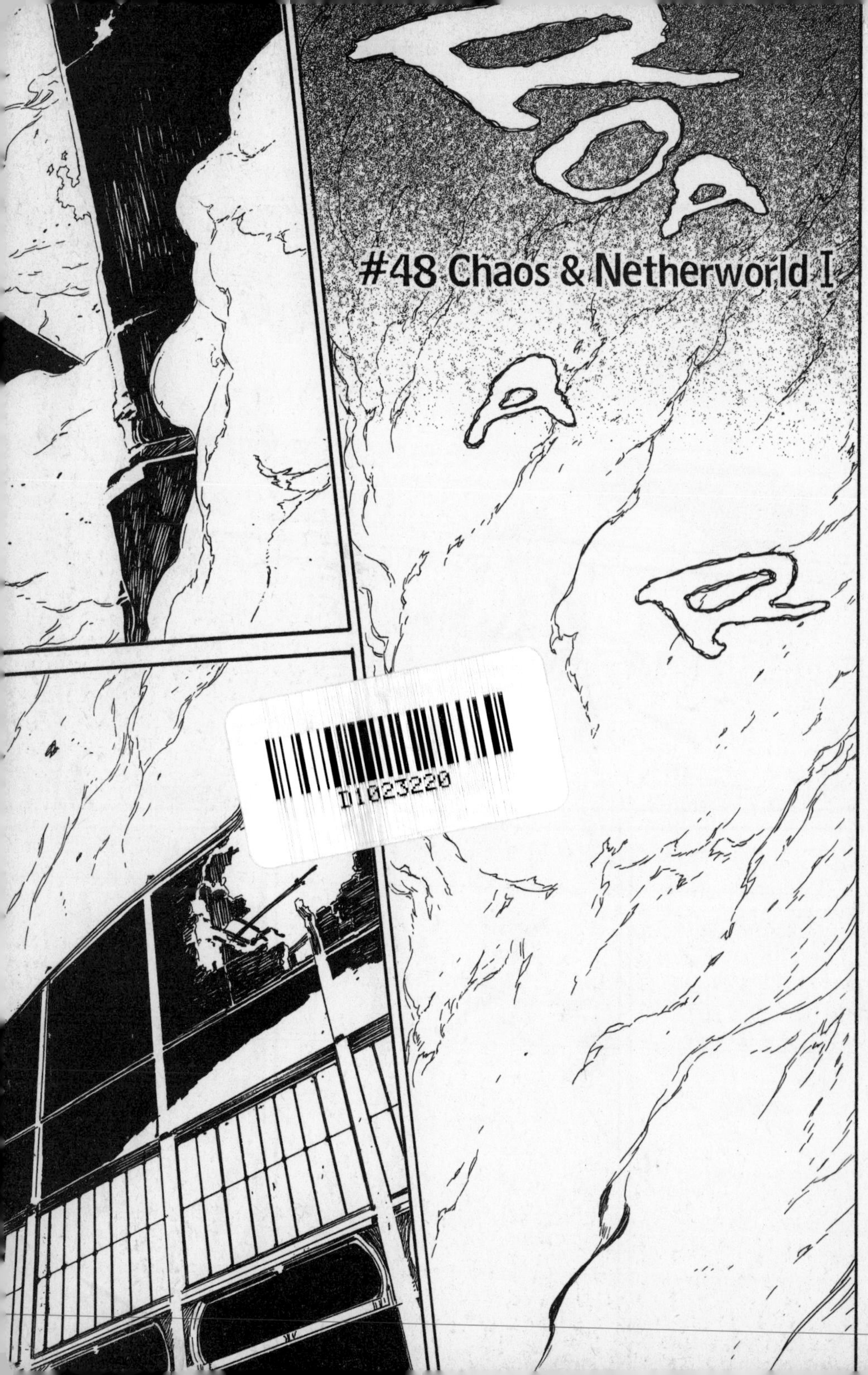

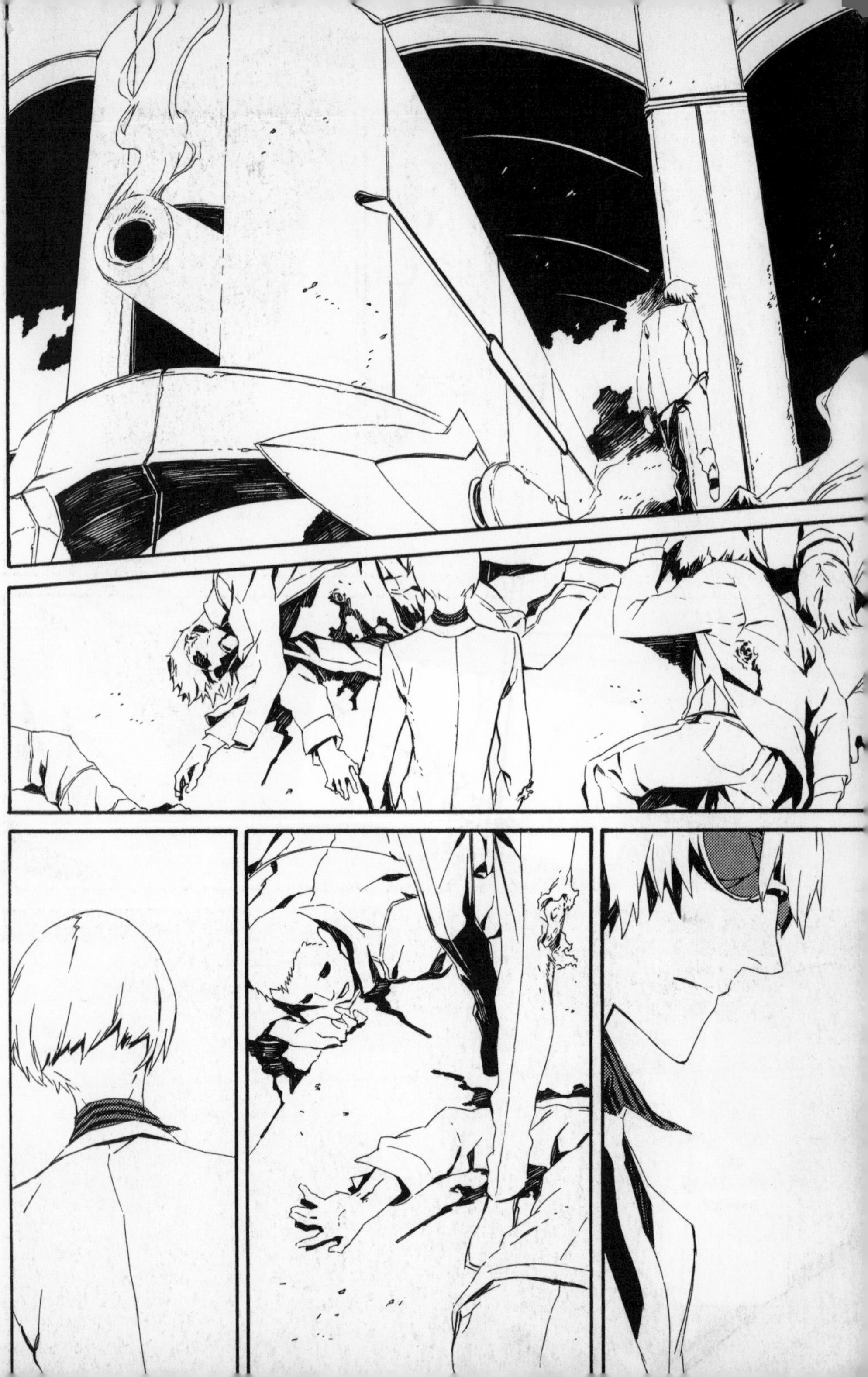

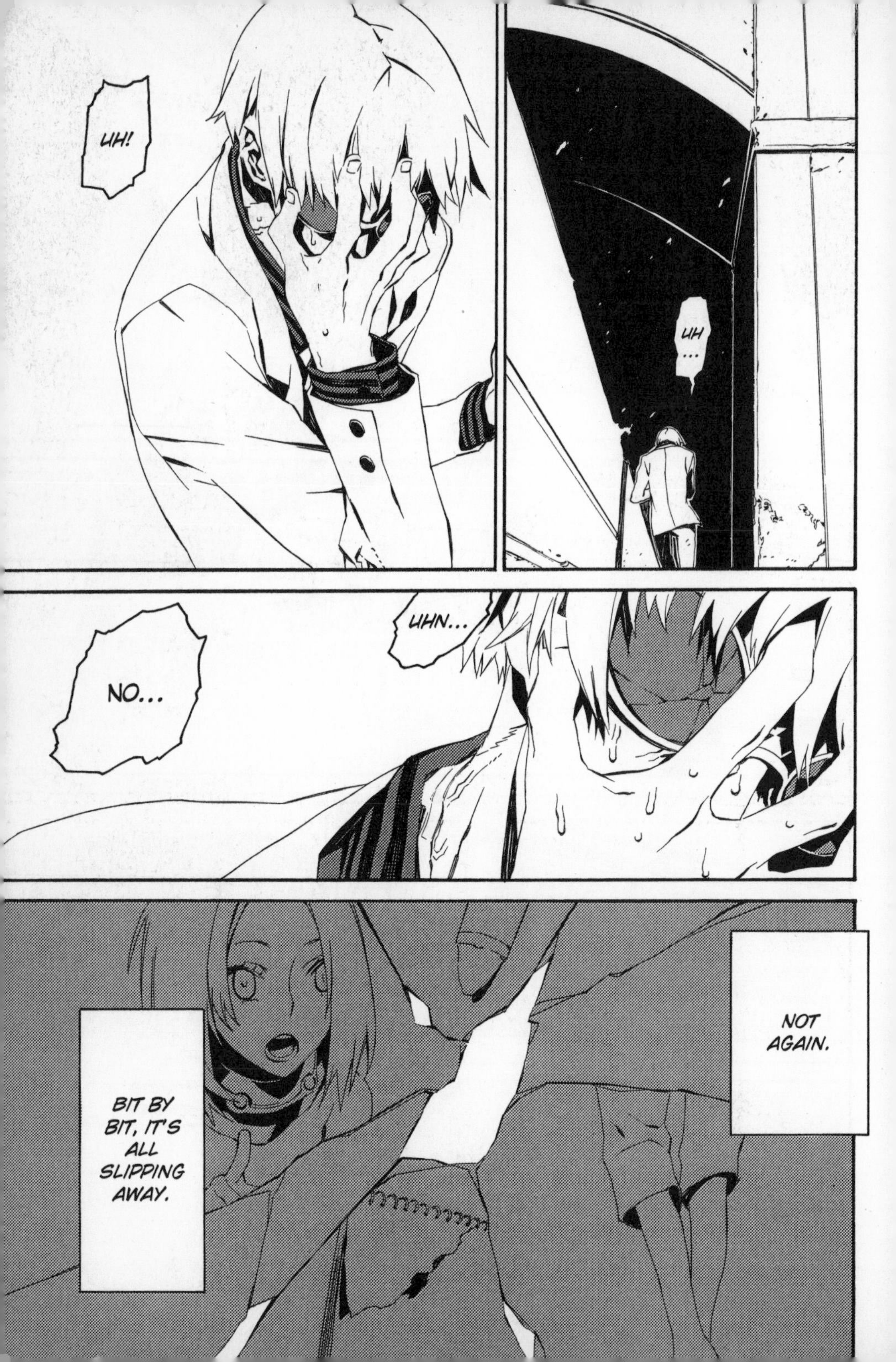
UH...
UH!
UHN...
NO...
NOT AGAIN.
BIT BY BIT, IT'S ALL SLIPPING AWAY.

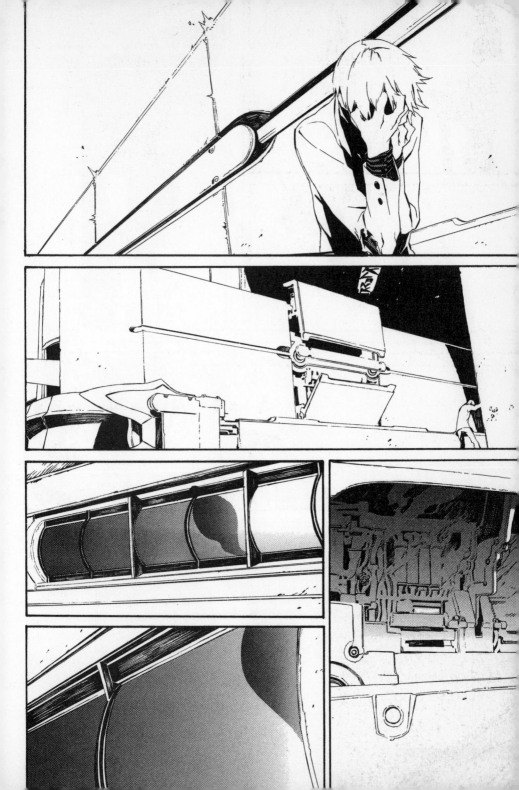

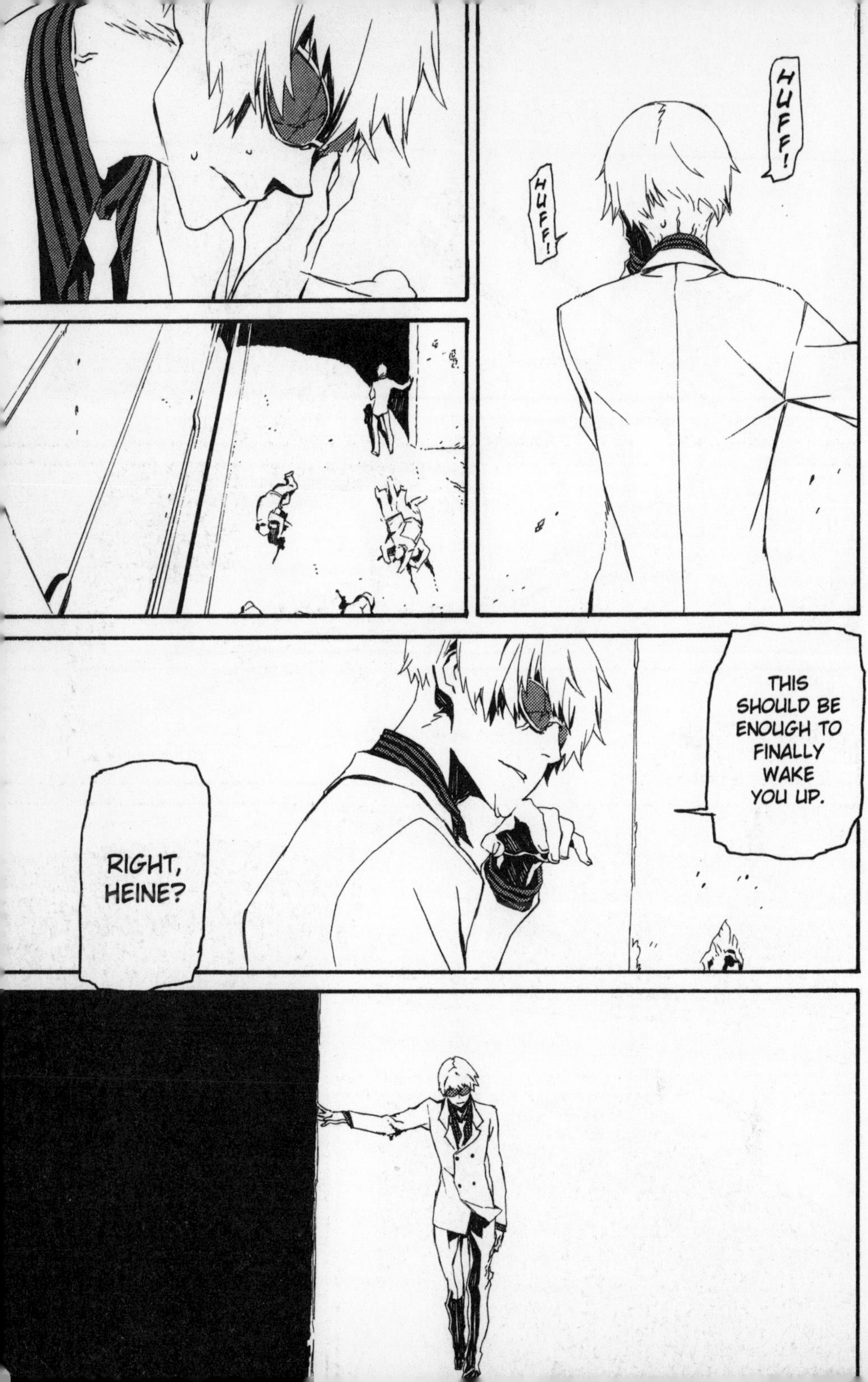
HUFF!
HUFF!
THIS SHOULD BE ENOUGH TO FINALLY WAKE YOU UP.
RIGHT, HEINE?

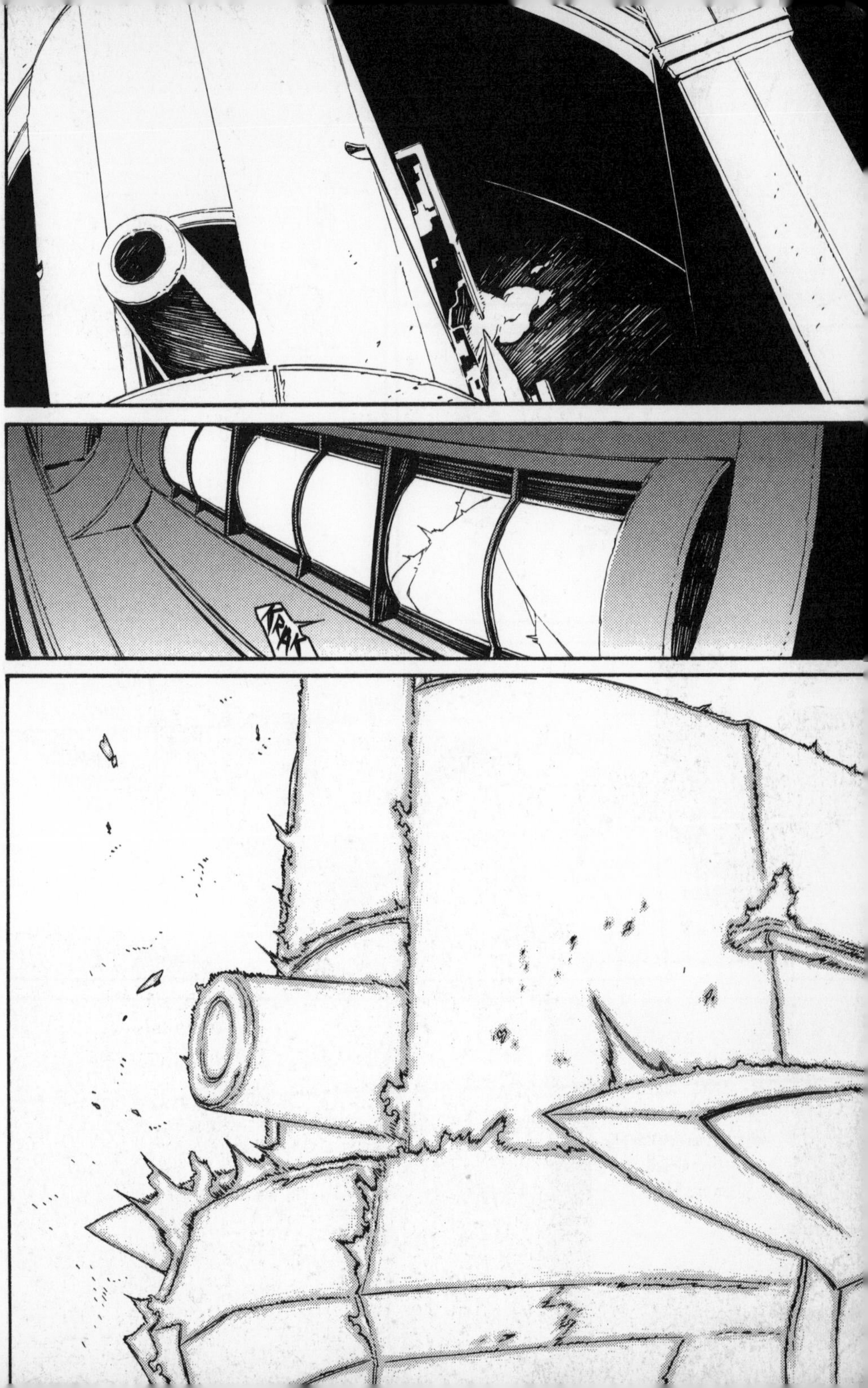
KRAK

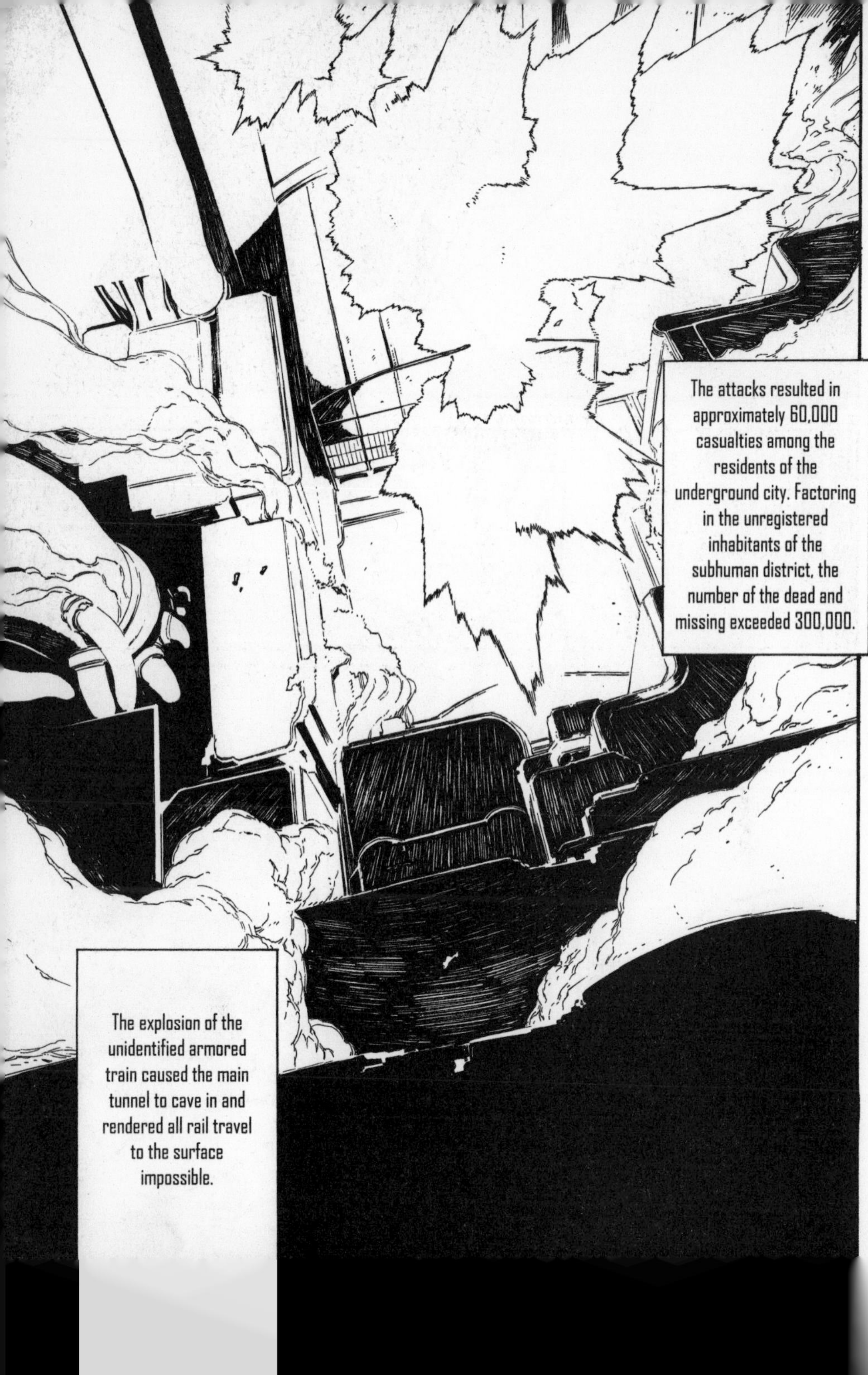
The attacks resulted in approximately 60,000 casualties among the residents of the underground city. Factoring in the unregistered inhabitants of the subhuman district, the number of the dead and missing exceeded 300,000.
The explosion of the unidentified armored train caused the main tunnel to cave in and rendered all rail travel to the surface impossible.

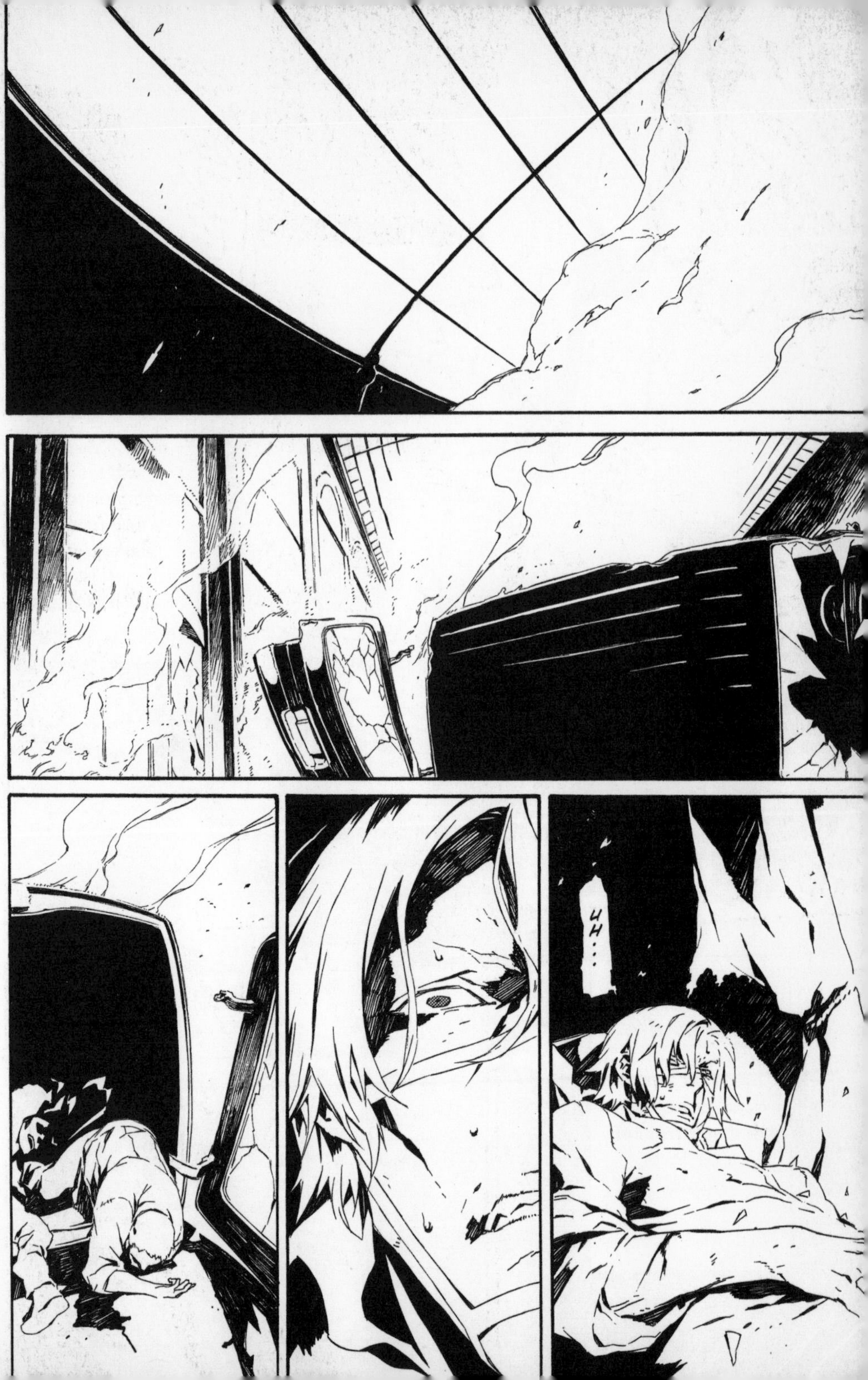
UH...

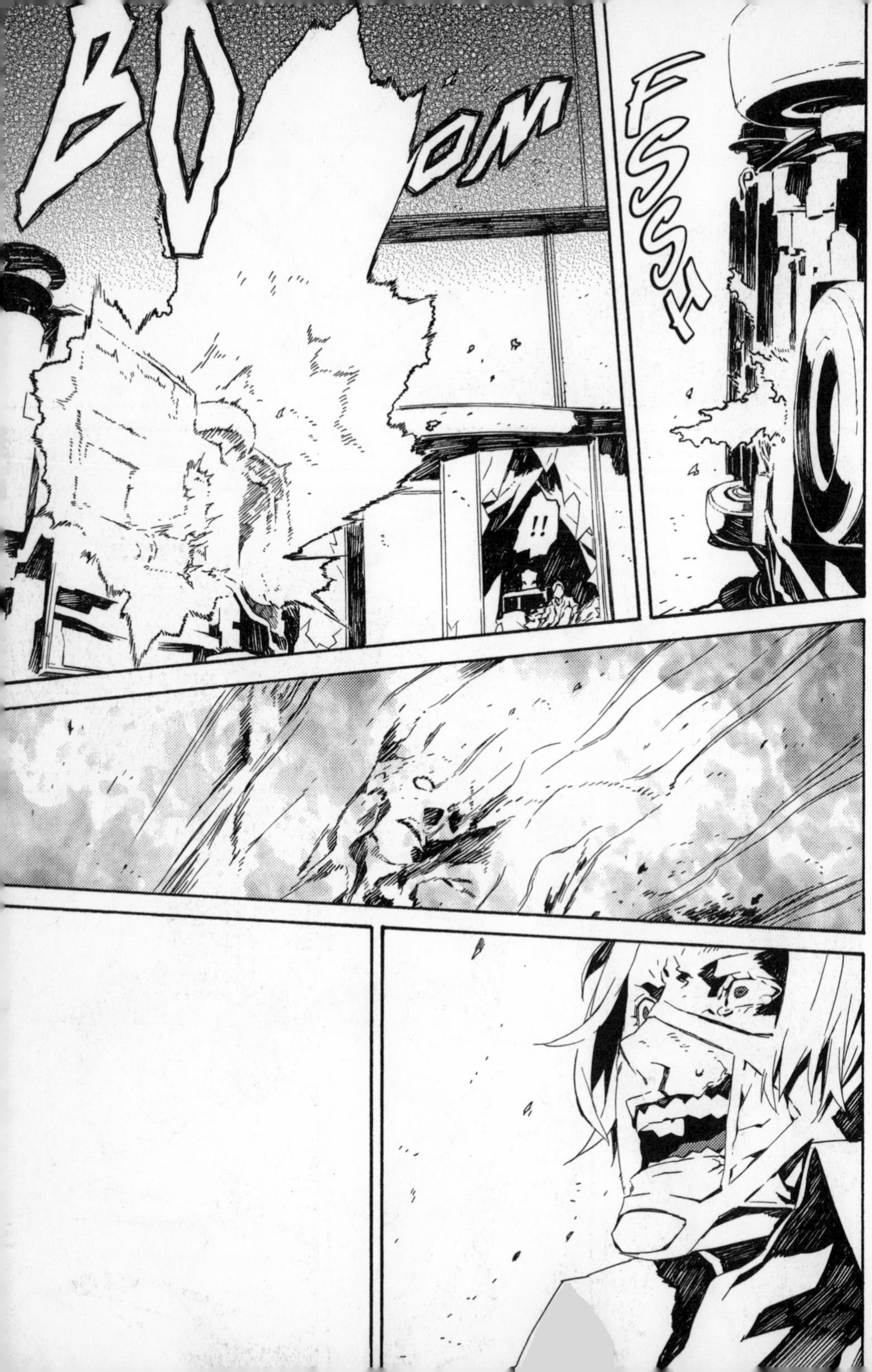
FSSH
BOOM
!!

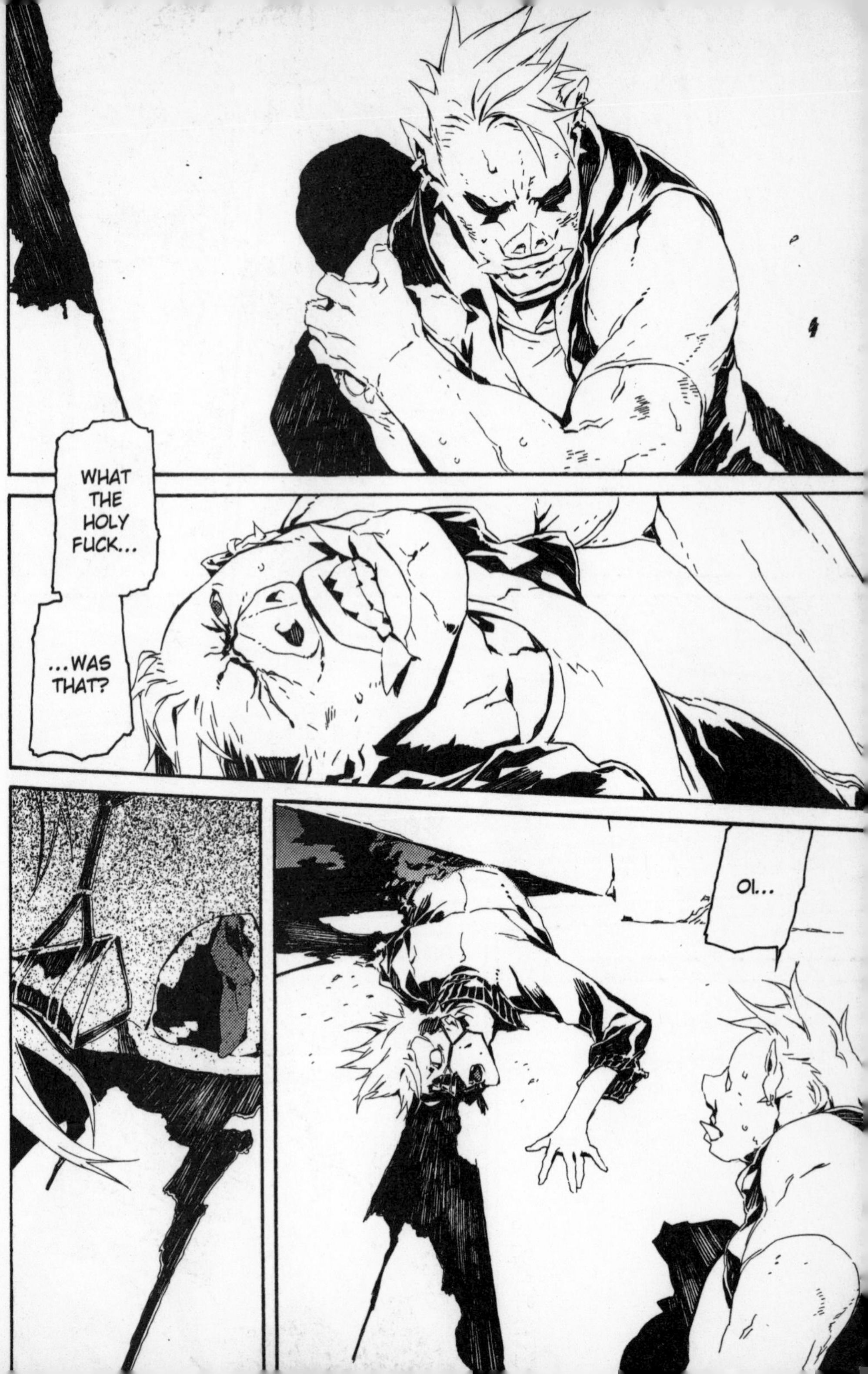
WHAT THE HOLY FUCK...
...WAS THAT?
OI...

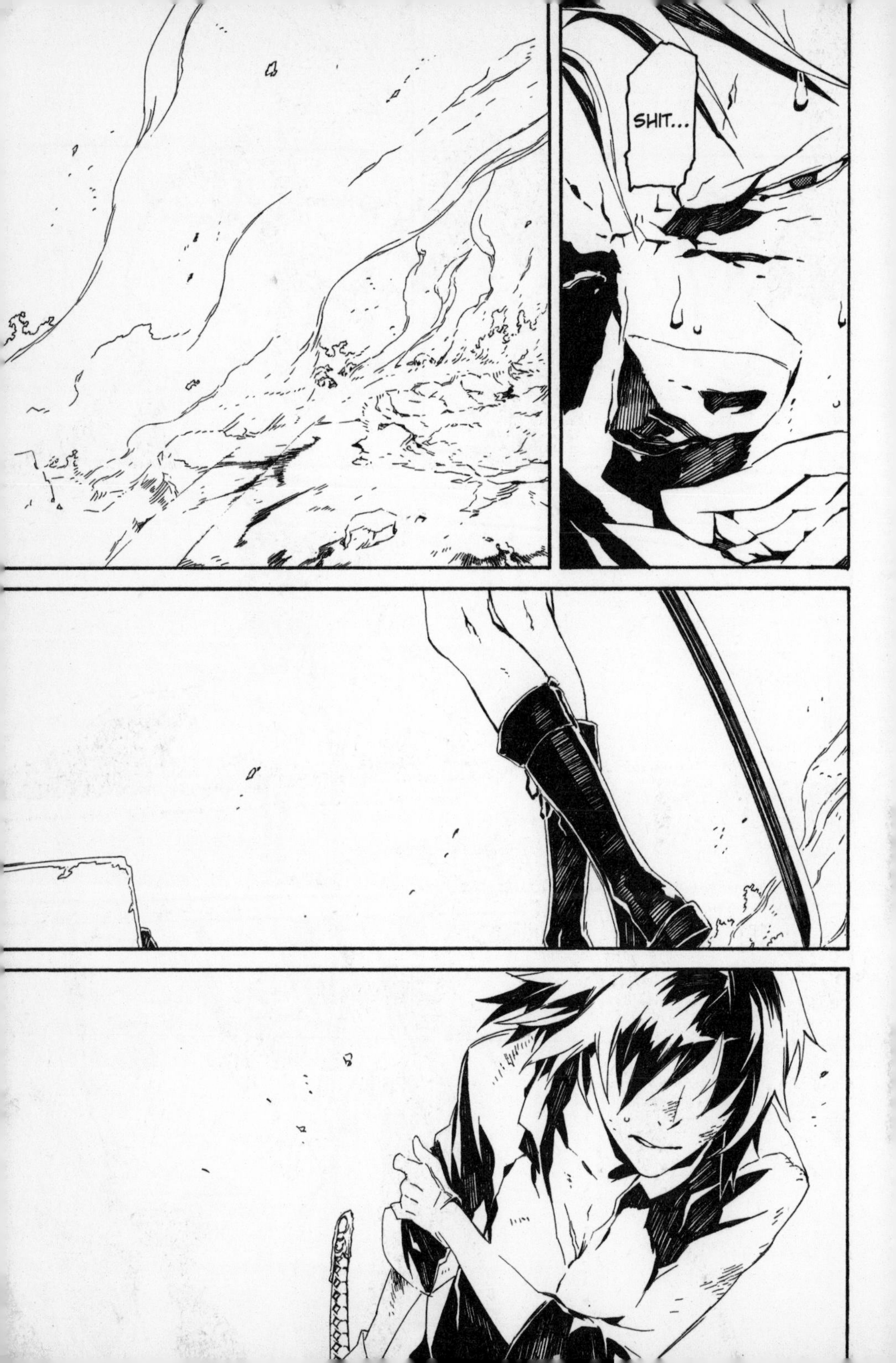
SHIT...

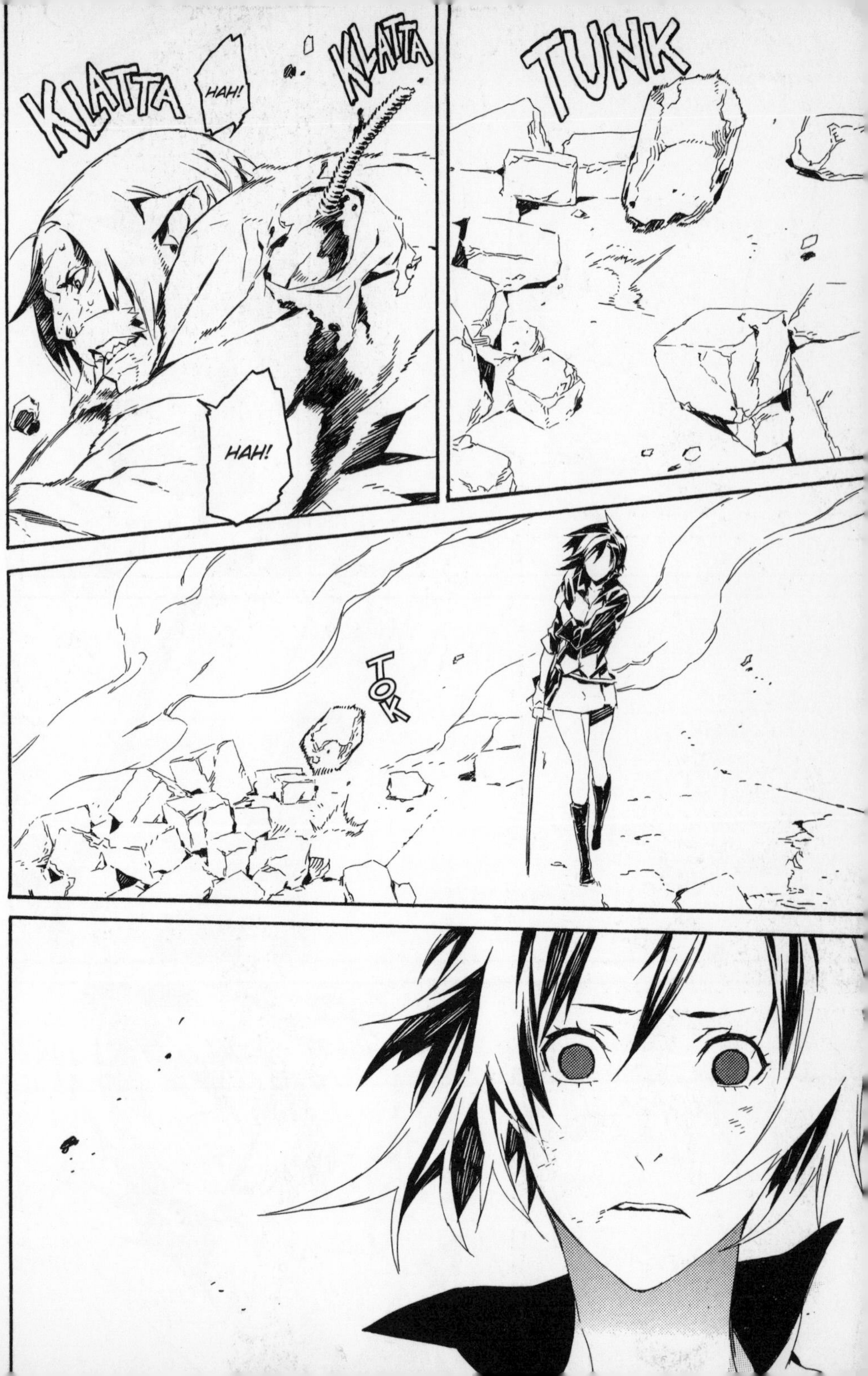
TUNK
KLATTA
HAH!
KLATTA
HAH!
TOK

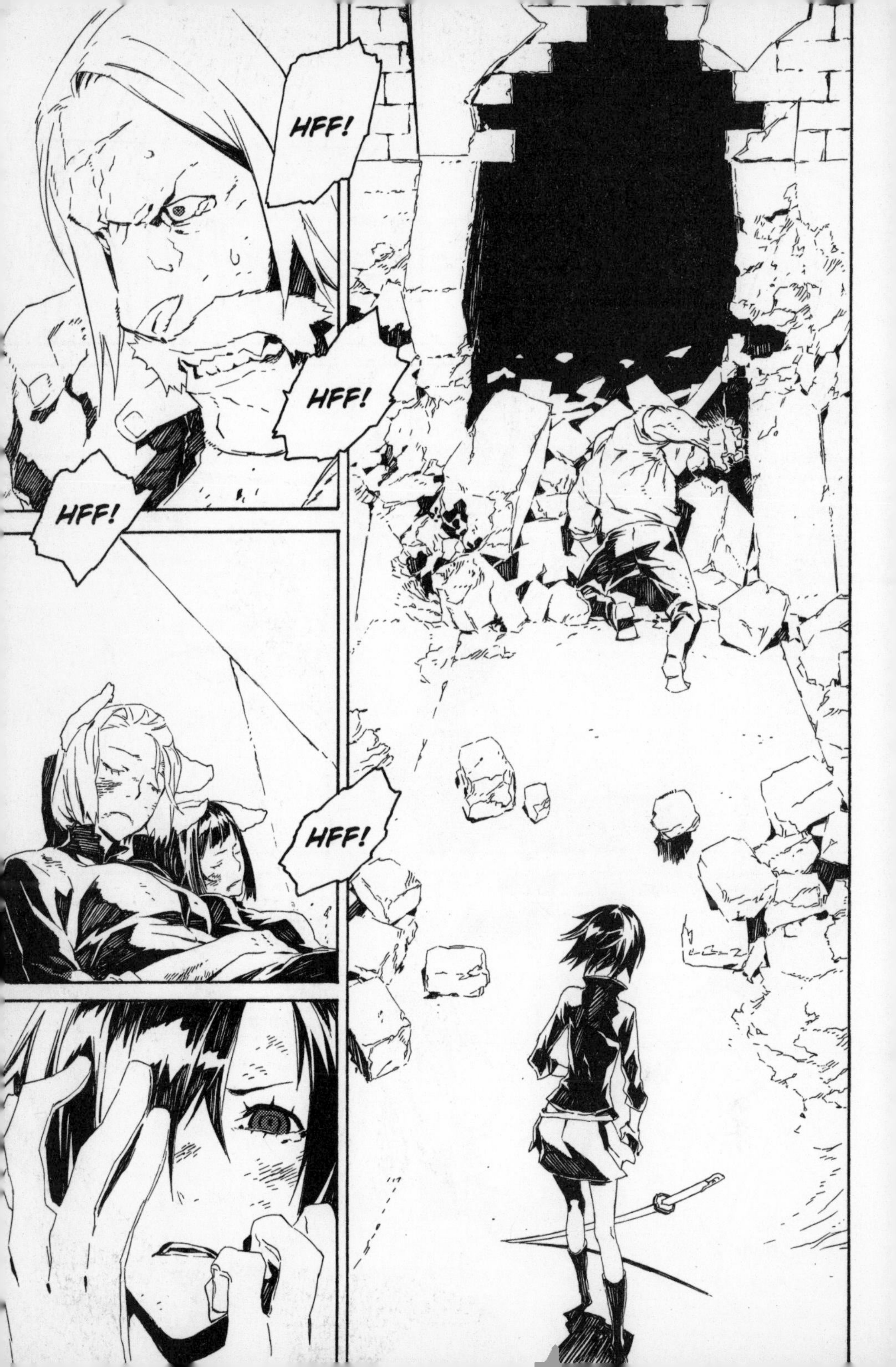
HFF!
HFF!
HFF!
HFF!

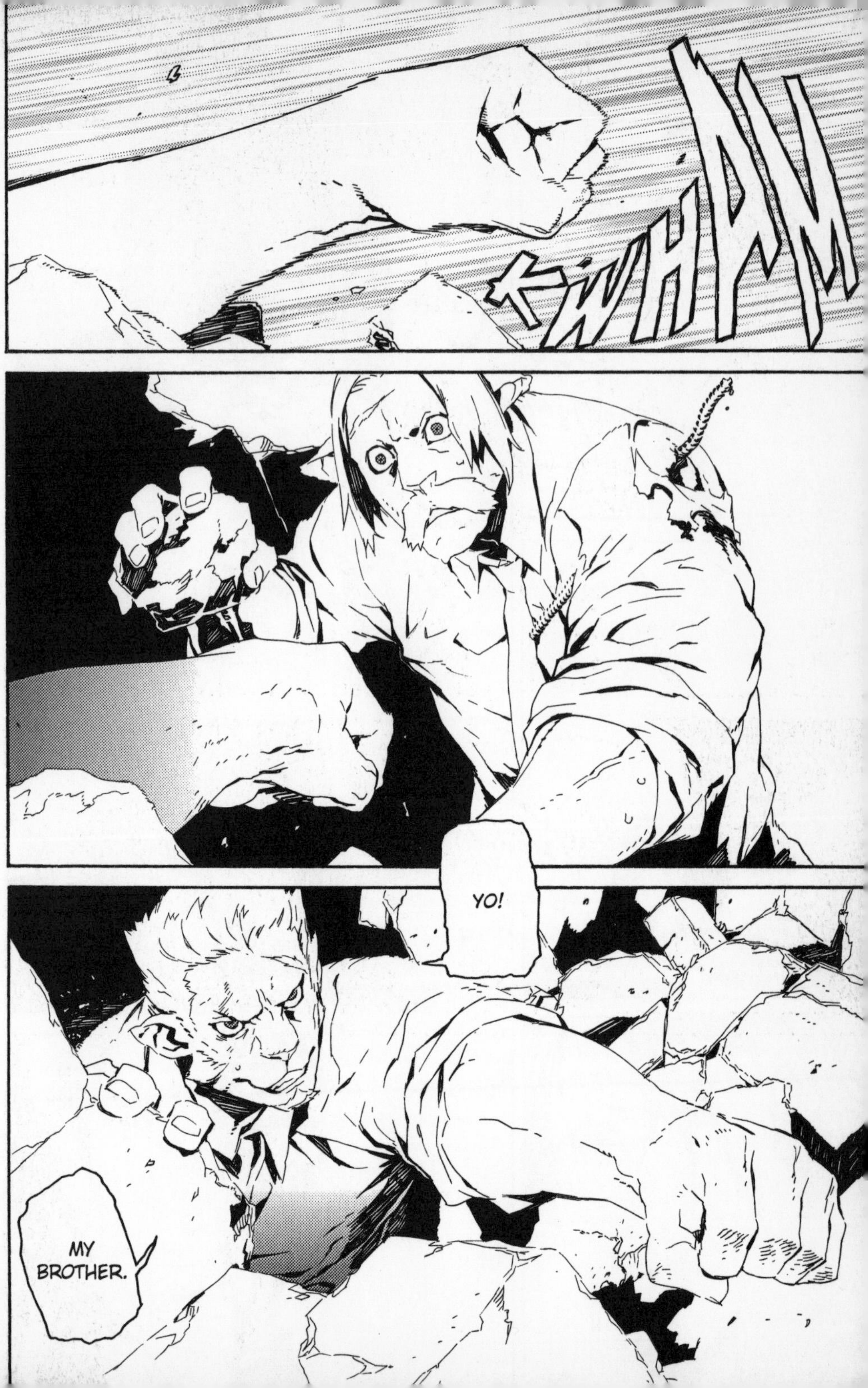
KWHAM
YO!
MY BROTHER.

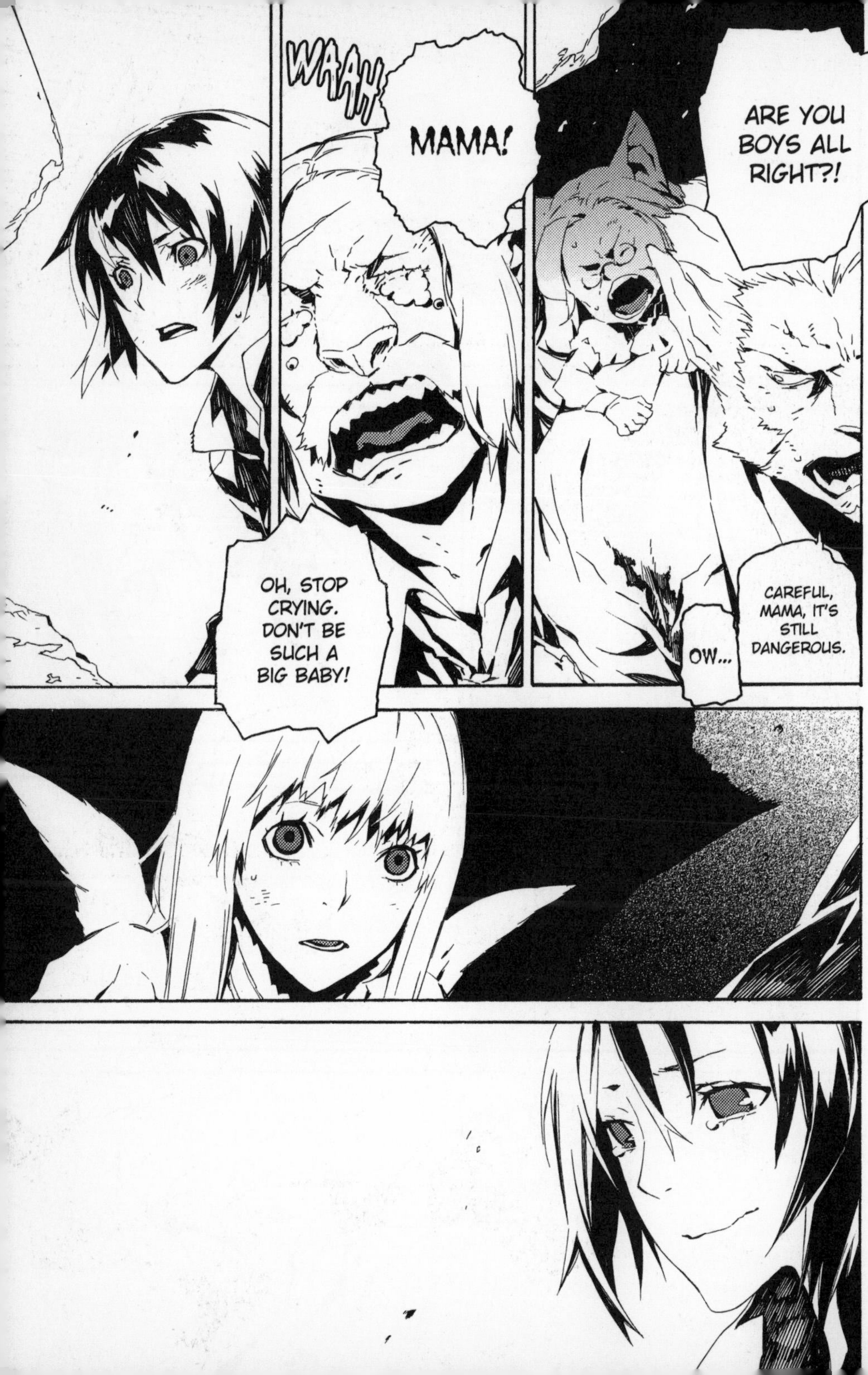
ARE YOU BOYS ALL RIGHT?!
CAREFUL, MAMA, IT'S STILL DANGEROUS.
OW...
WAAH
MAMA!
OH, STOP CRYING. DON'T BE SUCH A BIG BABY!

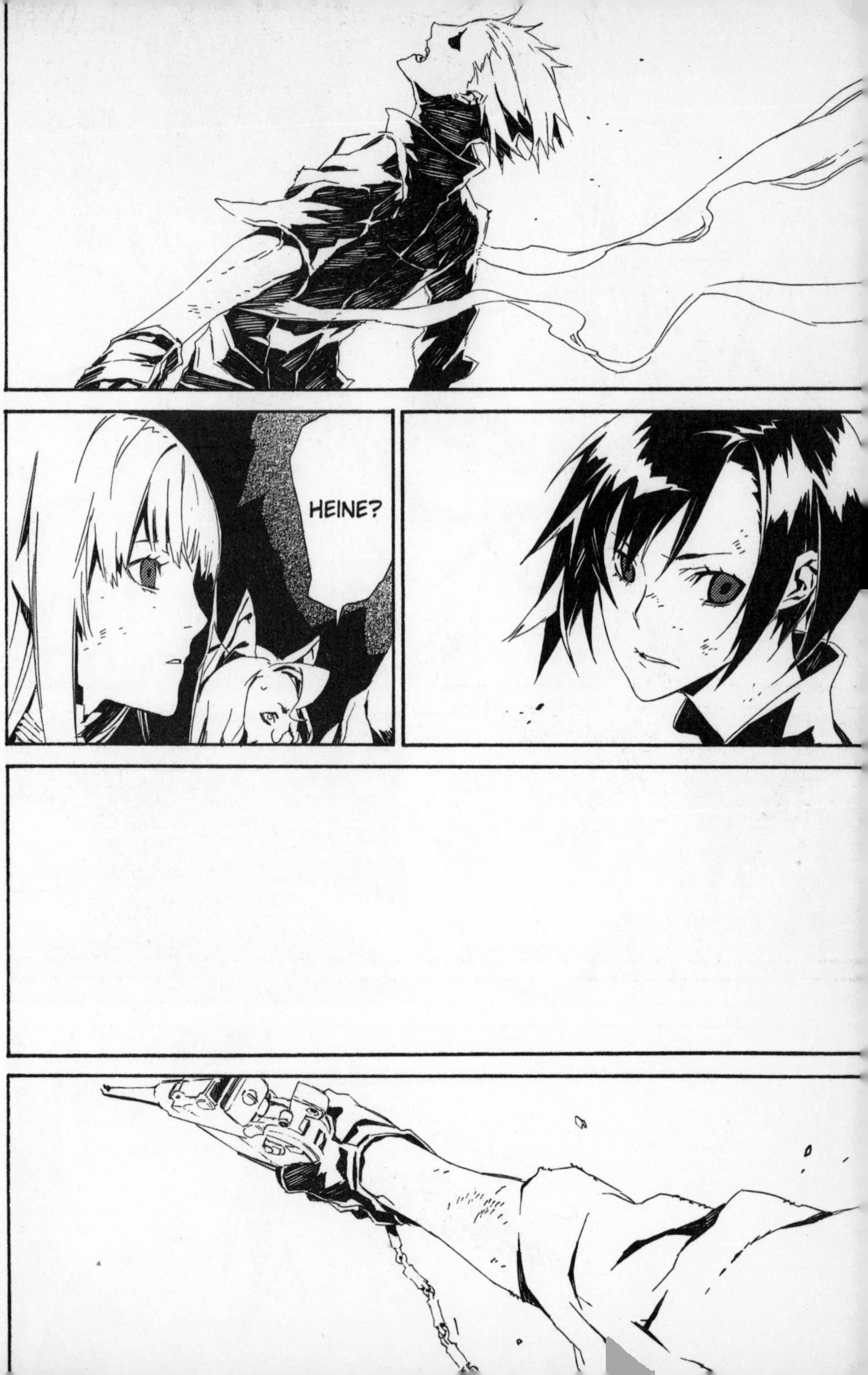
HEINE?

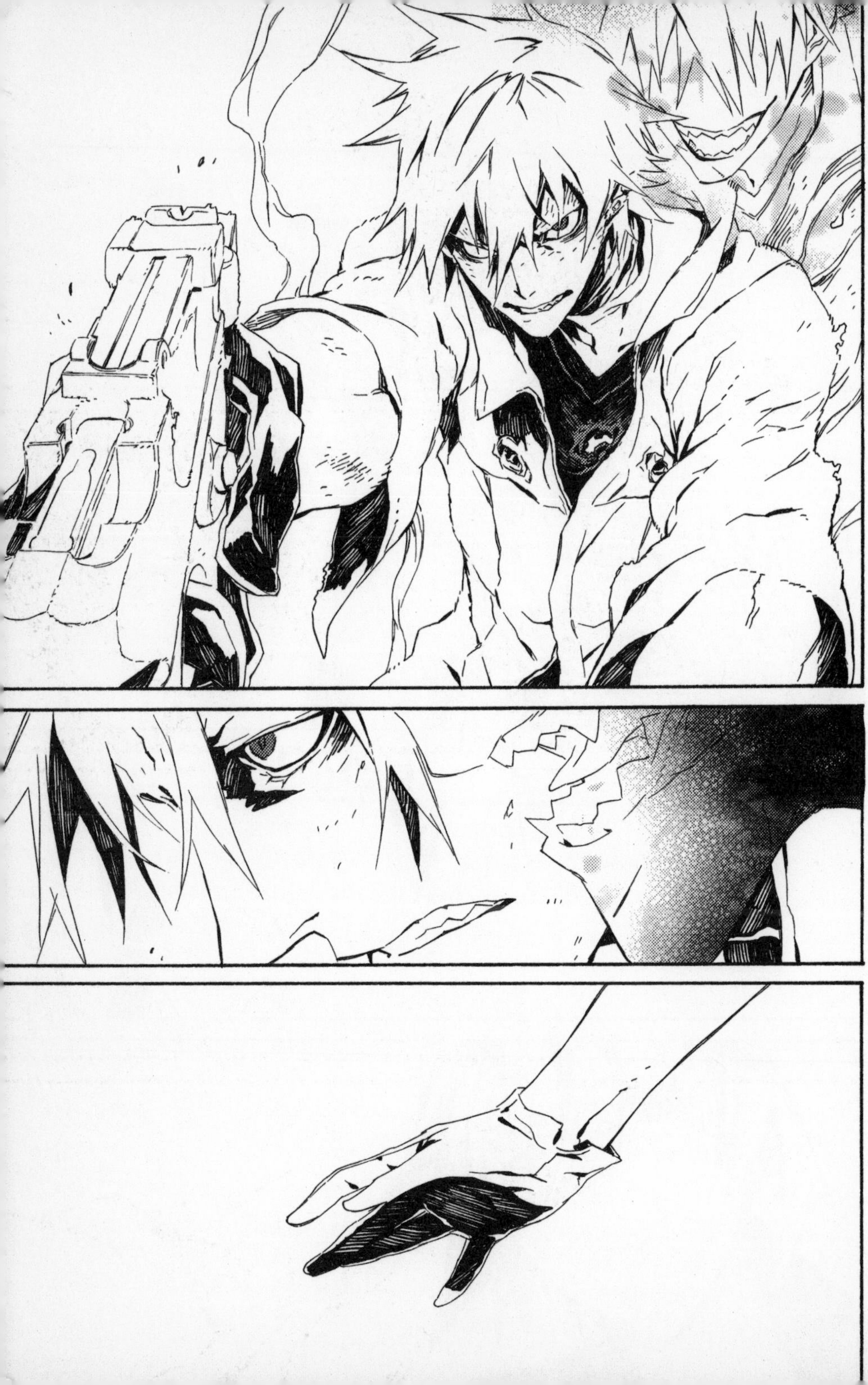

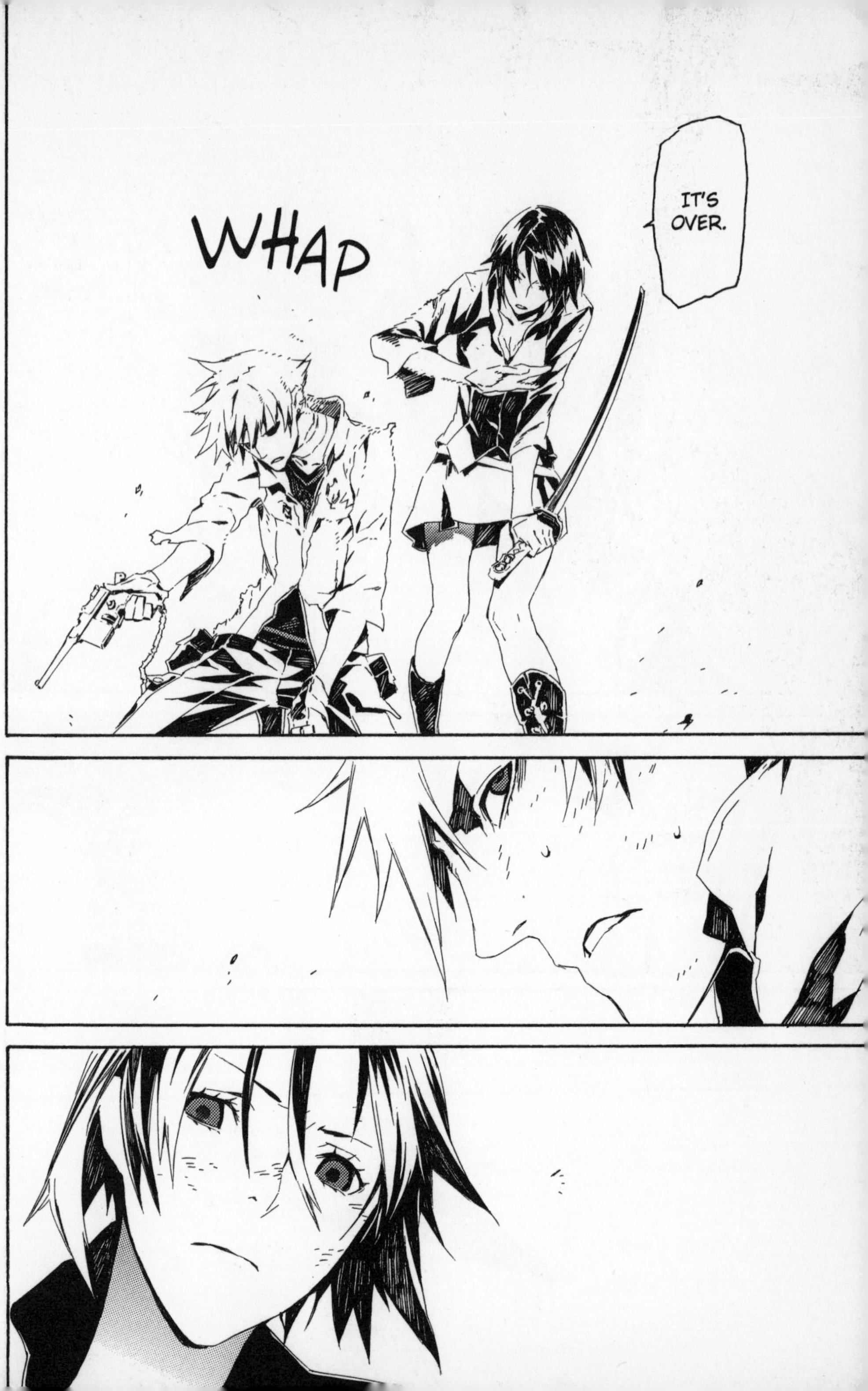
IT'S OVER.
WHAP

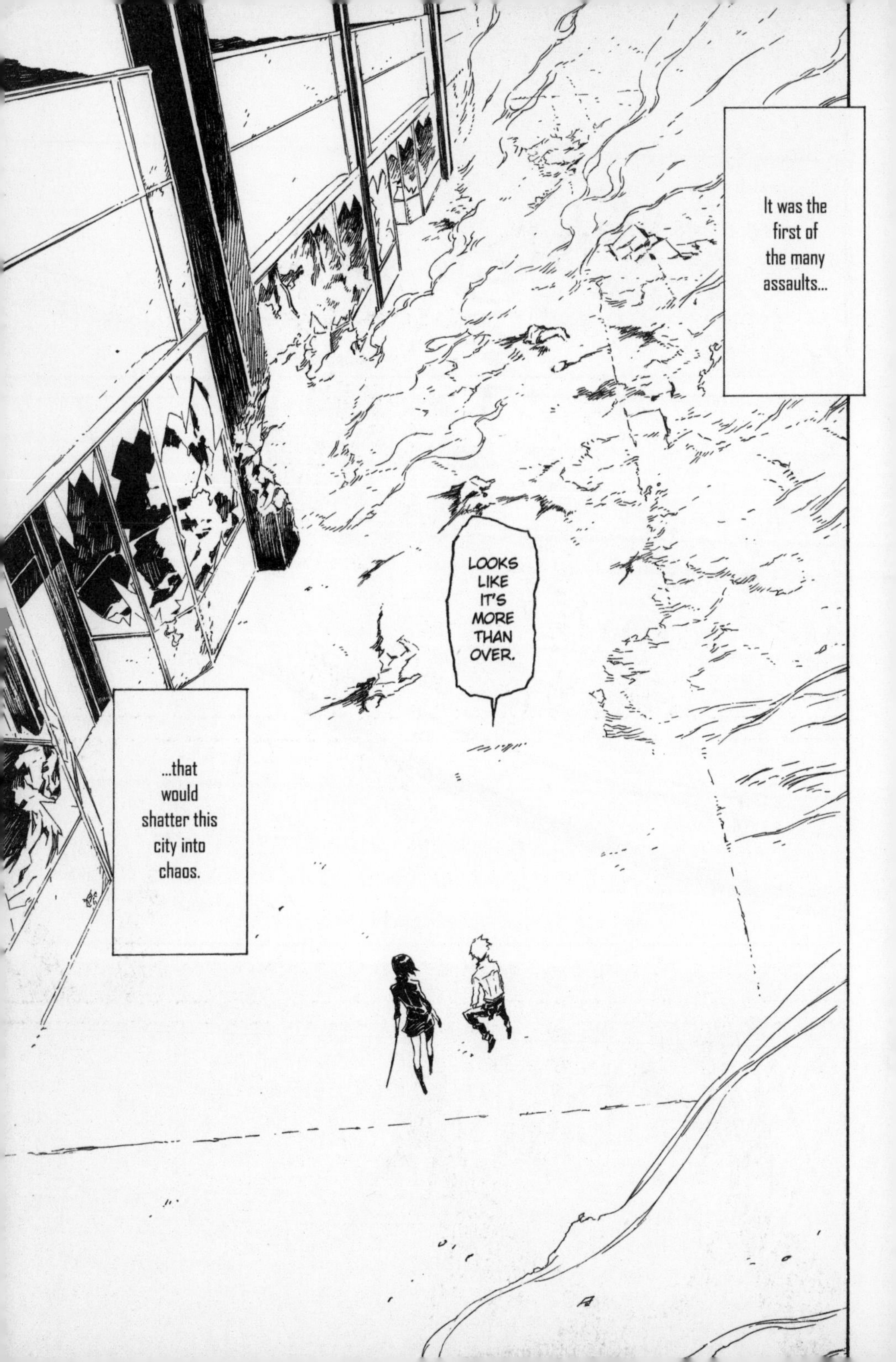
It was the first of the many assaults...
LOOKS LIKE IT'S MORE THAN OVER.
...that would shatter this city into chaos.

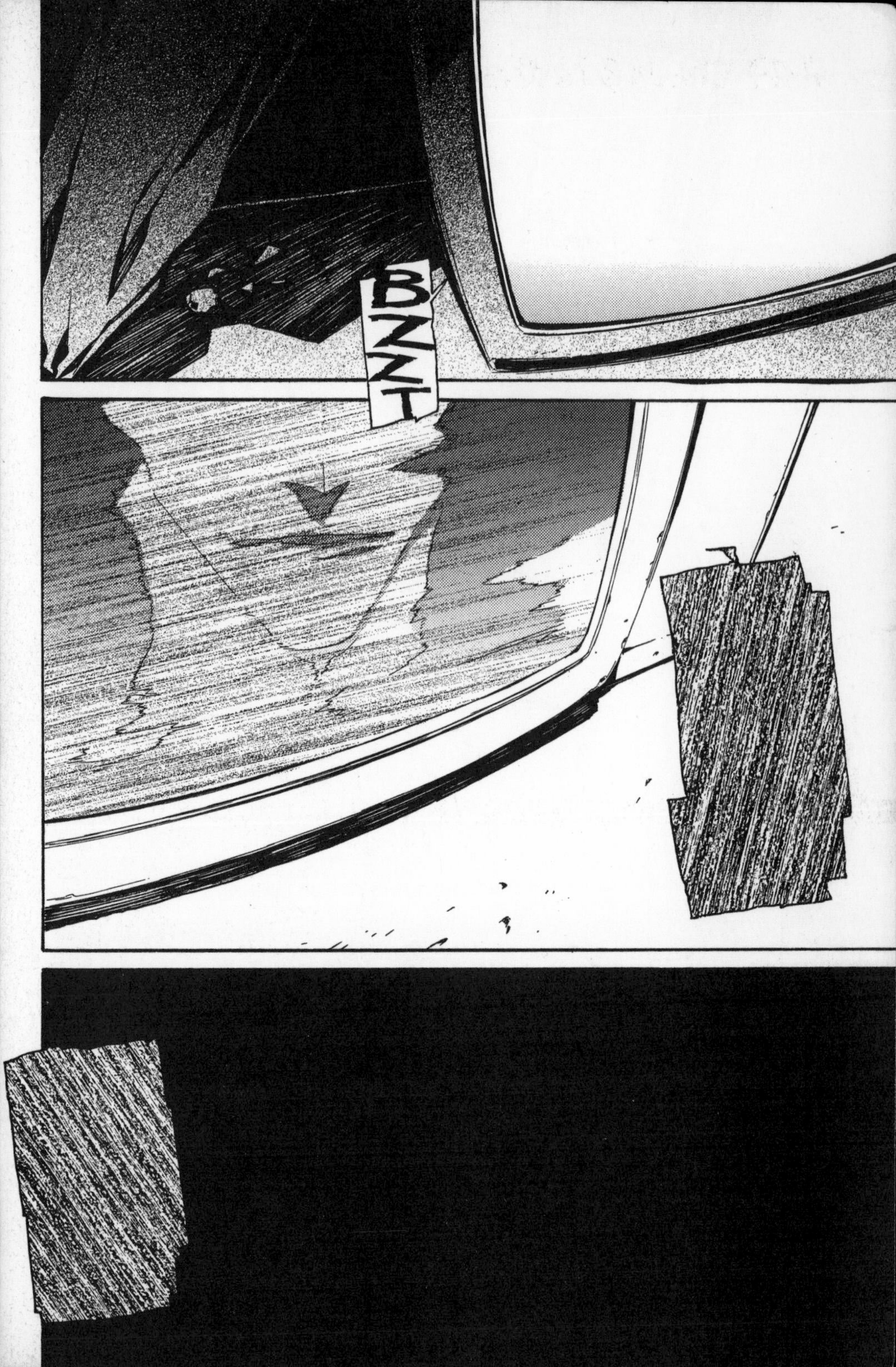
BZZT

# #49 Chaos & Netherworld II

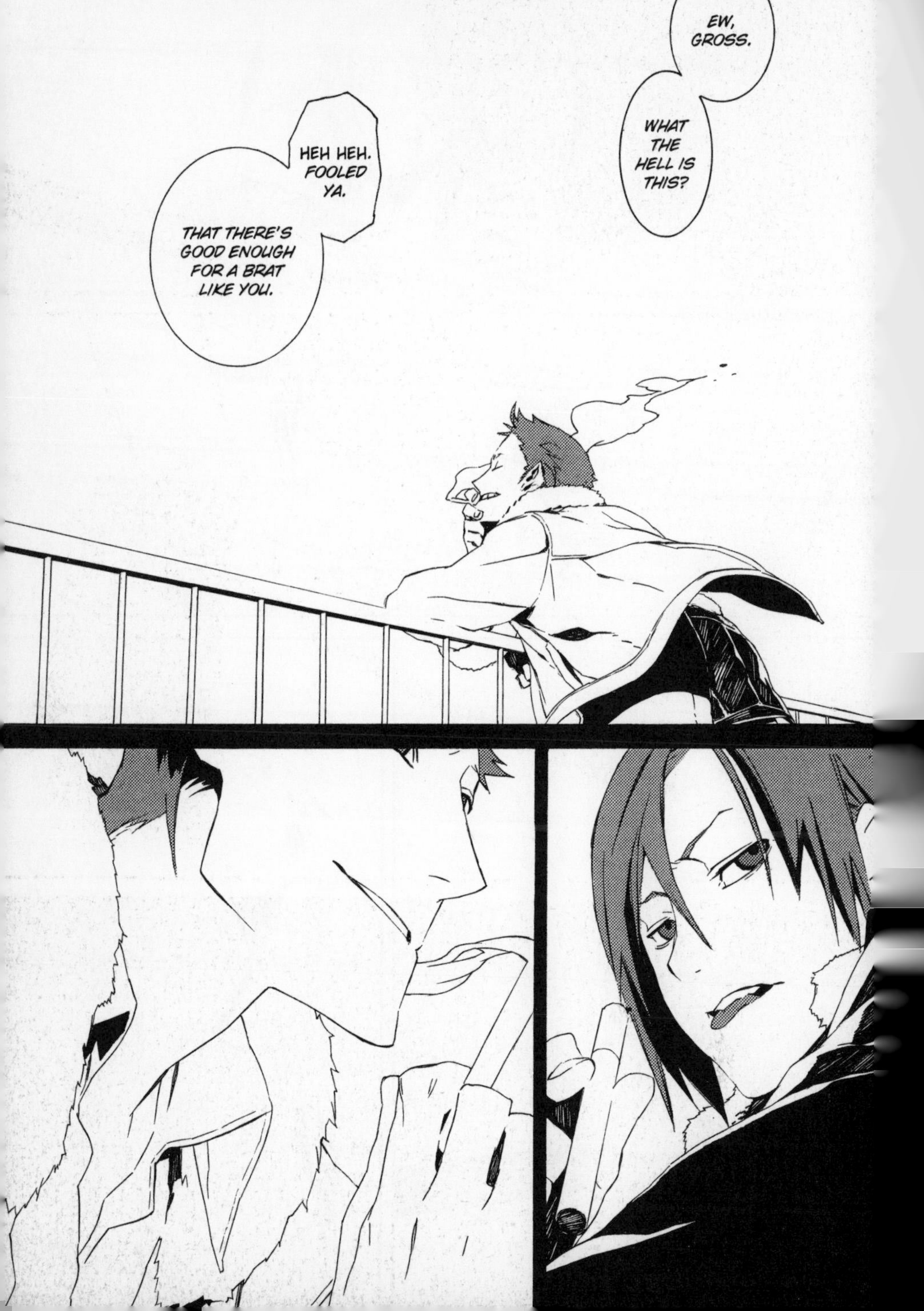
EW, GROSS.
WHAT THE HELL IS THIS?
HEH HEH. FOOLED YA.
THAT THERE'S GOOD ENOUGH FOR A BRAT LIKE YOU.

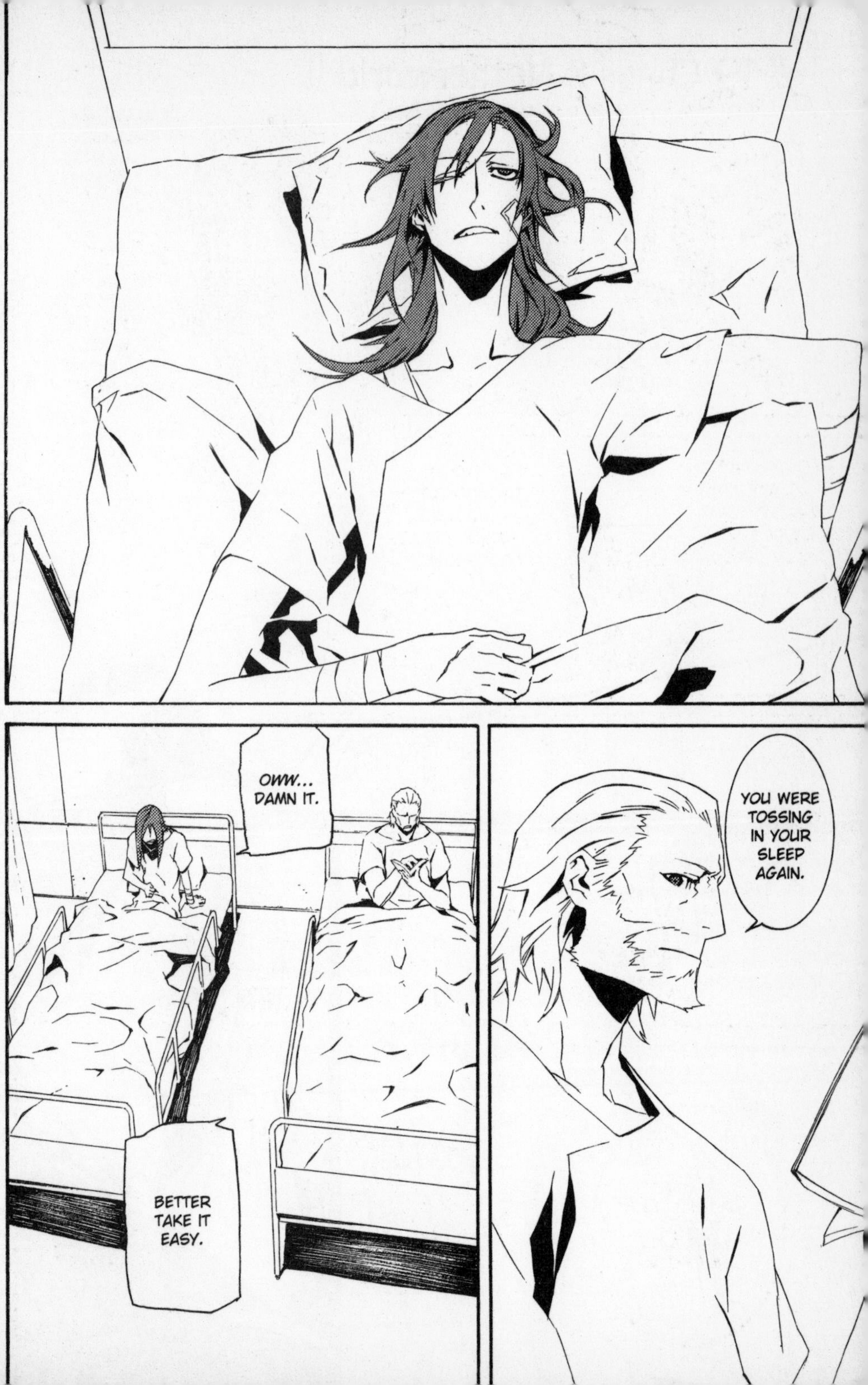
YOU WERE TOSSING IN YOUR SLEEP AGAIN.
OWW... DAMN IT.
BETTER TAKE IT EASY.

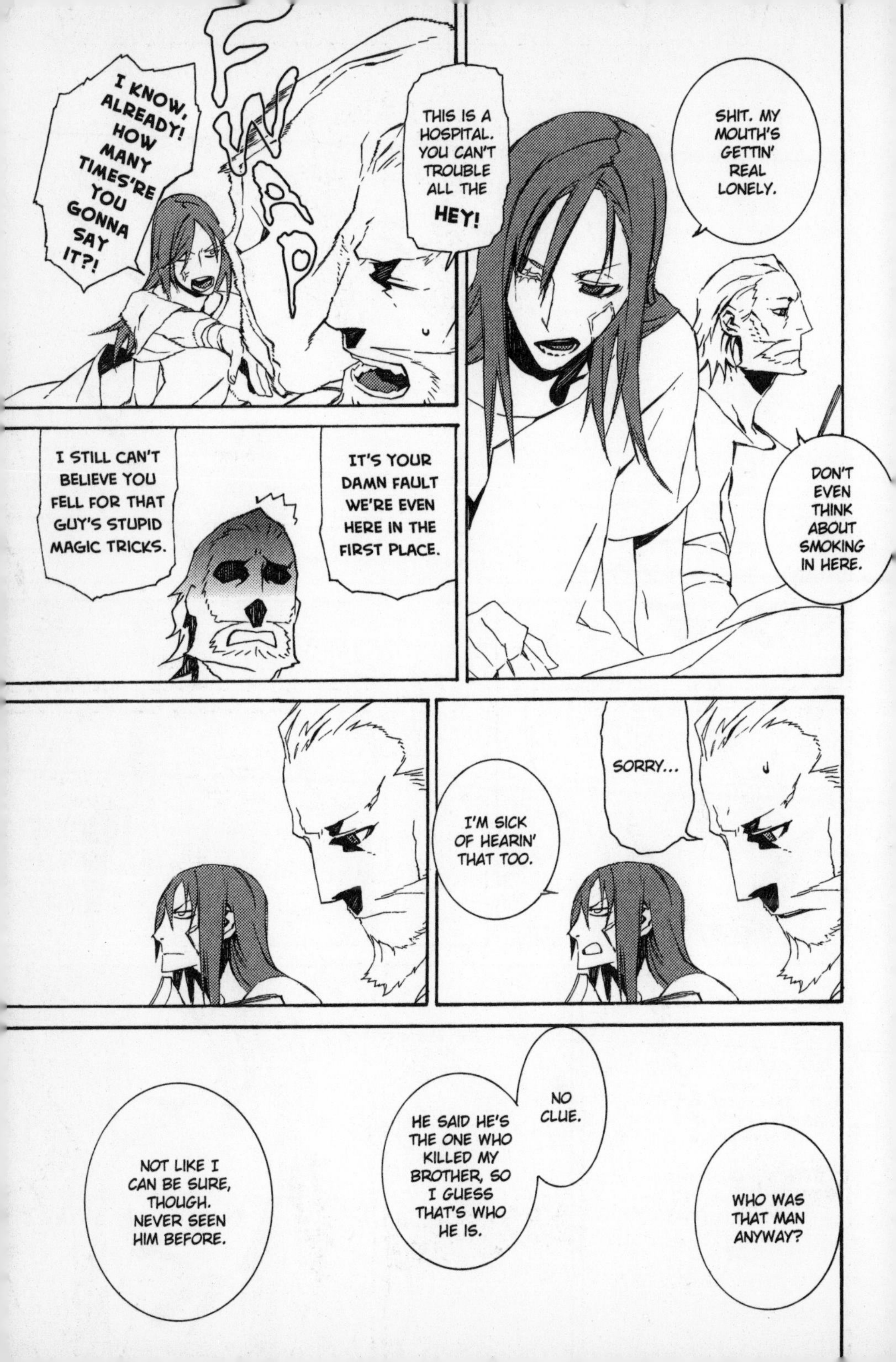
SHIT. MY MOUTH'S GETTIN' REAL LONELY.
DON'T EVEN THINK ABOUT SMOKING IN HERE.
THIS IS A HOSPITAL. YOU CAN'T TROUBLE ALL THE HEY!
FWAP
I KNOW, ALREADY! HOW MANY TIMES'RE YOU GONNA SAY IT?!
IT'S YOUR DAMN FAULT WE'RE EVEN HERE IN THE FIRST PLACE.
I STILL CAN'T BELIEVE YOU FELL FOR THAT GUY'S STUPID MAGIC TRICKS.
SORRY...
I'M SICK OF HEARIN' THAT TOO.
WHO WAS THAT MAN ANYWAY?
NO CLUE.
HE SAID HE'S THE ONE WHO KILLED MY BROTHER, SO I GUESS THAT'S WHO HE IS.
NOT LIKE I CAN BE SURE, THOUGH. NEVER SEEN HIM BEFORE.

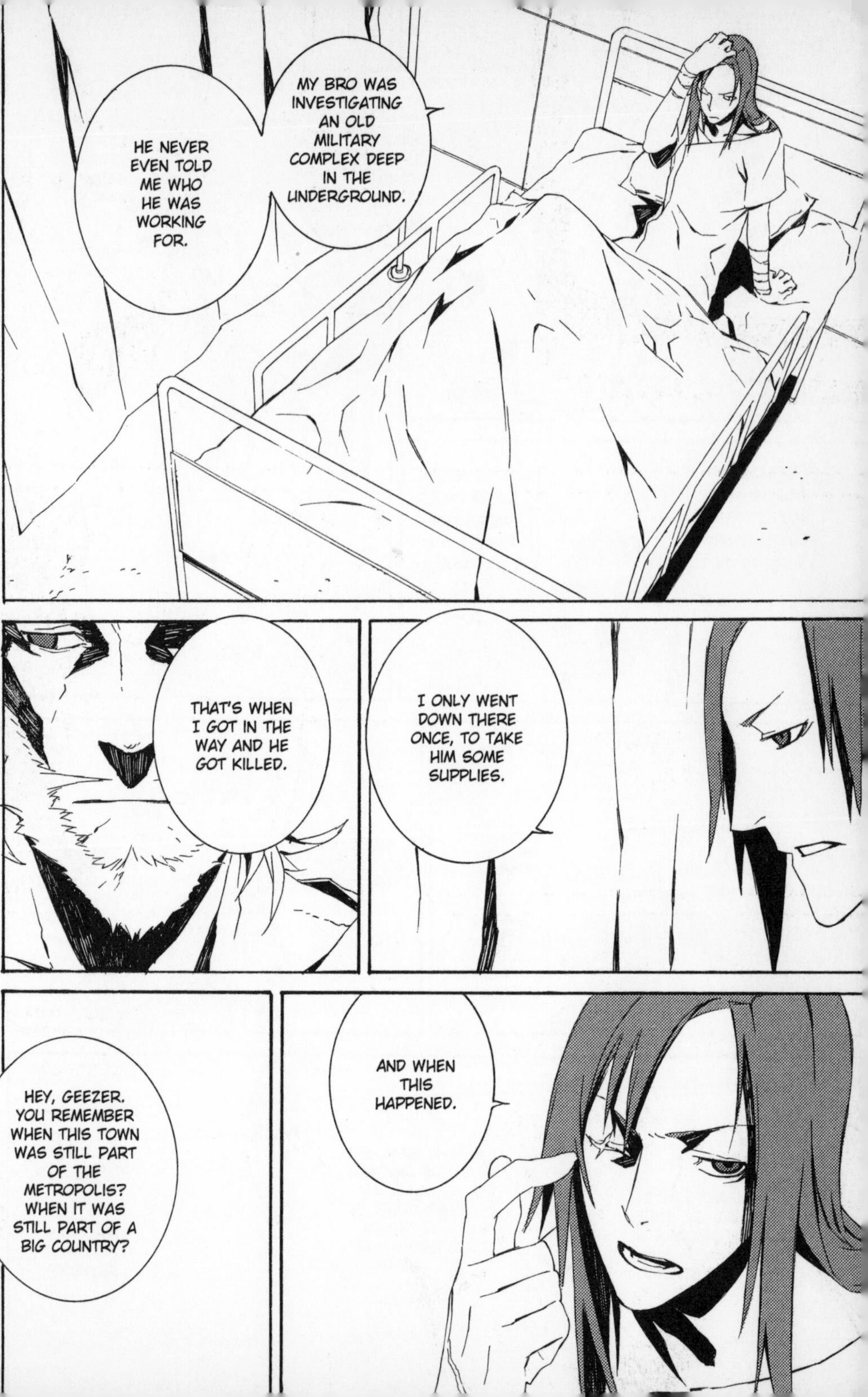
MY BRO WAS INVESTIGATING AN OLD MILITARY COMPLEX DEEP IN THE UNDERGROUND.
HE NEVER EVEN TOLD ME WHO HE WAS WORKING FOR.
I ONLY WENT DOWN THERE ONCE, TO TAKE HIM SOME SUPPLIES.
THAT'S WHEN I GOT IN THE WAY AND HE GOT KILLED.
AND WHEN THIS HAPPENED.
HEY, GEEZER. YOU REMEMBER WHEN THIS TOWN WAS STILL PART OF THE METROPOLIS? WHEN IT WAS STILL PART OF A BIG COUNTRY?

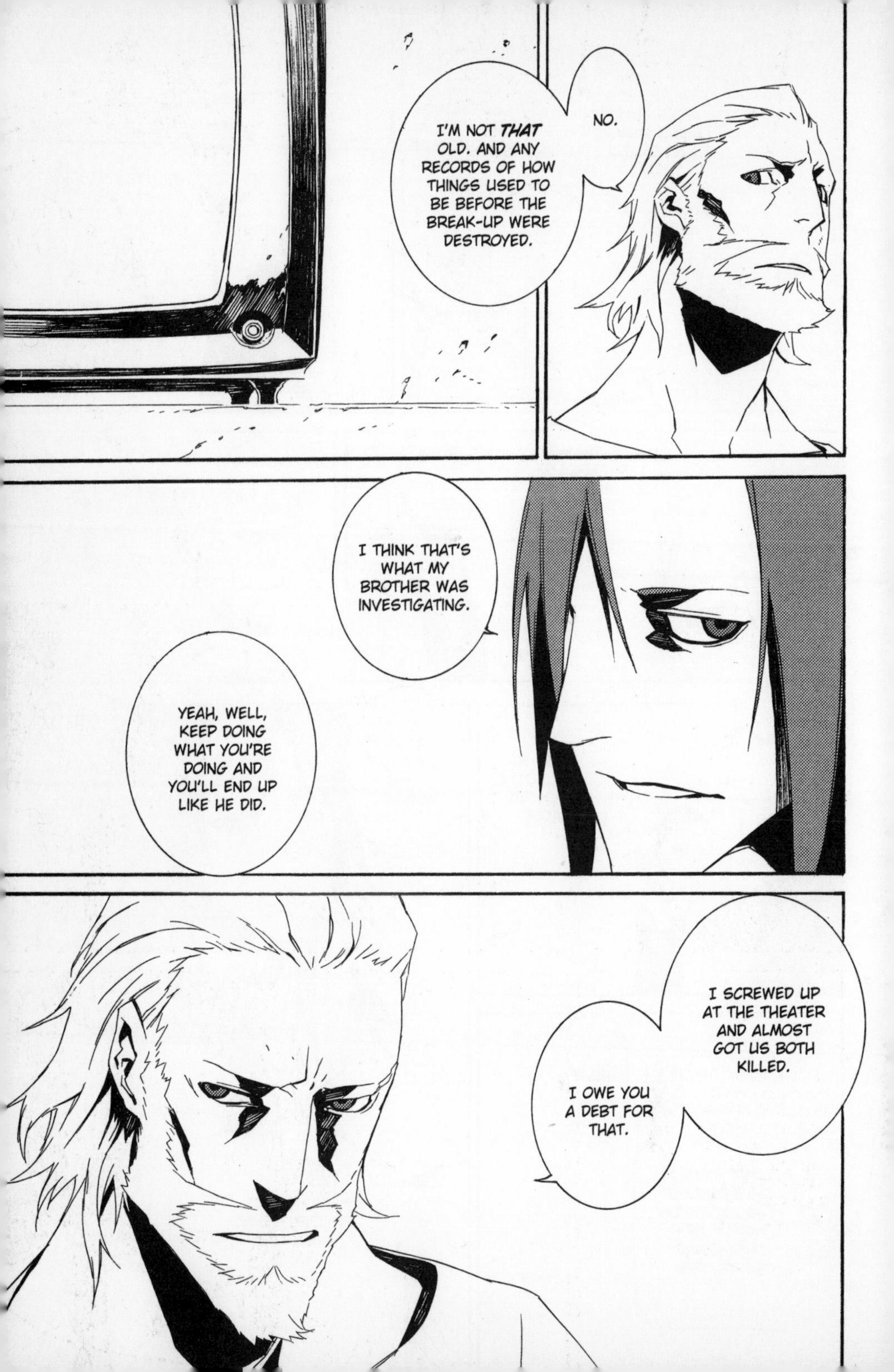
NO.
I'M NOT *THAT* OLD. AND ANY RECORDS OF HOW THINGS USED TO BE BEFORE THE BREAK-UP WERE DESTROYED.
I THINK THAT'S WHAT MY BROTHER WAS INVESTIGATING.
YEAH, WELL, KEEP DOING WHAT YOU'RE DOING AND YOU'LL END UP LIKE HE DID.
I SCREWED UP AT THE THEATER AND ALMOST GOT US BOTH KILLED.
I OWE YOU A DEBT FOR THAT.

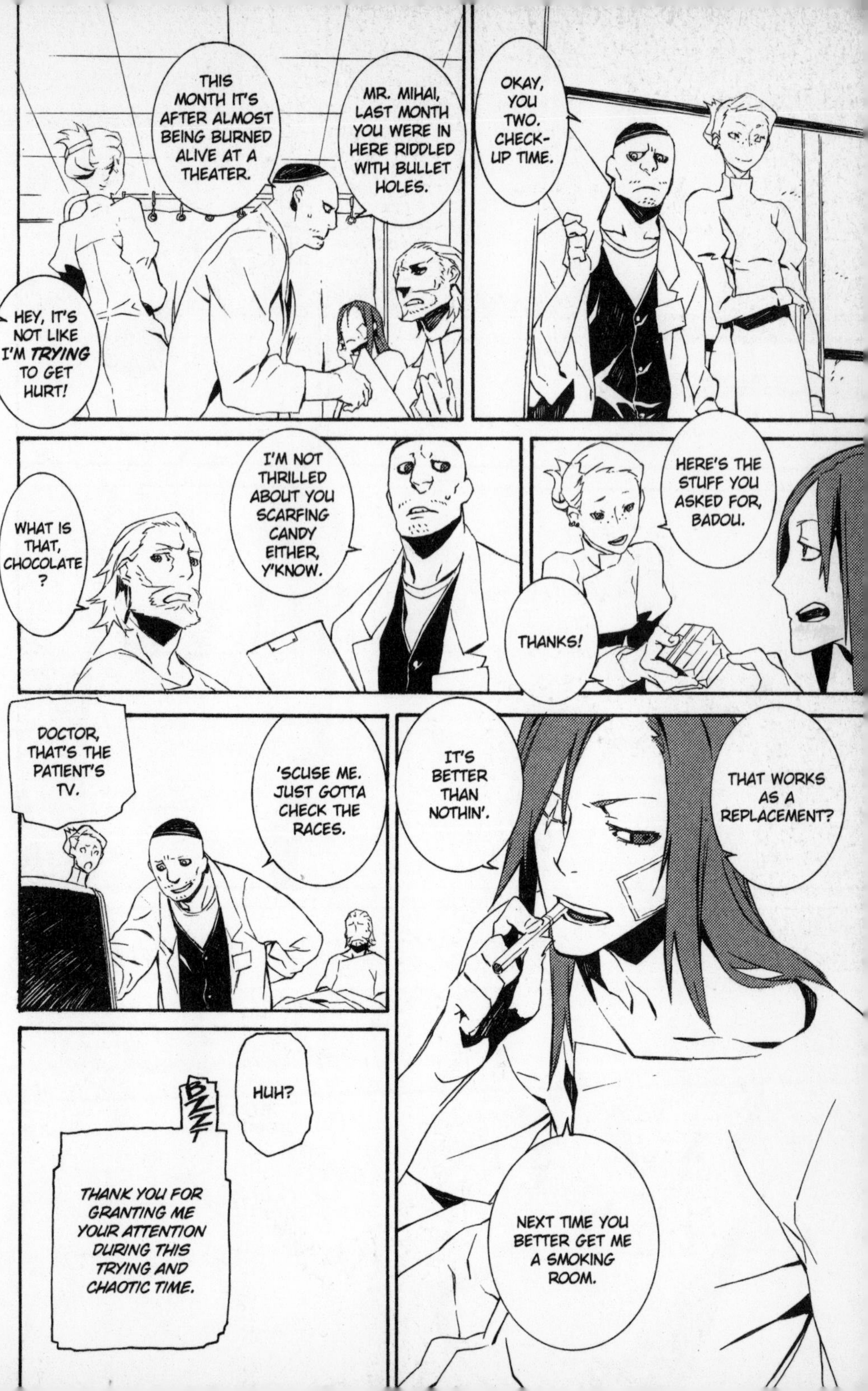
OKAY, YOU TWO. CHECK-UP TIME.
MR. MIHAI, LAST MONTH YOU WERE IN HERE RIDDLED WITH BULLET HOLES.
THIS MONTH IT'S AFTER ALMOST BEING BURNED ALIVE AT A THEATER.
HEY, IT'S NOT LIKE I'M *TRYING* TO GET HURT!
HERE'S THE STUFF YOU ASKED FOR, BADOU.
THANKS!
I'M NOT THRILLED ABOUT YOU SCARFING CANDY EITHER, Y'KNOW.
WHAT IS THAT, CHOCOLATE?
THAT WORKS AS A REPLACEMENT?
IT'S BETTER THAN NOTHIN'.
NEXT TIME YOU BETTER GET ME A SMOKING ROOM.
'SCUSE ME. JUST GOTTA CHECK THE RACES.
DOCTOR, THAT'S THE PATIENT'S TV.
HUH?
BZZT
THANK YOU FOR GRANTING ME YOUR ATTENTION DURING THIS TRYING AND CHAOTIC TIME.

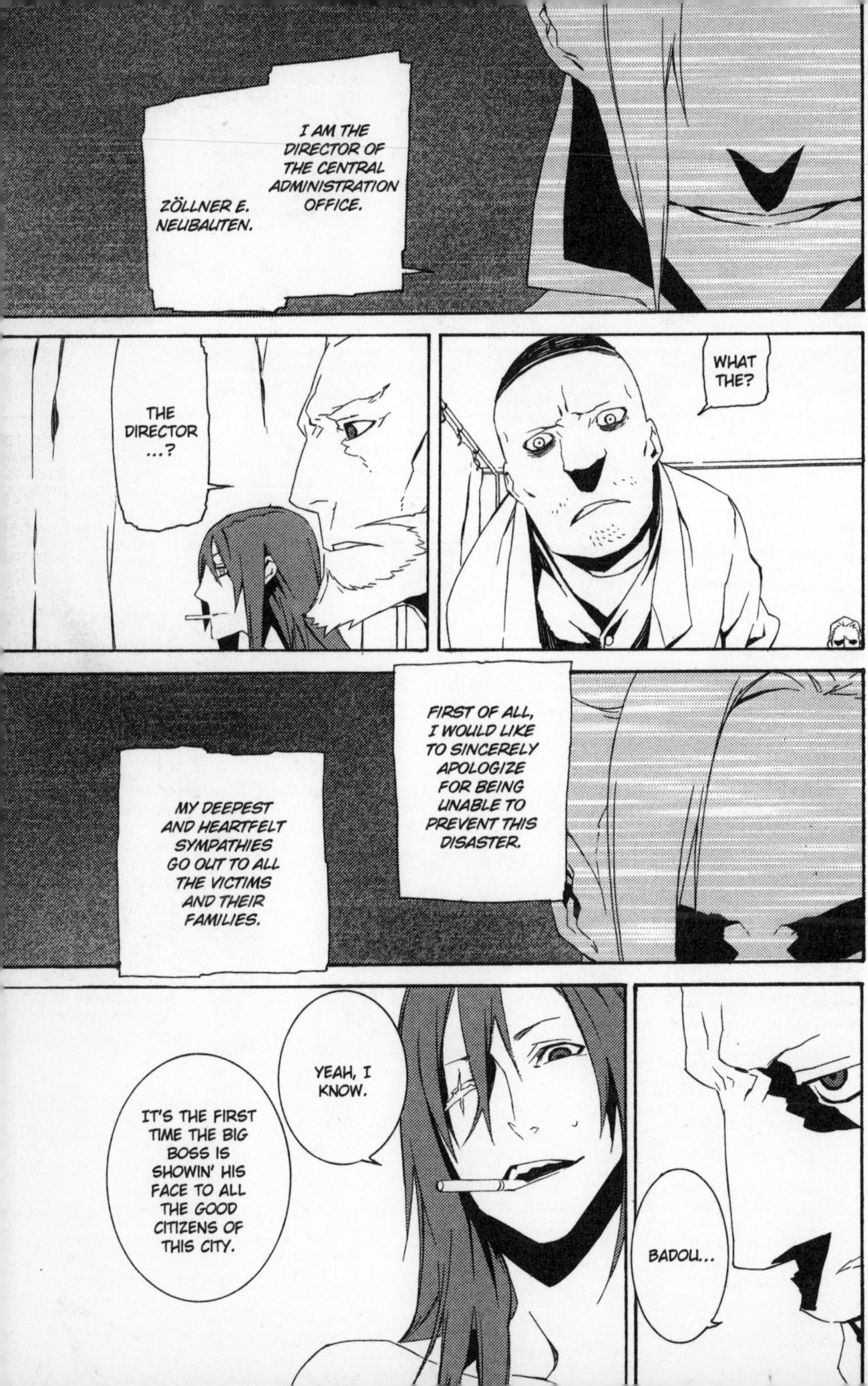
I AM THE DIRECTOR OF THE CENTRAL ADMINISTRATION OFFICE.
ZÖLLNER E. NEUBAUTEN.
WHAT THE?
THE DIRECTOR ...?
FIRST OF ALL, I WOULD LIKE TO SINCERELY APOLOGIZE FOR BEING UNABLE TO PREVENT THIS DISASTER.
MY DEEPEST AND HEARTFELT SYMPATHIES GO OUT TO ALL THE VICTIMS AND THEIR FAMILIES.
BADOU...
YEAH, I KNOW.
IT'S THE FIRST TIME THE BIG BOSS IS SHOWIN' HIS FACE TO ALL THE GOOD CITIZENS OF THIS CITY.

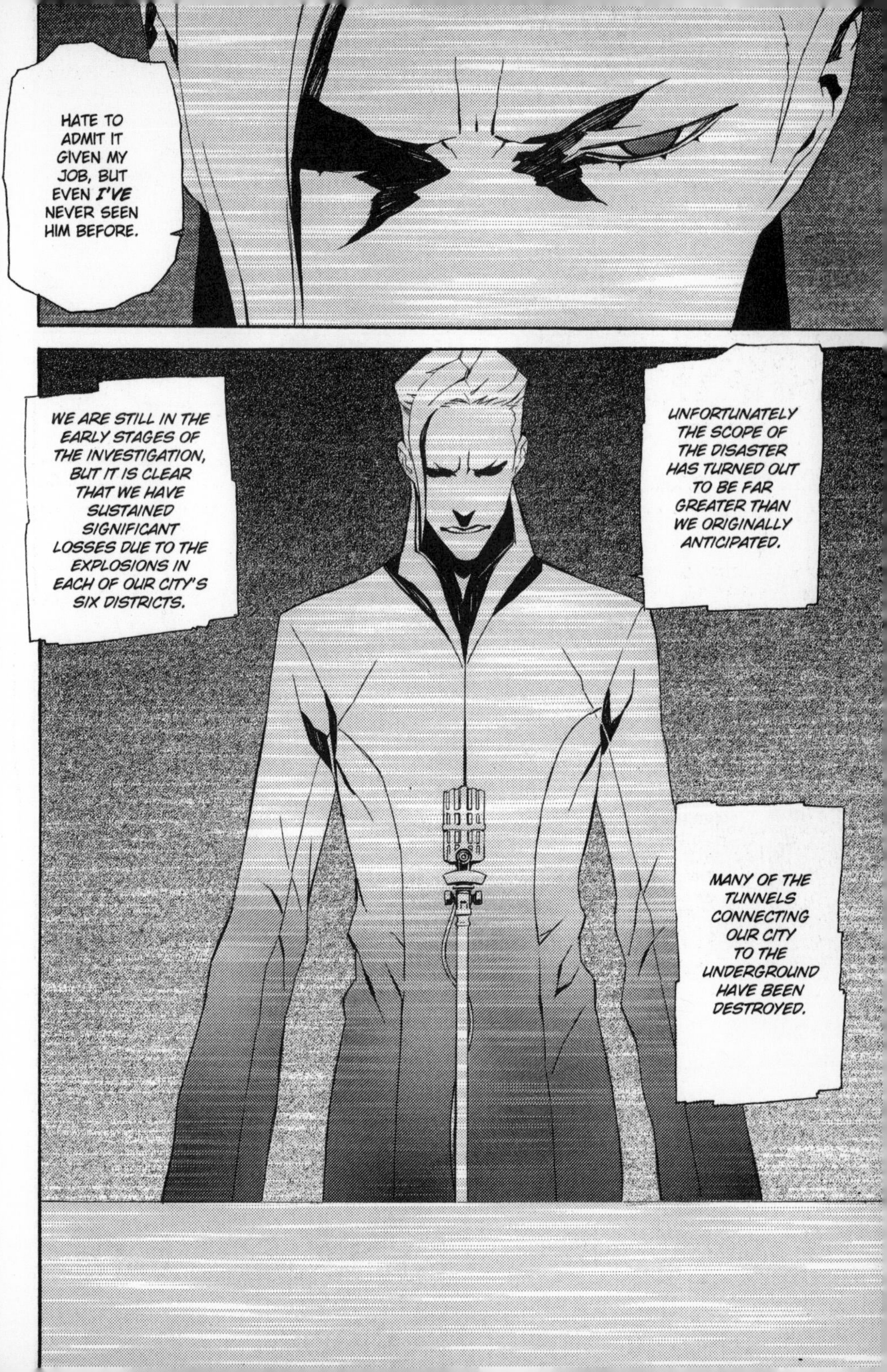
HATE TO ADMIT IT GIVEN MY JOB, BUT EVEN ***I'VE*** NEVER SEEN HIM BEFORE.
*UNFORTUNATELY THE SCOPE OF THE DISASTER HAS TURNED OUT TO BE FAR GREATER THAN WE ORIGINALLY ANTICIPATED.*
*WE ARE STILL IN THE EARLY STAGES OF THE INVESTIGATION, BUT IT IS CLEAR THAT WE HAVE SUSTAINED SIGNIFICANT LOSSES DUE TO THE EXPLOSIONS IN EACH OF OUR CITY'S SIX DISTRICTS.*
*MANY OF THE TUNNELS CONNECTING OUR CITY TO THE UNDERGROUND HAVE BEEN DESTROYED.*

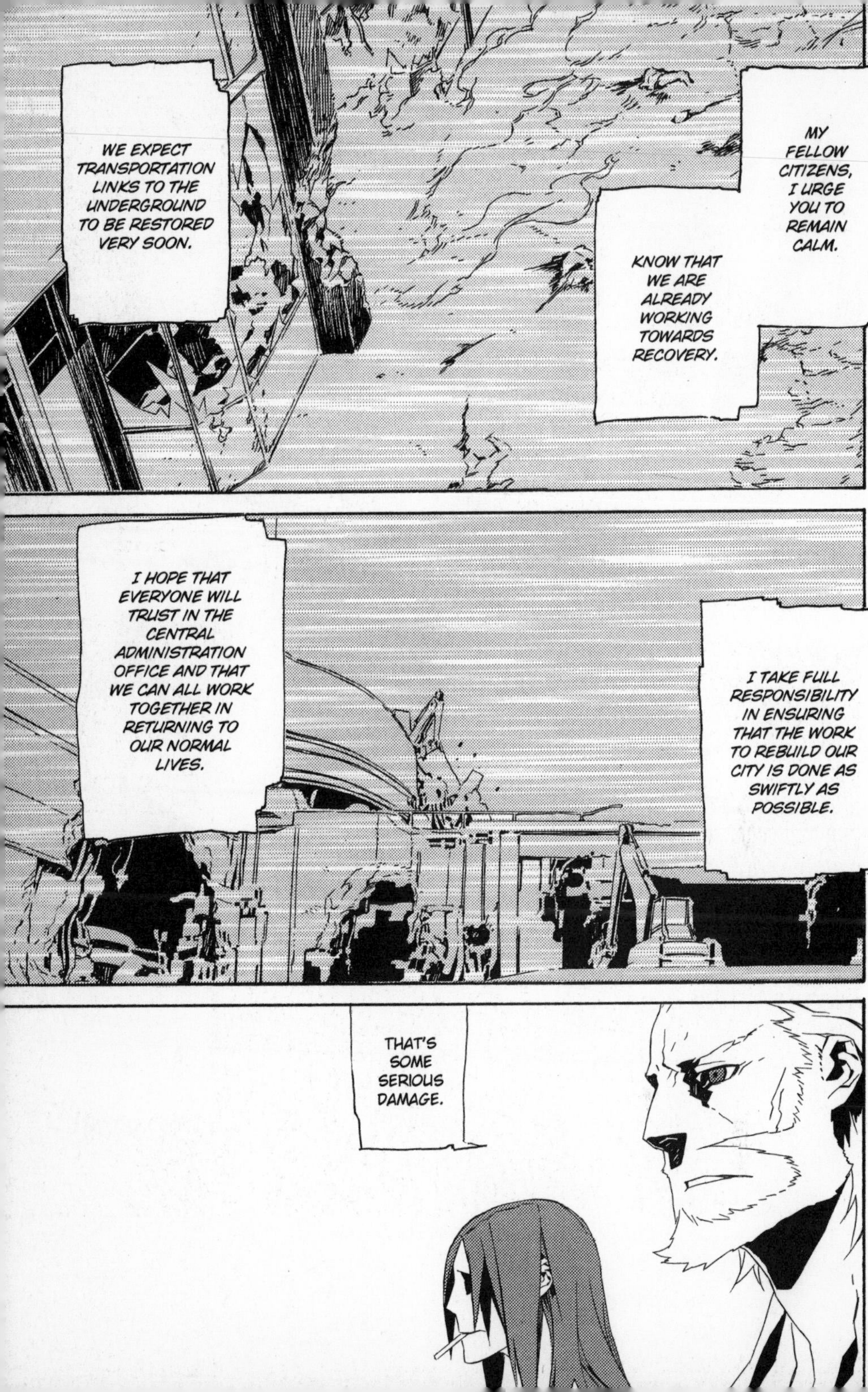
MY FELLOW CITIZENS, I URGE YOU TO REMAIN CALM.
KNOW THAT WE ARE ALREADY WORKING TOWARDS RECOVERY.
WE EXPECT TRANSPORTATION LINKS TO THE UNDERGROUND TO BE RESTORED VERY SOON.
I TAKE FULL RESPONSIBILITY IN ENSURING THAT THE WORK TO REBUILD OUR CITY IS DONE AS SWIFTLY AS POSSIBLE.
I HOPE THAT EVERYONE WILL TRUST IN THE CENTRAL ADMINISTRATION OFFICE AND THAT WE CAN ALL WORK TOGETHER IN RETURNING TO OUR NORMAL LIVES.
THAT'S SOME SERIOUS DAMAGE.

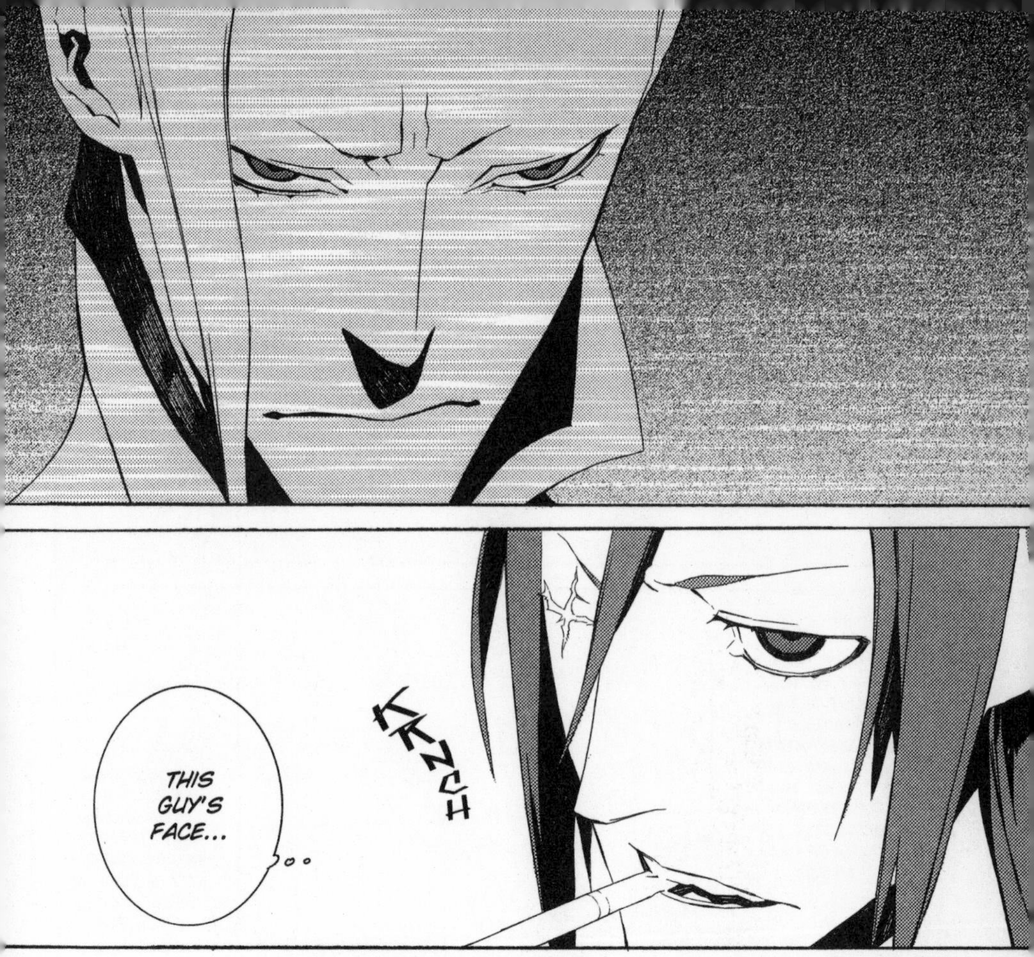
KRNCH
THIS GUY'S FACE...

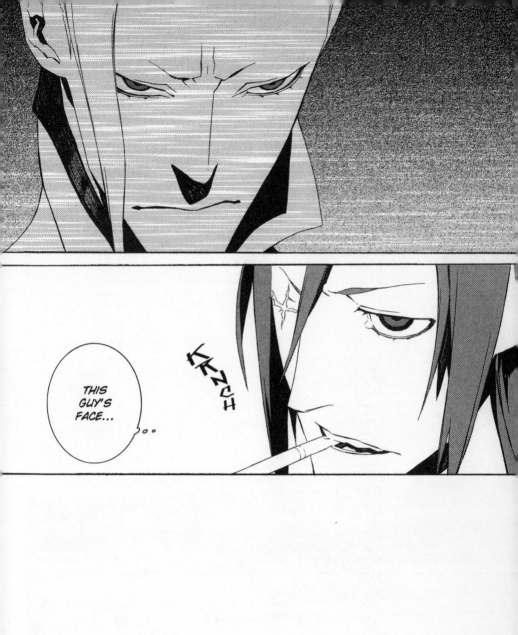

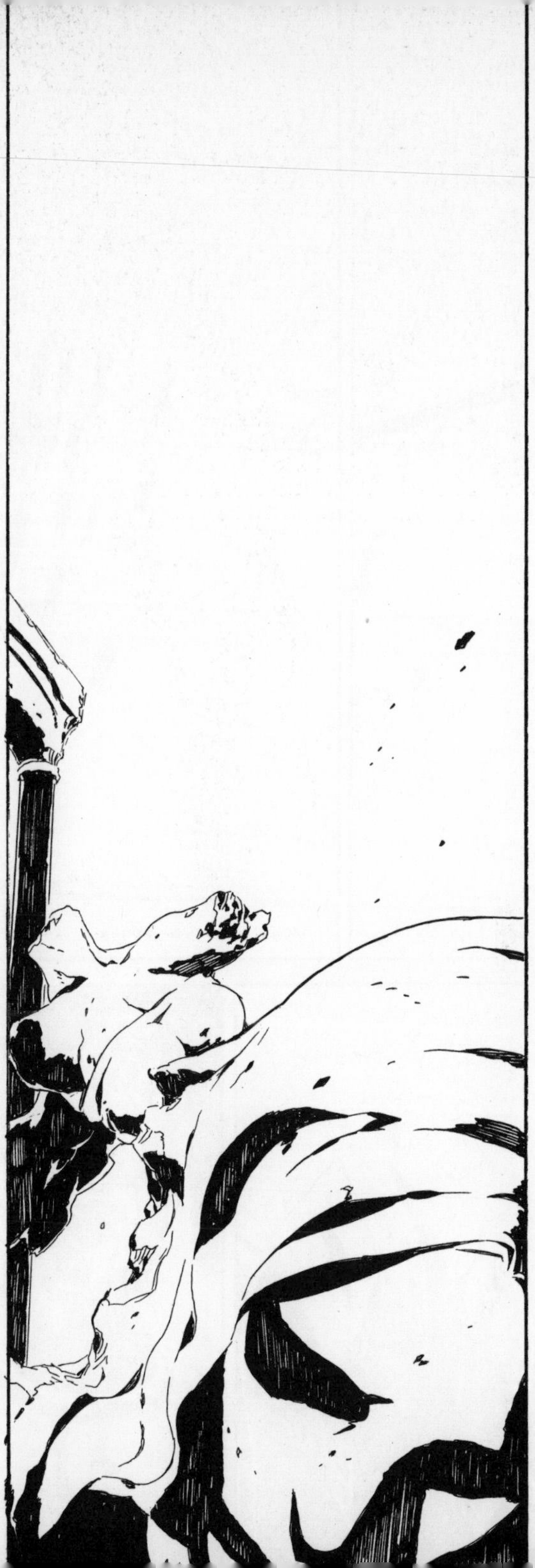

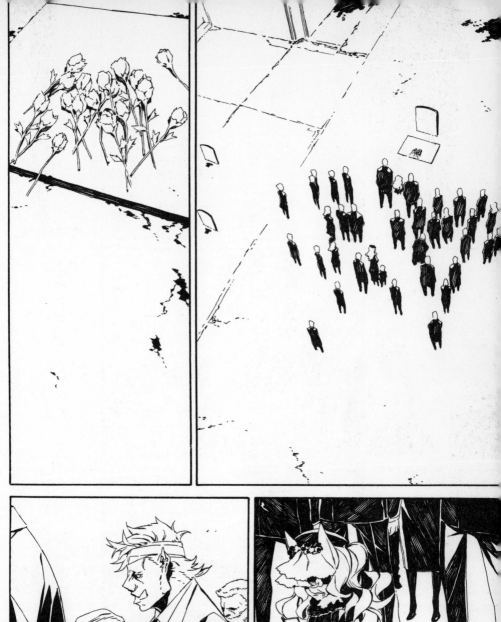

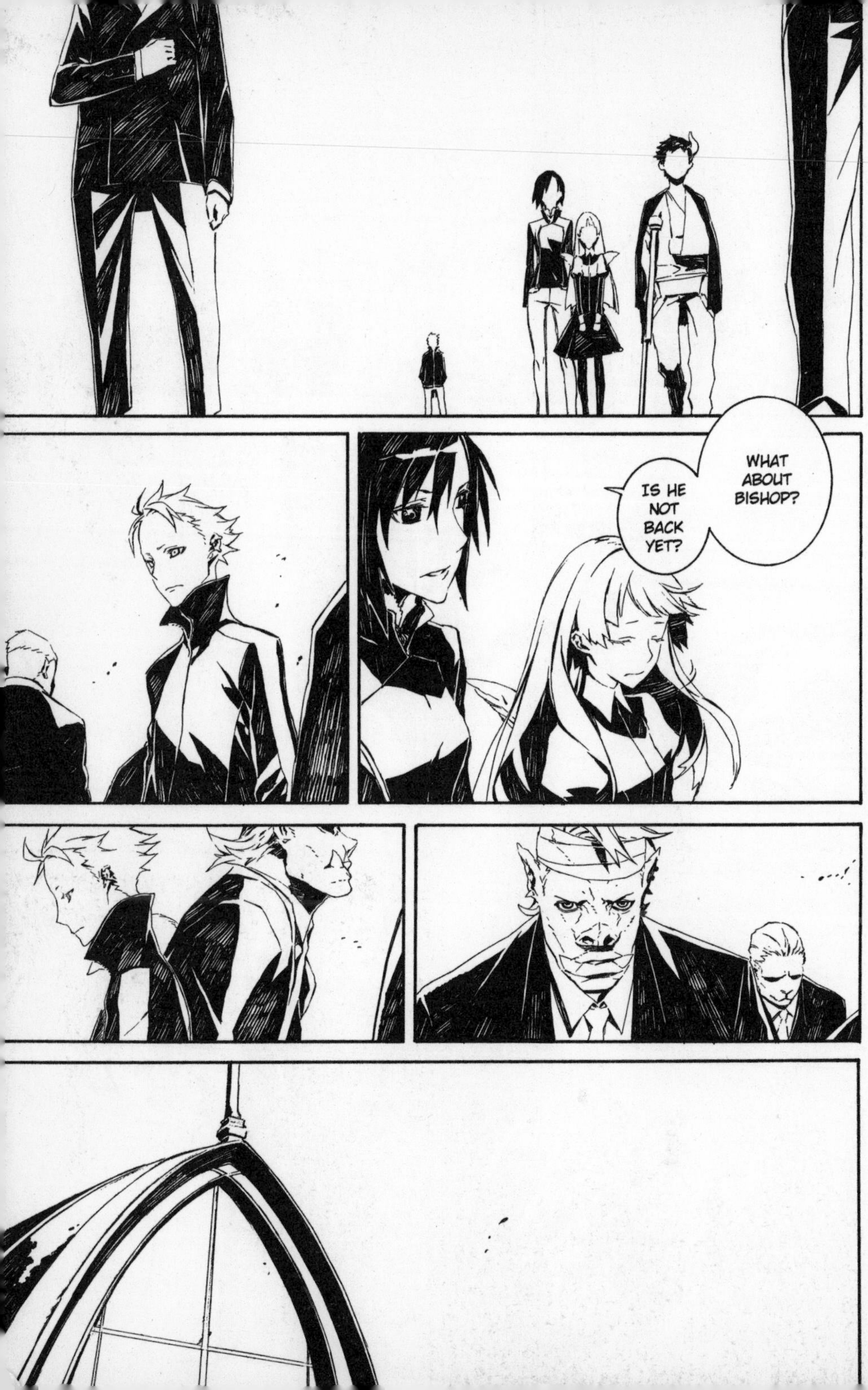
WHAT ABOUT BISHOP?
IS HE NOT BACK YET?

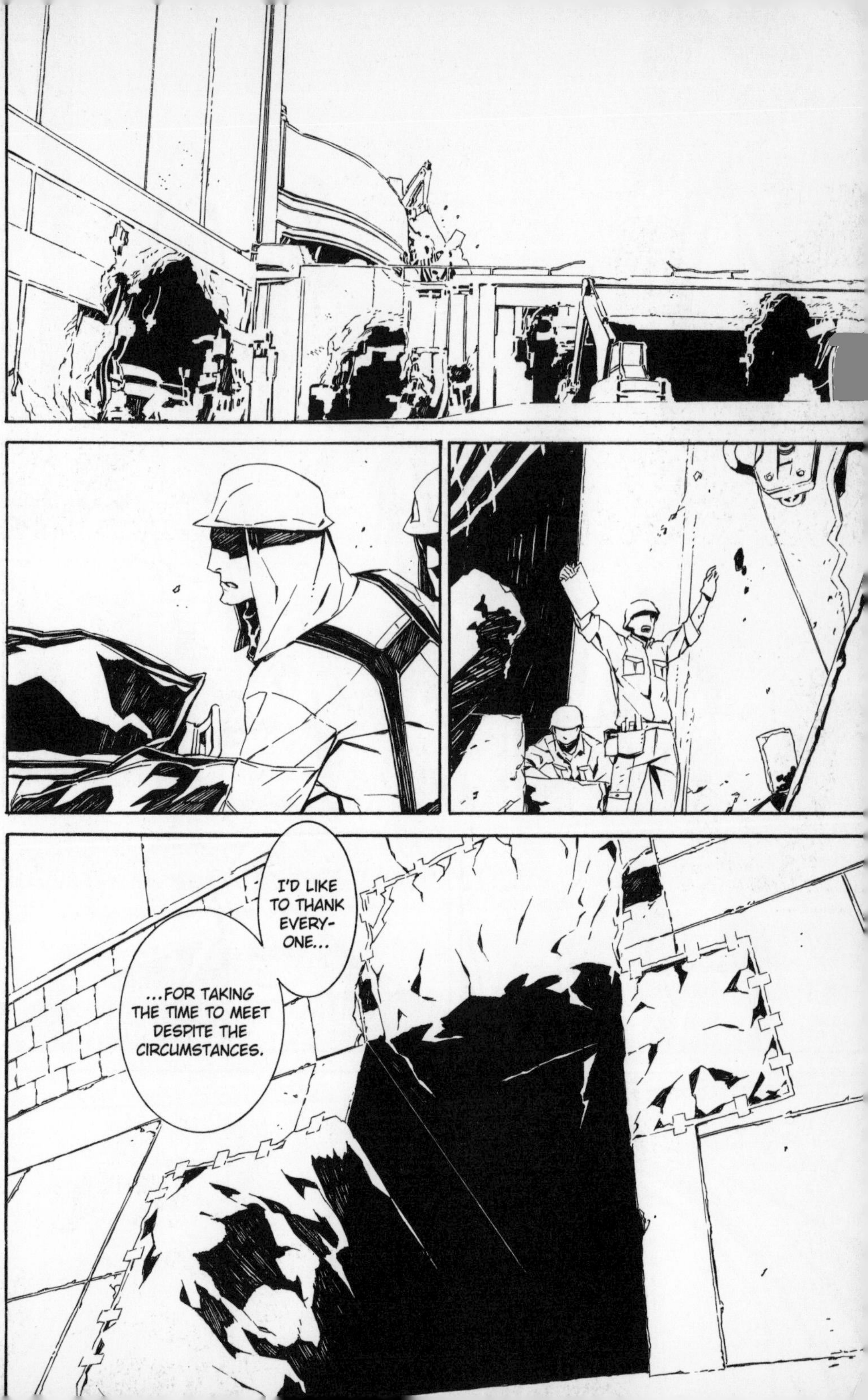
I'D LIKE TO THANK EVERY-ONE...
...FOR TAKING THE TIME TO MEET DESPITE THE CIRCUMSTANCES.

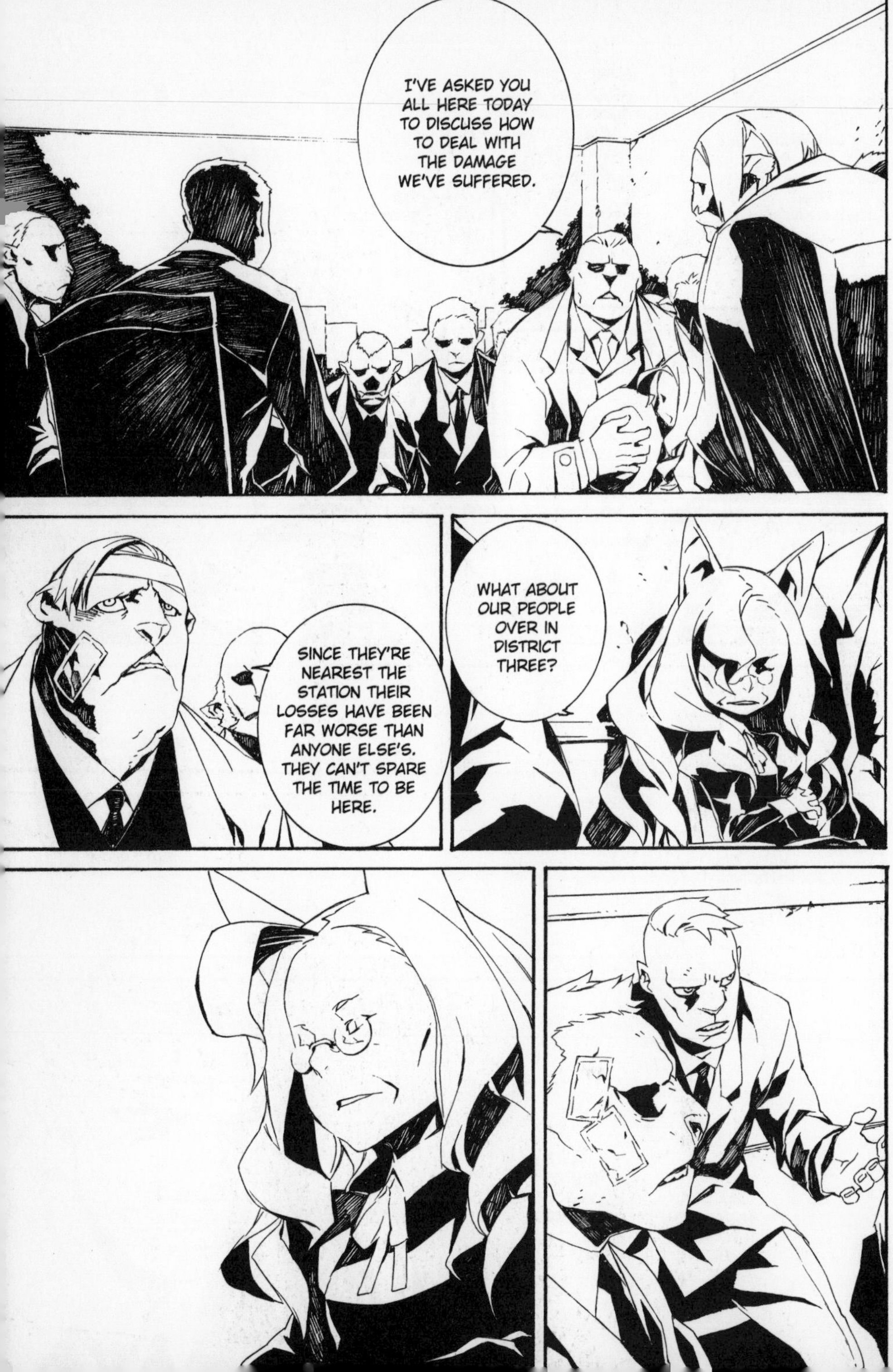
I'VE ASKED YOU ALL HERE TODAY TO DISCUSS HOW TO DEAL WITH THE DAMAGE WE'VE SUFFERED.
WHAT ABOUT OUR PEOPLE OVER IN DISTRICT THREE?
SINCE THEY'RE NEAREST THE STATION THEIR LOSSES HAVE BEEN FAR WORSE THAN ANYONE ELSE'S. THEY CAN'T SPARE THE TIME TO BE HERE.

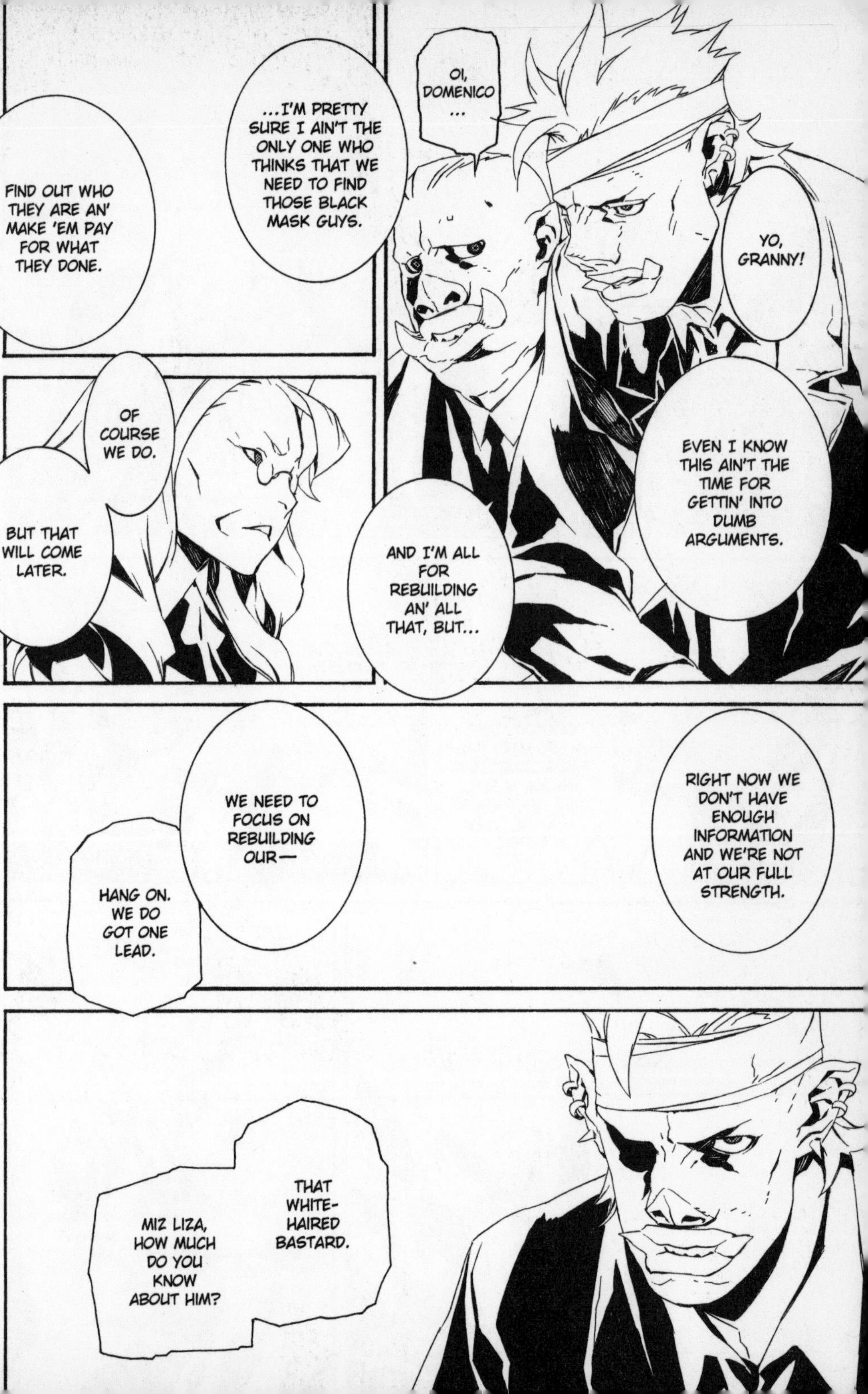
YO, GRANNY!
EVEN I KNOW THIS AIN'T THE TIME FOR GETTIN' INTO DUMB ARGUMENTS.
AND I'M ALL FOR REBUILDING AN' ALL THAT, BUT...
OI, DOMENICO...
...I'M PRETTY SURE I AIN'T THE ONLY ONE WHO THINKS THAT WE NEED TO FIND THOSE BLACK MASK GUYS.
FIND OUT WHO THEY ARE AN' MAKE 'EM PAY FOR WHAT THEY DONE.
OF COURSE WE DO.
BUT THAT WILL COME LATER.
RIGHT NOW WE DON'T HAVE ENOUGH INFORMATION AND WE'RE NOT AT OUR FULL STRENGTH.
WE NEED TO FOCUS ON REBUILDING OUR—
HANG ON. WE DO GOT ONE LEAD.
THAT WHITE-HAIRED BASTARD.
MIZ LIZA, HOW MUCH DO YOU KNOW ABOUT HIM?

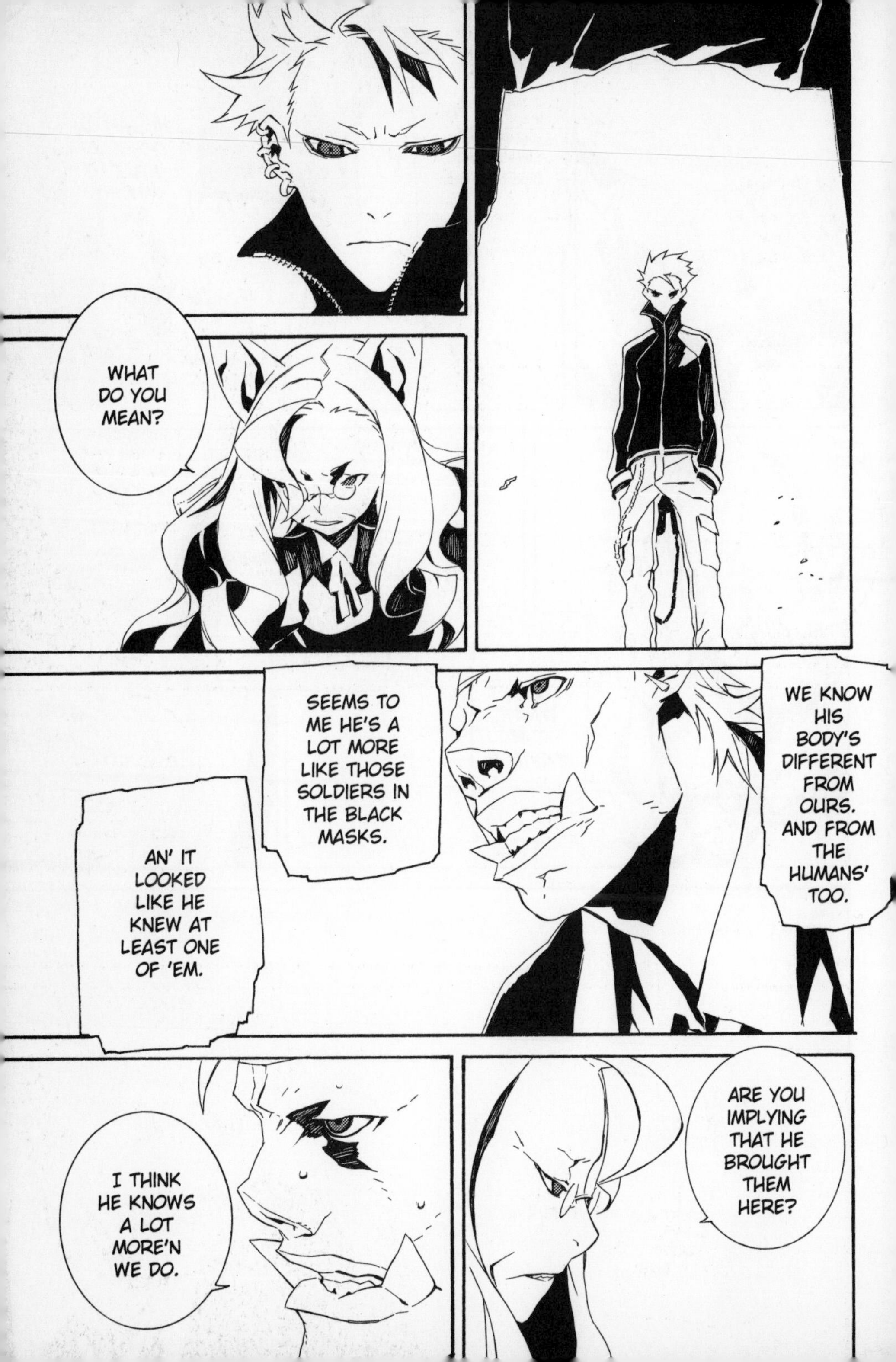
WHAT DO YOU MEAN?
WE KNOW HIS BODY'S DIFFERENT FROM OURS. AND FROM THE HUMANS' TOO.
SEEMS TO ME HE'S A LOT MORE LIKE THOSE SOLDIERS IN THE BLACK MASKS.
AN' IT LOOKED LIKE HE KNEW AT LEAST ONE OF 'EM.
ARE YOU IMPLYING THAT HE BROUGHT THEM HERE?
I THINK HE KNOWS A LOT MORE'N WE DO.

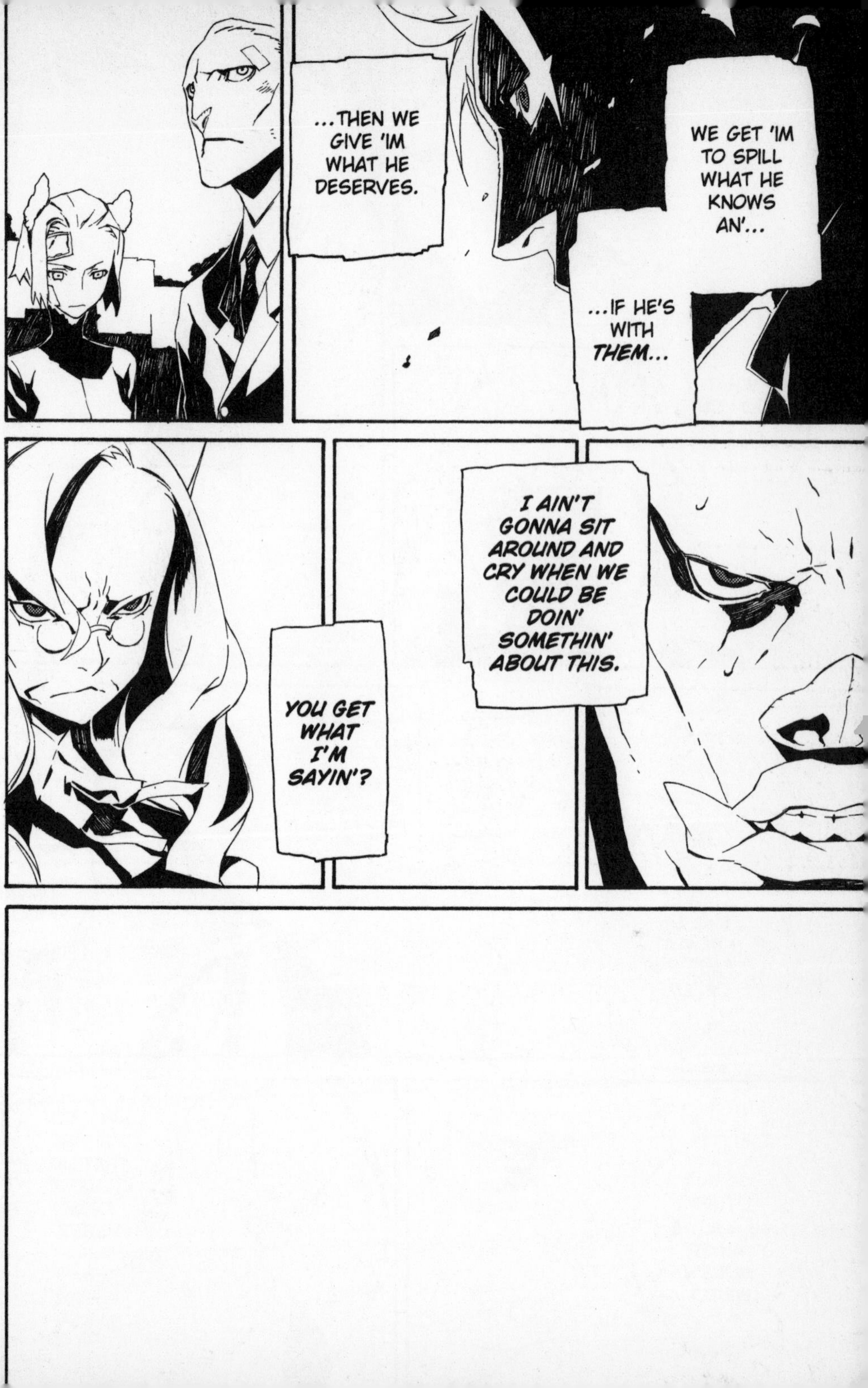
WE GET 'IM TO SPILL WHAT HE KNOWS AN'...
...IF HE'S WITH *THEM*...
...THEN WE GIVE 'IM WHAT HE DESERVES.
I AIN'T GONNA SIT AROUND AND CRY WHEN WE COULD BE DOIN' SOMETHIN' ABOUT THIS.
YOU GET WHAT I'M SAYIN'?

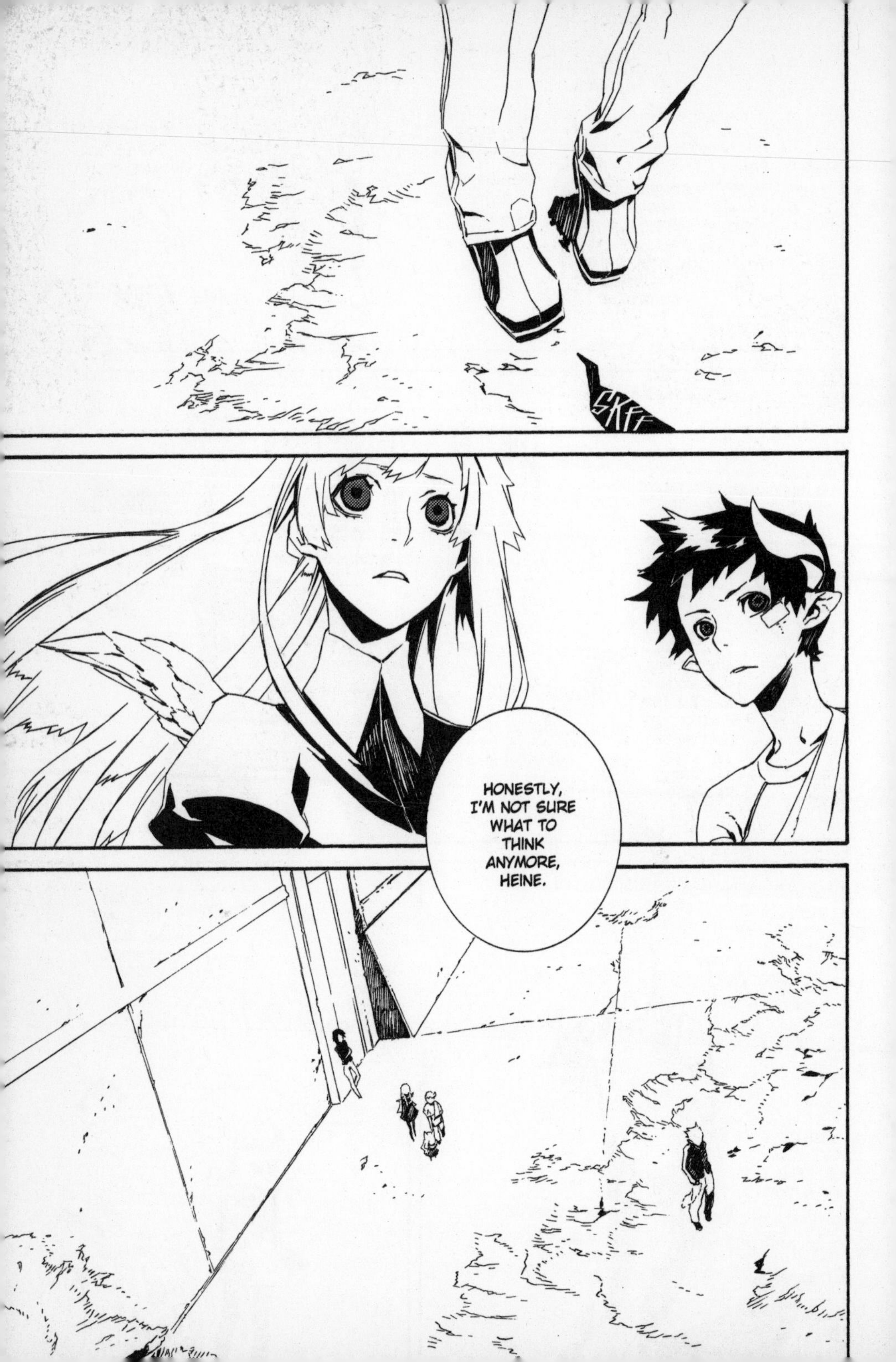
SKFF
HONESTLY, I'M NOT SURE WHAT TO THINK ANYMORE, HEINE.

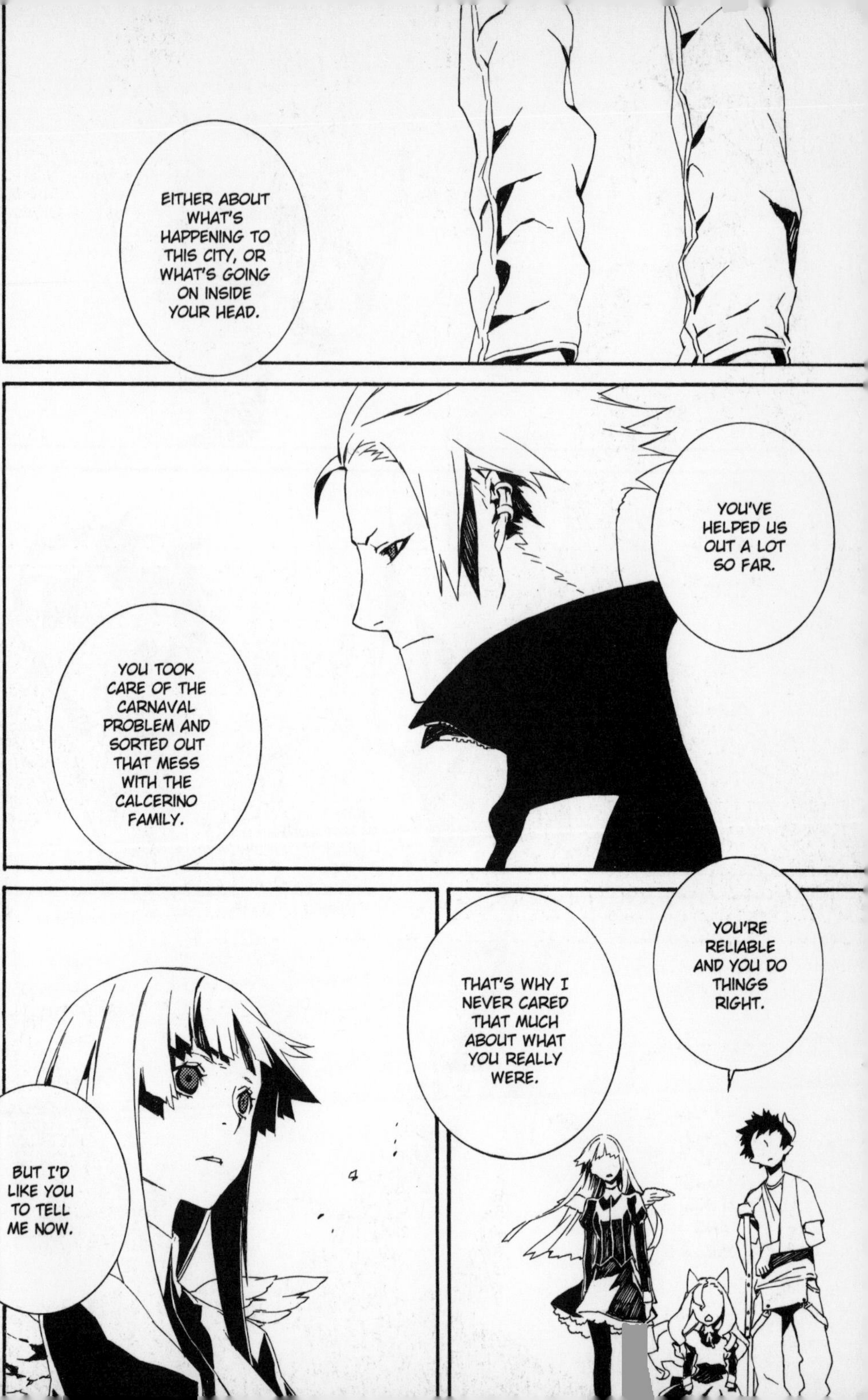
EITHER ABOUT WHAT'S HAPPENING TO THIS CITY, OR WHAT'S GOING ON INSIDE YOUR HEAD.
YOU'VE HELPED US OUT A LOT SO FAR.
YOU TOOK CARE OF THE CARNAVAL PROBLEM AND SORTED OUT THAT MESS WITH THE CALCERINO FAMILY.
YOU'RE RELIABLE AND YOU DO THINGS RIGHT.
THAT'S WHY I NEVER CARED THAT MUCH ABOUT WHAT YOU REALLY WERE.
BUT I'D LIKE YOU TO TELL ME NOW.

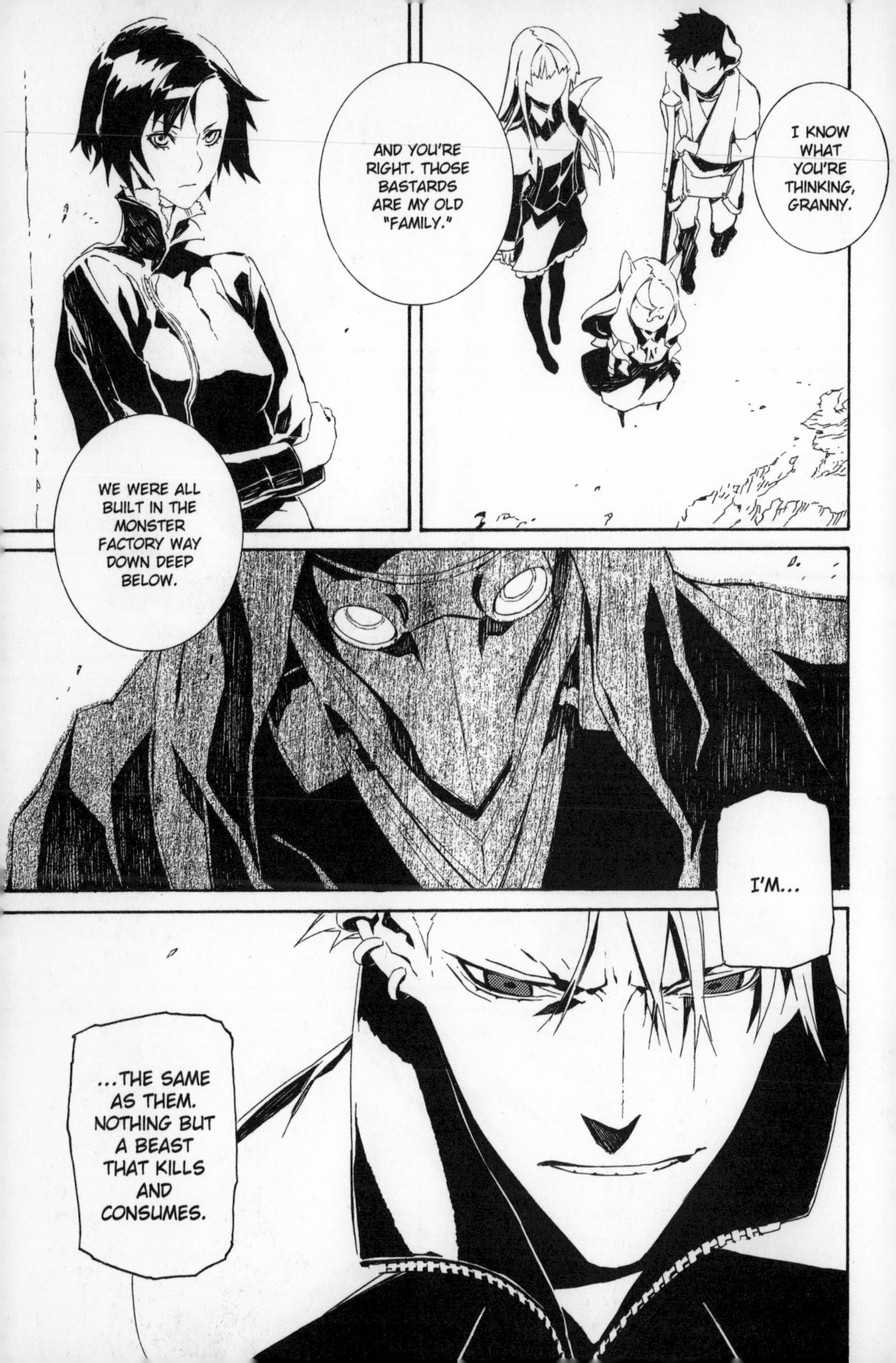
I KNOW WHAT YOU'RE THINKING, GRANNY.
AND YOU'RE RIGHT. THOSE BASTARDS ARE MY OLD "FAMILY."
WE WERE ALL BUILT IN THE MONSTER FACTORY WAY DOWN DEEP BELOW.
I'M...
...THE SAME AS THEM. NOTHING BUT A BEAST THAT KILLS AND CONSUMES.

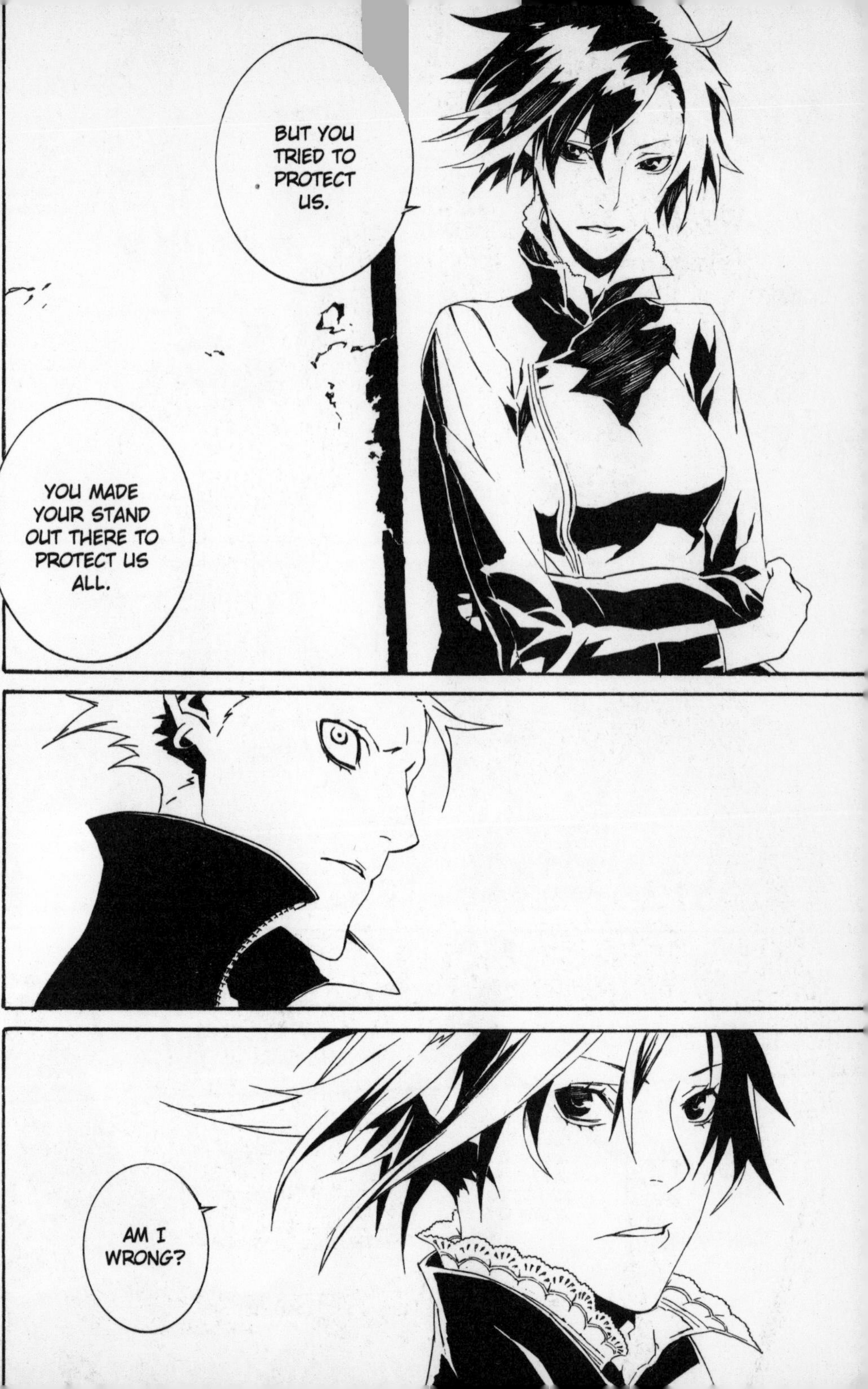
BUT YOU TRIED TO PROTECT US.
YOU MADE YOUR STAND OUT THERE TO PROTECT US ALL.
AM I WRONG?

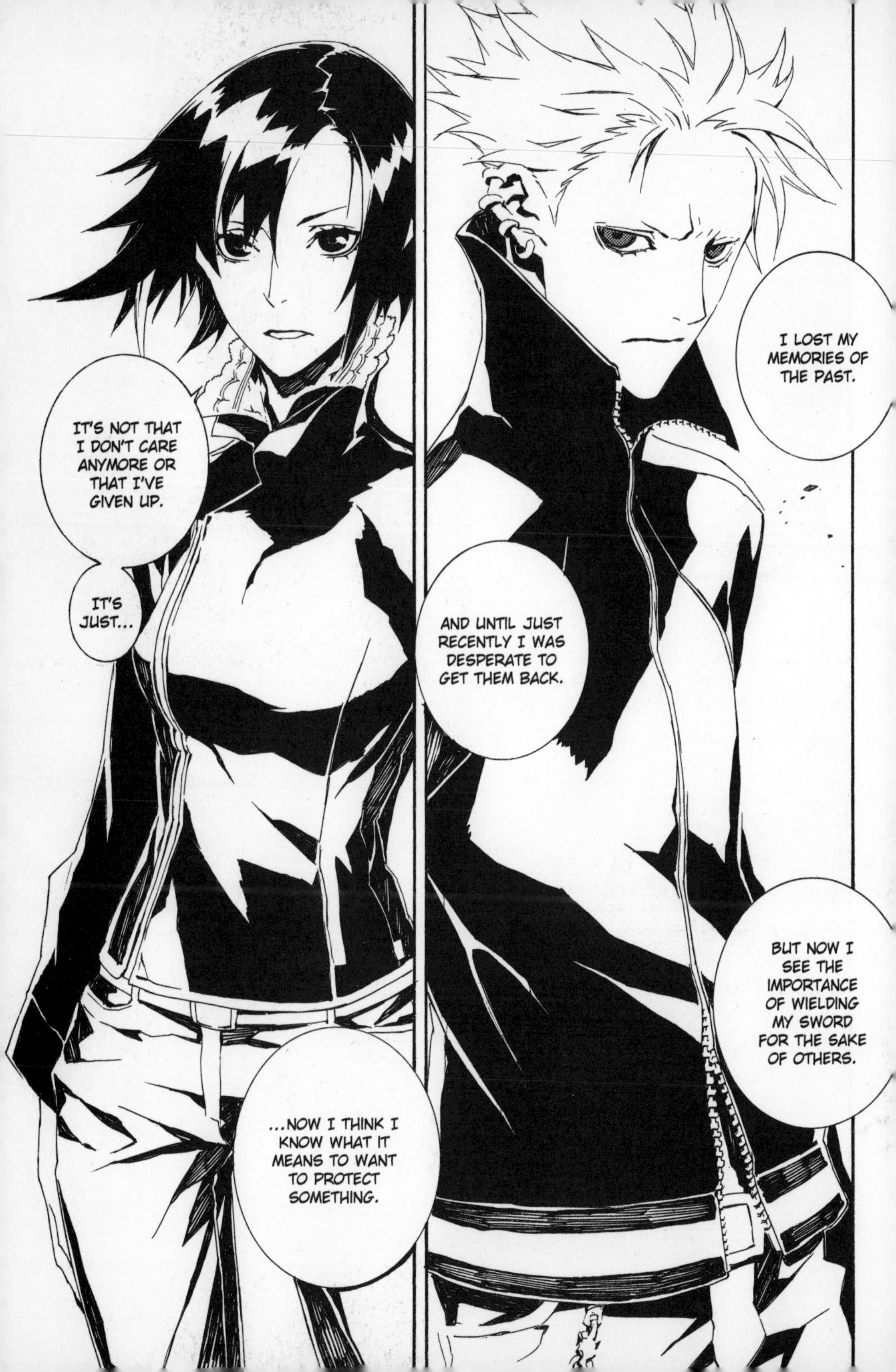
I LOST MY MEMORIES OF THE PAST.
AND UNTIL JUST RECENTLY I WAS DESPERATE TO GET THEM BACK.
BUT NOW I SEE THE IMPORTANCE OF WIELDING MY SWORD FOR THE SAKE OF OTHERS.
IT'S NOT THAT I DON'T CARE ANYMORE OR THAT I'VE GIVEN UP.
IT'S JUST...
...NOW I THINK I KNOW WHAT IT MEANS TO WANT TO PROTECT SOMETHING.

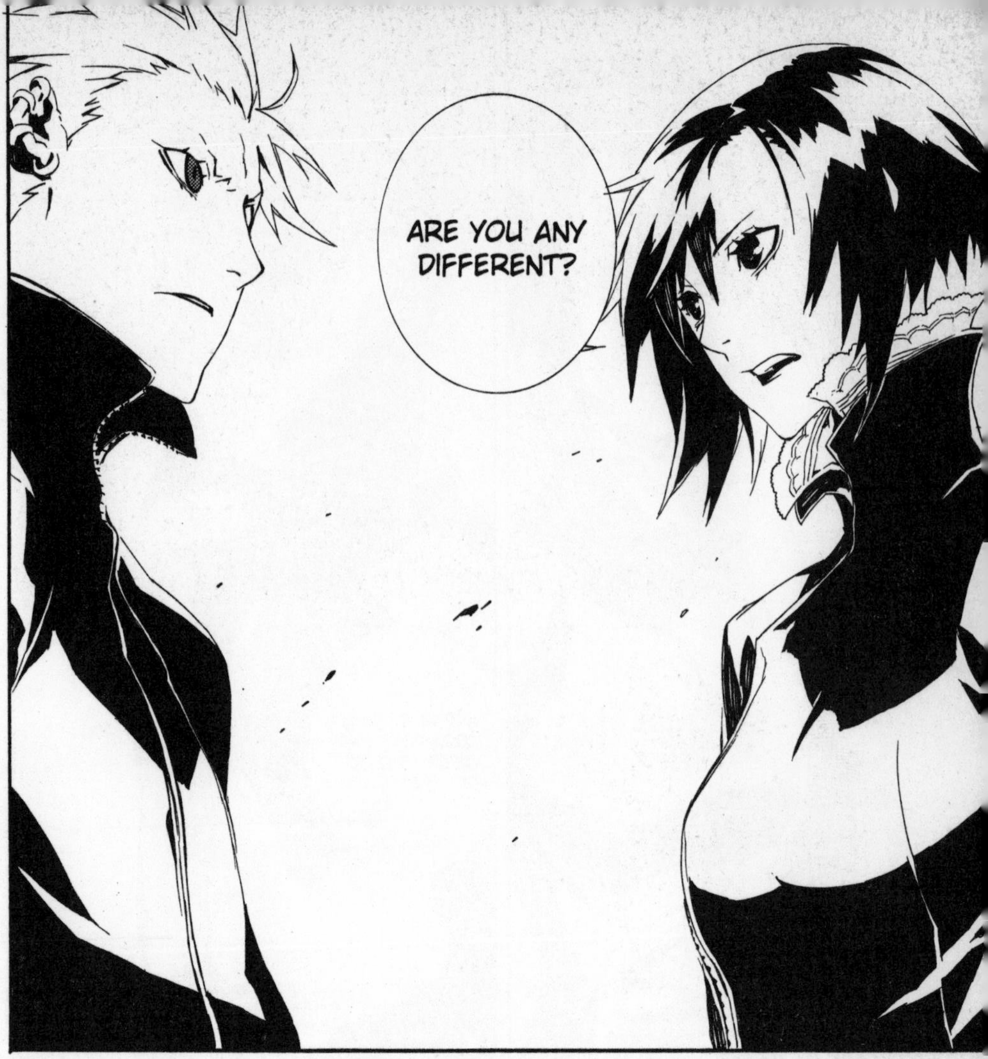
ARE YOU ANY DIFFERENT?

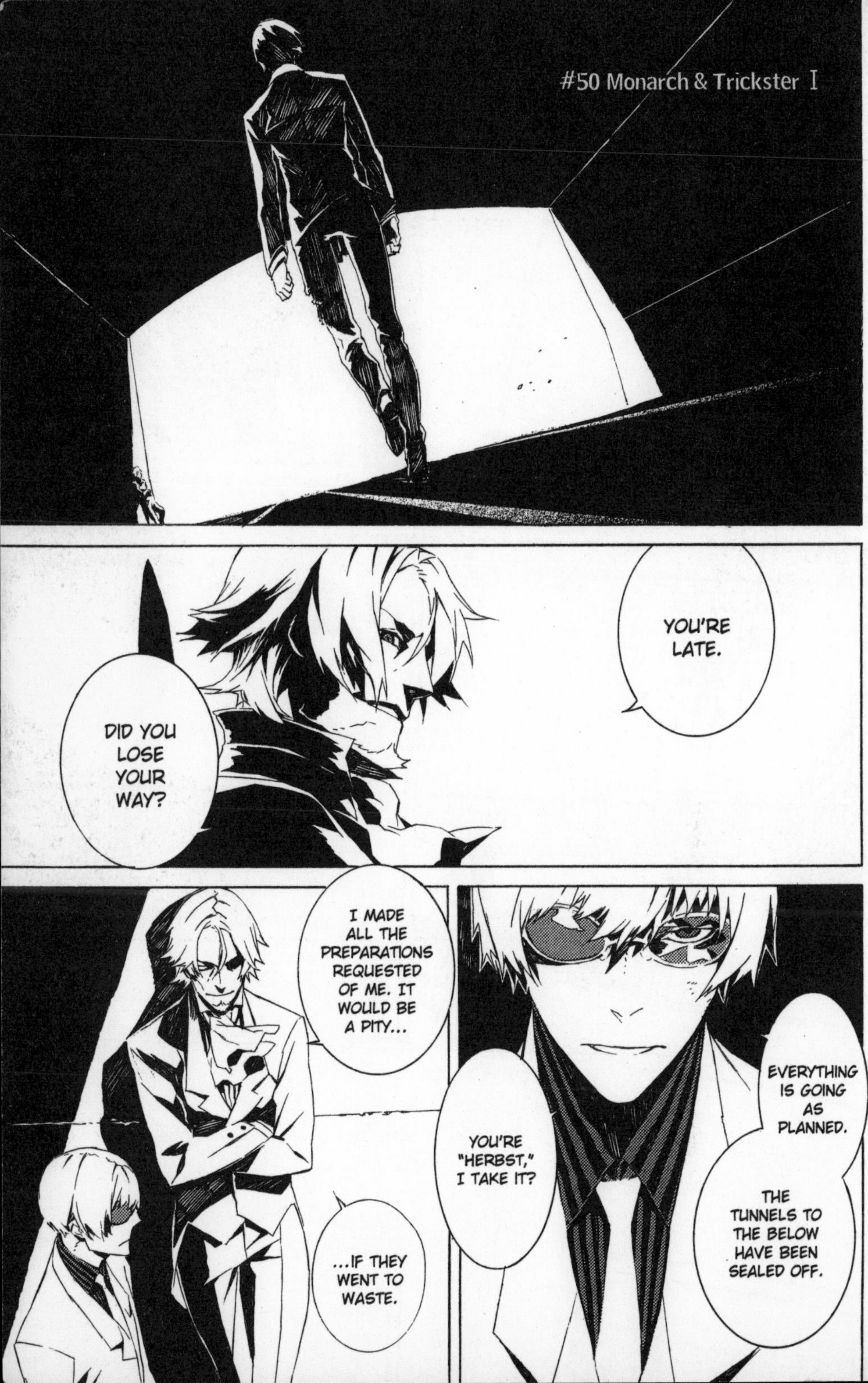
#50 Monarch & Trickster I
YOU'RE LATE.
DID YOU LOSE YOUR WAY?
EVERYTHING IS GOING AS PLANNED.
THE TUNNELS TO THE BELOW HAVE BEEN SEALED OFF.
YOU'RE "HERBST," I TAKE IT?
I MADE ALL THE PREPARATIONS REQUESTED OF ME. IT WOULD BE A PITY...
...IF THEY WENT TO WASTE.

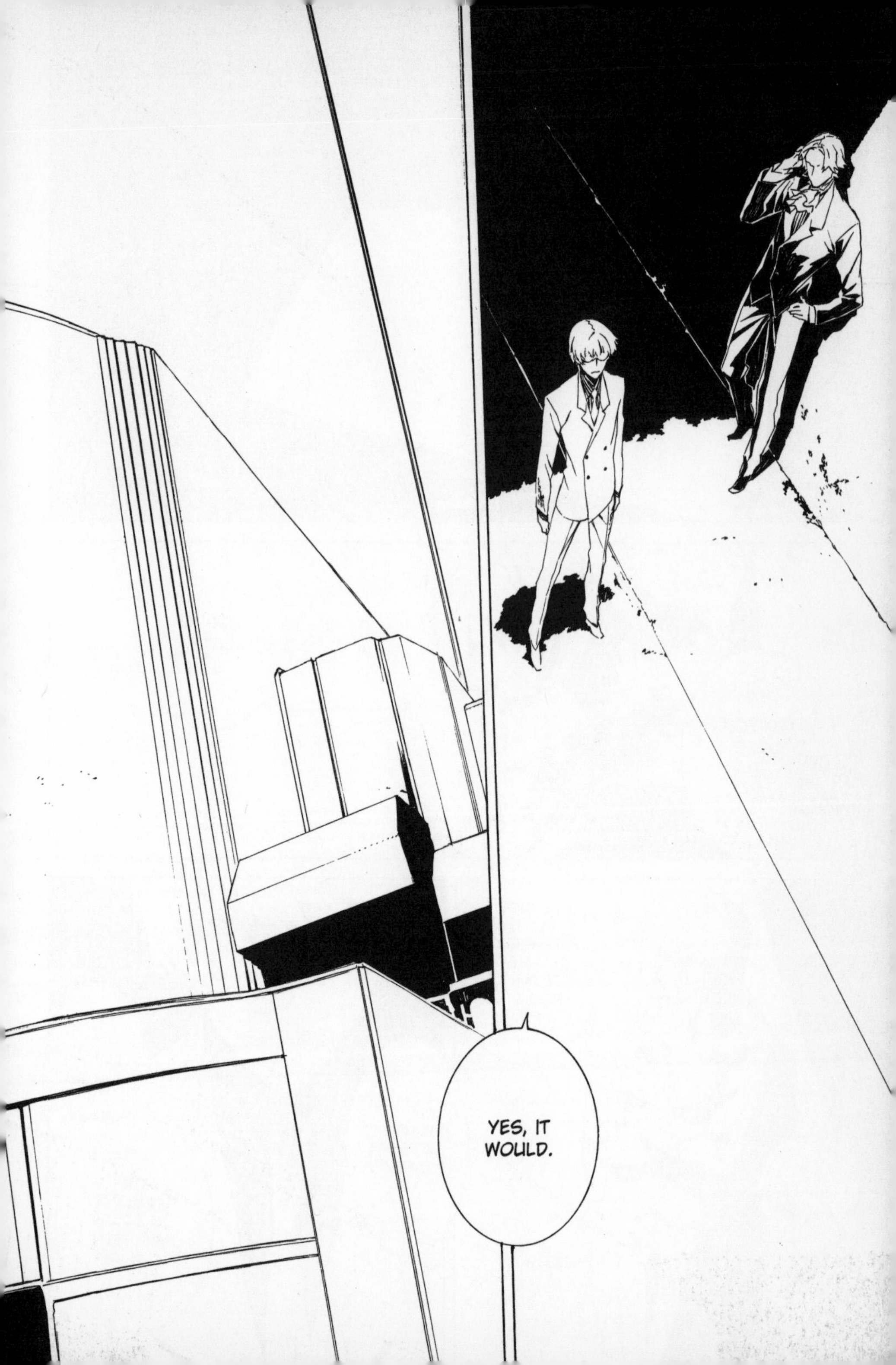
YES, IT WOULD.

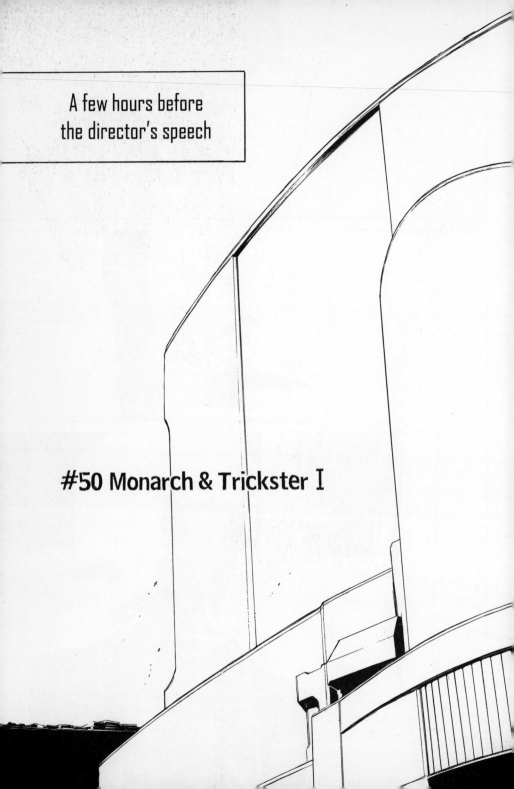

A few hours before
the director's speech

#50 Monarch & Trickster I

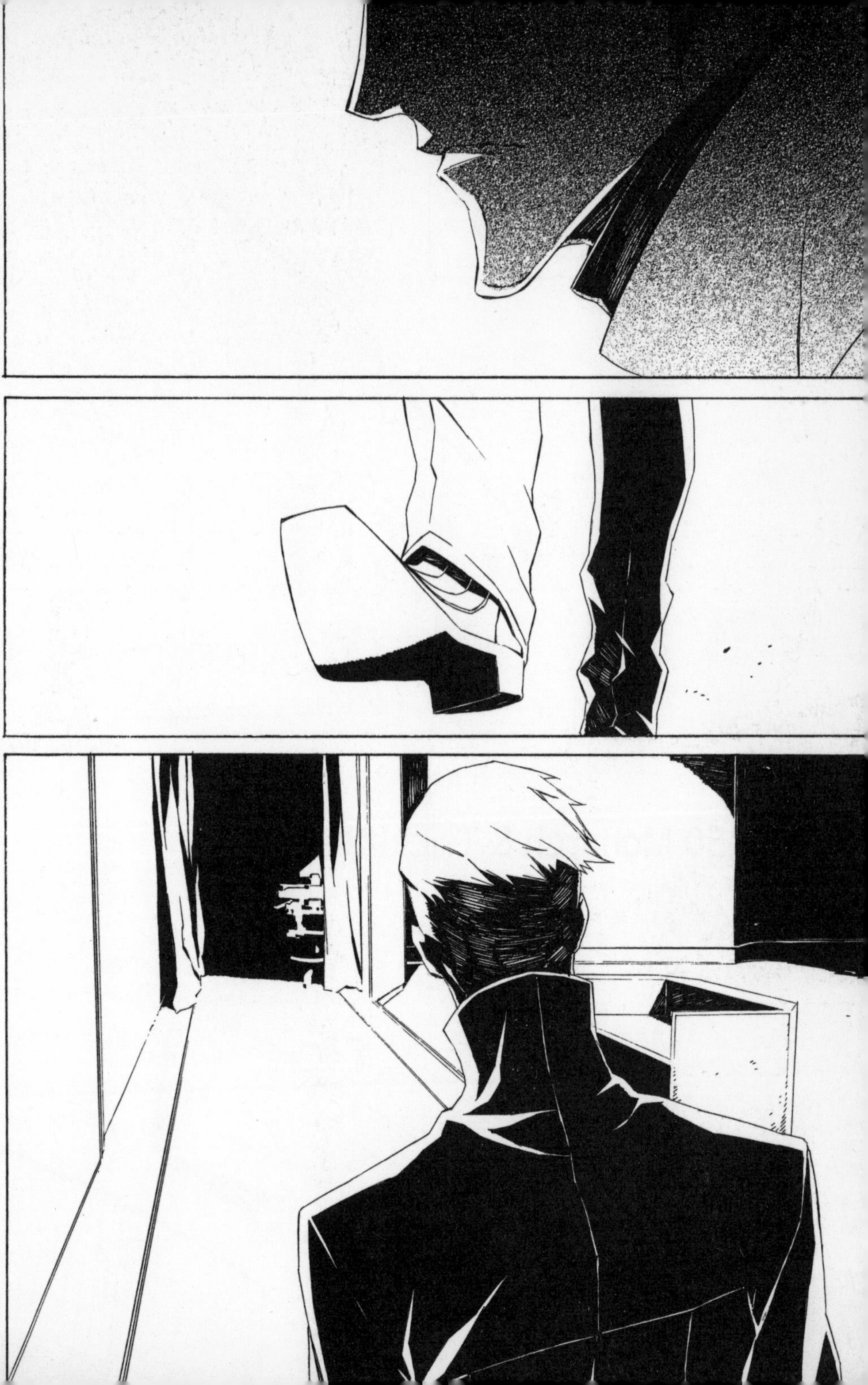

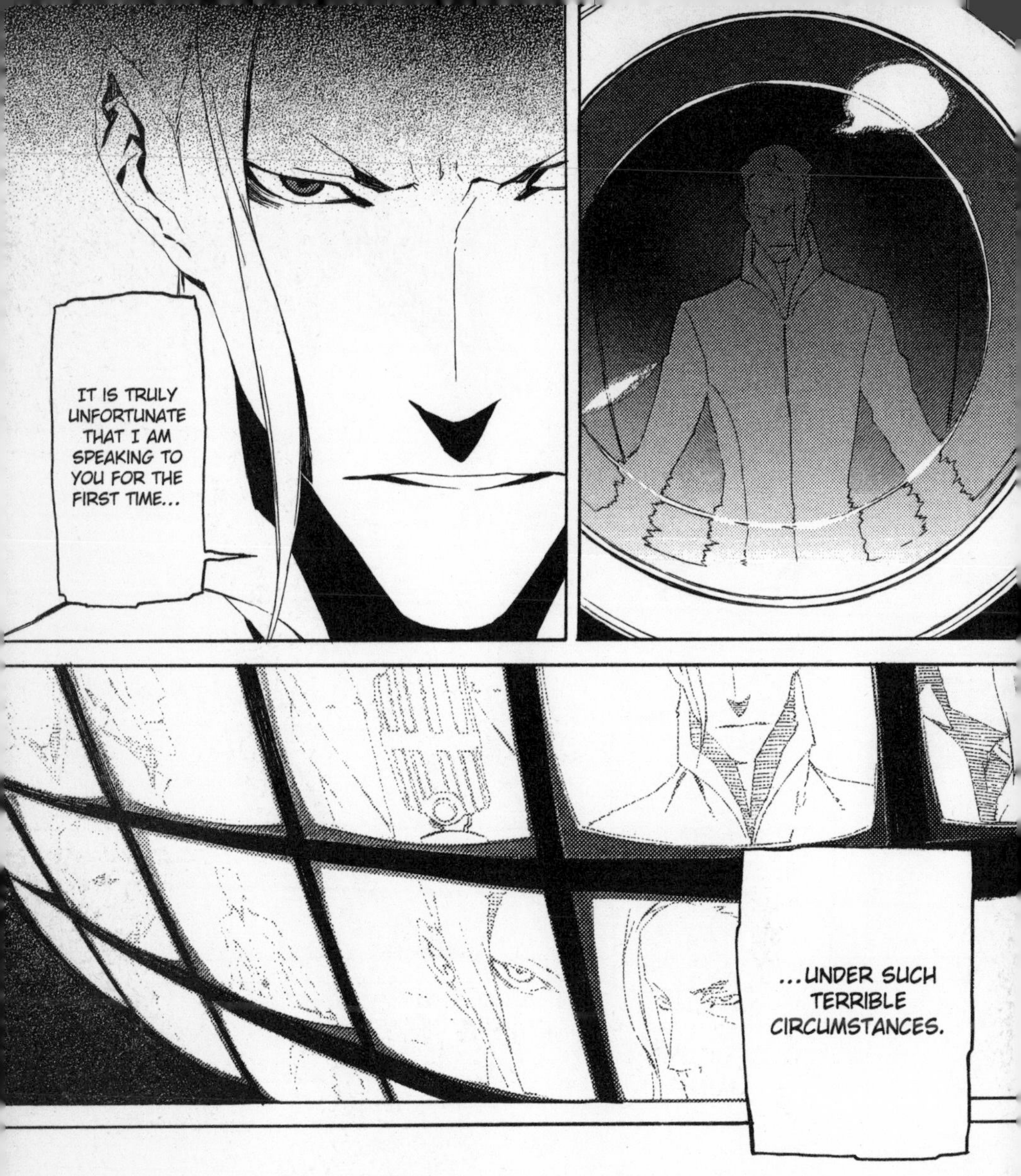
IT IS TRULY UNFORTUNATE THAT I AM SPEAKING TO YOU FOR THE FIRST TIME...
...UNDER SUCH TERRIBLE CIRCUMSTANCES.

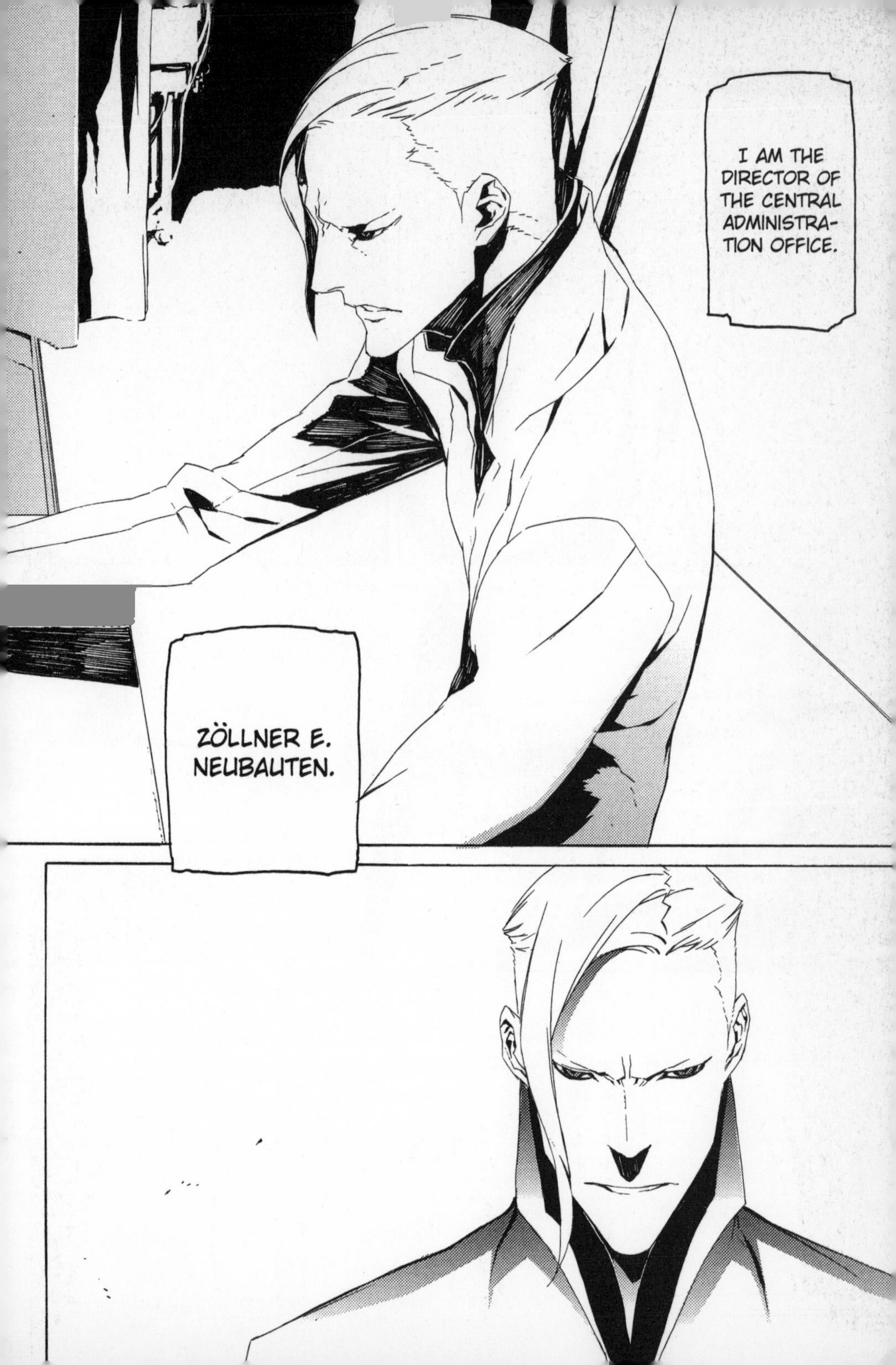
I AM THE DIRECTOR OF THE CENTRAL ADMINISTRATION OFFICE.
ZÖLLNER E. NEUBAUTEN.

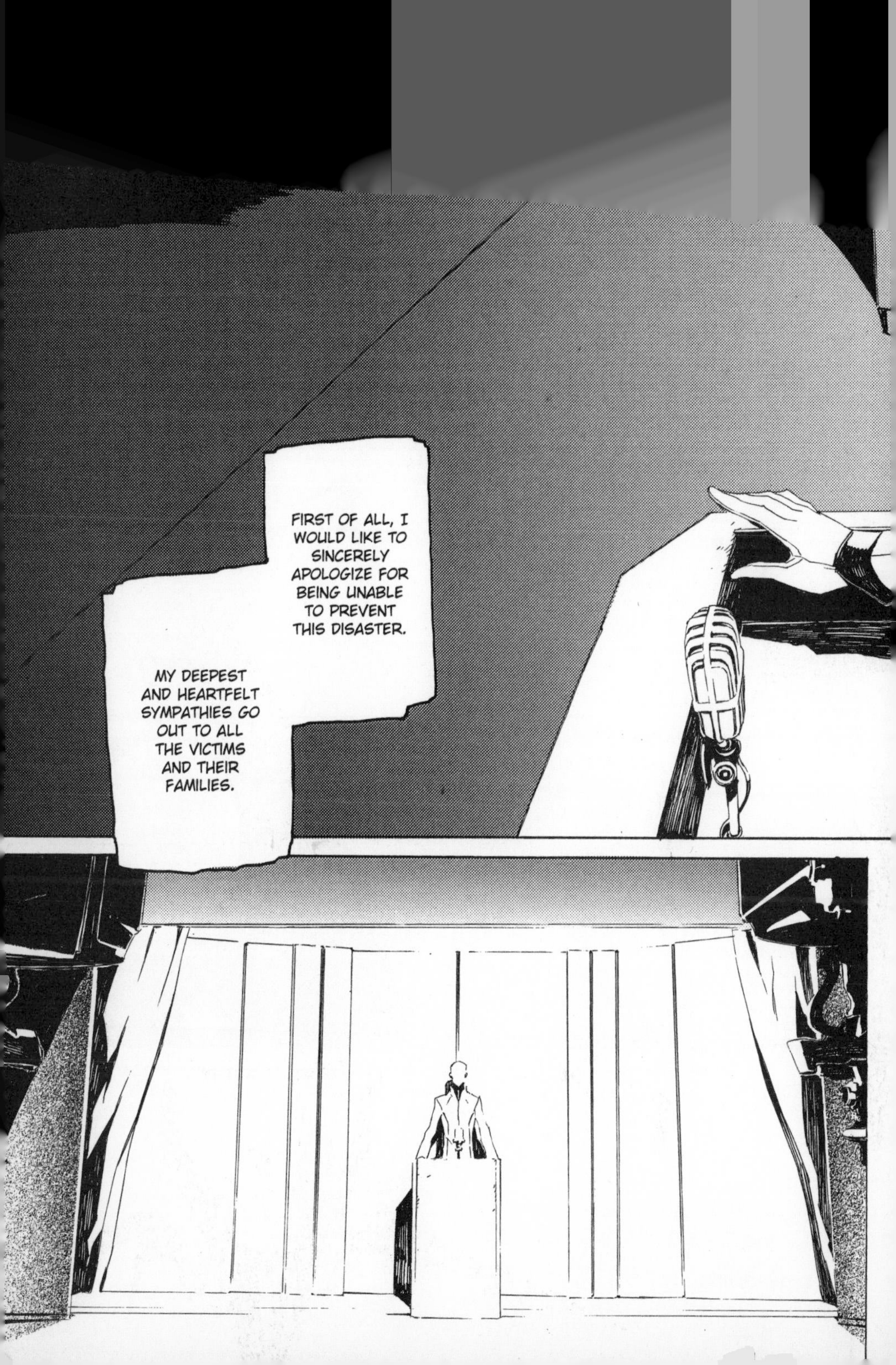
FIRST OF ALL, I WOULD LIKE TO SINCERELY APOLOGIZE FOR BEING UNABLE TO PREVENT THIS DISASTER.
MY DEEPEST AND HEARTFELT SYMPATHIES GO OUT TO ALL THE VICTIMS AND THEIR FAMILIES.

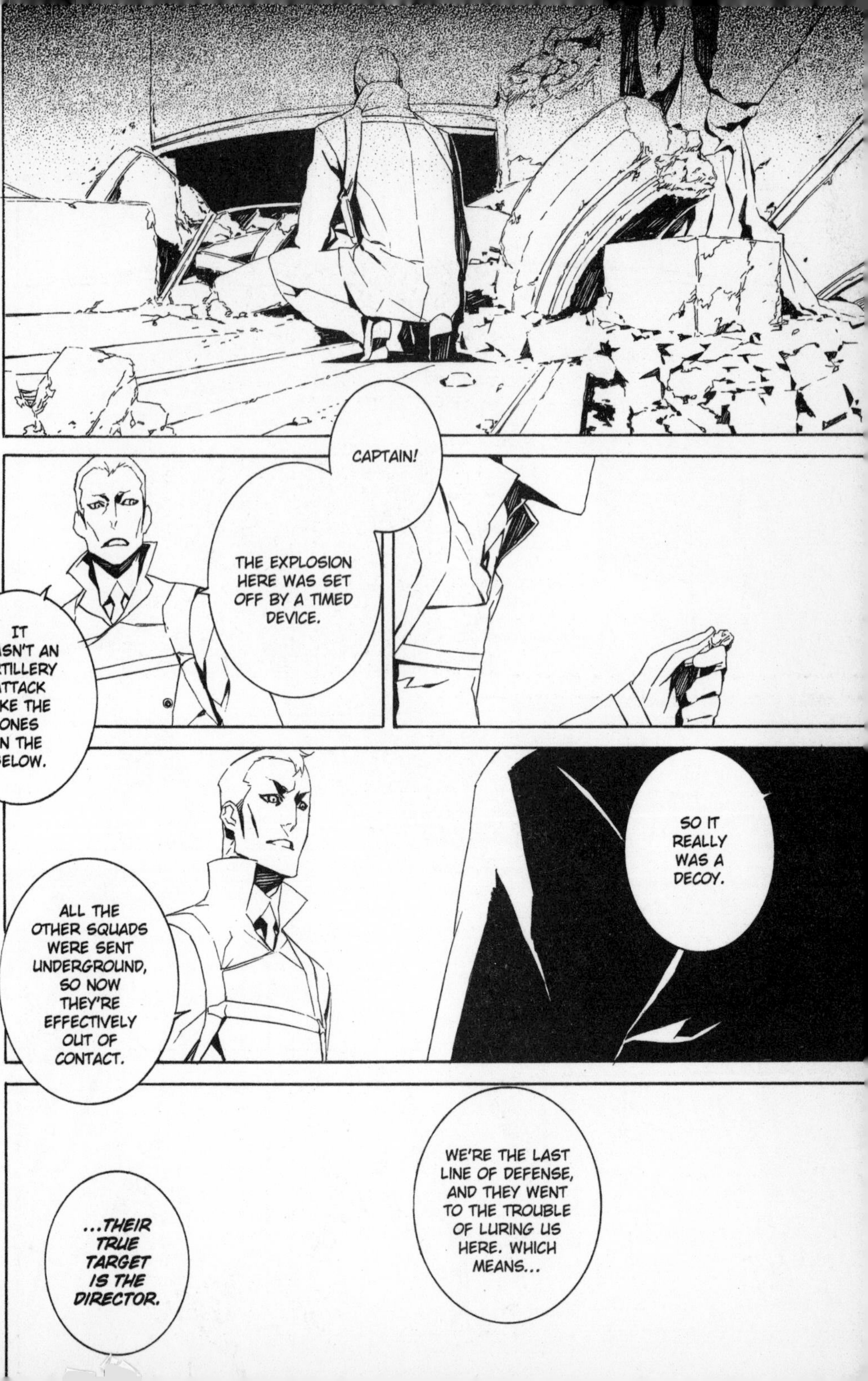
CAPTAIN!
THE EXPLOSION HERE WAS SET OFF BY A TIMED DEVICE.
IT WASN'T AN ARTILLERY ATTACK LIKE THE ONES IN THE BELOW.
SO IT REALLY WAS A DECOY.
ALL THE OTHER SQUADS WERE SENT UNDERGROUND, SO NOW THEY'RE EFFECTIVELY OUT OF CONTACT.
WE'RE THE LAST LINE OF DEFENSE, AND THEY WENT TO THE TROUBLE OF LURING US HERE. WHICH MEANS...
...THEIR TRUE TARGET IS THE DIRECTOR.

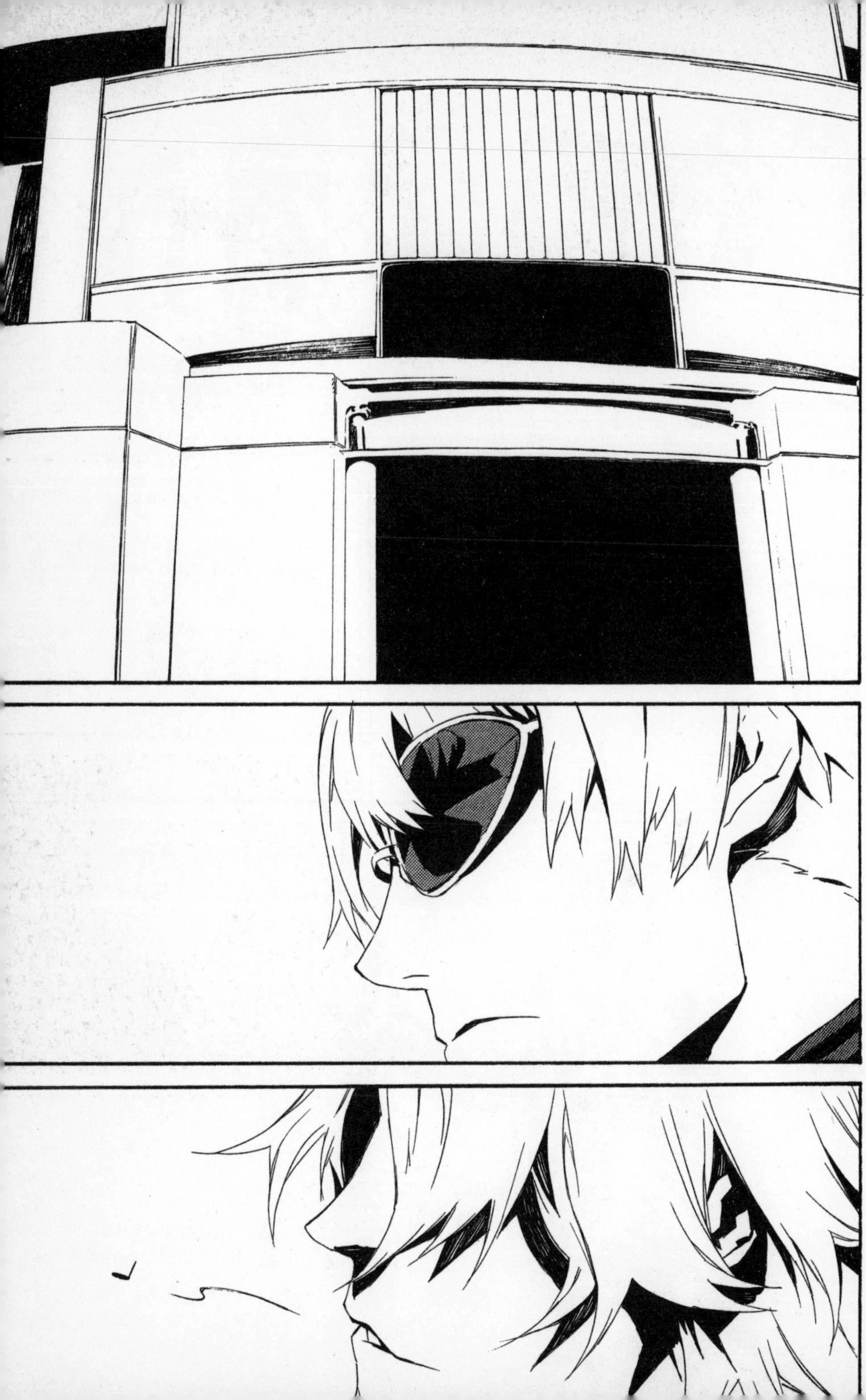

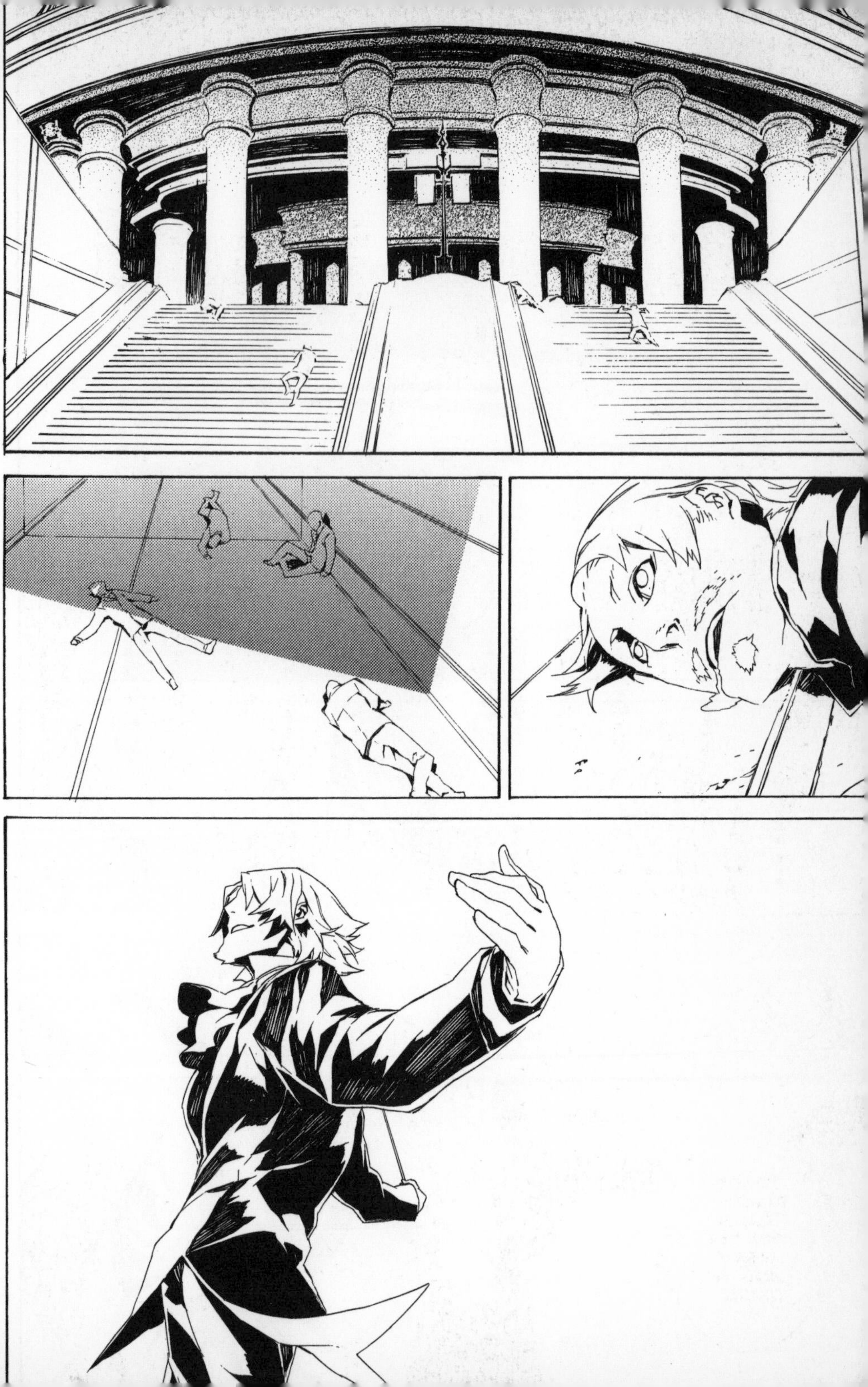

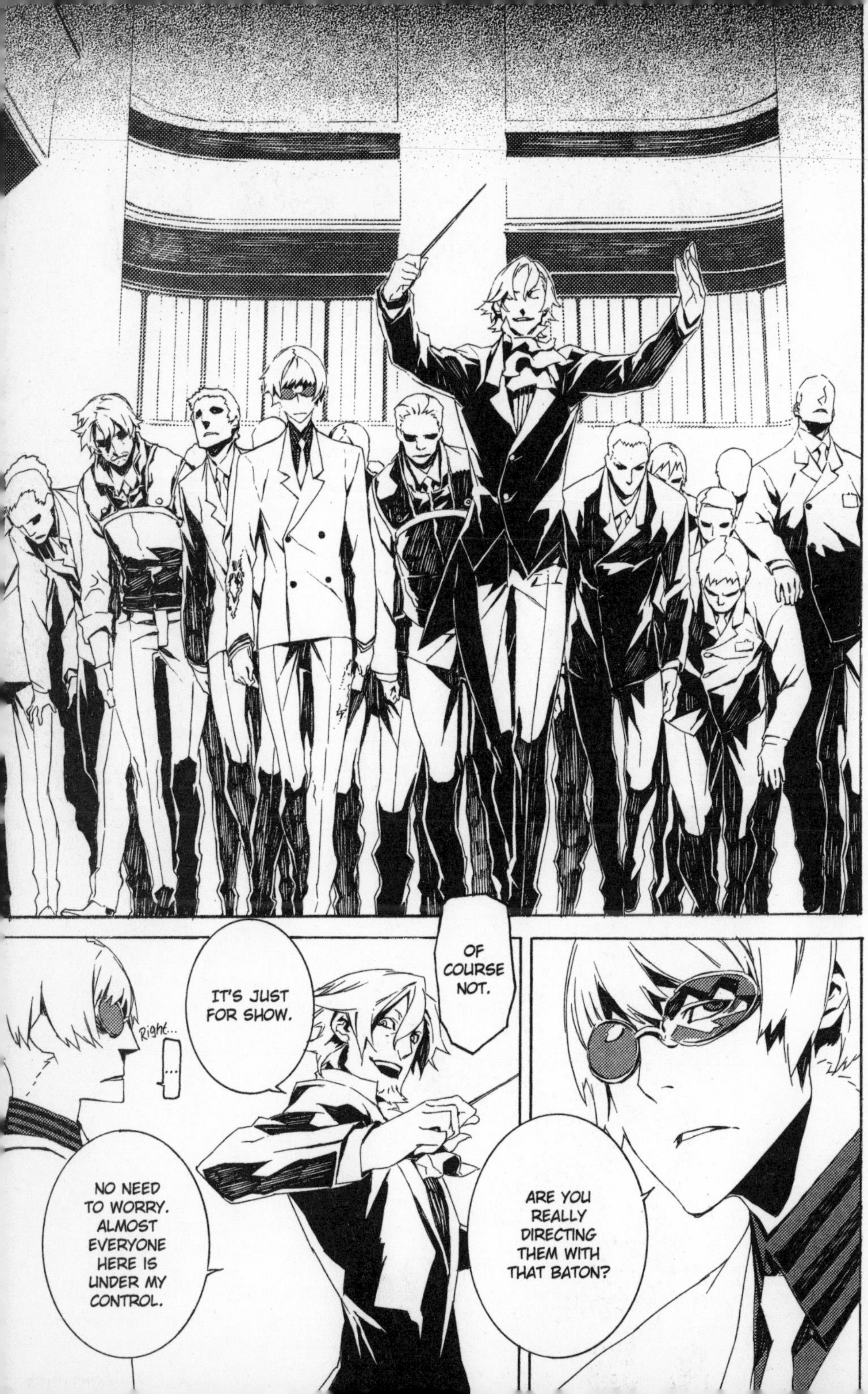
ARE YOU REALLY DIRECTING THEM WITH THAT BATON?
OF COURSE NOT.
IT'S JUST FOR SHOW.
Right...
...
NO NEED TO WORRY. ALMOST EVERYONE HERE IS UNDER MY CONTROL.

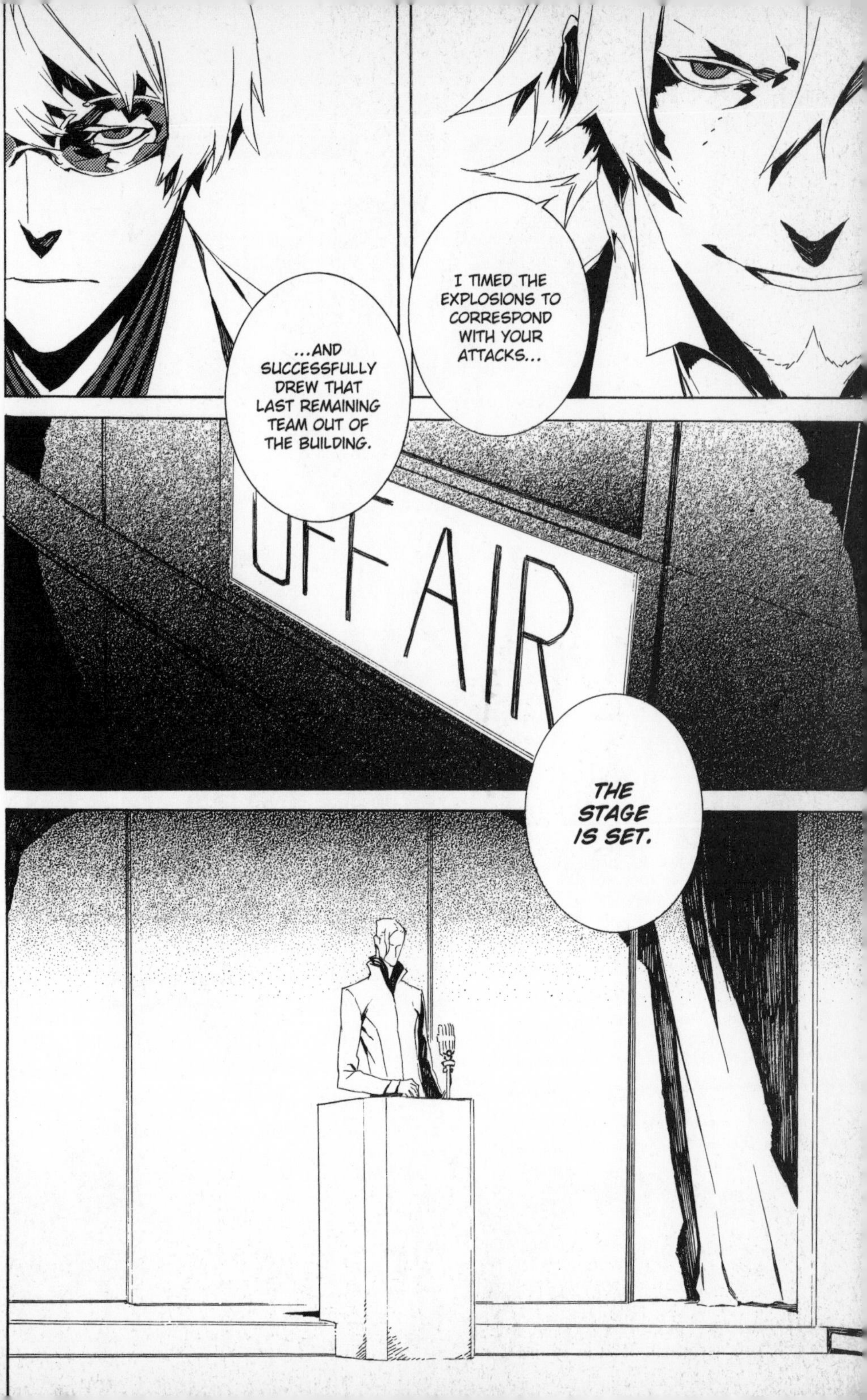
I TIMED THE EXPLOSIONS TO CORRESPOND WITH YOUR ATTACKS...
...AND SUCCESSFULLY DREW THAT LAST REMAINING TEAM OUT OF THE BUILDING.
THE STAGE IS SET.

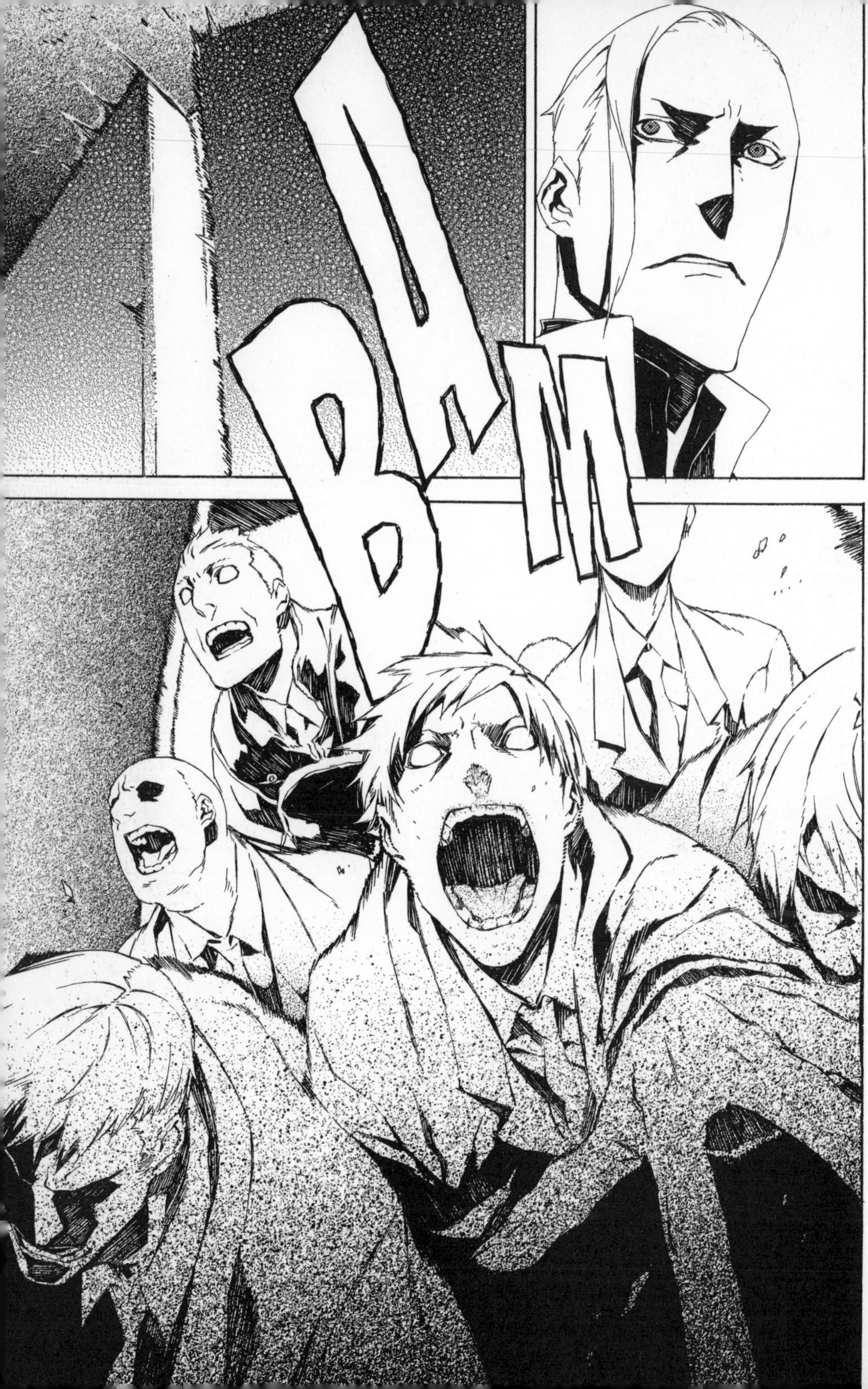
BAM

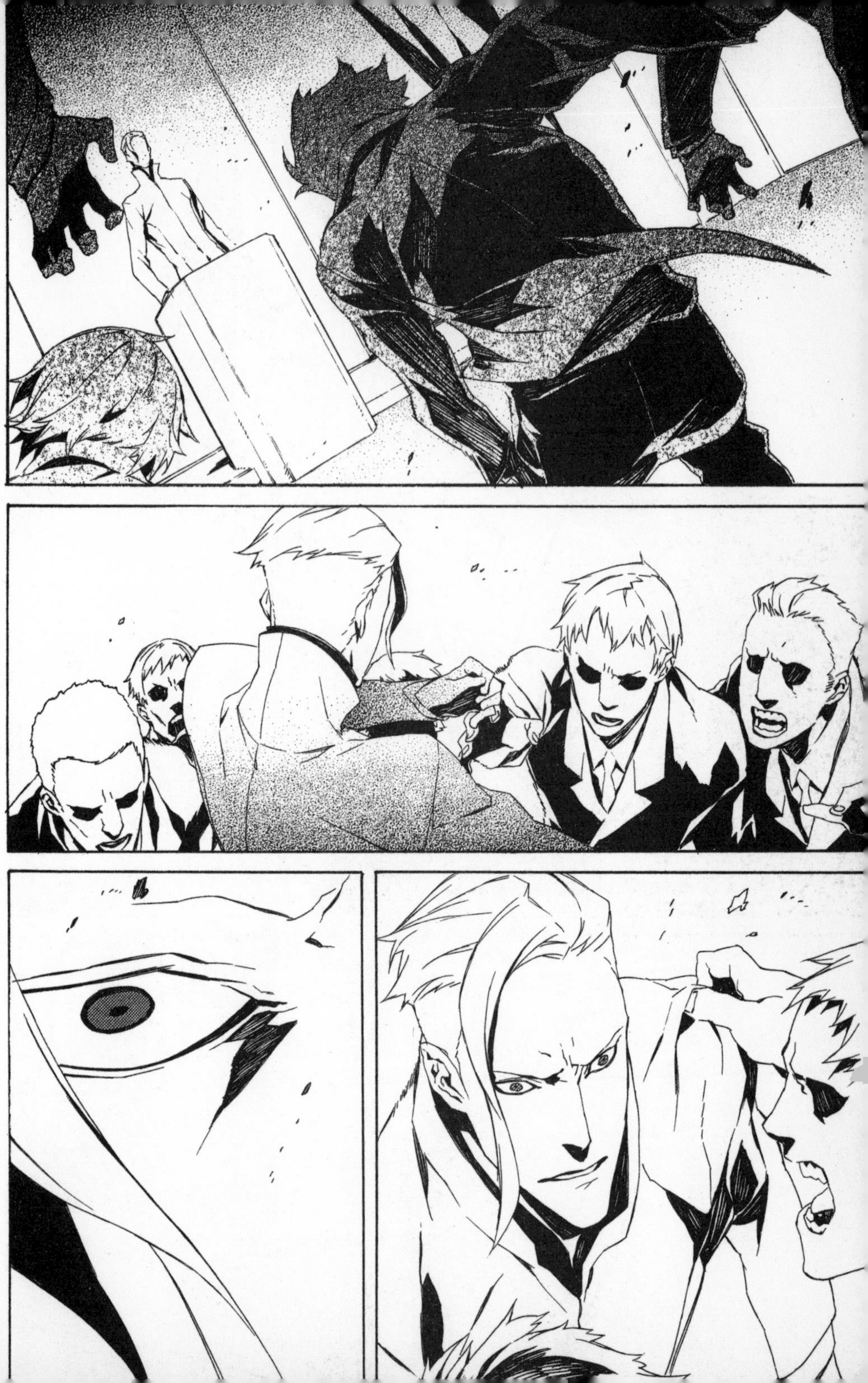

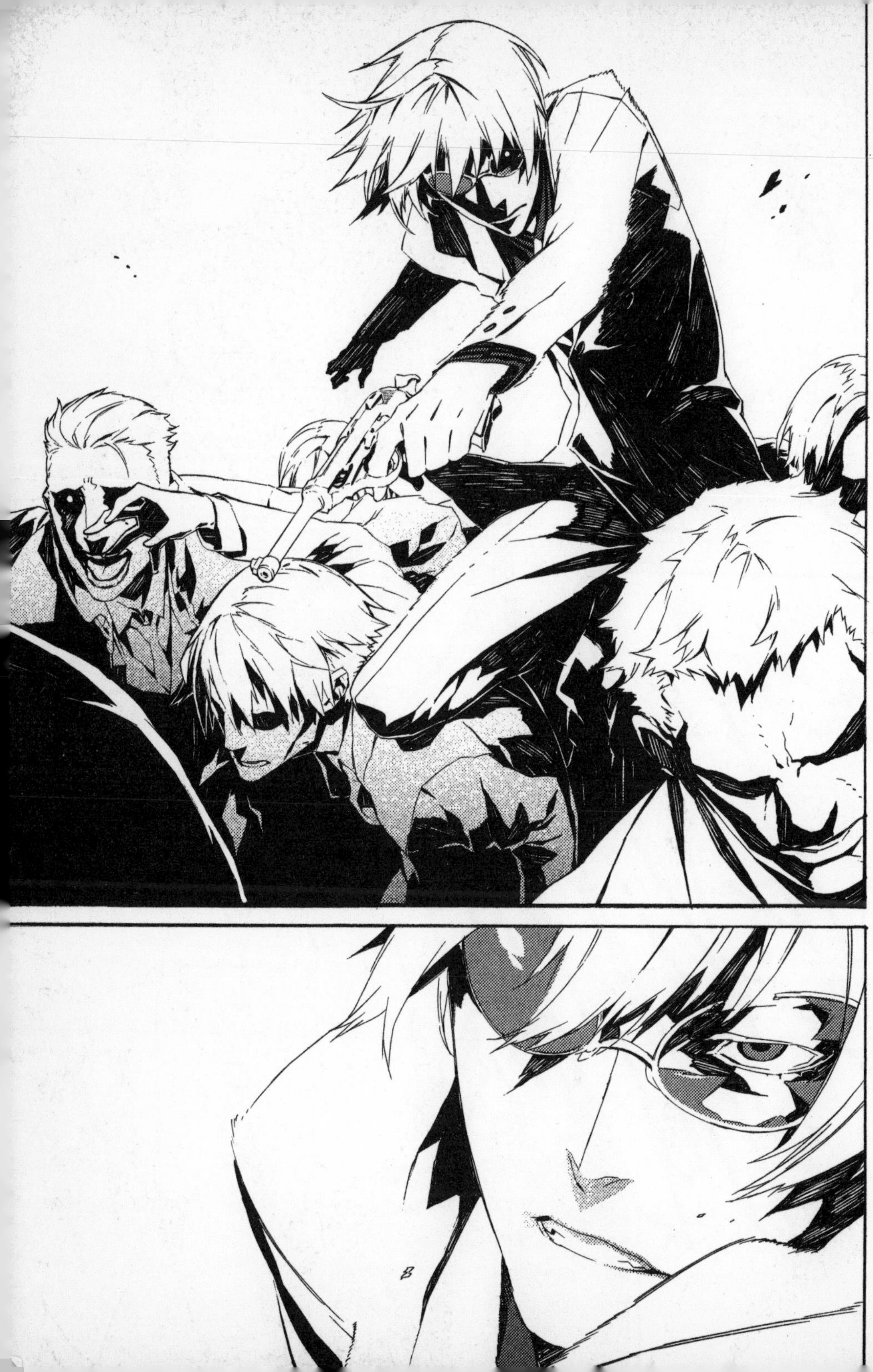

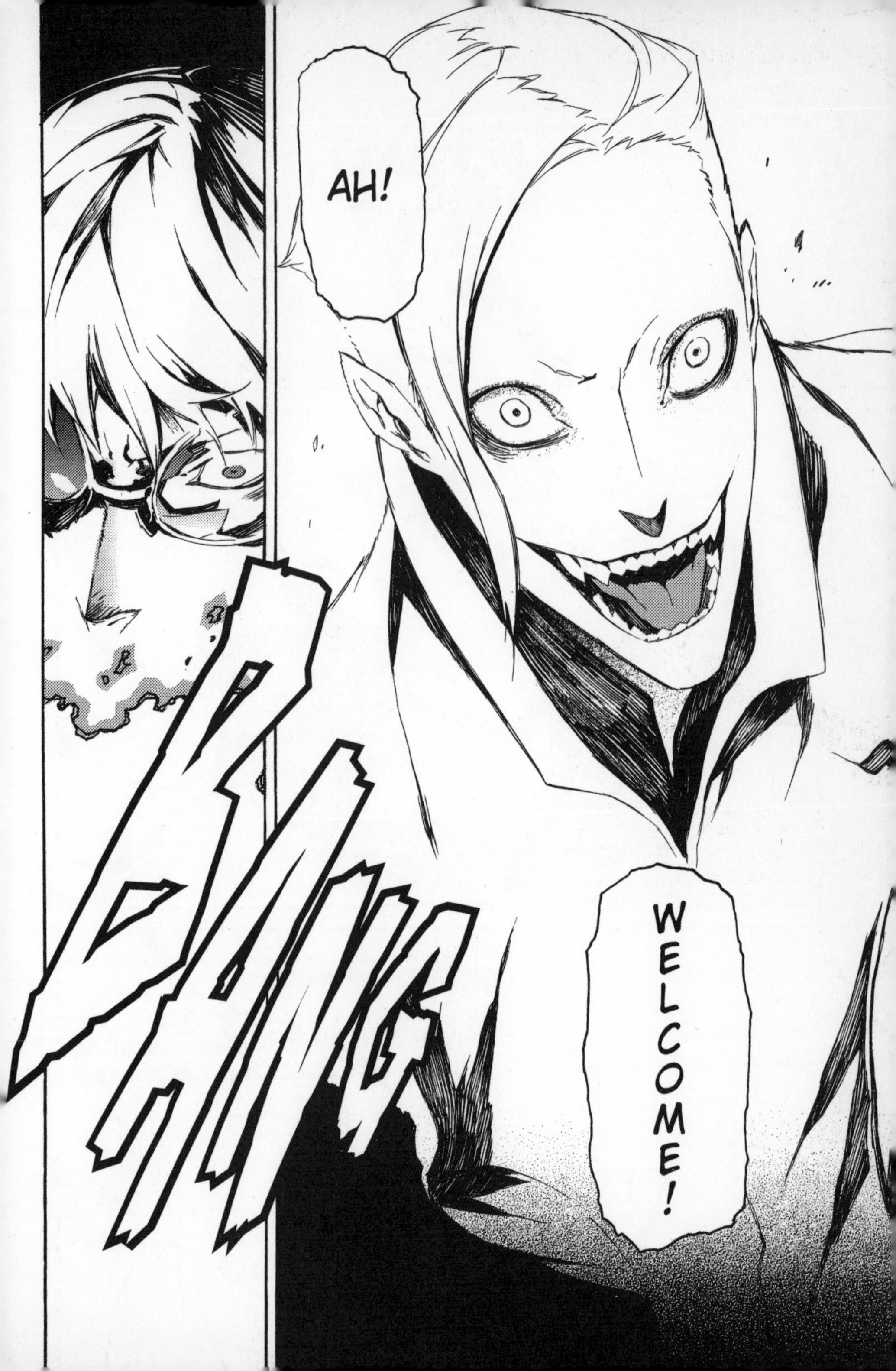
AH!
WELCOME!

# #51 Monarch & Trickster Ⅱ

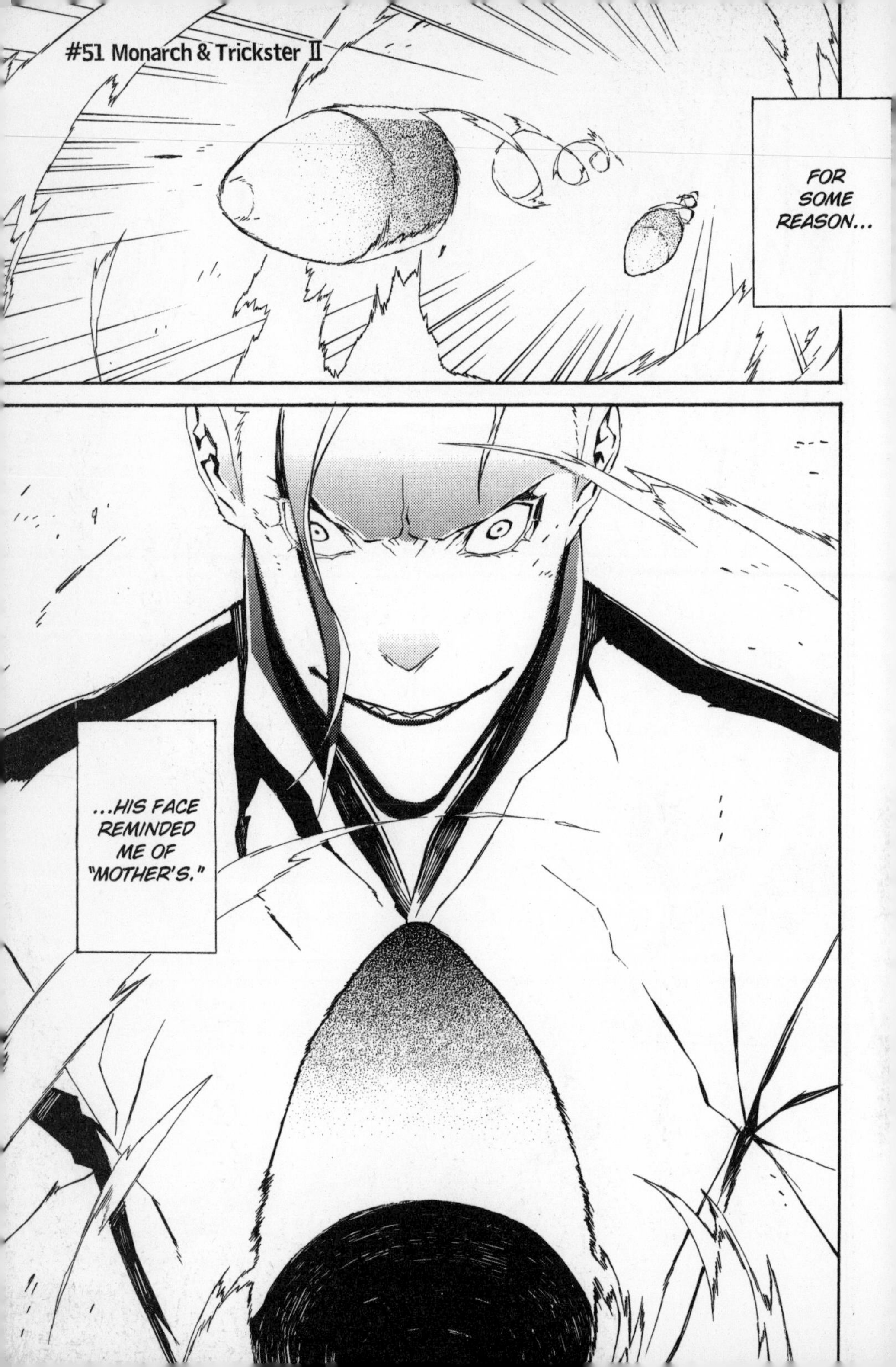
FOR SOME REASON...
...HIS FACE REMINDED ME OF "MOTHER'S."

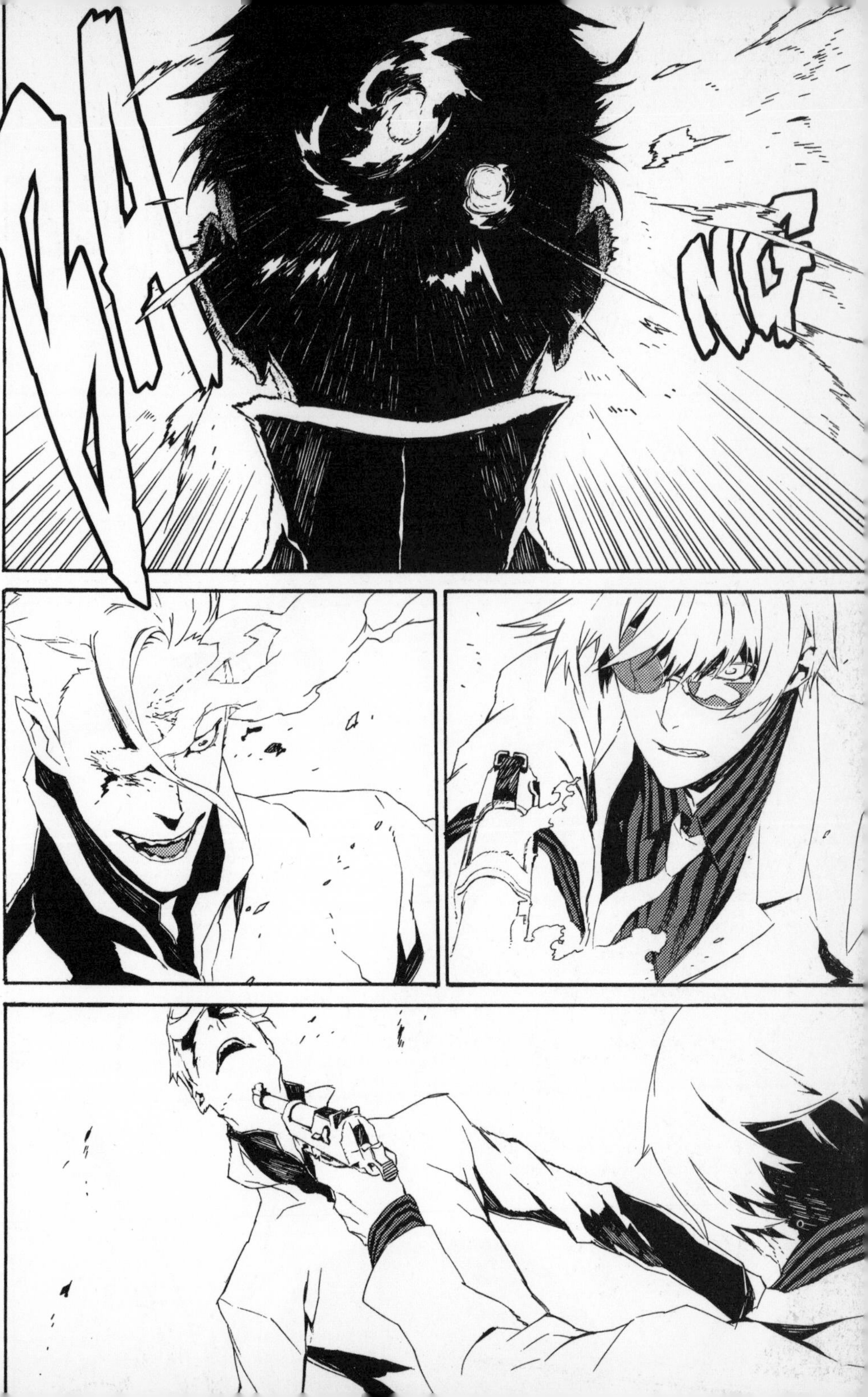
NG

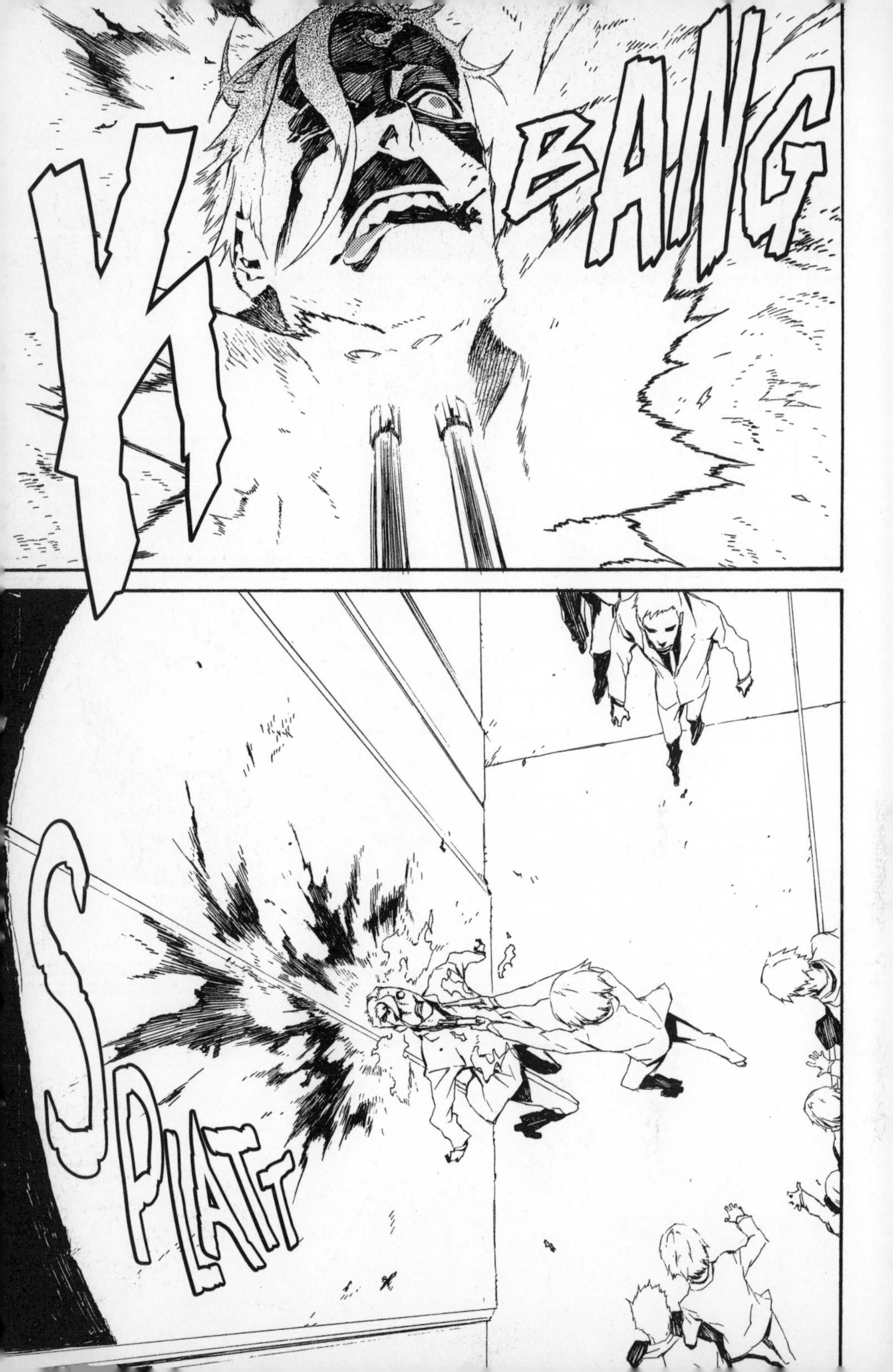
KBANG
SPLATT

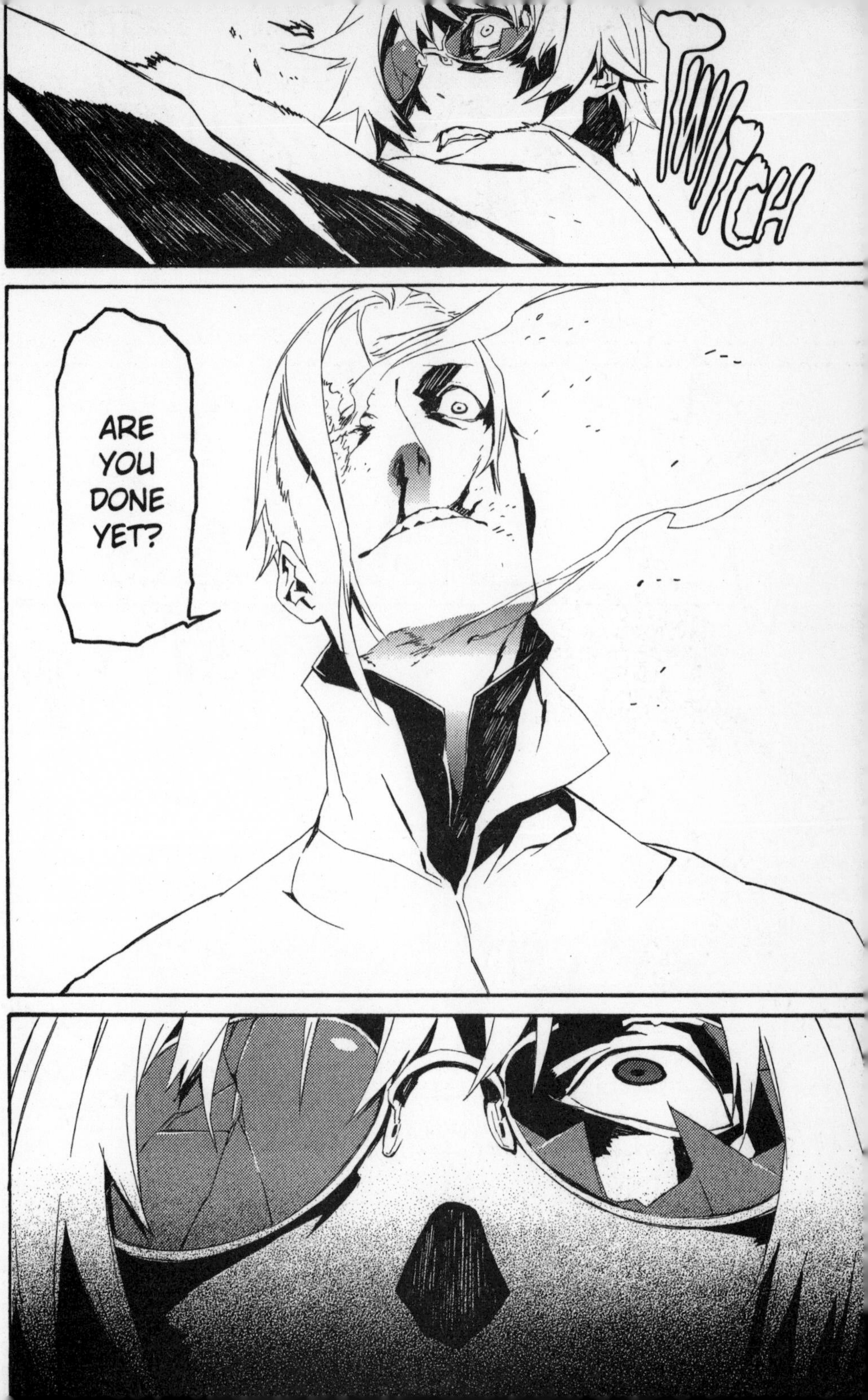
TWITCH
ARE YOU DONE YET?

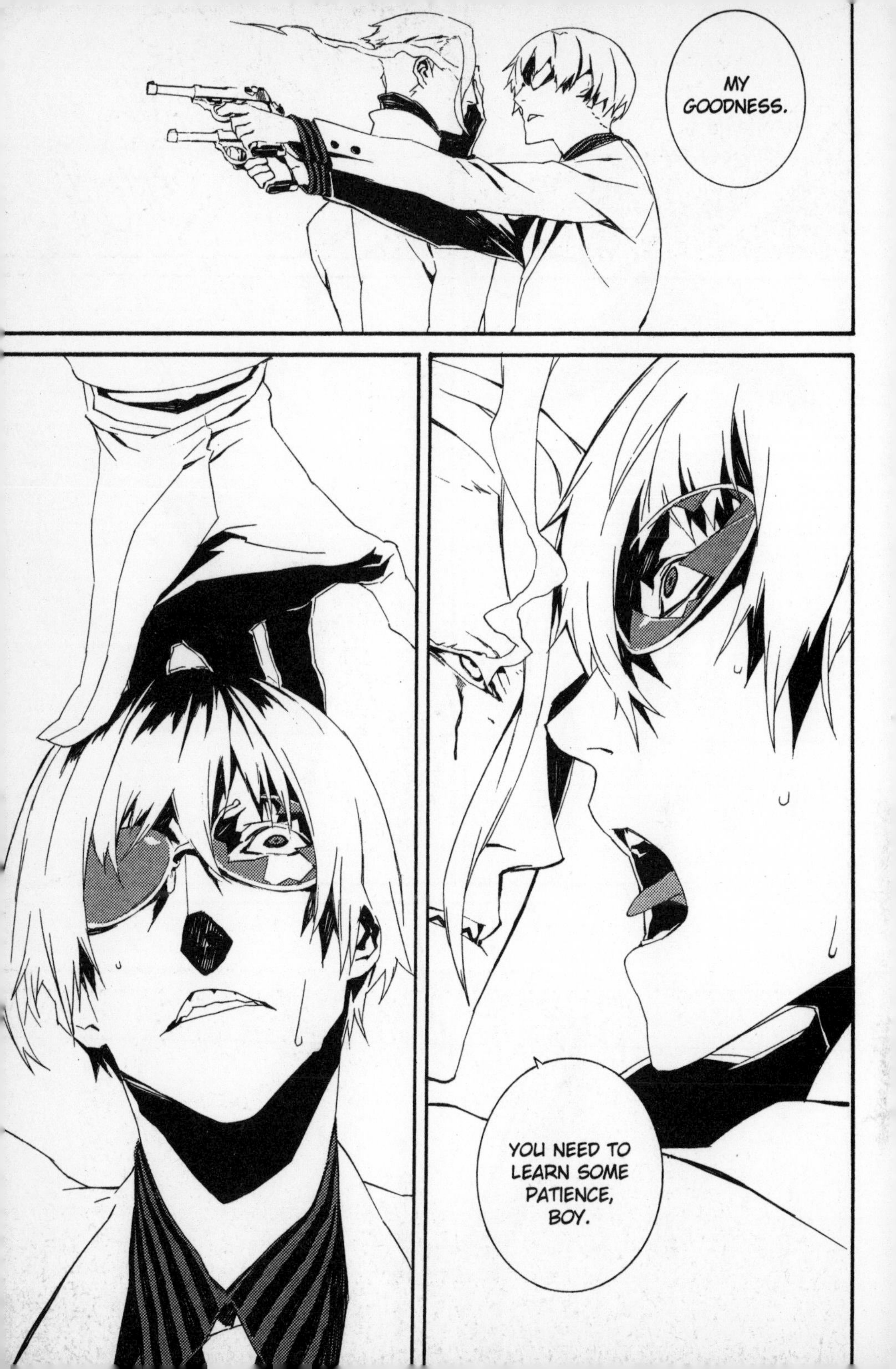
MY GOODNESS.
YOU NEED TO LEARN SOME PATIENCE, BOY.

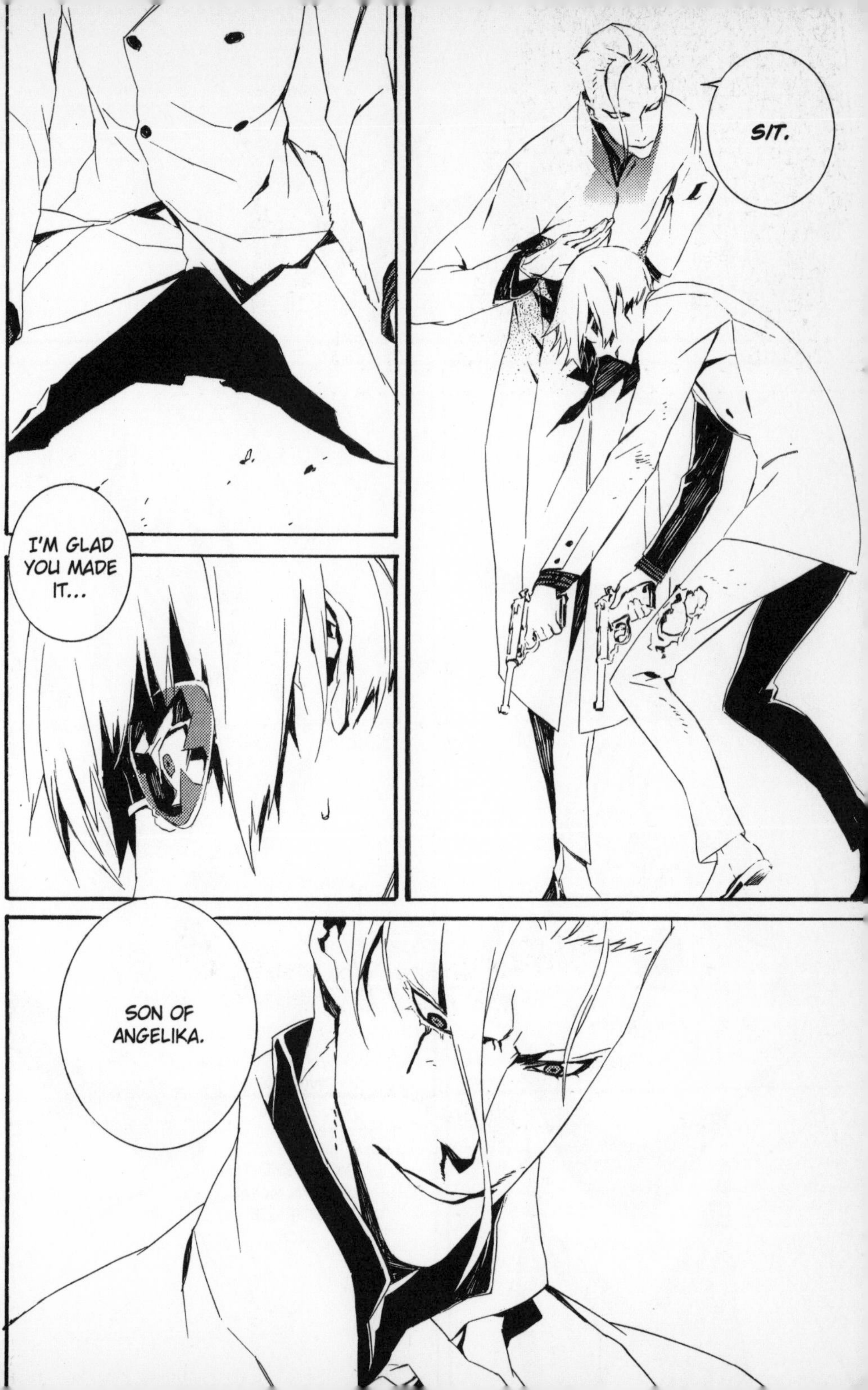
SIT.
I'M GLAD YOU MADE IT...
SON OF ANGELIKA.

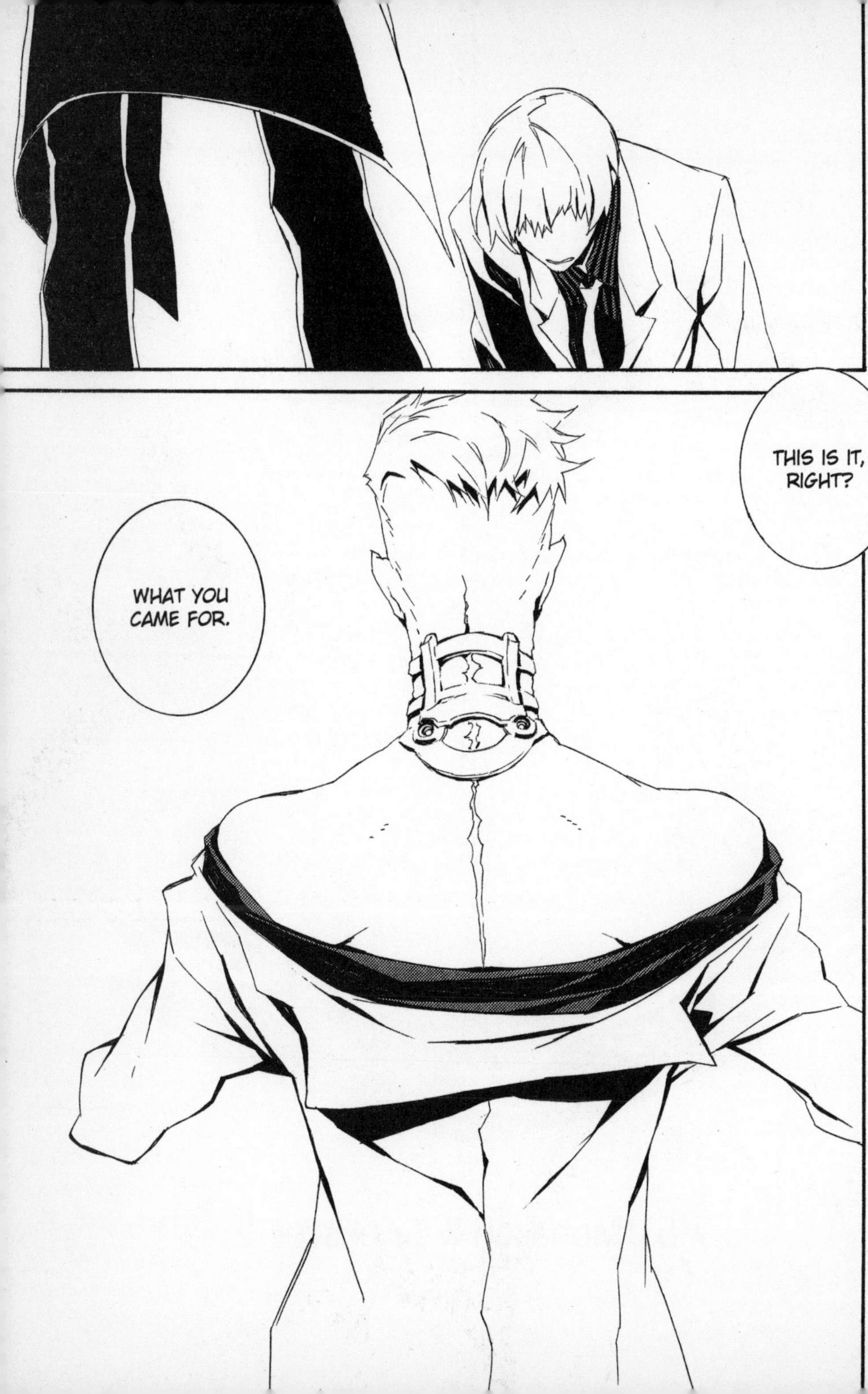
THIS IS IT, RIGHT?
WHAT YOU CAME FOR.

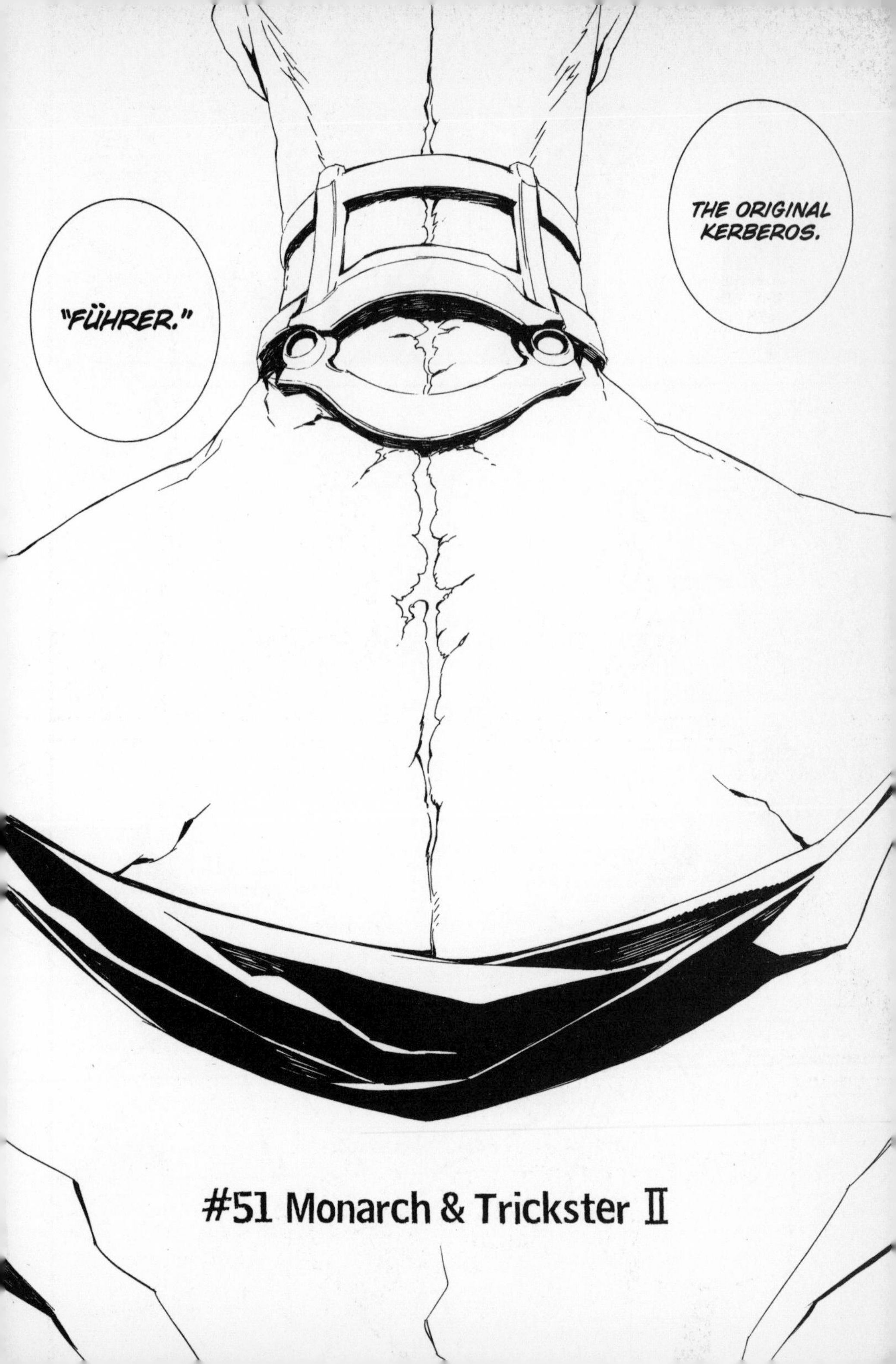
THE ORIGINAL KERBEROS.
"FÜHRER."

#51 Monarch & Trickster II

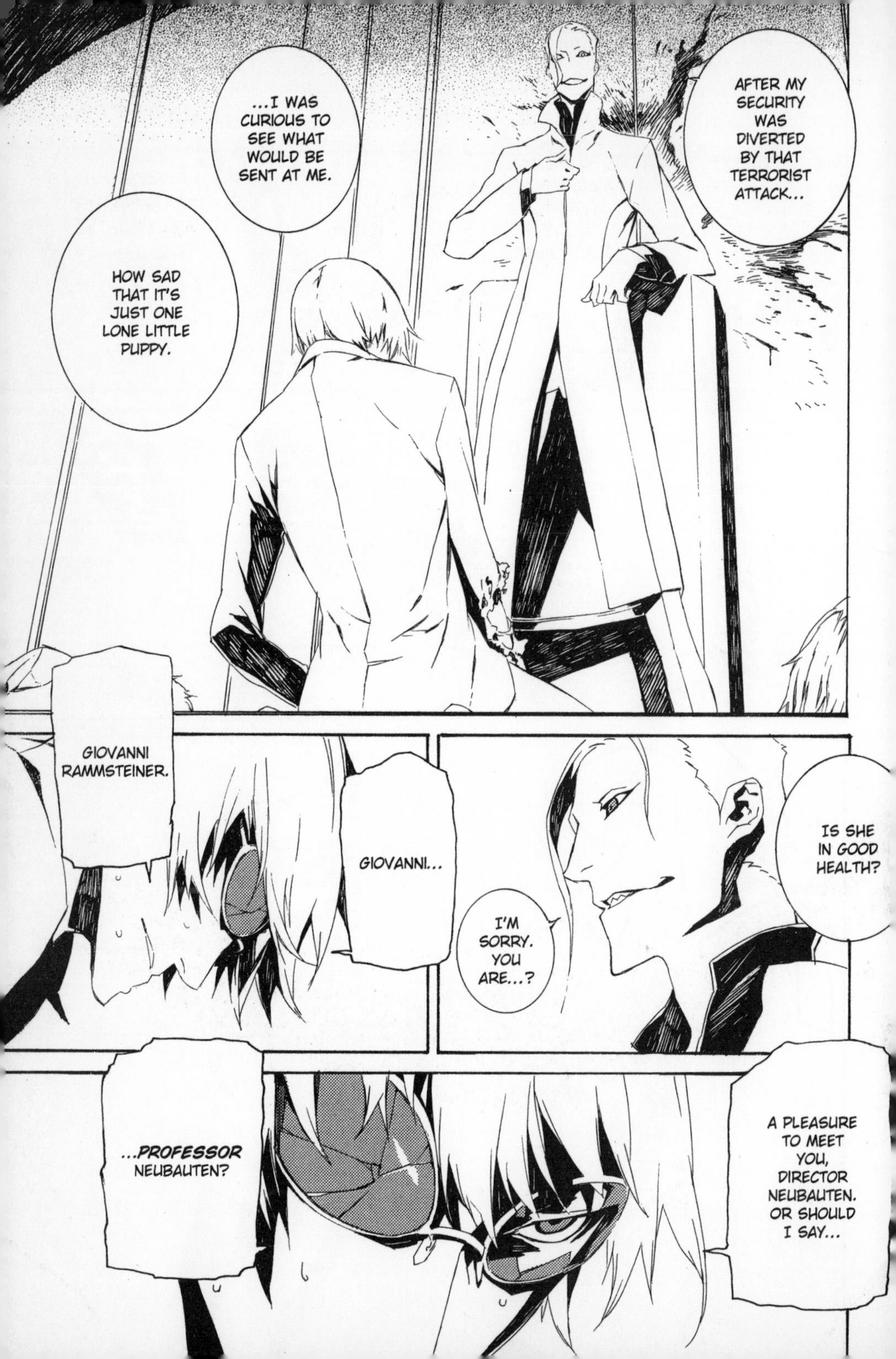
AFTER MY SECURITY WAS DIVERTED BY THAT TERRORIST ATTACK...
...I WAS CURIOUS TO SEE WHAT WOULD BE SENT AT ME.
HOW SAD THAT IT'S JUST ONE LONE LITTLE PUPPY.
IS SHE IN GOOD HEALTH?
I'M SORRY. YOU ARE...?
GIOVANNI...
GIOVANNI RAMMSTEINER.
A PLEASURE TO MEET YOU, DIRECTOR NEUBAUTEN. OR SHOULD I SAY...
...*PROFESSOR* NEUBAUTEN?

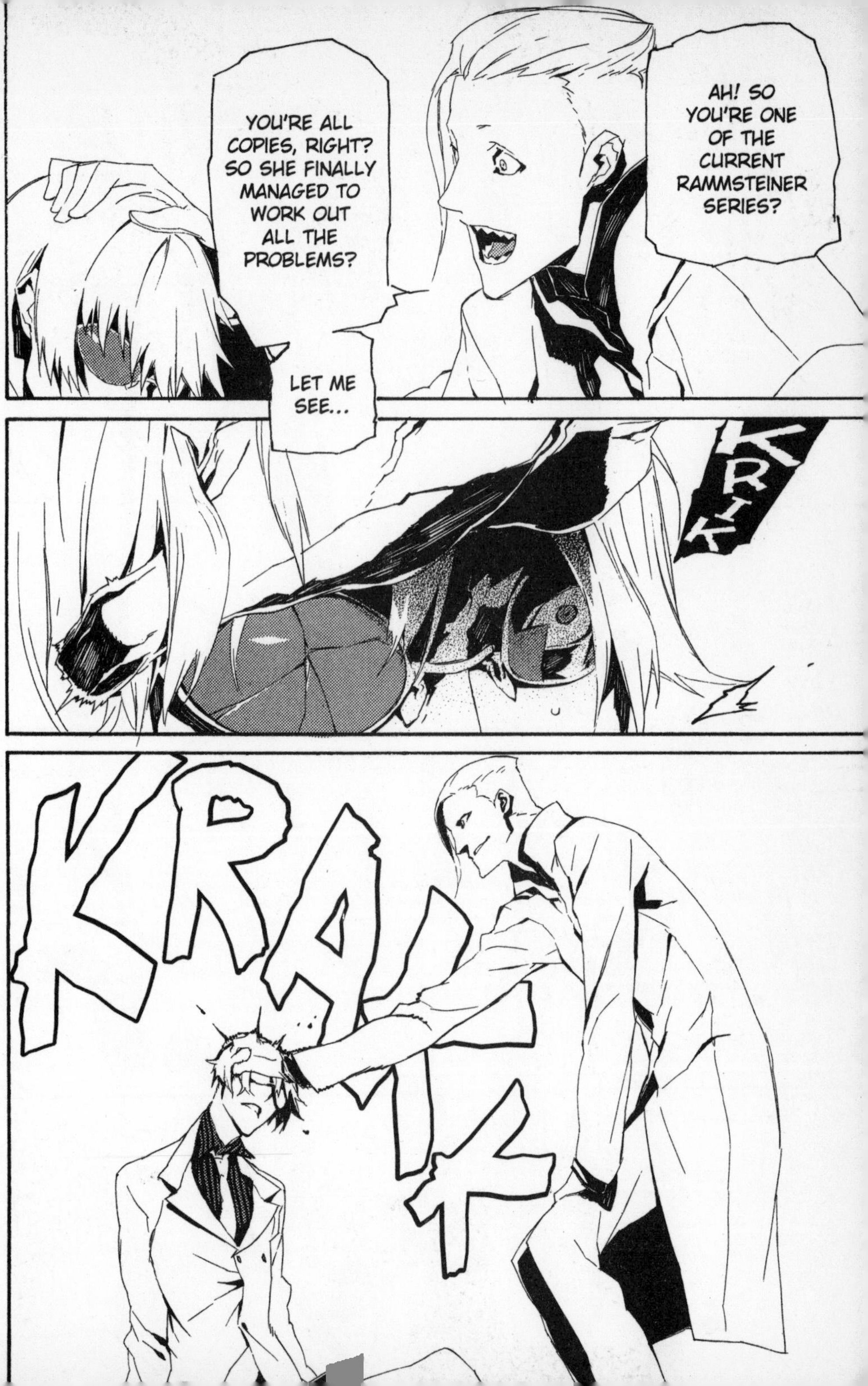
AH! SO YOU'RE ONE OF THE CURRENT RAMMSTEINER SERIES?
YOU'RE ALL COPIES, RIGHT? SO SHE FINALLY MANAGED TO WORK OUT ALL THE PROBLEMS?
LET ME SEE...
KRIK
KRAK

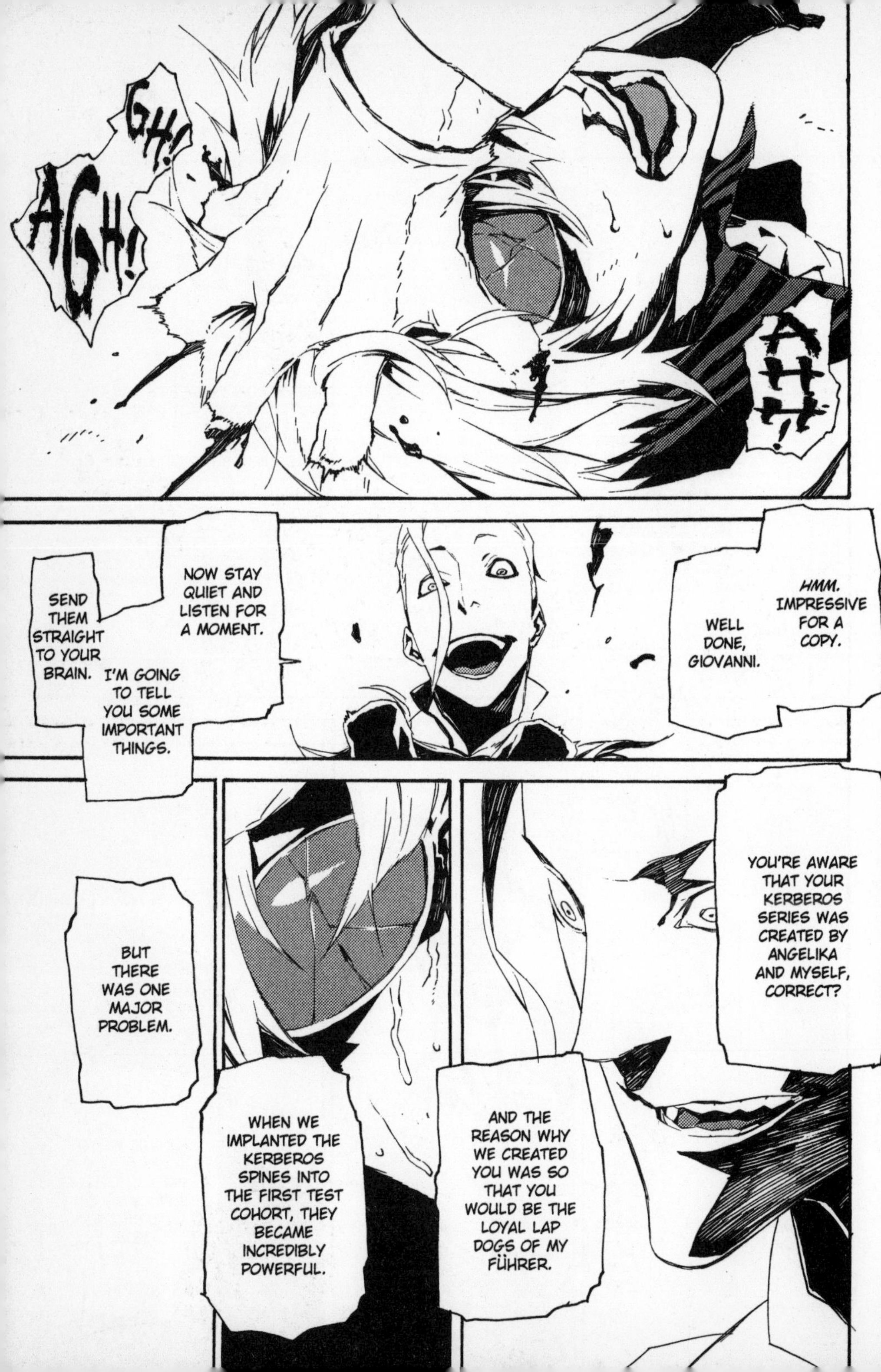
AHH!
GH!
AGH!
HMM. IMPRESSIVE FOR A COPY.
WELL DONE, GIOVANNI.
NOW STAY QUIET AND LISTEN FOR A MOMENT.
I'M GOING TO TELL YOU SOME IMPORTANT THINGS.
SEND THEM STRAIGHT TO YOUR BRAIN.
YOU'RE AWARE THAT YOUR KERBEROS SERIES WAS CREATED BY ANGELIKA AND MYSELF, CORRECT?
AND THE REASON WHY WE CREATED YOU WAS SO THAT YOU WOULD BE THE LOYAL LAP DOGS OF MY FÜHRER.
WHEN WE IMPLANTED THE KERBEROS SPINES INTO THE FIRST TEST COHORT, THEY BECAME INCREDIBLY POWERFUL.
BUT THERE WAS ONE MAJOR PROBLEM.

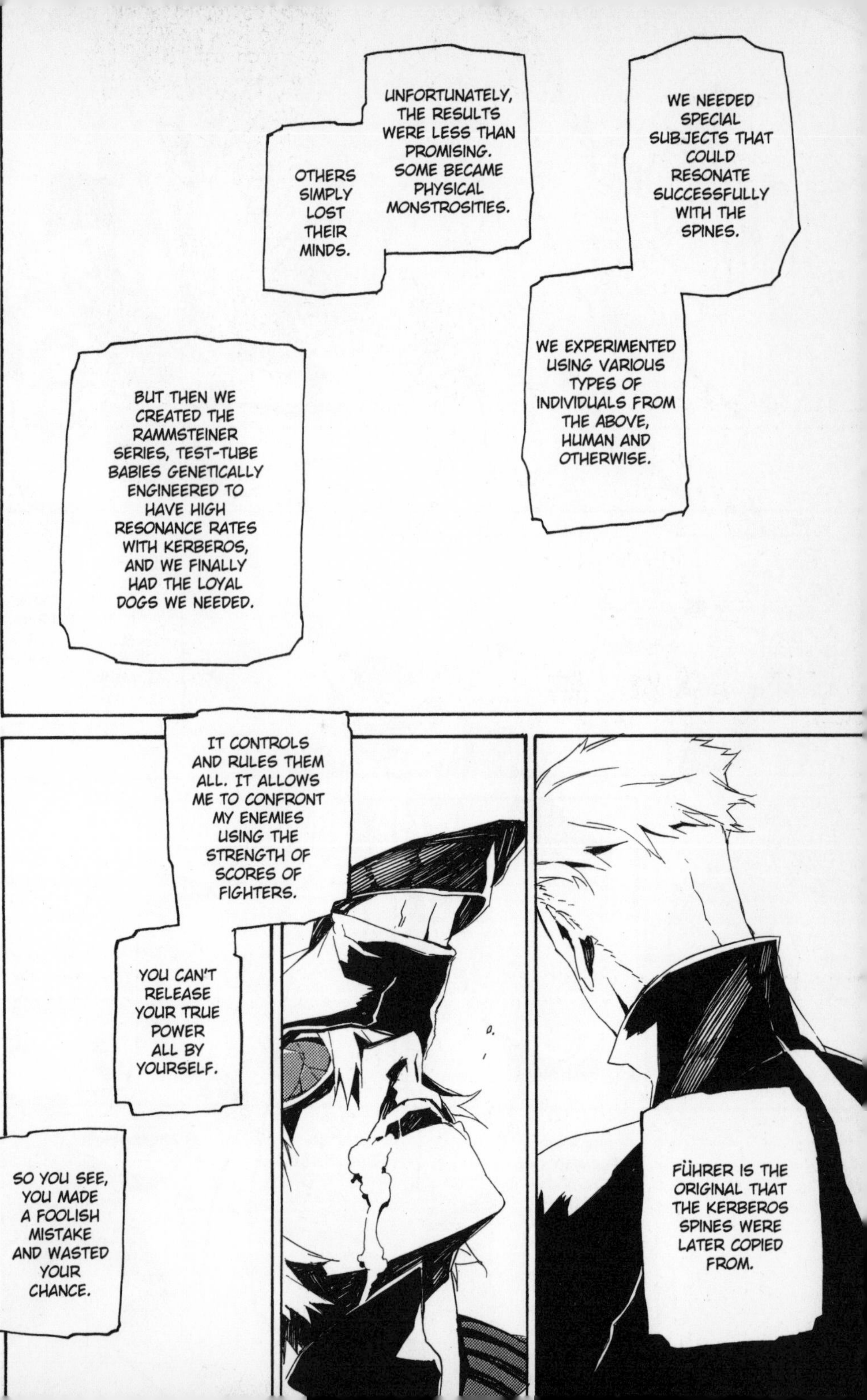
WE NEEDED SPECIAL SUBJECTS THAT COULD RESONATE SUCCESSFULLY WITH THE SPINES.
WE EXPERIMENTED USING VARIOUS TYPES OF INDIVIDUALS FROM THE ABOVE, HUMAN AND OTHERWISE.
UNFORTUNATELY, THE RESULTS WERE LESS THAN PROMISING. SOME BECAME PHYSICAL MONSTROSITIES.
OTHERS SIMPLY LOST THEIR MINDS.
BUT THEN WE CREATED THE RAMMSTEINER SERIES, TEST-TUBE BABIES GENETICALLY ENGINEERED TO HAVE HIGH RESONANCE RATES WITH KERBEROS, AND WE FINALLY HAD THE LOYAL DOGS WE NEEDED.
FÜHRER IS THE ORIGINAL THAT THE KERBEROS SPINES WERE LATER COPIED FROM.
IT CONTROLS AND RULES THEM ALL. IT ALLOWS ME TO CONFRONT MY ENEMIES USING THE STRENGTH OF SCORES OF FIGHTERS.
YOU CAN'T RELEASE YOUR TRUE POWER ALL BY YOURSELF.
SO YOU SEE, YOU MADE A FOOLISH MISTAKE AND WASTED YOUR CHANCE.

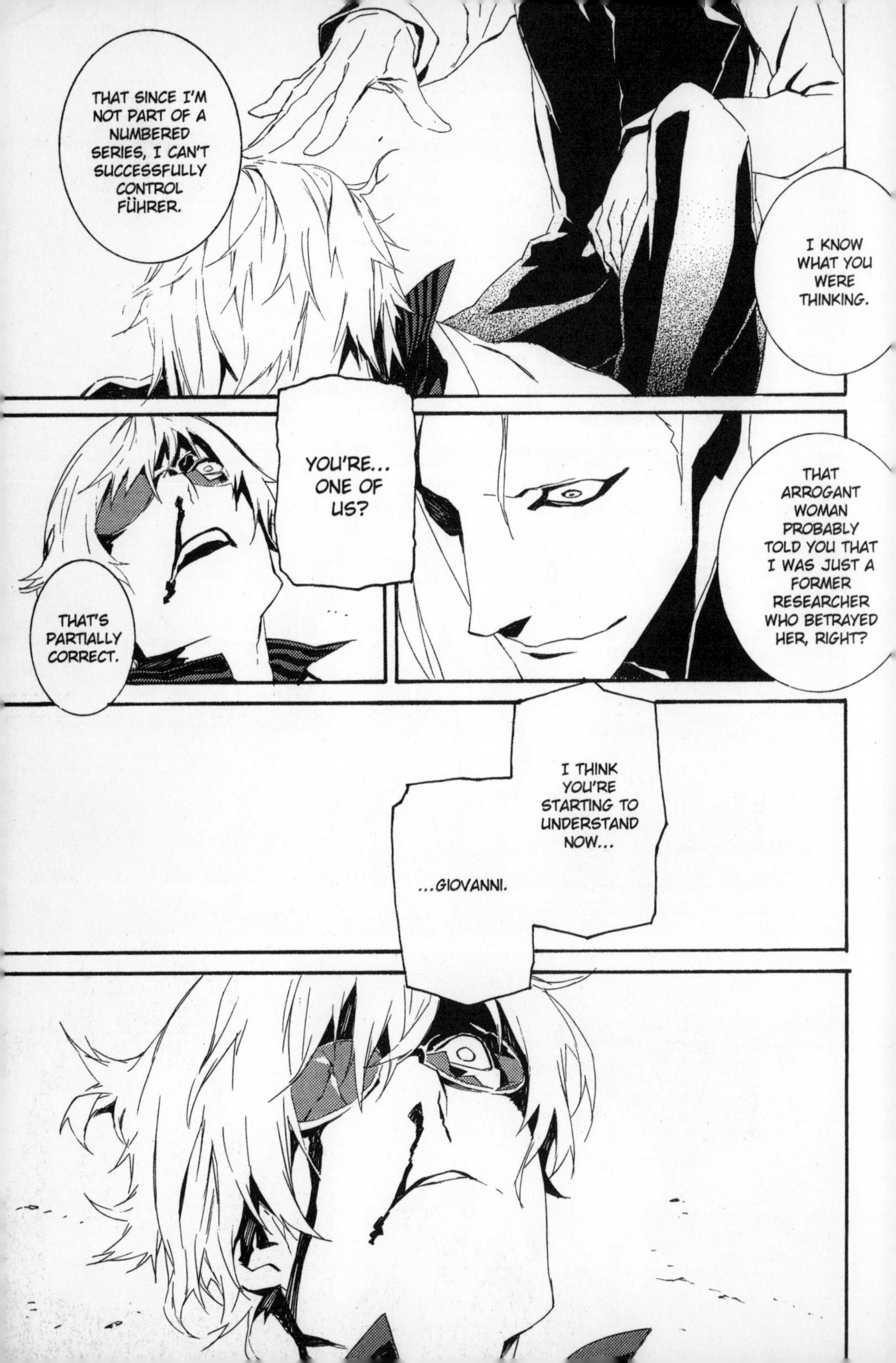
I KNOW WHAT YOU WERE THINKING.
THAT SINCE I'M NOT PART OF A NUMBERED SERIES, I CAN'T SUCCESSFULLY CONTROL FÜHRER.
THAT ARROGANT WOMAN PROBABLY TOLD YOU THAT I WAS JUST A FORMER RESEARCHER WHO BETRAYED HER, RIGHT?
YOU'RE... ONE OF US?
THAT'S PARTIALLY CORRECT.
I THINK YOU'RE STARTING TO UNDERSTAND NOW...
...GIOVANNI.

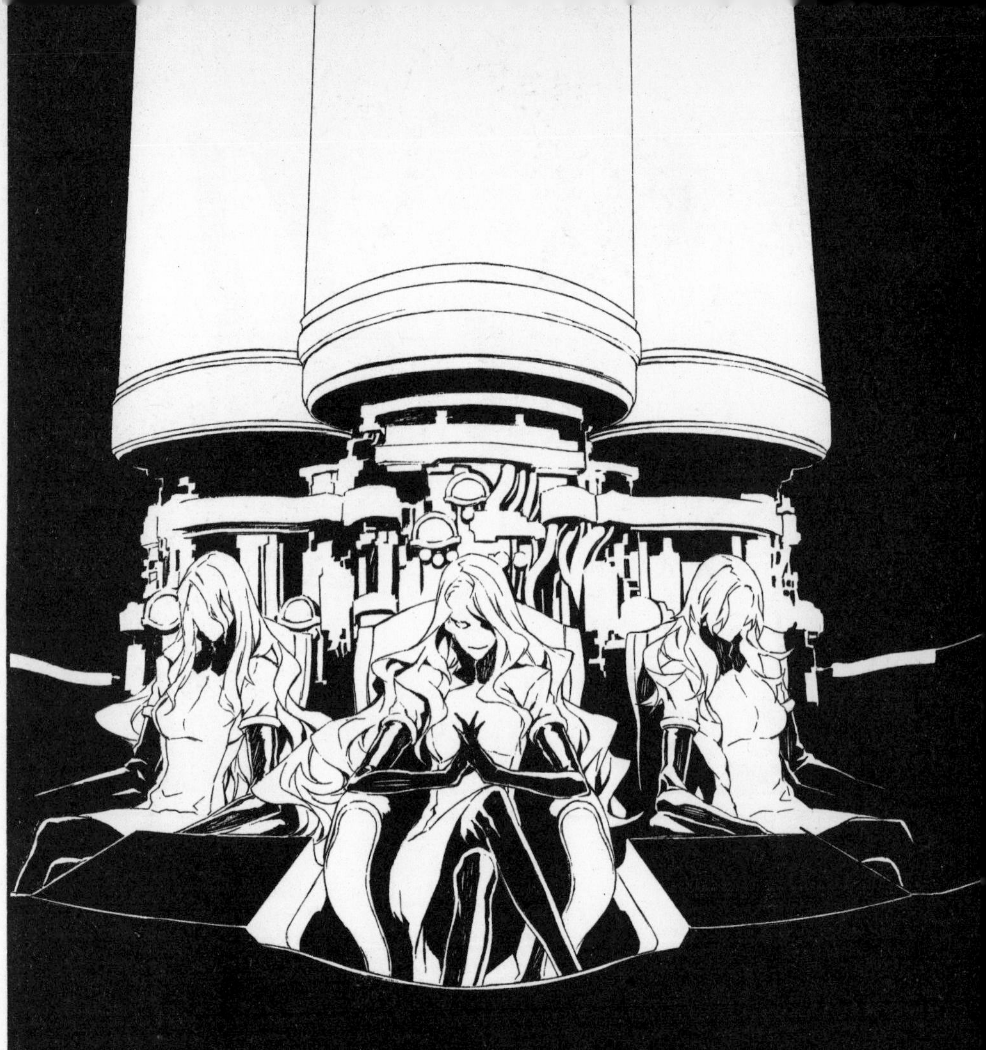
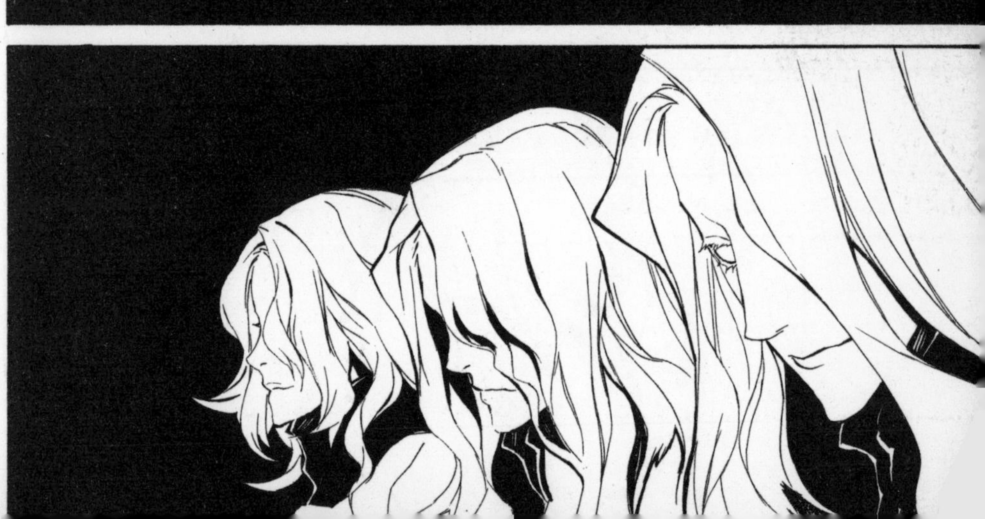

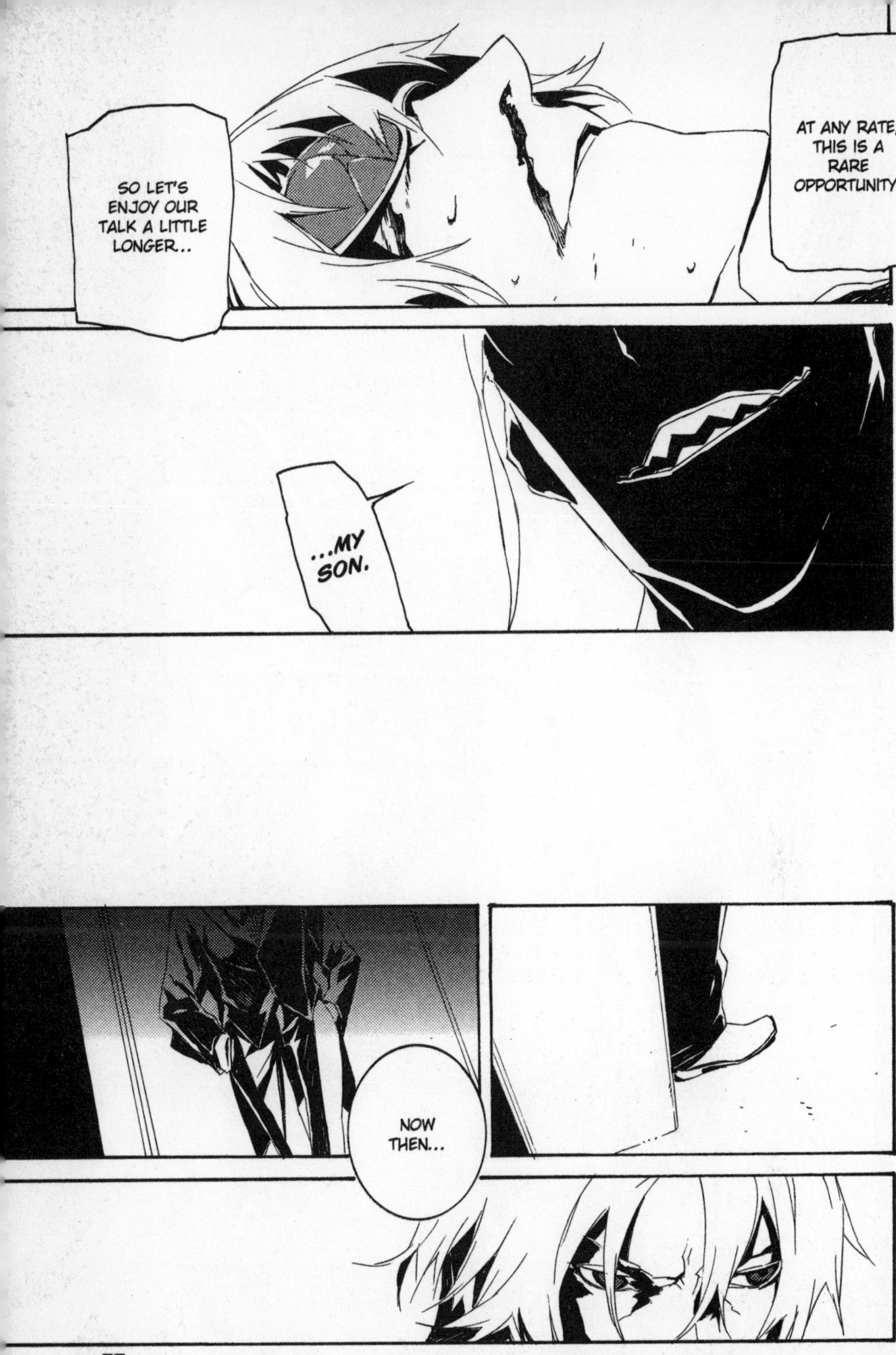
AT ANY RATE, THIS IS A RARE OPPORTUNITY.
SO LET'S ENJOY OUR TALK A LITTLE LONGER...
...MY SON.
NOW THEN...

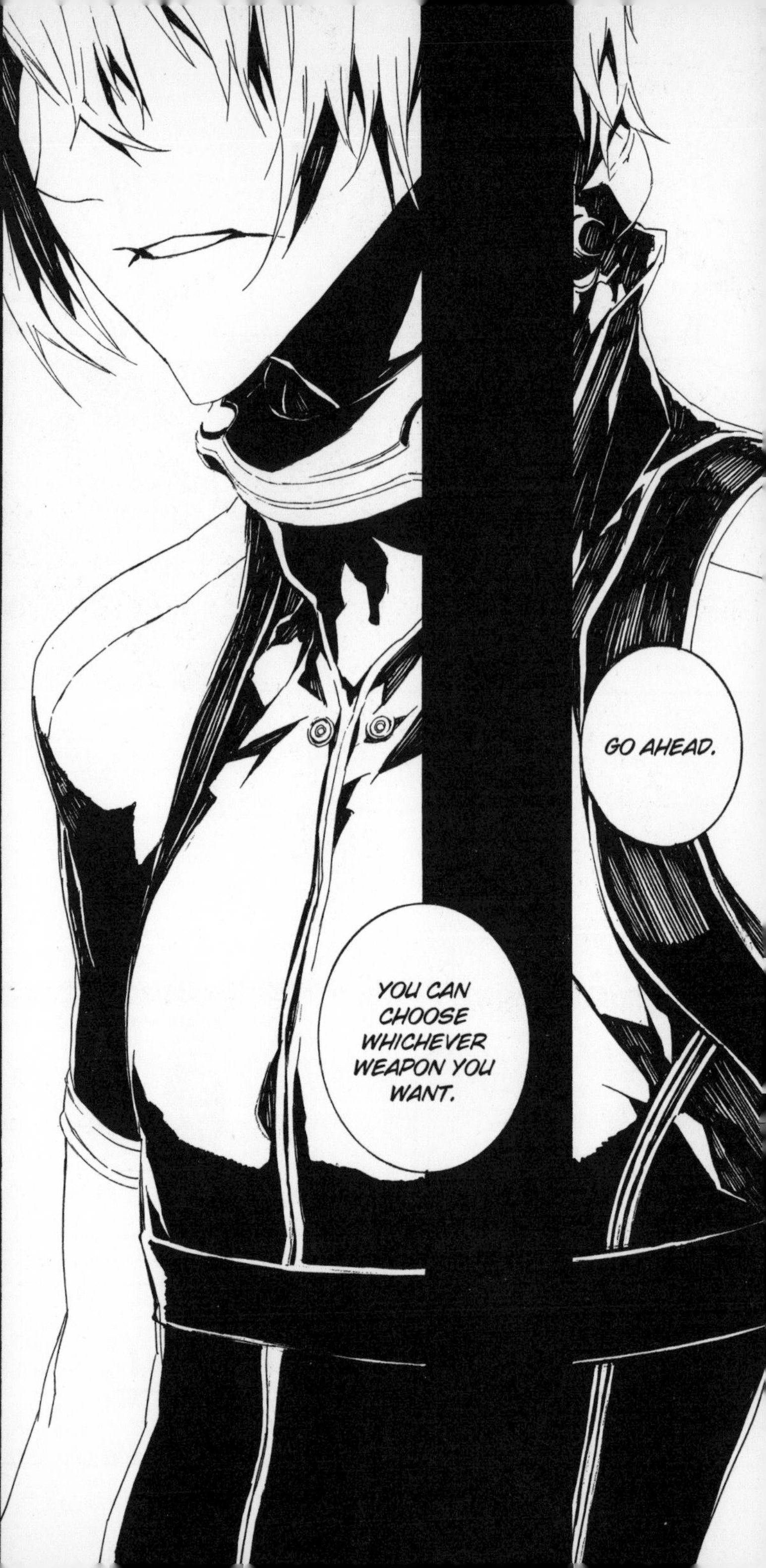
GO AHEAD.
YOU CAN CHOOSE WHICHEVER WEAPON YOU WANT.

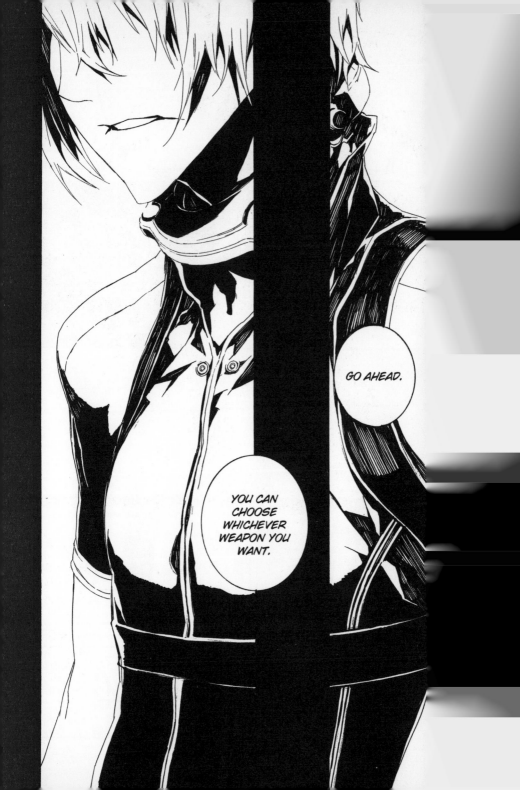

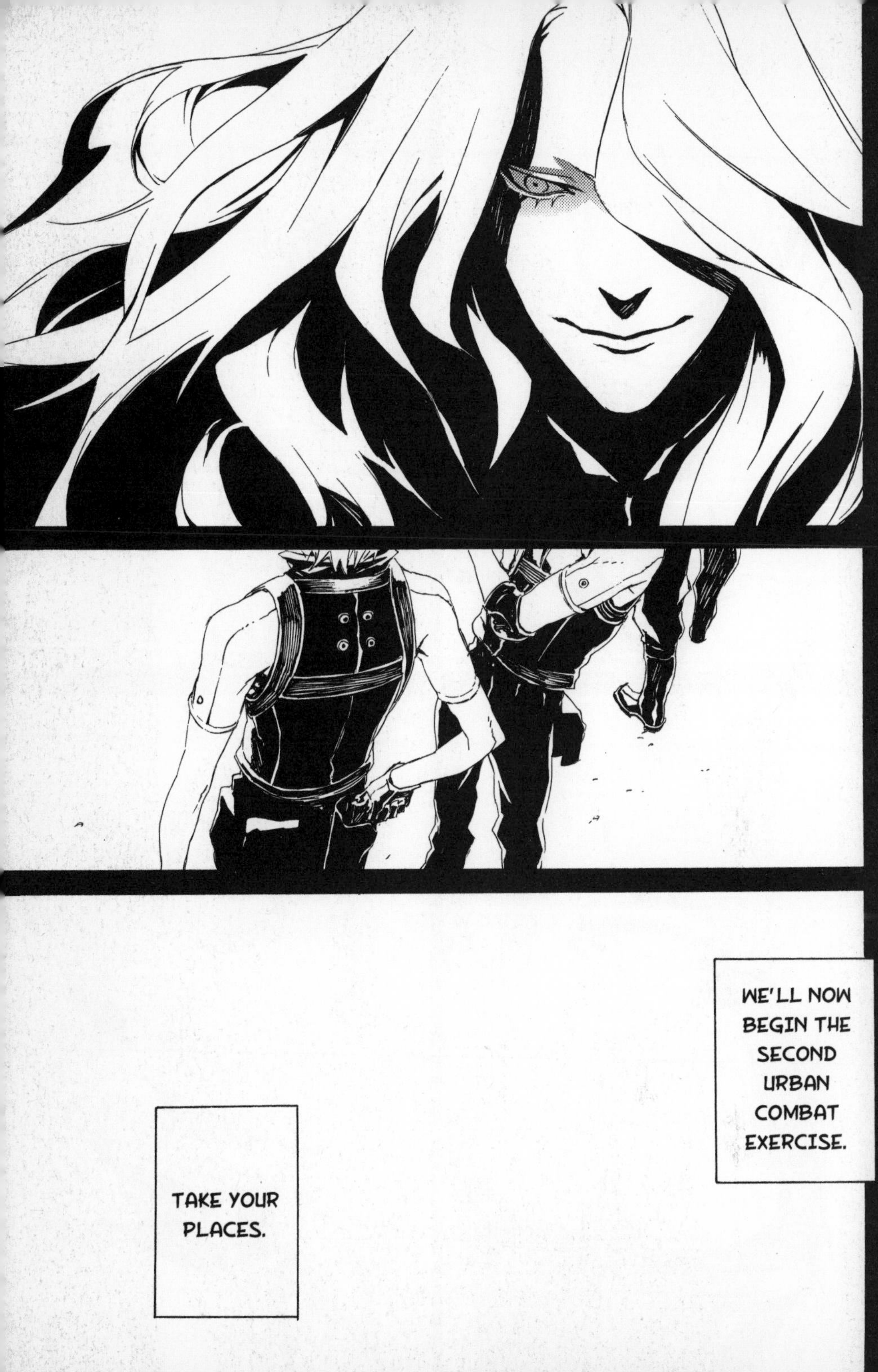
WE'LL NOW BEGIN THE SECOND URBAN COMBAT EXERCISE.
TAKE YOUR PLACES.

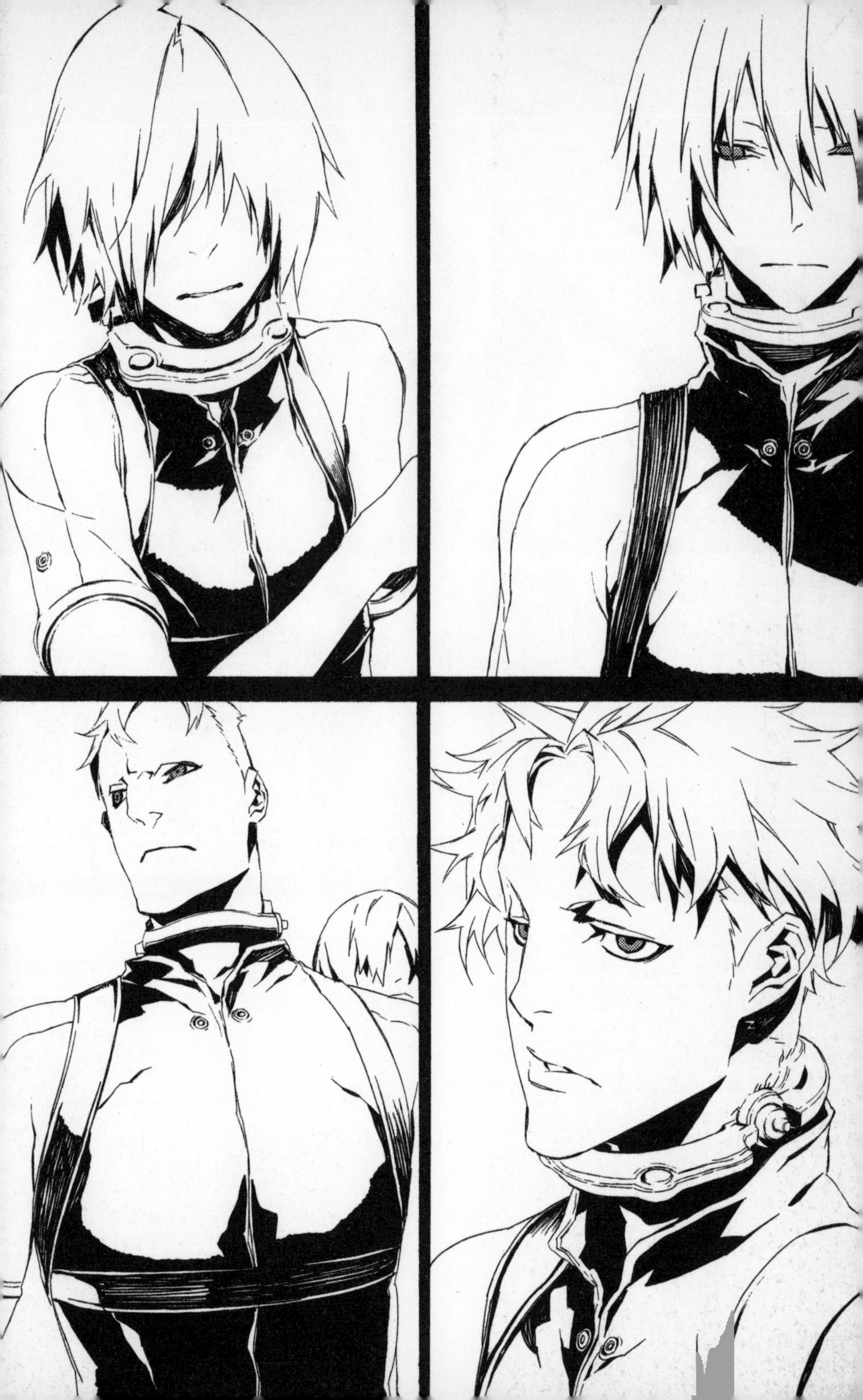

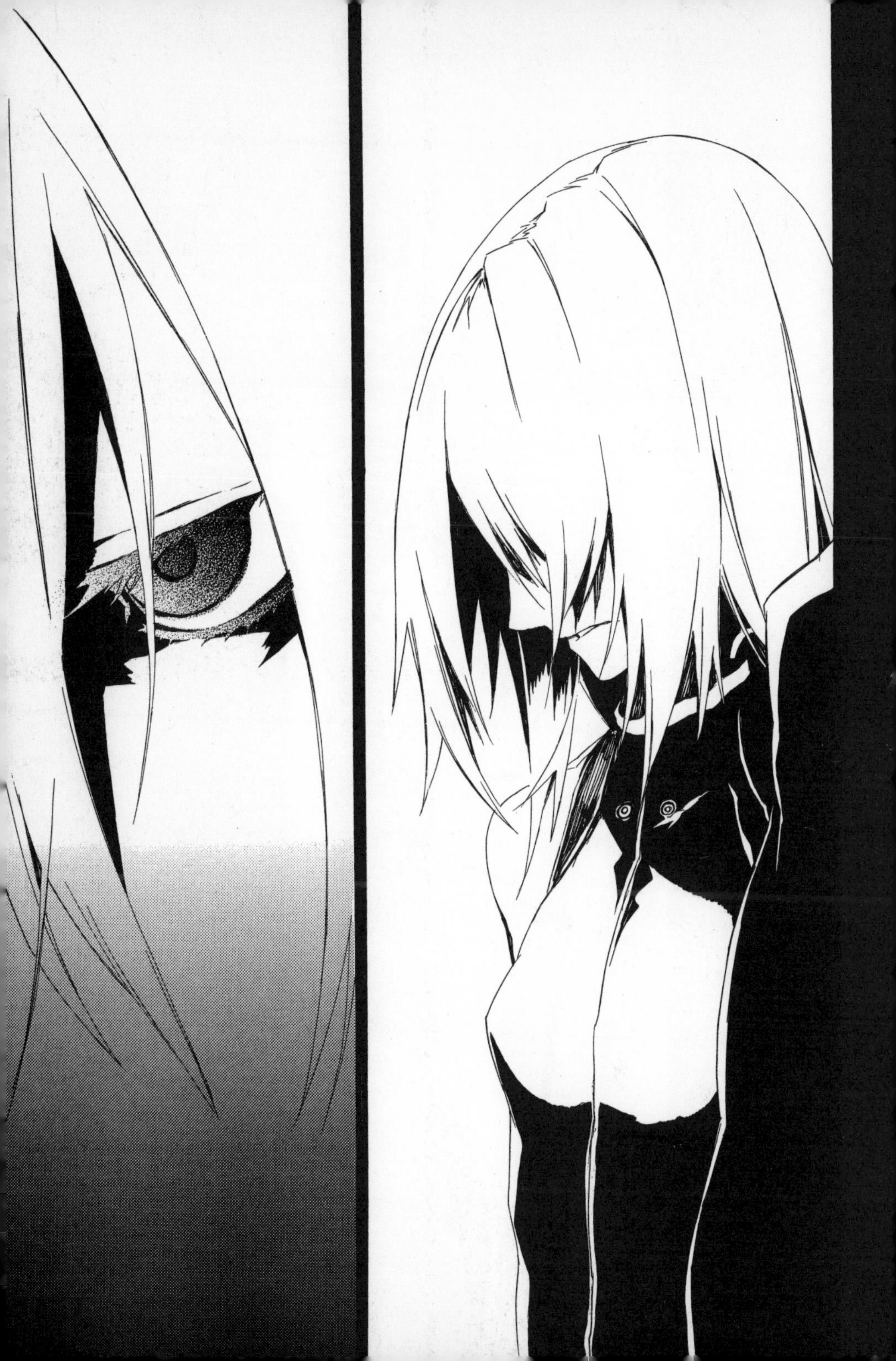

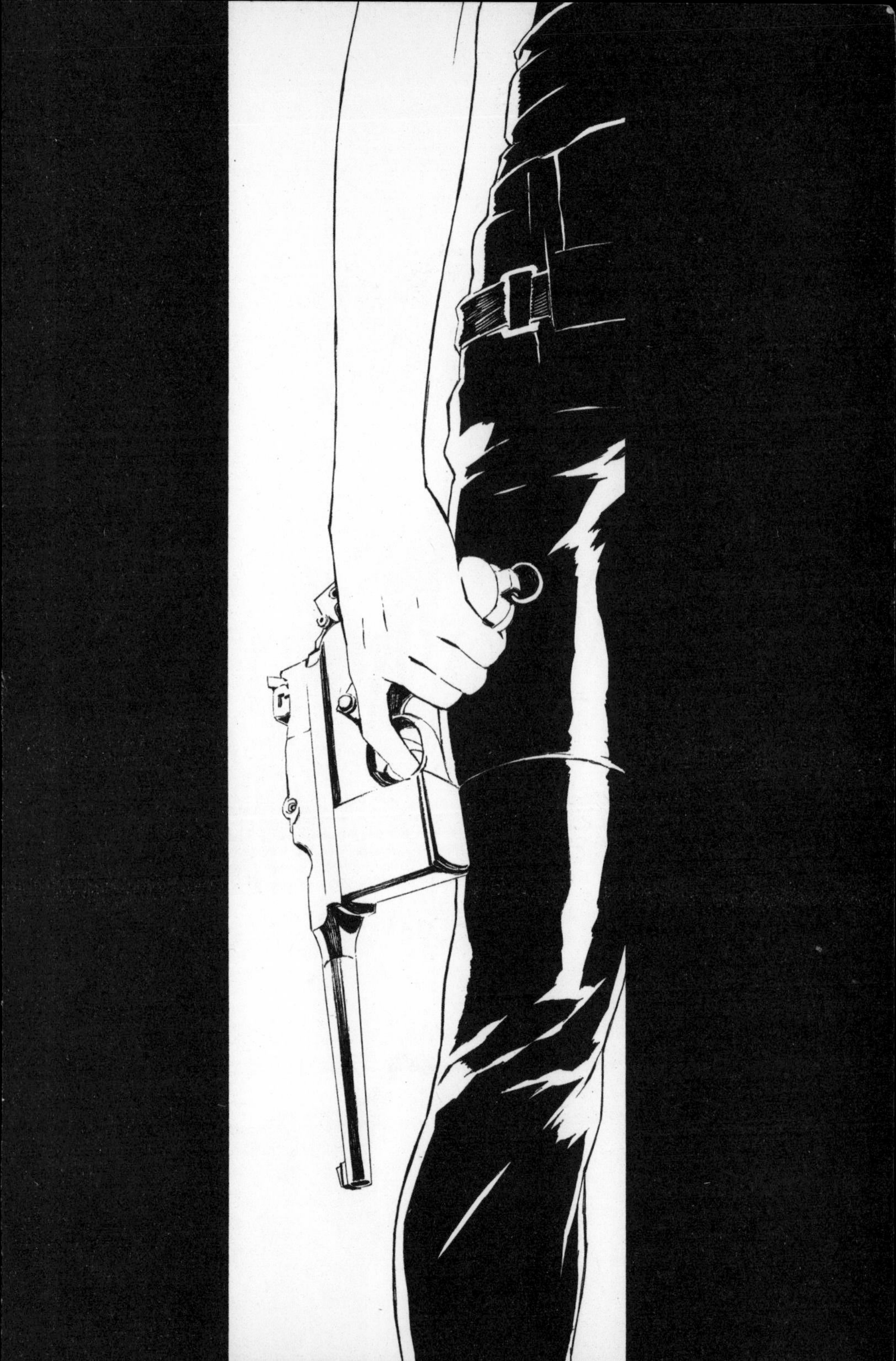

# #52 Cage & Puppies Ⅰ

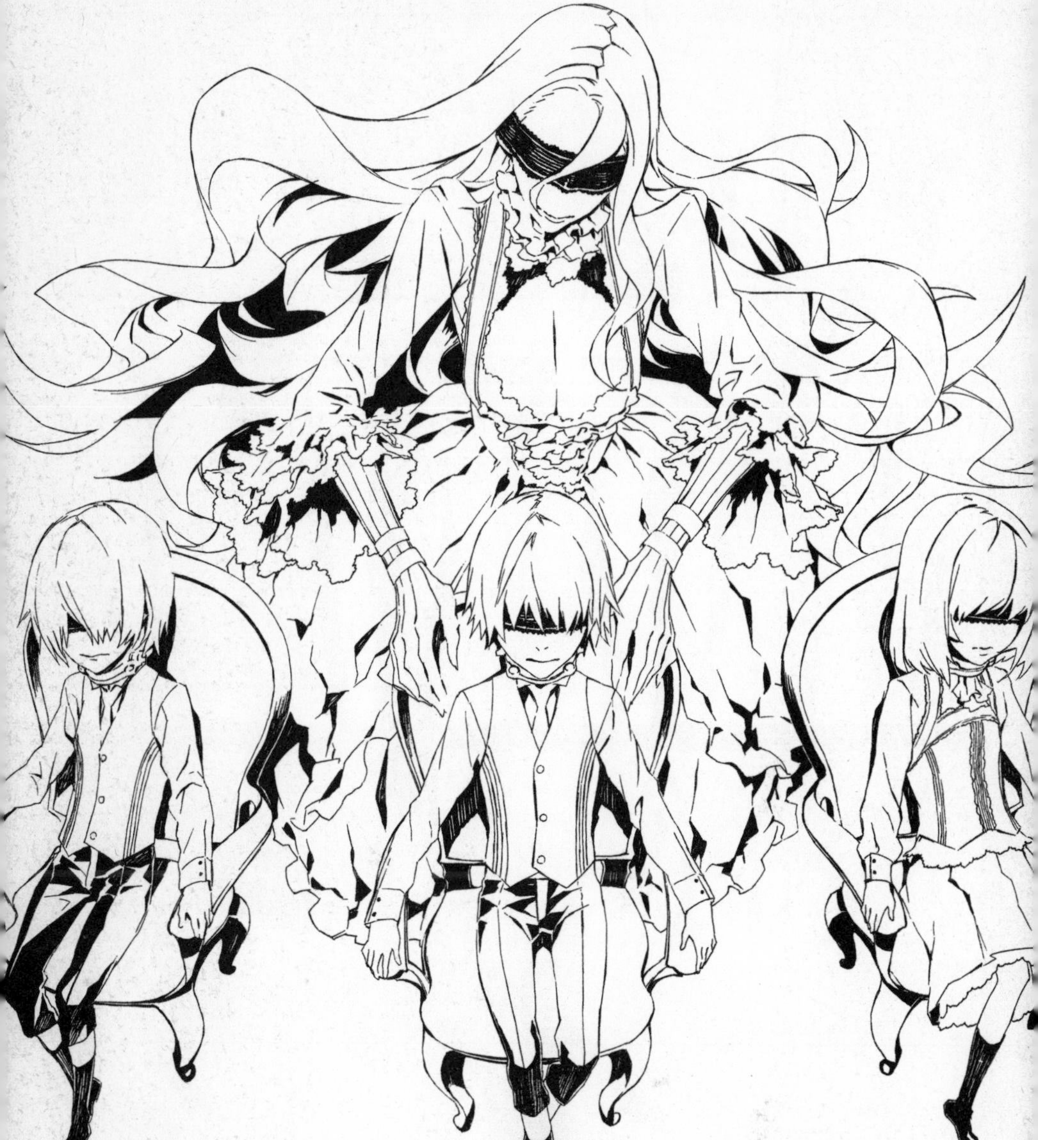

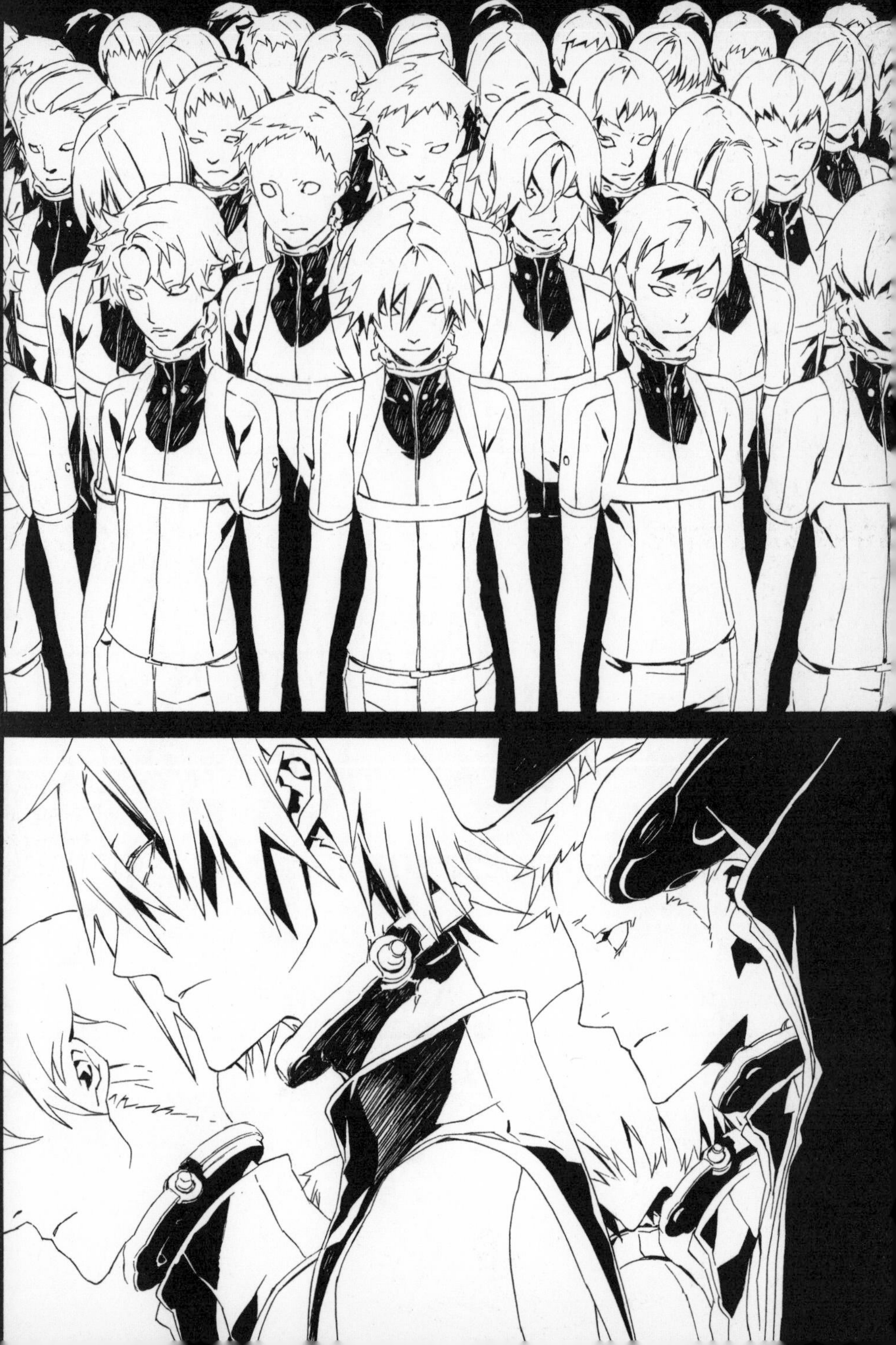

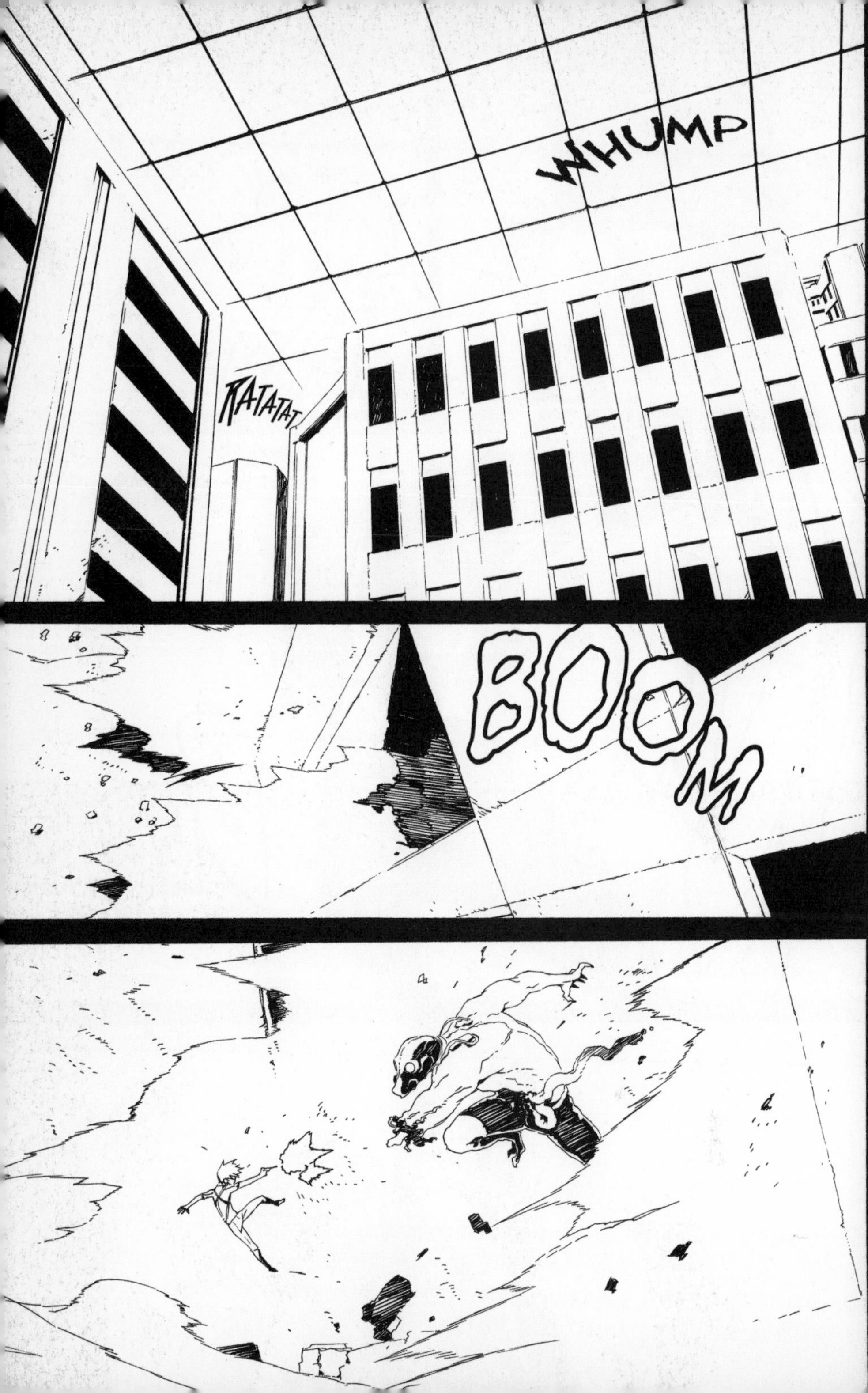
WHUMP
RATATAT
BOOM

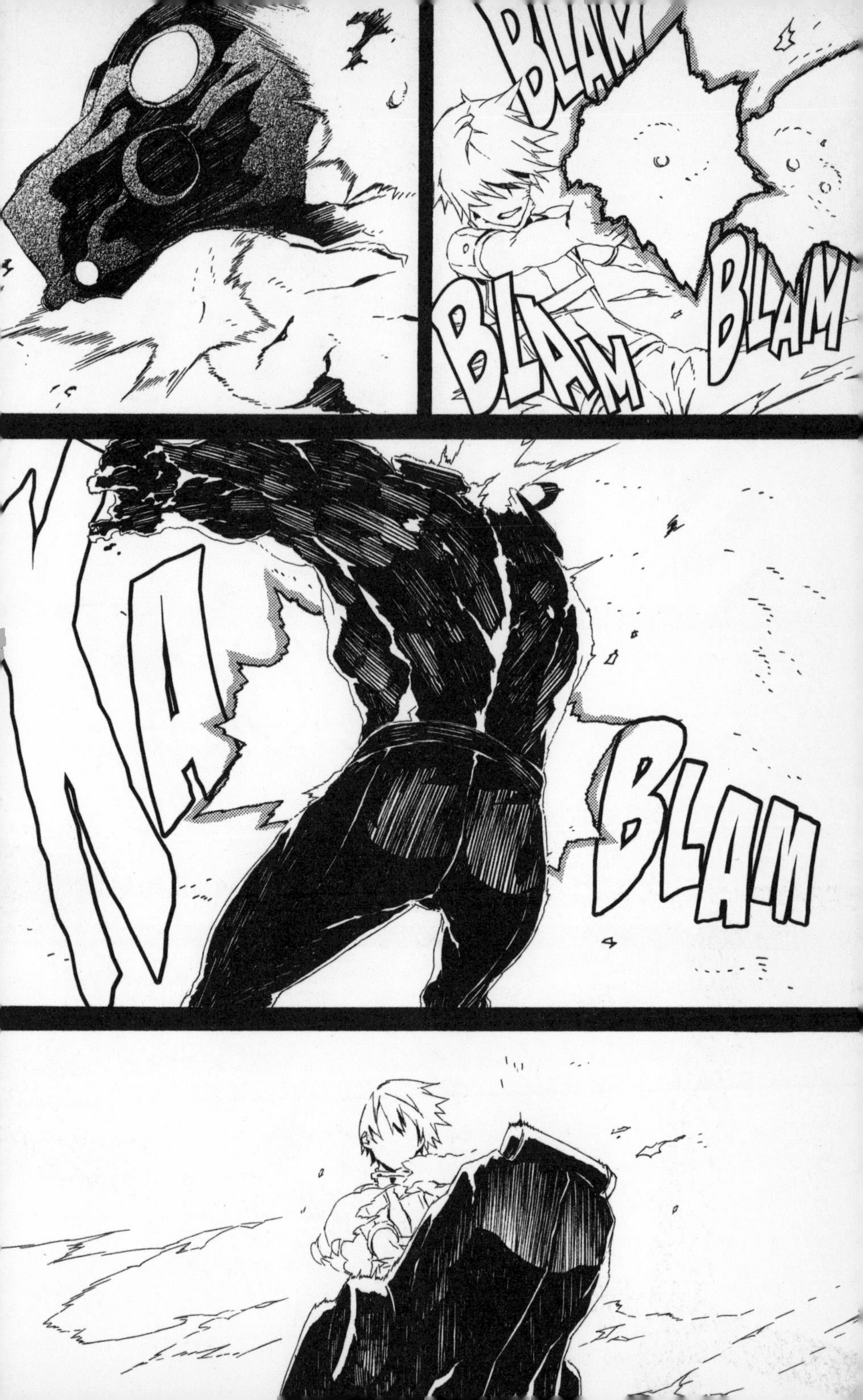
BLAM
BLAM
BLAM
BLAM

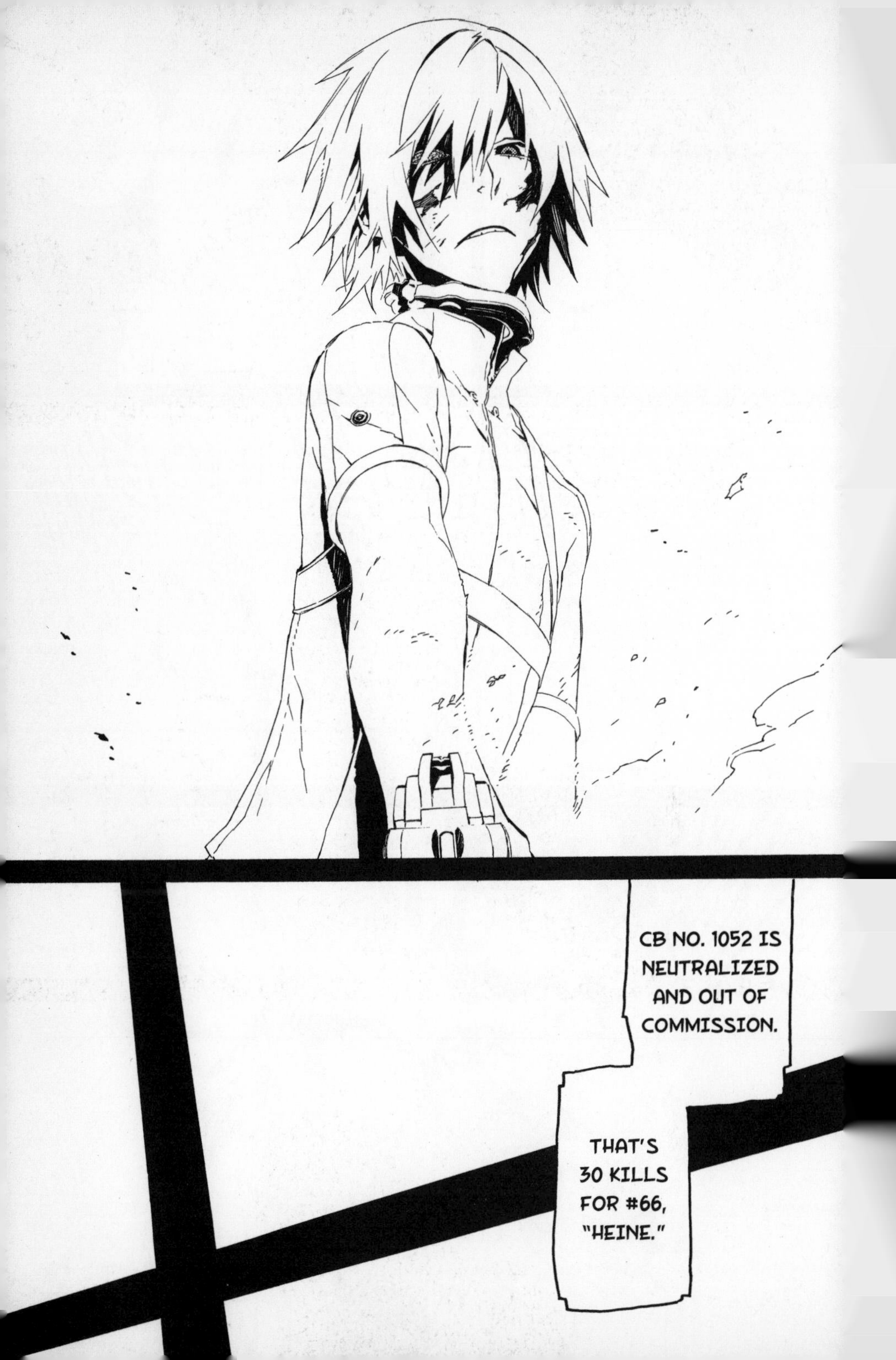
CB NO. 1052 IS NEUTRALIZED AND OUT OF COMMISSION.
THAT'S 30 KILLS FOR #66, "HEINE."

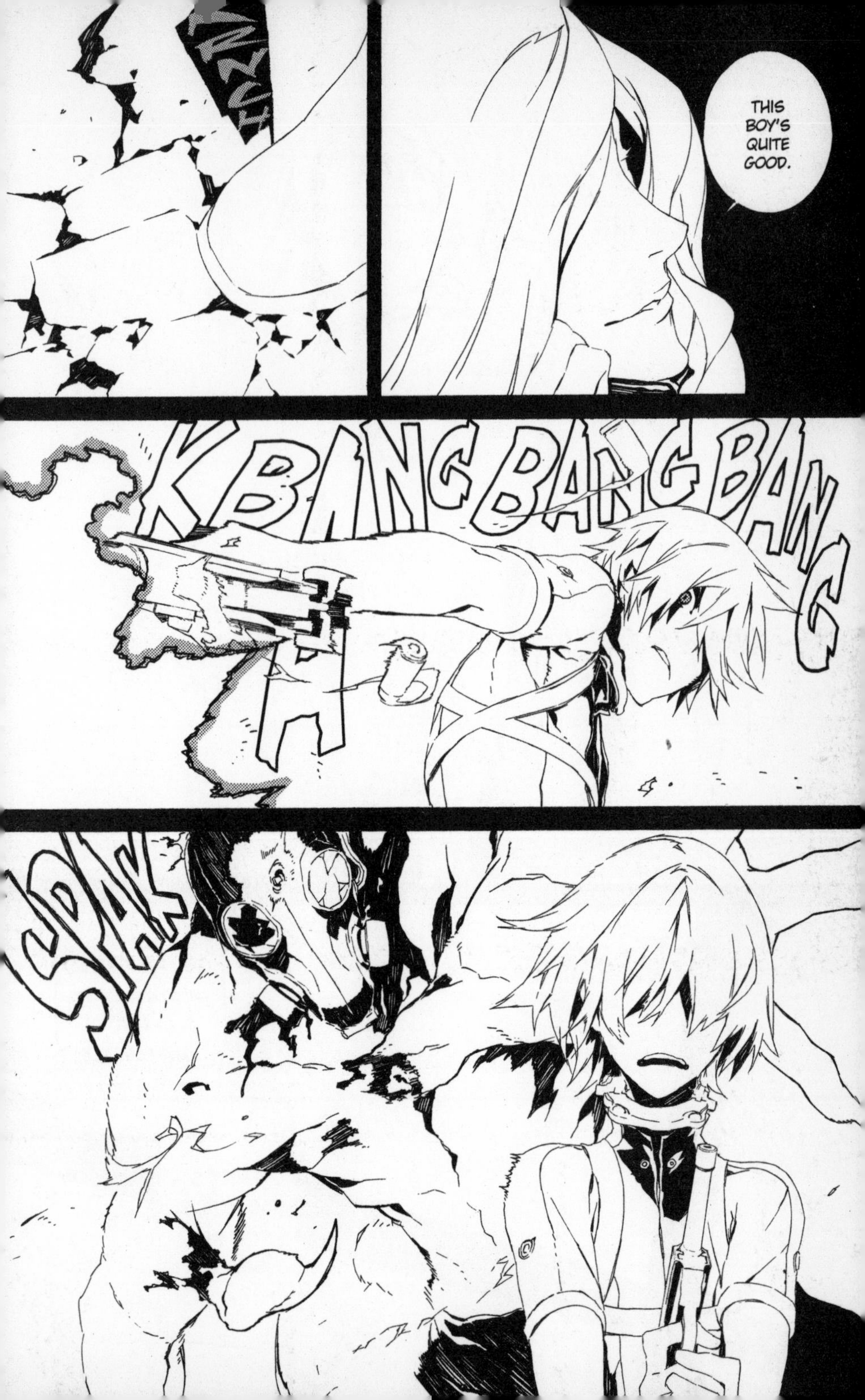
THIS BOY'S QUITE GOOD.
K BANG BANG BANG
SPAK

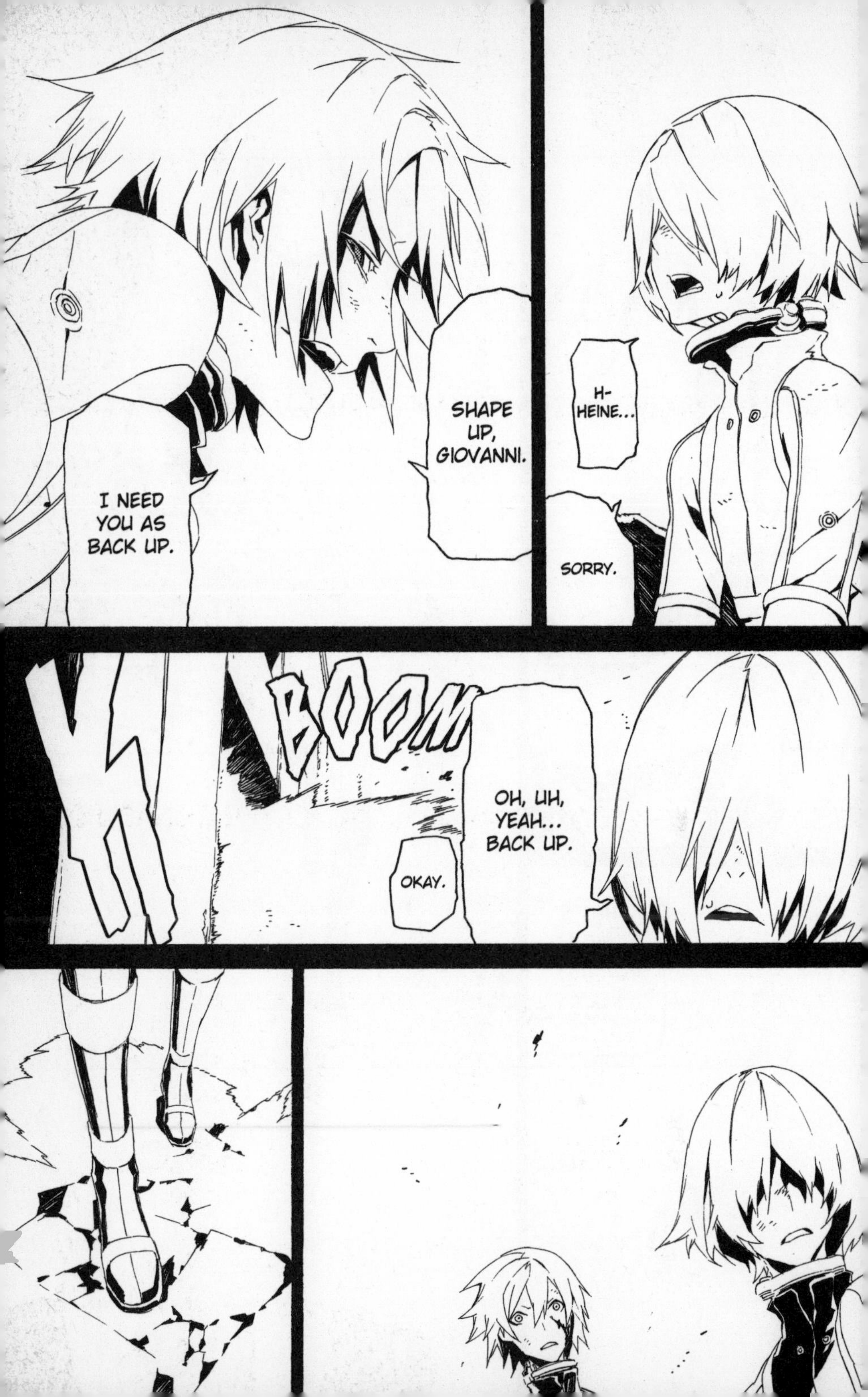
H-HEINE...
SORRY.
SHAPE UP, GIOVANNI.
I NEED YOU AS BACK UP.
OH, UH, YEAH... BACK UP.
OKAY.
BOOM

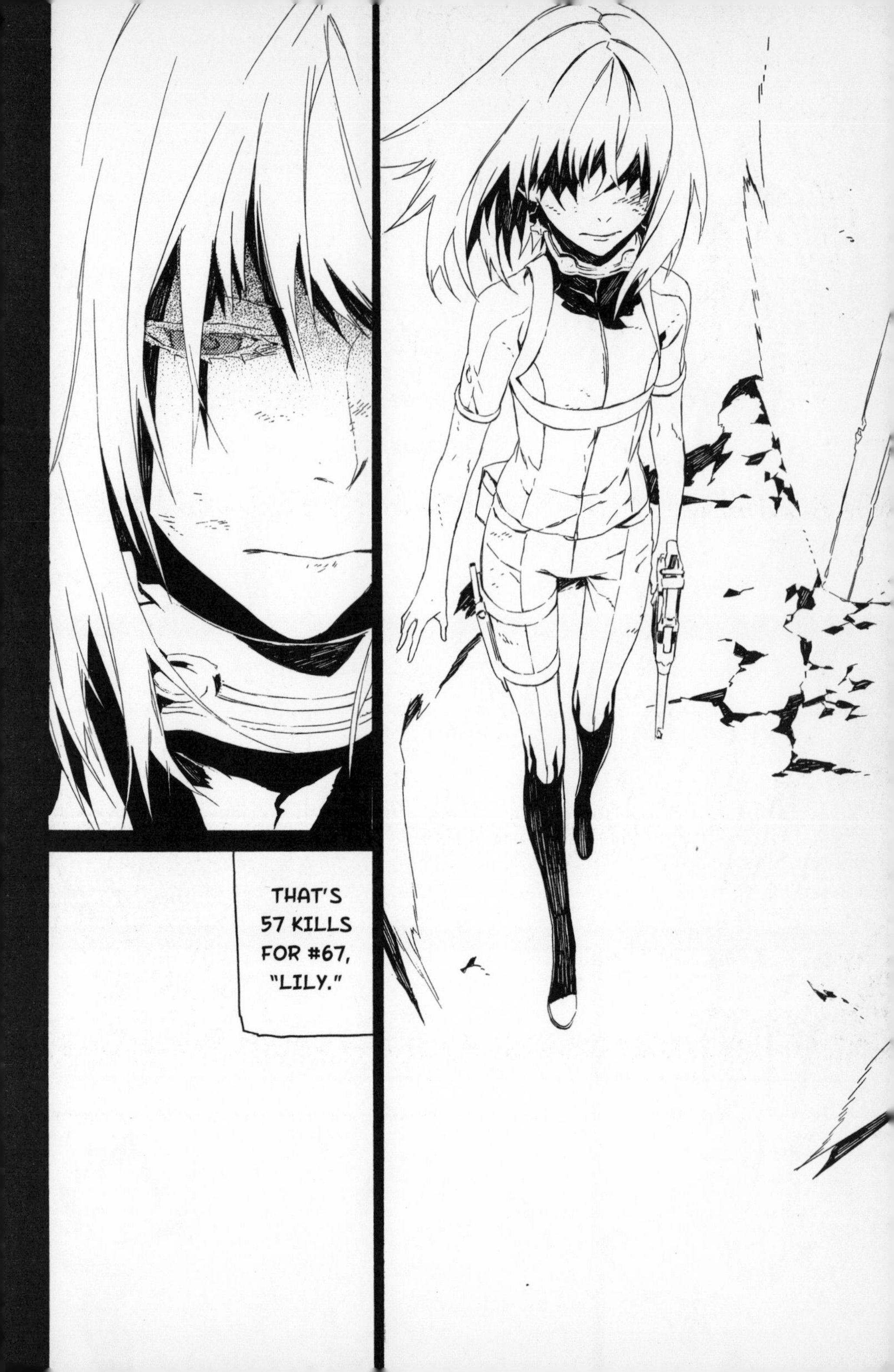
THAT'S 57 KILLS FOR #67, "LILY."

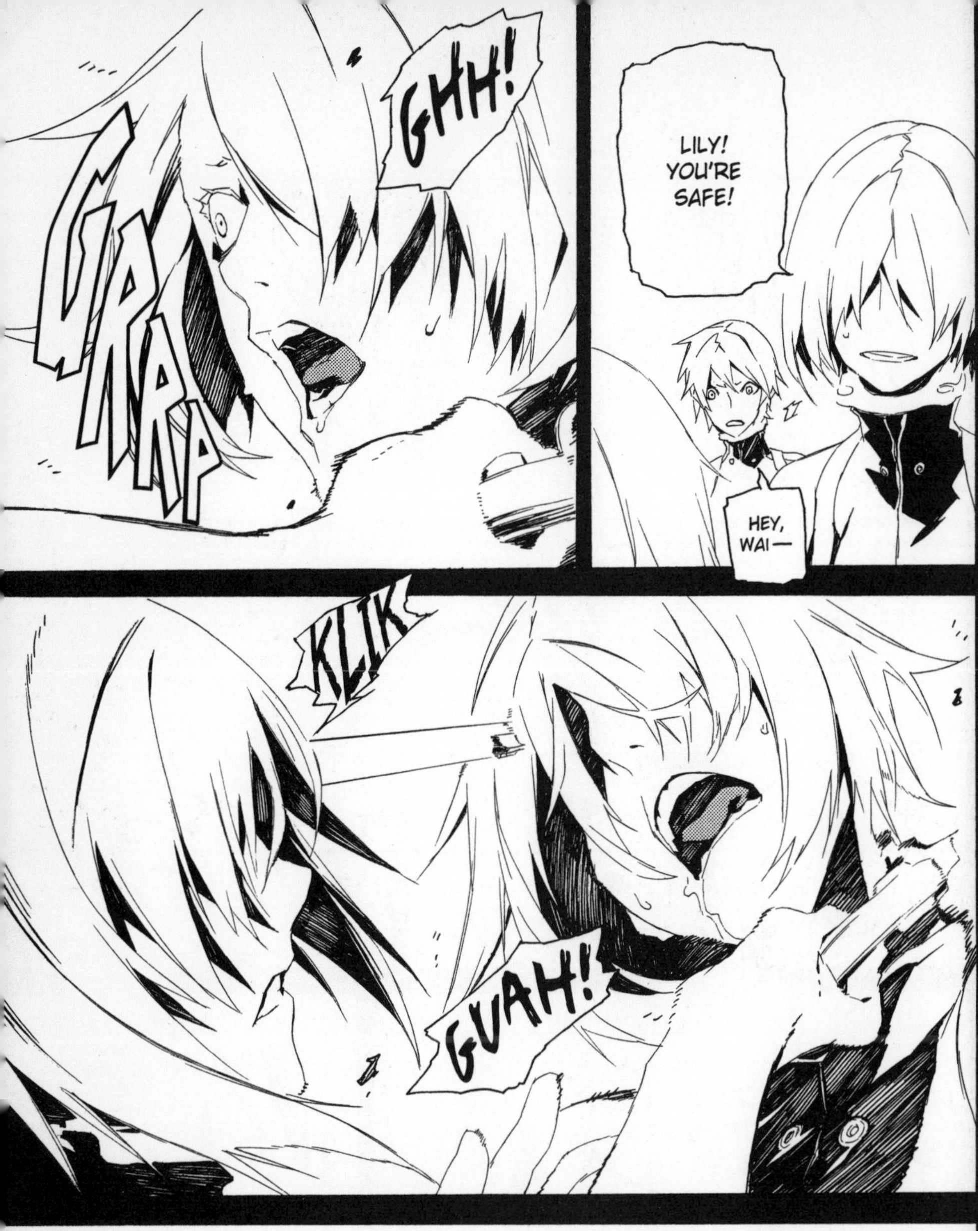
LILY! YOU'RE SAFE!
HEY, WAI—
GHH!
GRAP
KLIK
GUAH!

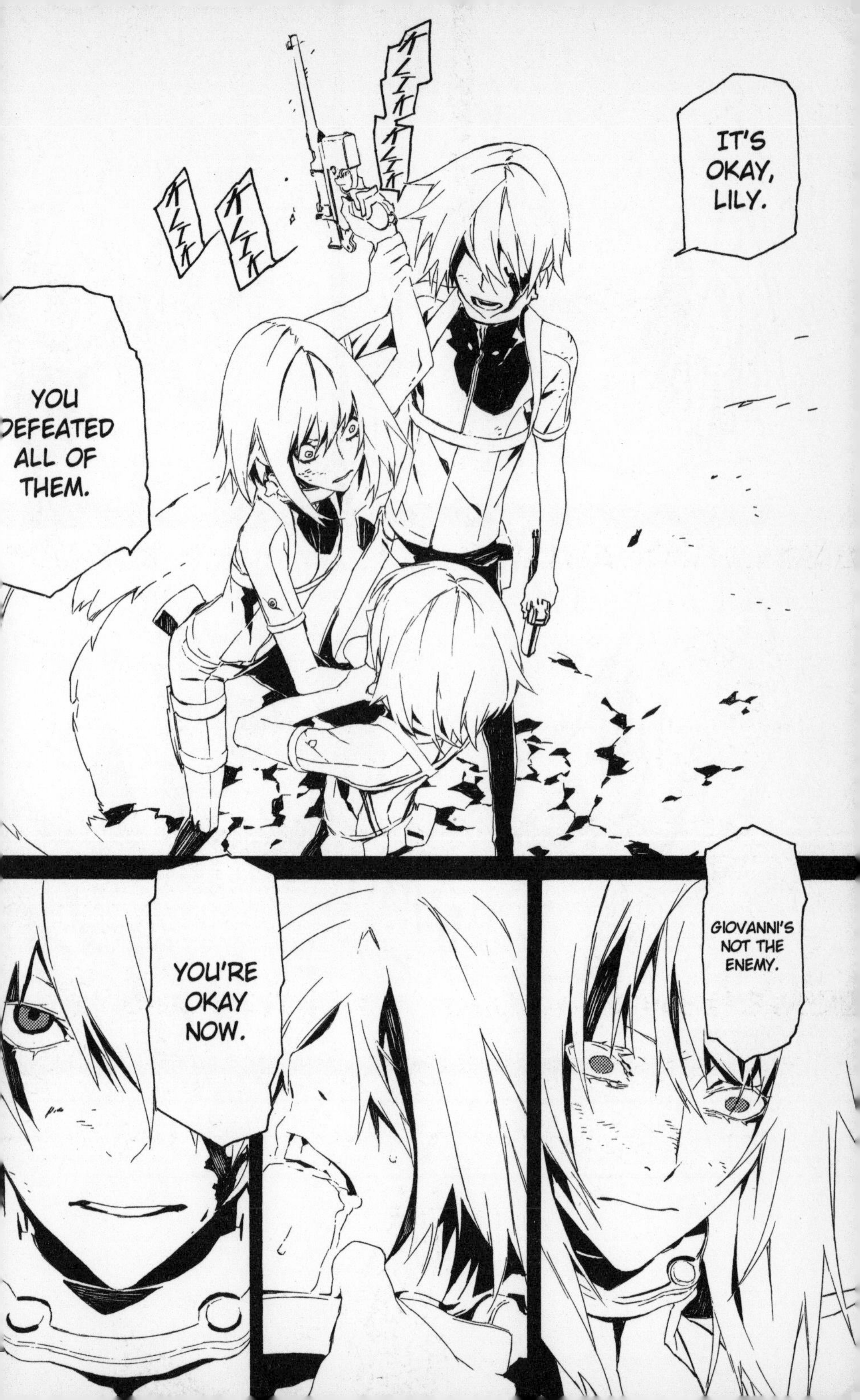
IT'S OKAY, LILY.
YOU DEFEATED ALL OF THEM.
GIOVANNI'S NOT THE ENEMY.
YOU'RE OKAY NOW.

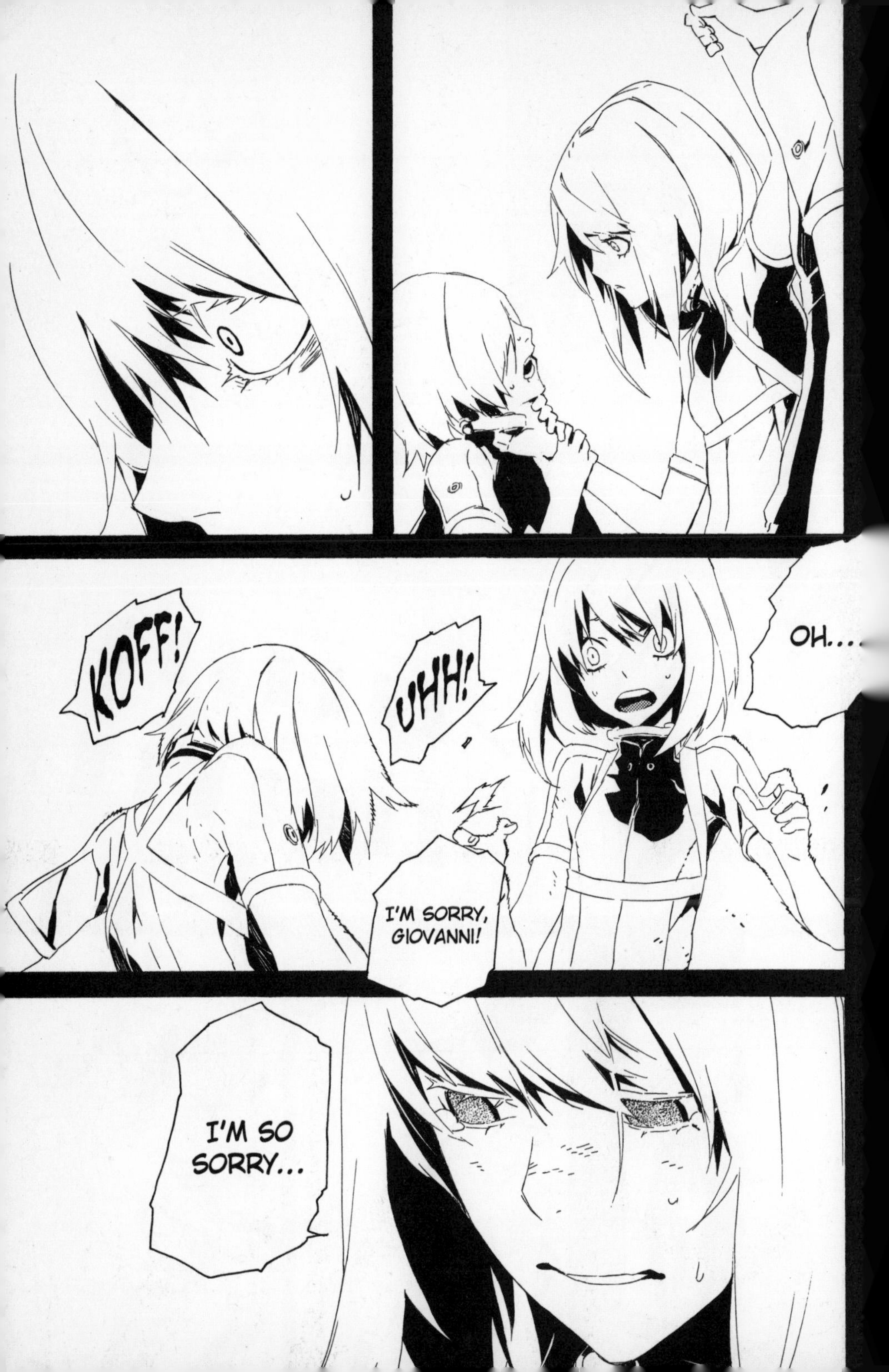
OH....
UHH!
KOFF!
I'M SORRY, GIOVANNI!
I'M SO SORRY...

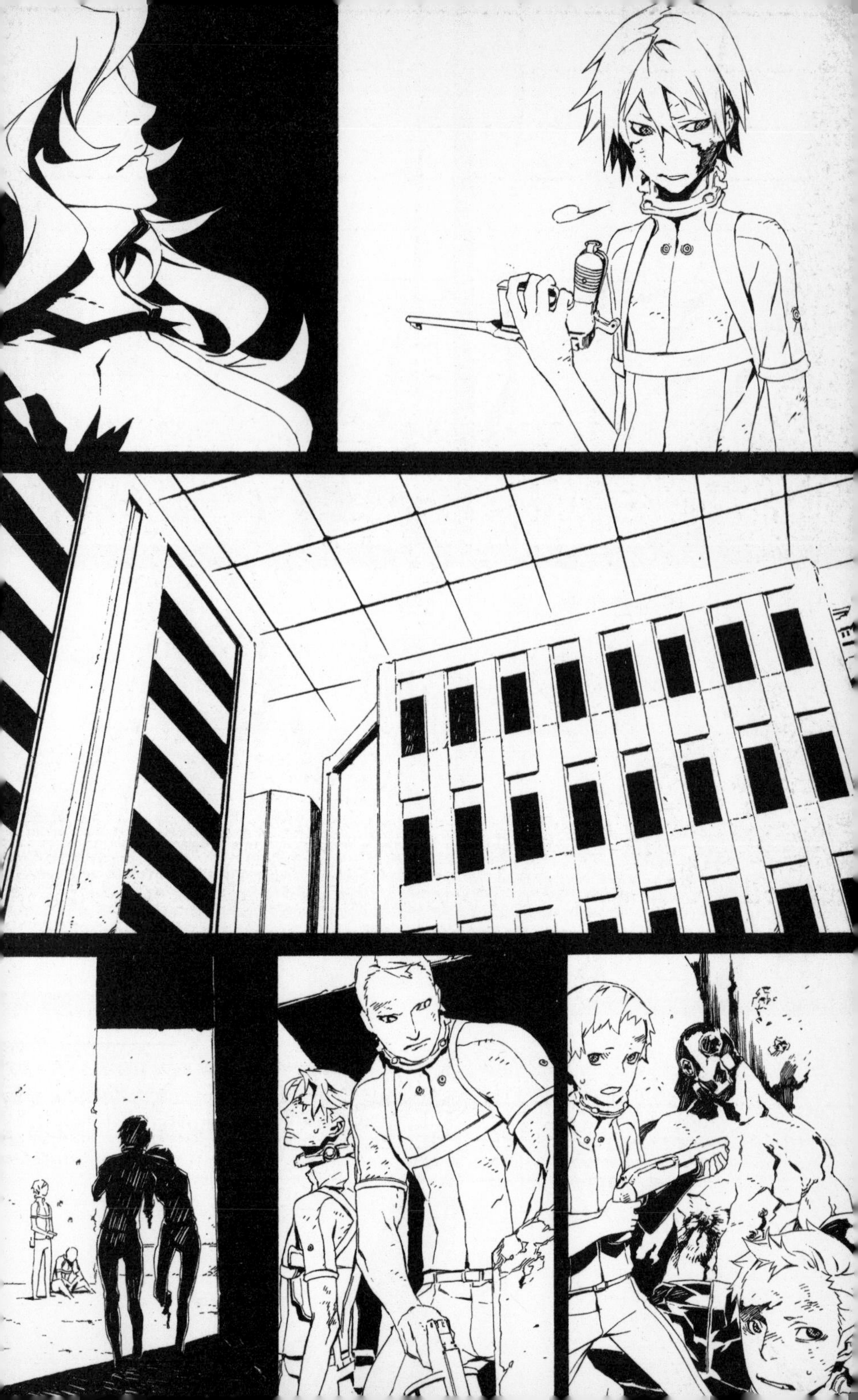

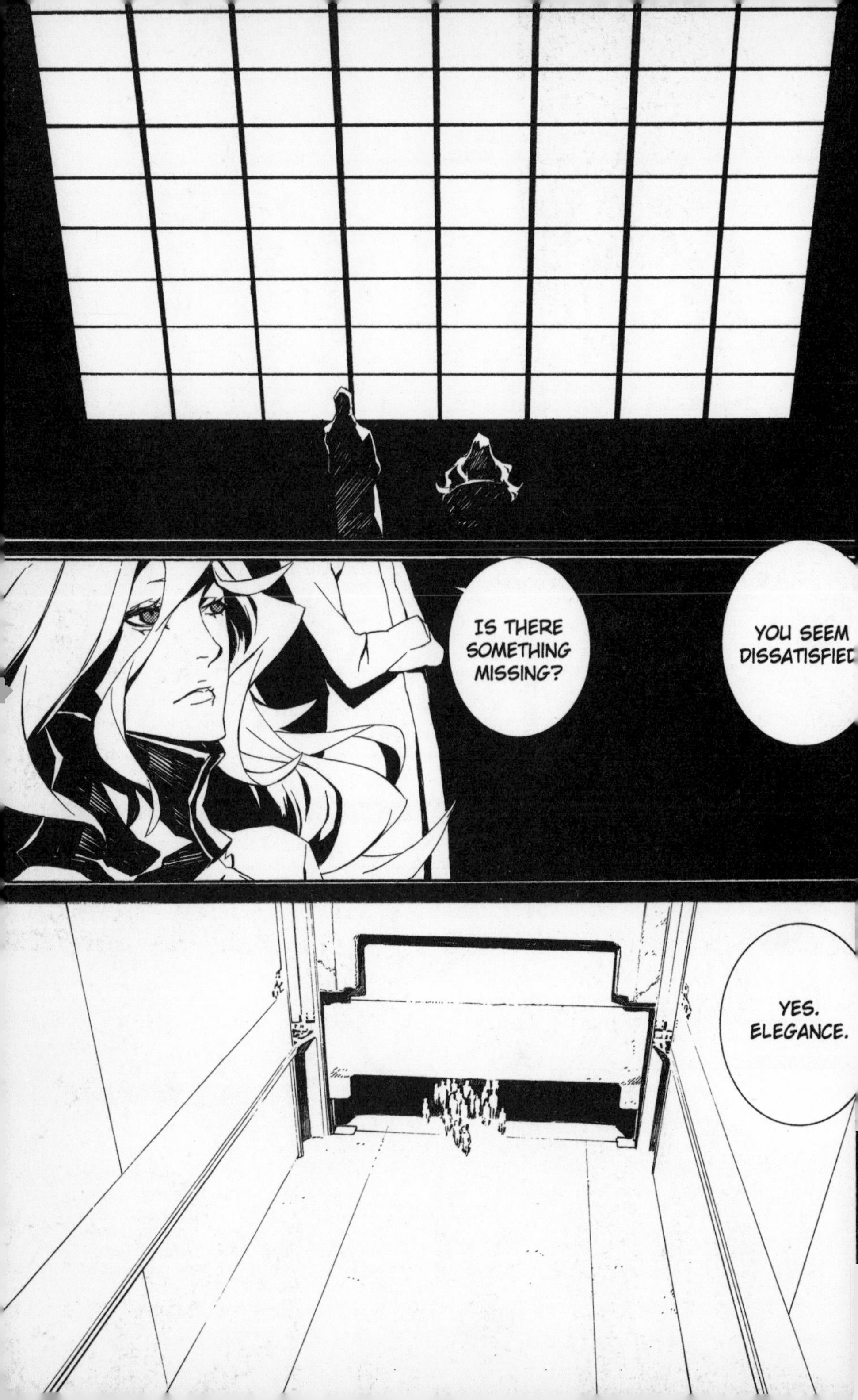
YOU SEEM DISSATISFIED
IS THERE SOMETHING MISSING?
YES. ELEGANCE.

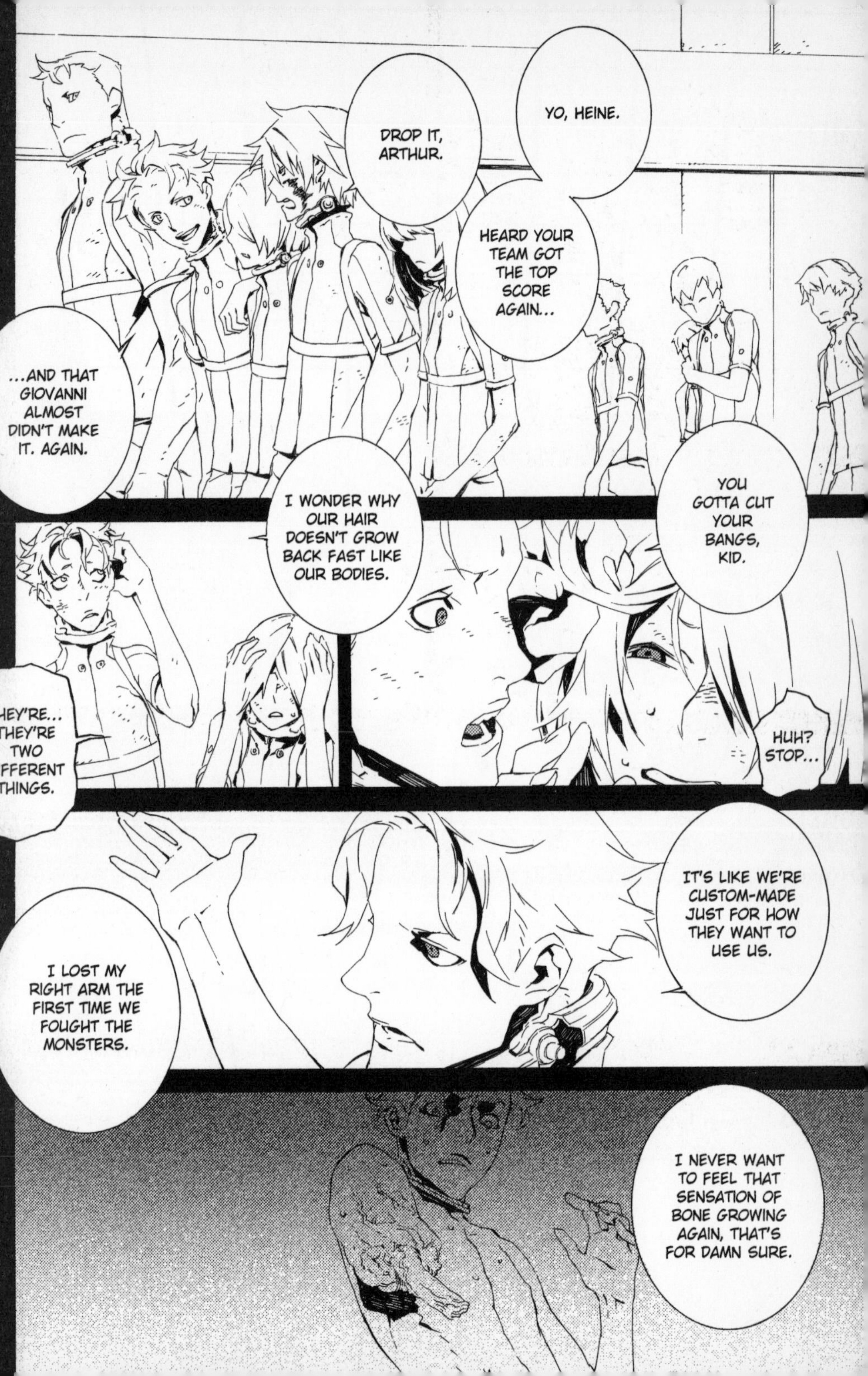
YO, HEINE.
DROP IT, ARTHUR.
HEARD YOUR TEAM GOT THE TOP SCORE AGAIN...
...AND THAT GIOVANNI ALMOST DIDN'T MAKE IT. AGAIN.
YOU GOTTA CUT YOUR BANGS, KID.
HUH? STOP...
I WONDER WHY OUR HAIR DOESN'T GROW BACK FAST LIKE OUR BODIES.
THEY'RE... THEY'RE TWO DIFFERENT THINGS.
IT'S LIKE WE'RE CUSTOM-MADE JUST FOR HOW THEY WANT TO USE US.
I LOST MY RIGHT ARM THE FIRST TIME WE FOUGHT THE MONSTERS.
I NEVER WANT TO FEEL THAT SENSATION OF BONE GROWING AGAIN, THAT'S FOR DAMN SURE.

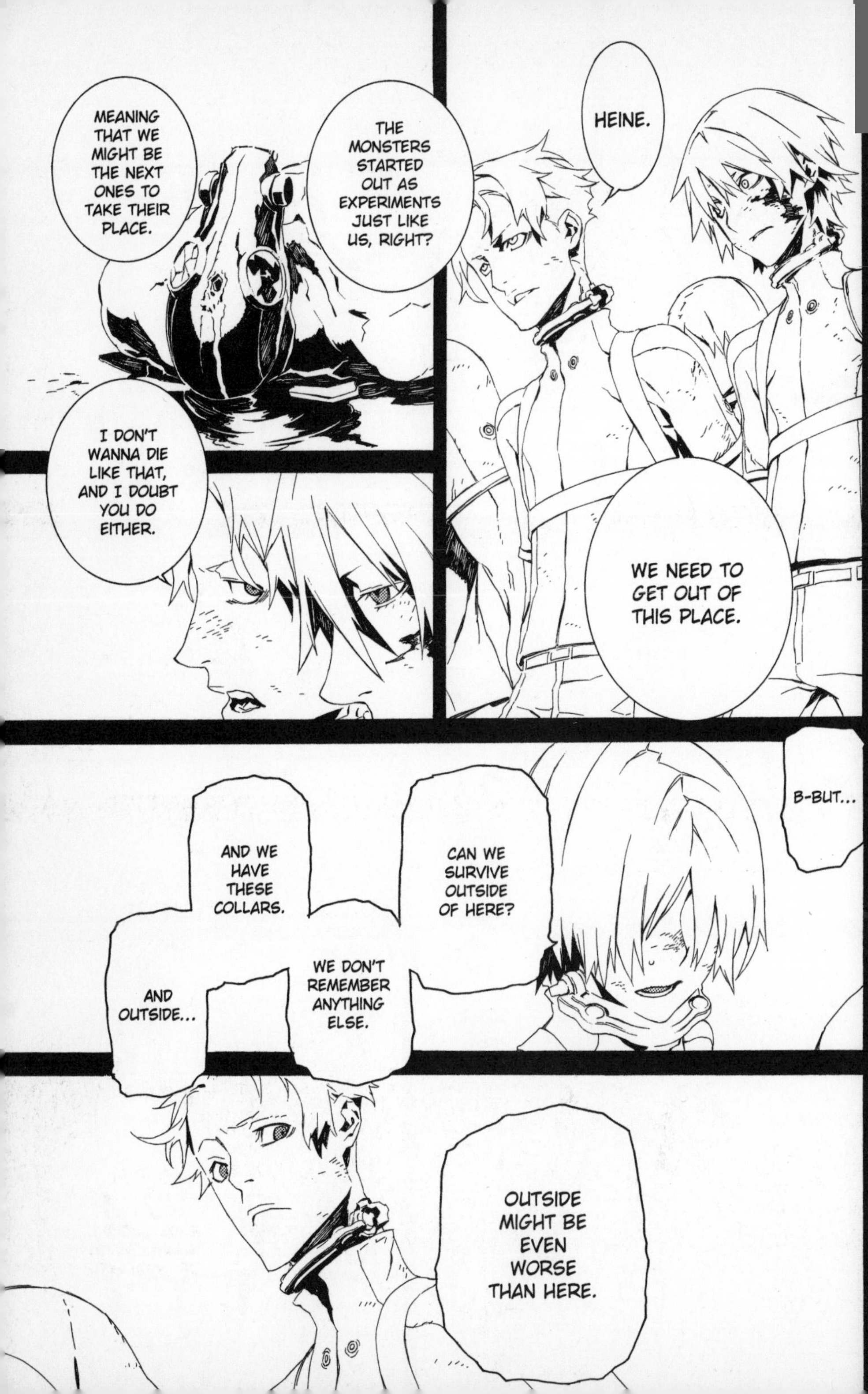
HEINE.
WE NEED TO GET OUT OF THIS PLACE.
THE MONSTERS STARTED OUT AS EXPERIMENTS JUST LIKE US, RIGHT?
MEANING THAT WE MIGHT BE THE NEXT ONES TO TAKE THEIR PLACE.
I DON'T WANNA DIE LIKE THAT, AND I DOUBT YOU DO EITHER.
B-BUT...
CAN WE SURVIVE OUTSIDE OF HERE?
AND WE HAVE THESE COLLARS.
WE DON'T REMEMBER ANYTHING ELSE.
AND OUTSIDE...
OUTSIDE MIGHT BE EVEN WORSE THAN HERE.

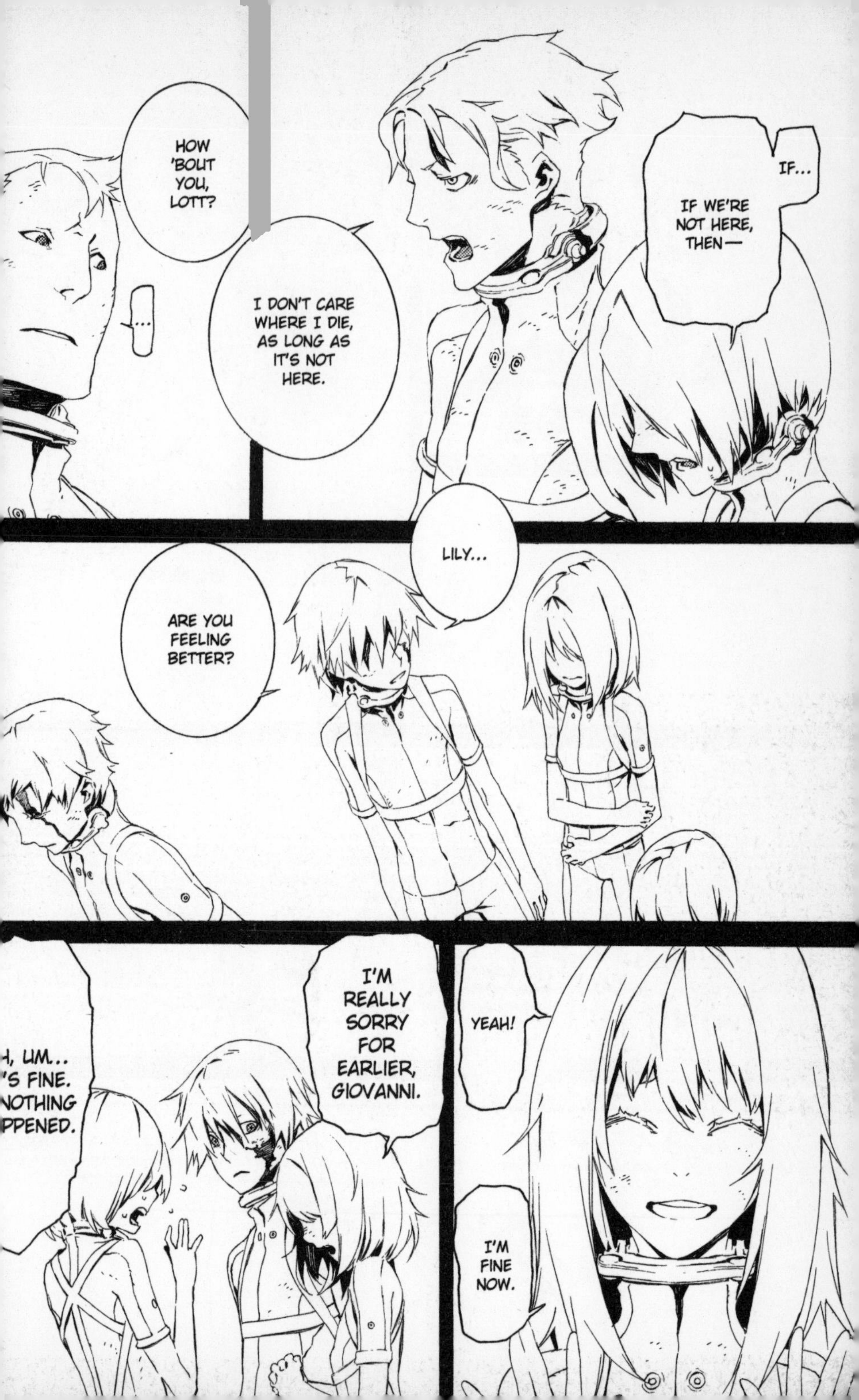
IF...
IF WE'RE NOT HERE, THEN—
I DON'T CARE WHERE I DIE, AS LONG AS IT'S NOT HERE.
HOW 'BOUT YOU, LOTT?
...
LILY...
ARE YOU FEELING BETTER?
YEAH!
I'M FINE NOW.
I'M REALLY SORRY FOR EARLIER, GIOVANNI.
H, UM... 'S FINE. NOTHING PPENED.

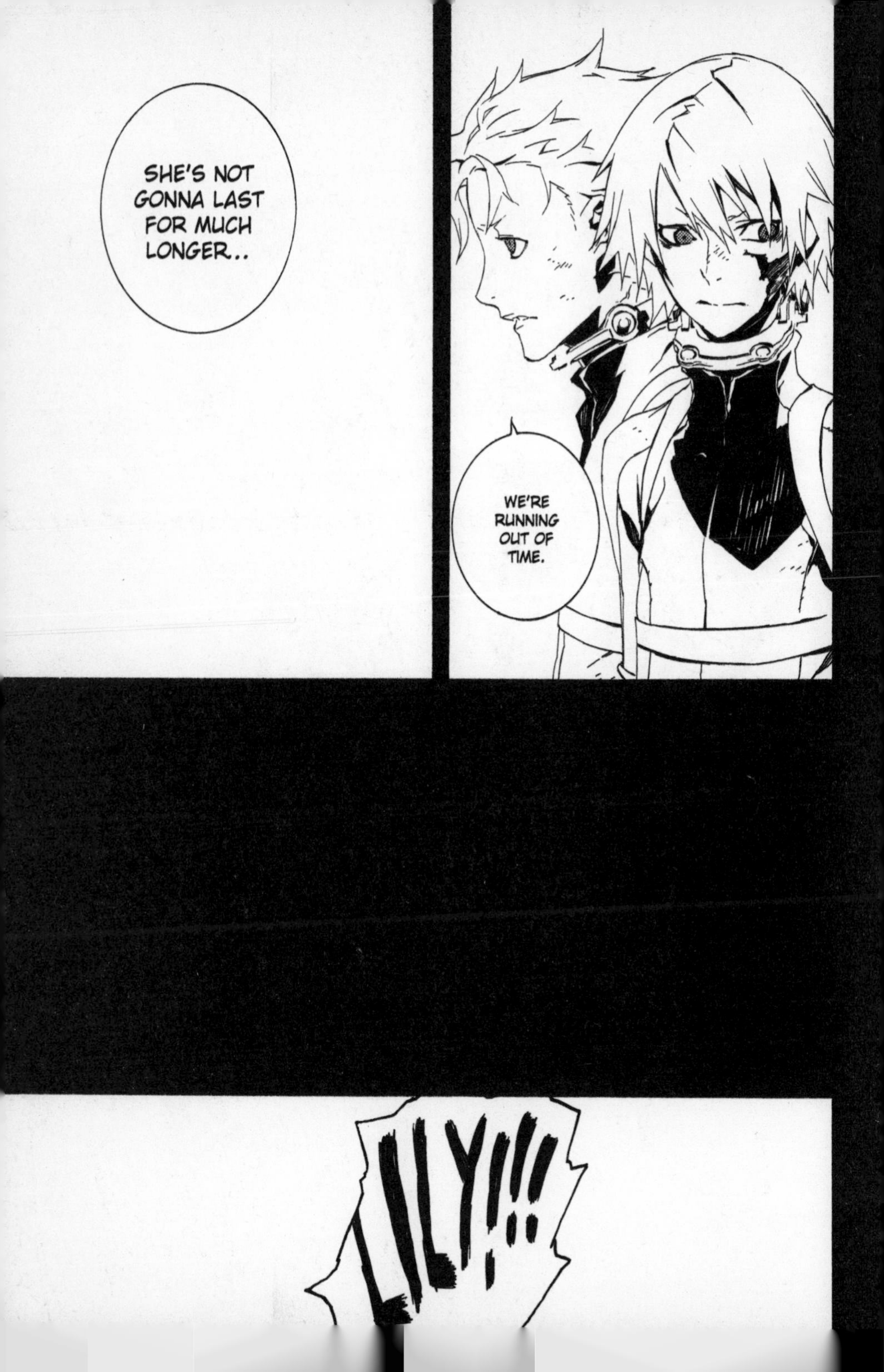
WE'RE RUNNING OUT OF TIME.
SHE'S NOT GONNA LAST FOR MUCH LONGER...
LILY!!!

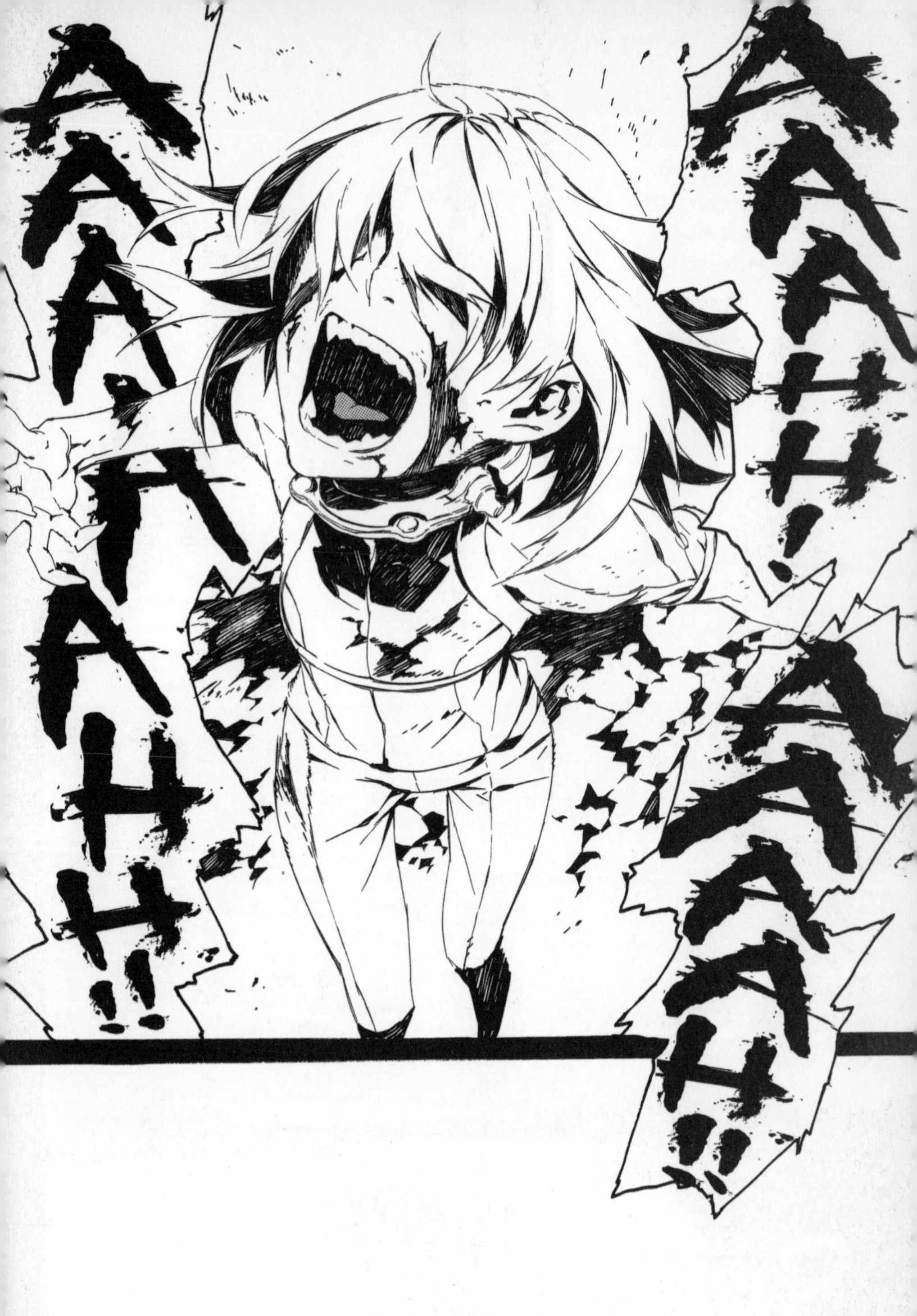
AAAHH!
AAAAH!!
AAAAAHH!!

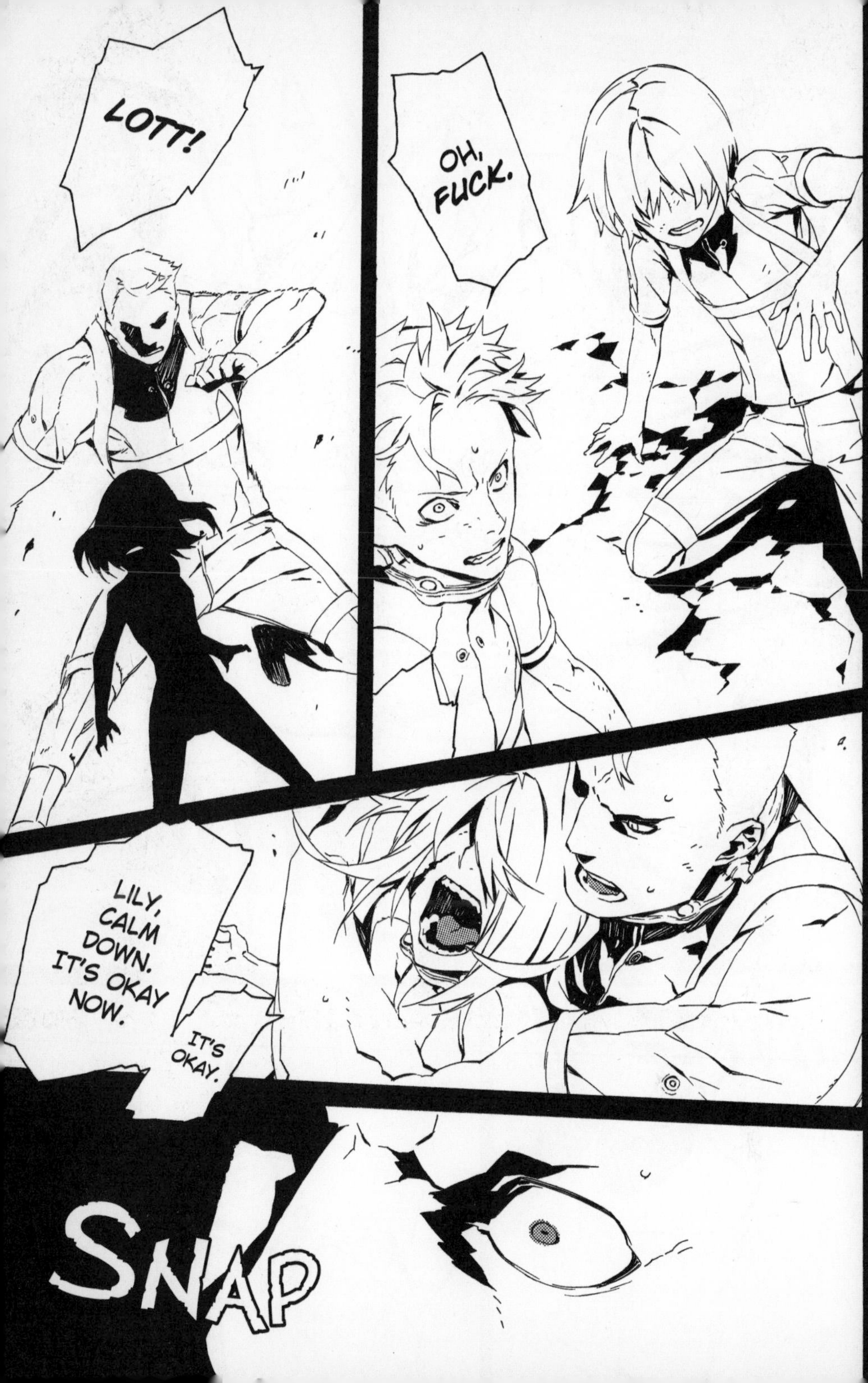
OH, FUCK.
LOTT!
LILY, CALM DOWN. IT'S OKAY NOW.
IT'S OKAY.
SNAP

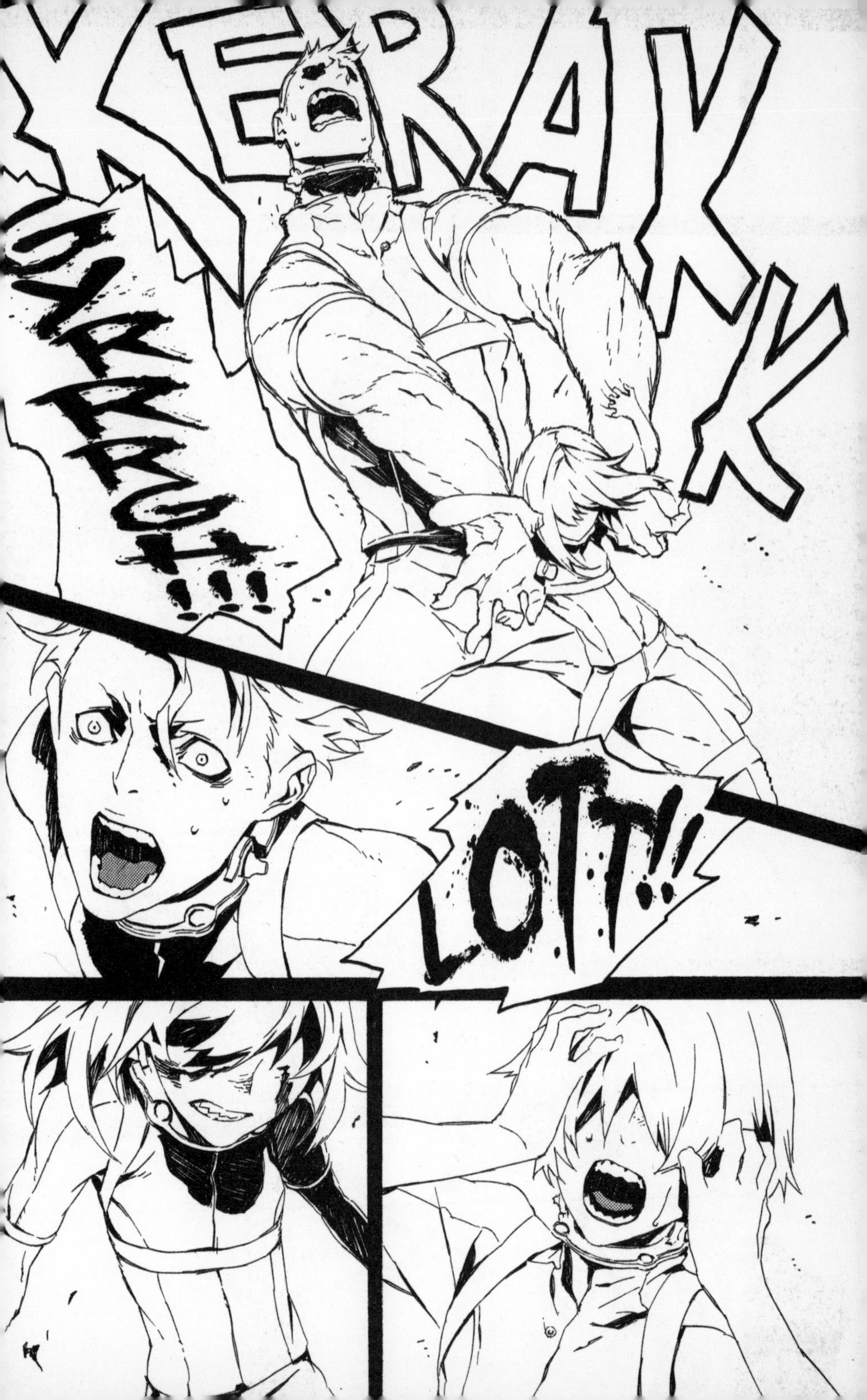
KRAK
GYARRGH!!!
LOTT!!

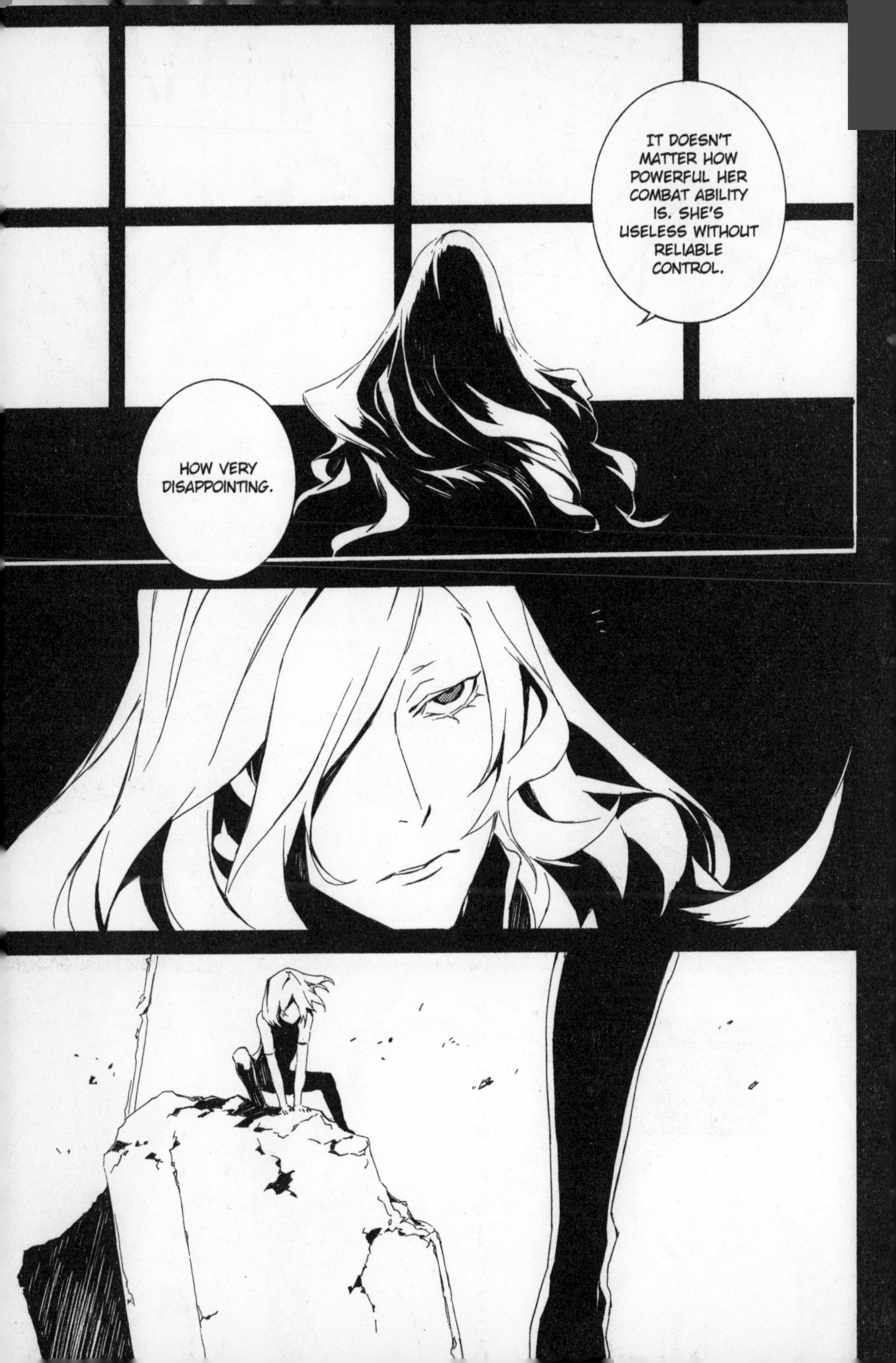
IT DOESN'T MATTER HOW POWERFUL HER COMBAT ABILITY IS. SHE'S USELESS WITHOUT RELIABLE CONTROL.
HOW VERY DISAPPOINTING.

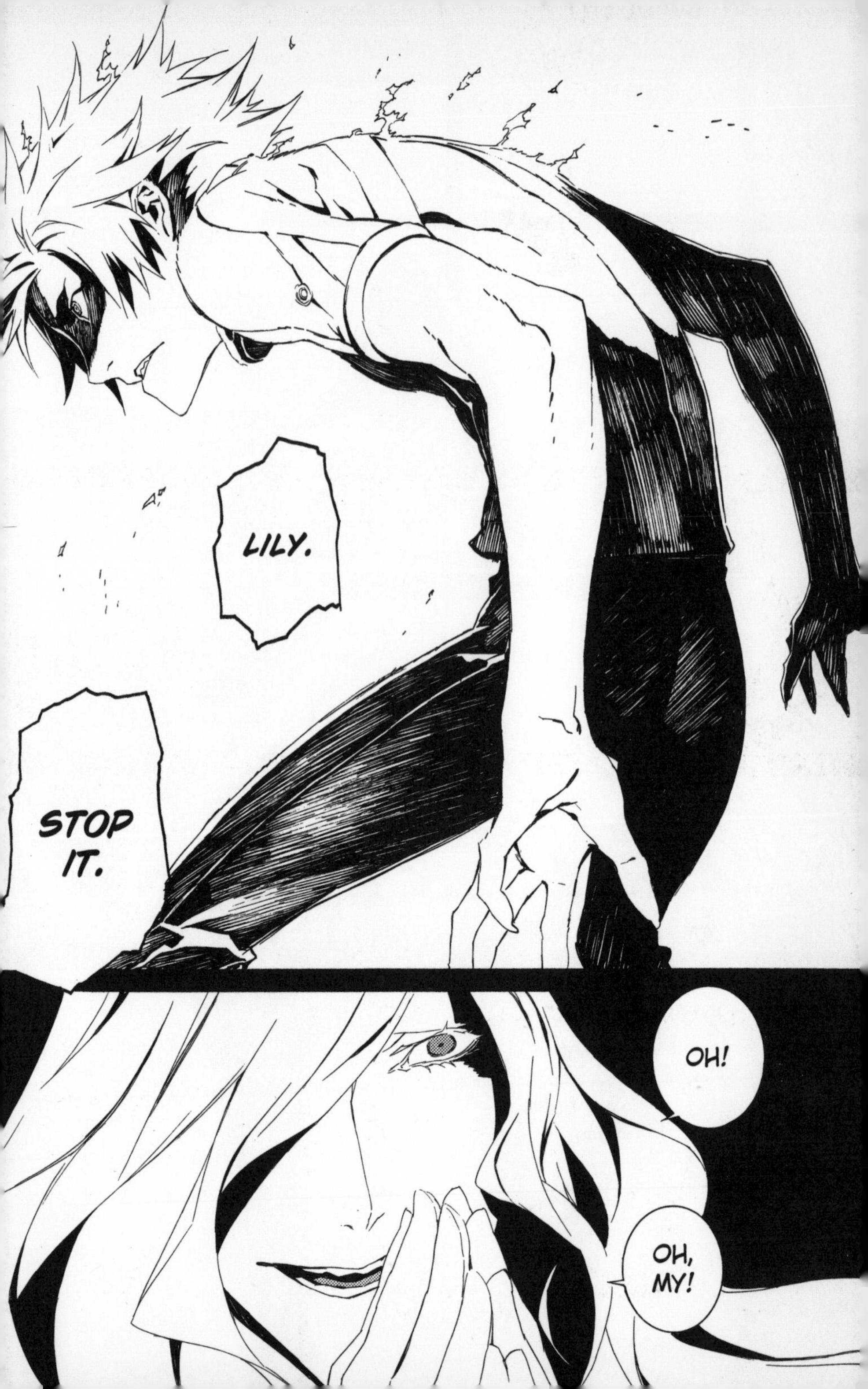
LILY.
STOP IT.
OH!
OH, MY!

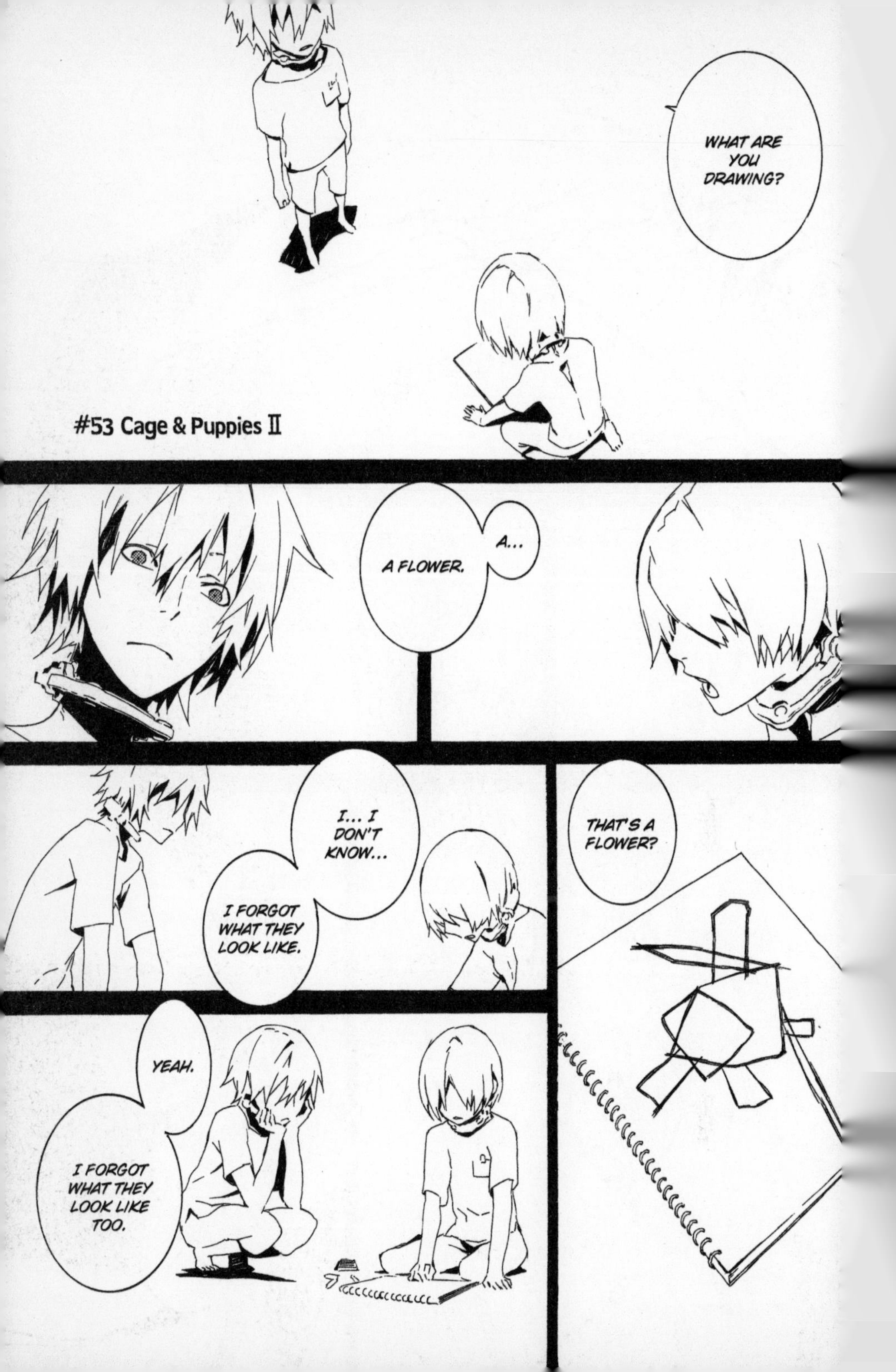
WHAT ARE YOU DRAWING?
#53 Cage & Puppies II
A...
A FLOWER.
THAT'S A FLOWER?
I... I DON'T KNOW...
I FORGOT WHAT THEY LOOK LIKE.
YEAH.
I FORGOT WHAT THEY LOOK LIKE TOO.

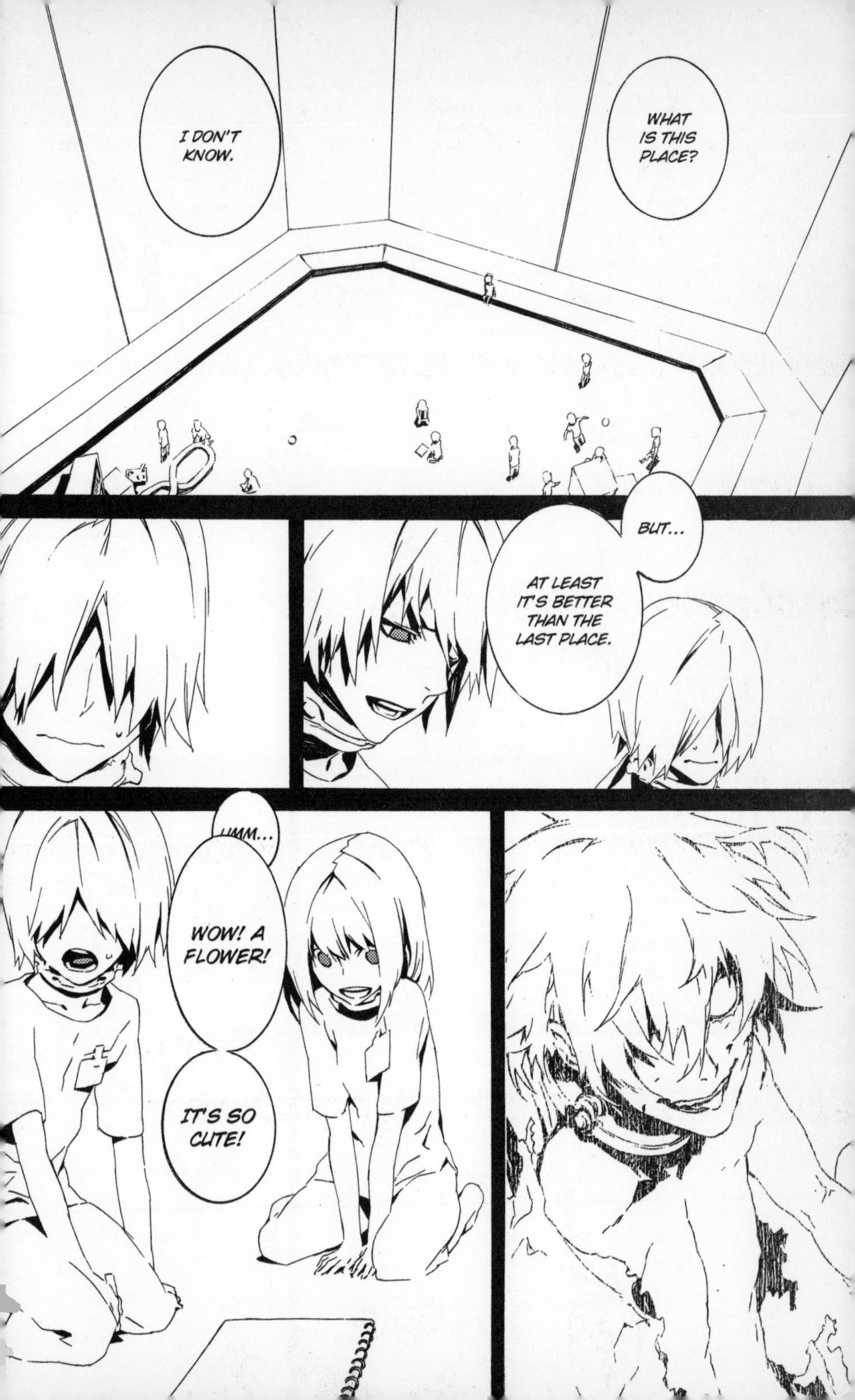
WHAT IS THIS PLACE?
I DON'T KNOW.
BUT...
AT LEAST IT'S BETTER THAN THE LAST PLACE.
UMM...
WOW! A FLOWER!
IT'S SO CUTE!

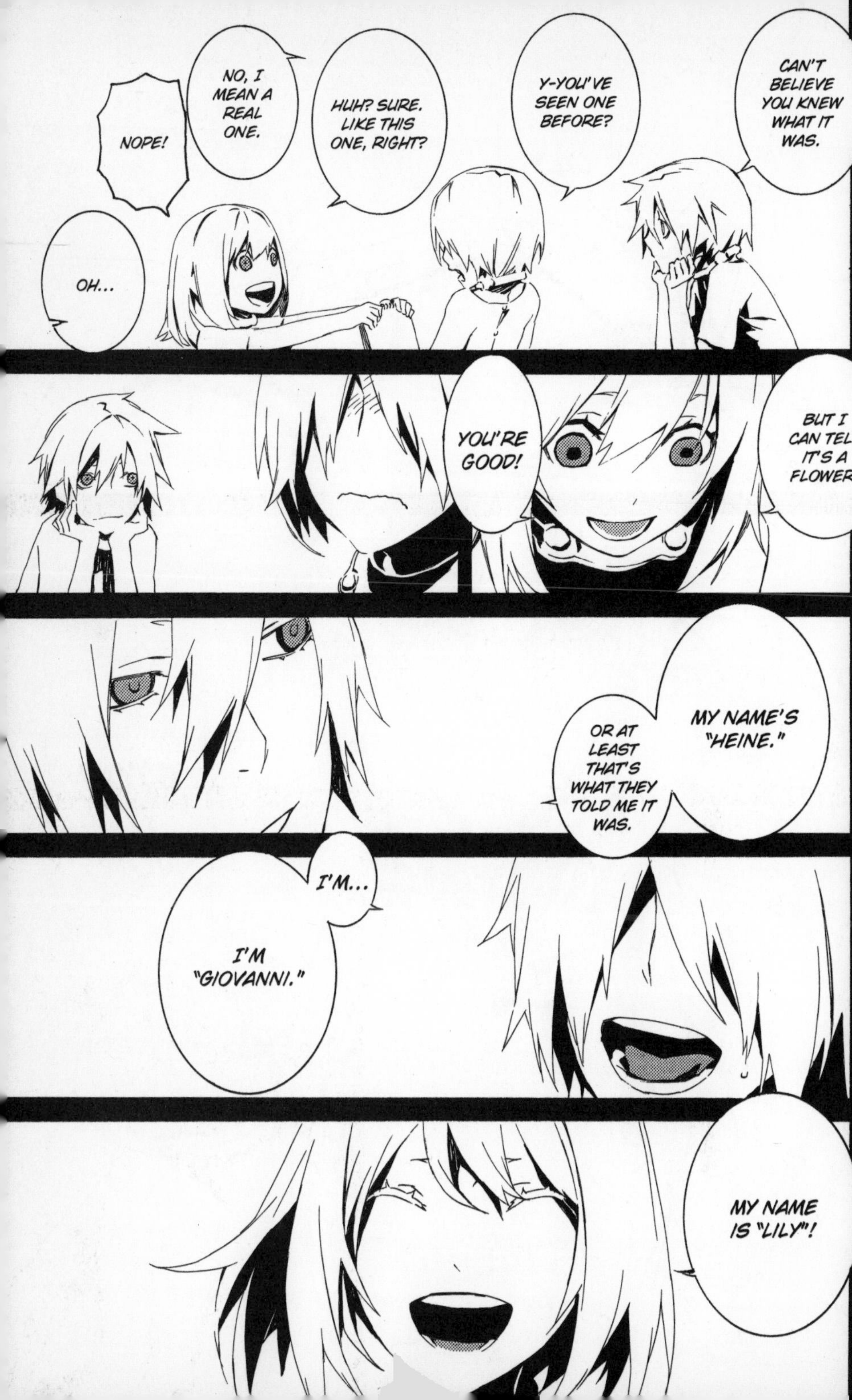
CAN'T BELIEVE YOU KNEW WHAT IT WAS.
Y-YOU'VE SEEN ONE BEFORE?
HUH? SURE. LIKE THIS ONE, RIGHT?
NO, I MEAN A REAL ONE.
NOPE!
OH...
BUT I CAN TELL IT'S A FLOWER.
YOU'RE GOOD!
MY NAME'S "HEINE."
OR AT LEAST THAT'S WHAT THEY TOLD ME IT WAS.
I'M...
I'M "GIOVANNI."
MY NAME IS "LILY"!

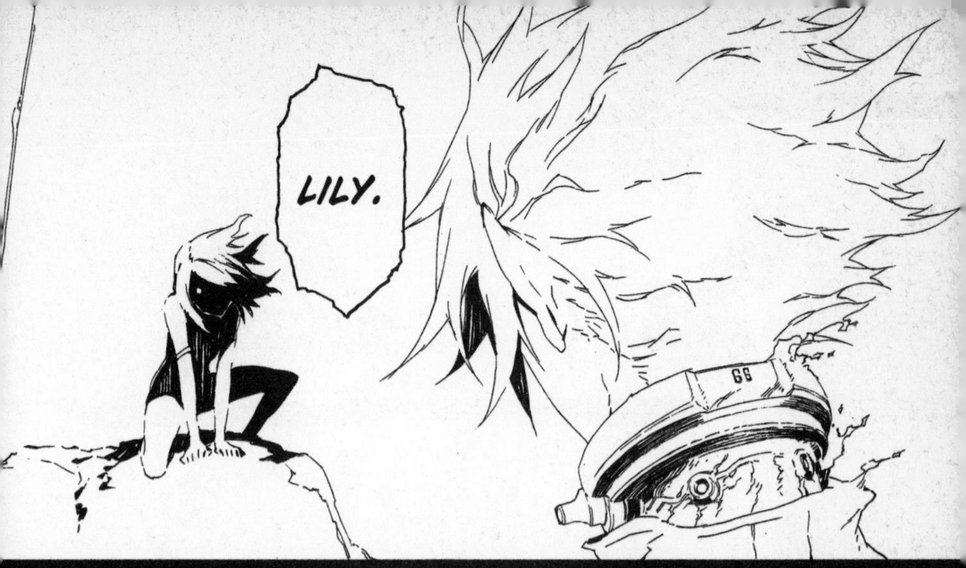
LILY.
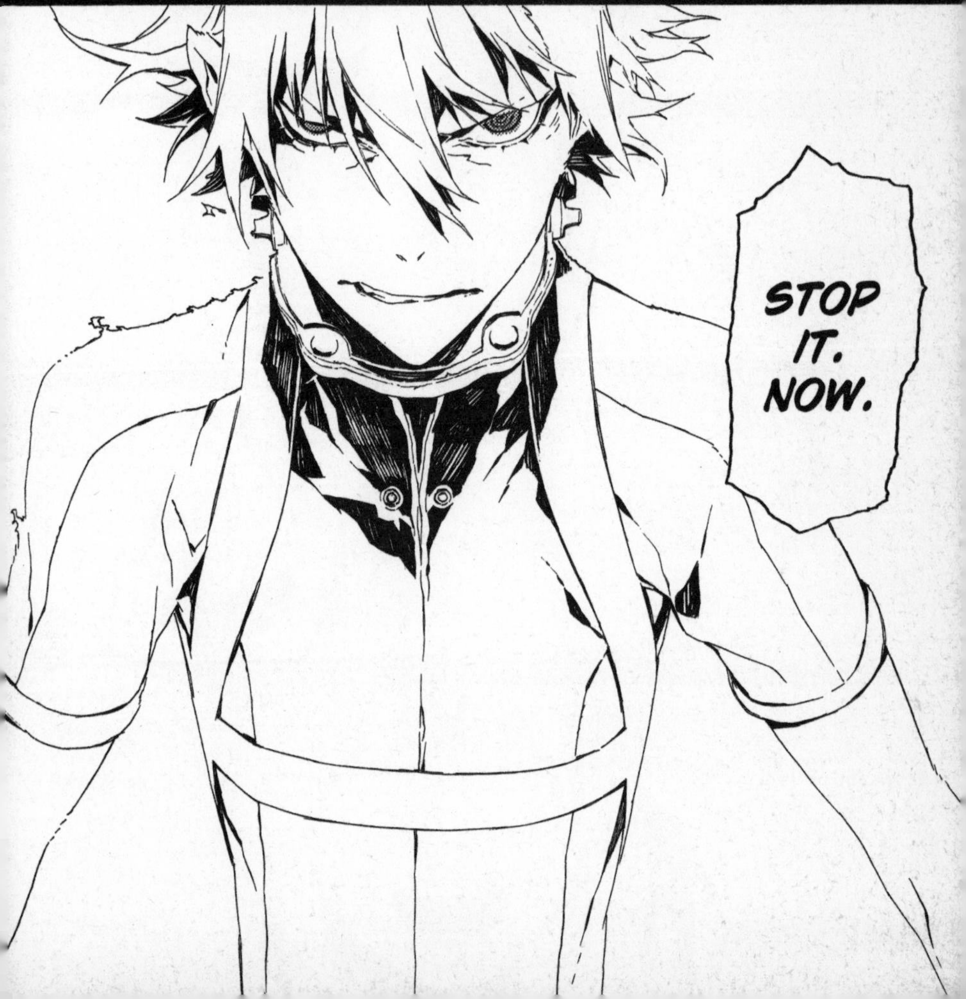
STOP IT. NOW.

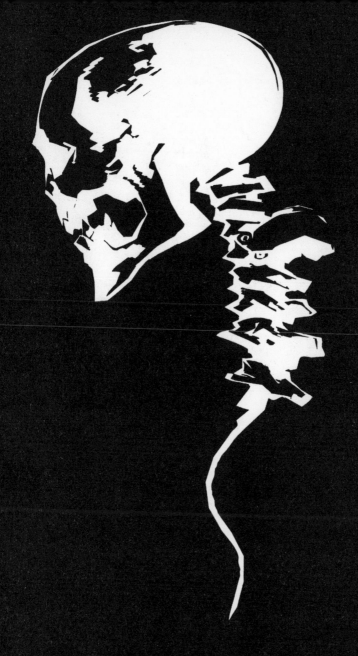

#53 Cage & Puppies Ⅱ

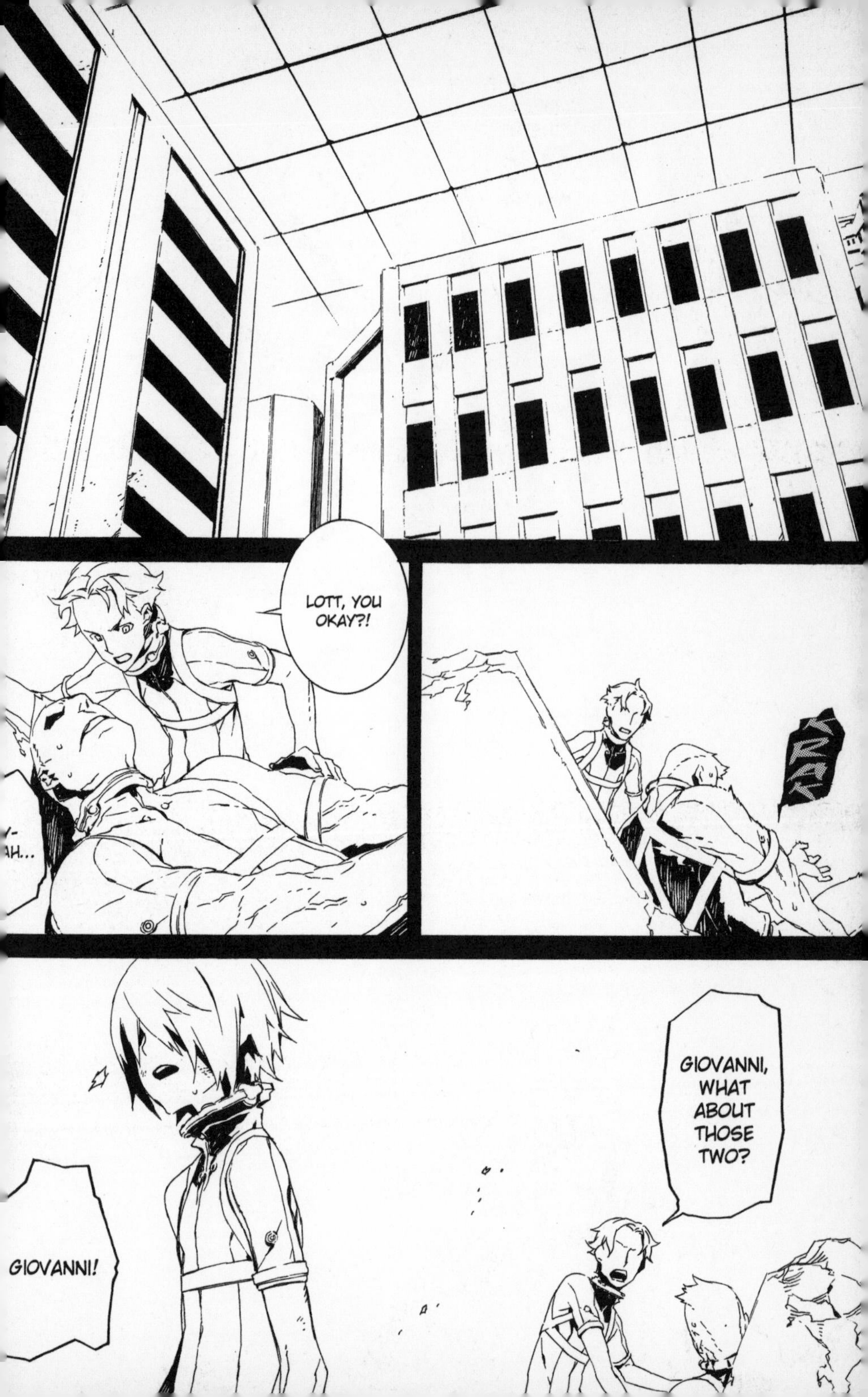
KRAK
LOTT, YOU OKAY?!
GIOVANNI, WHAT ABOUT THOSE TWO?
GIOVANNI!

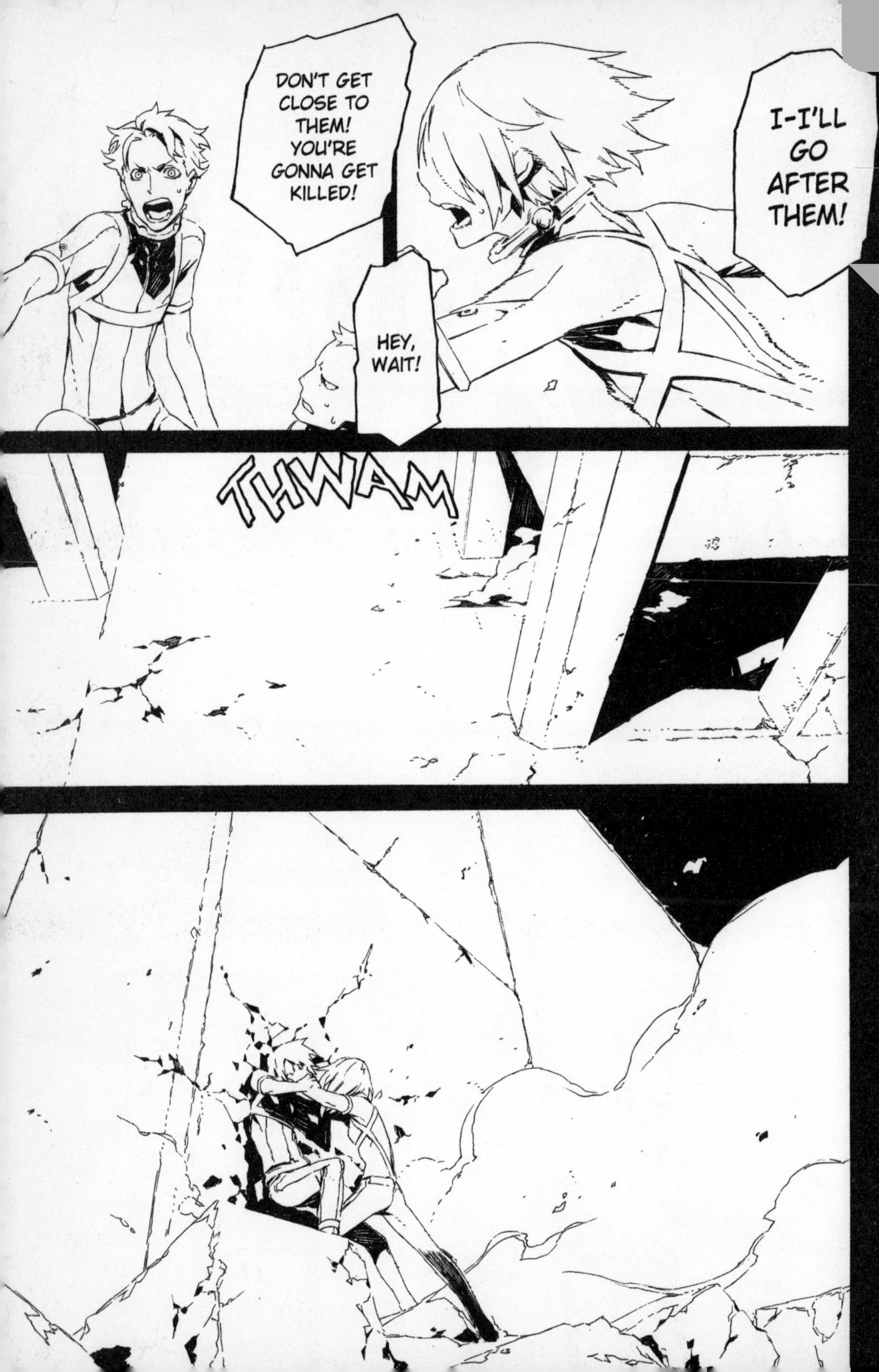
I-I'LL GO AFTER THEM!
DON'T GET CLOSE TO THEM! YOU'RE GONNA GET KILLED!
HEY, WAIT!
THWAM

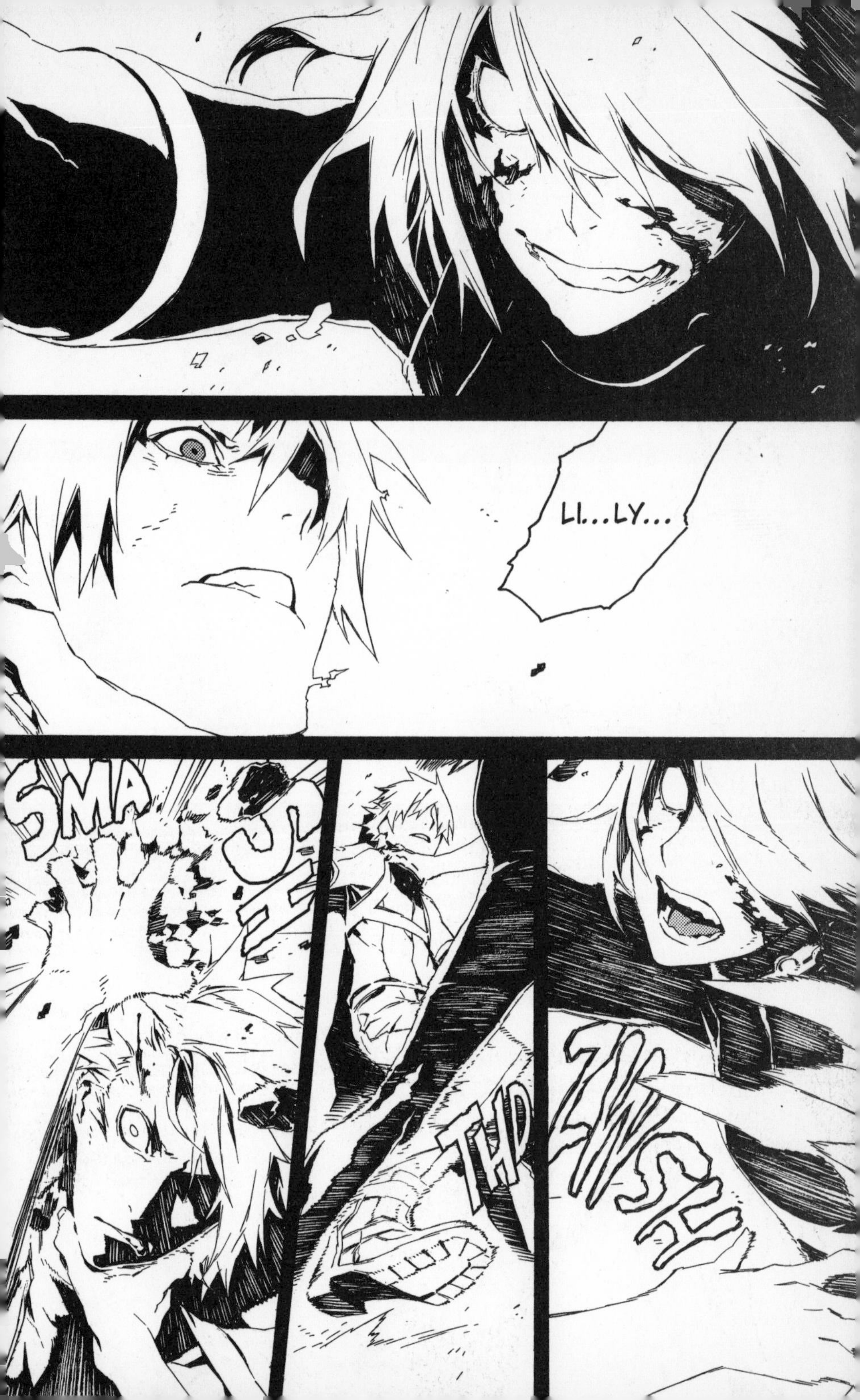
LI...LY...
ZWSH
THD
SMASH

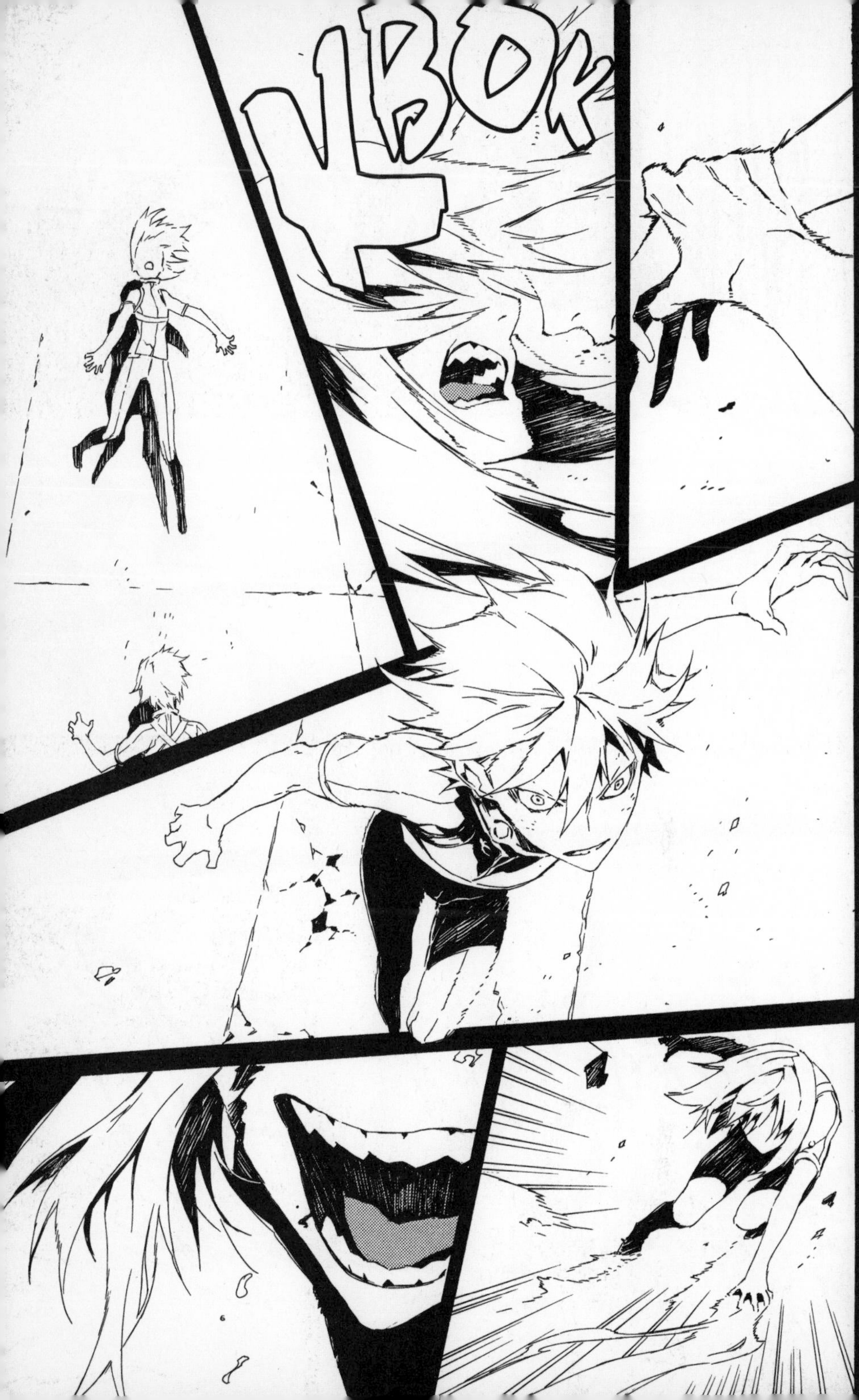
VBOK

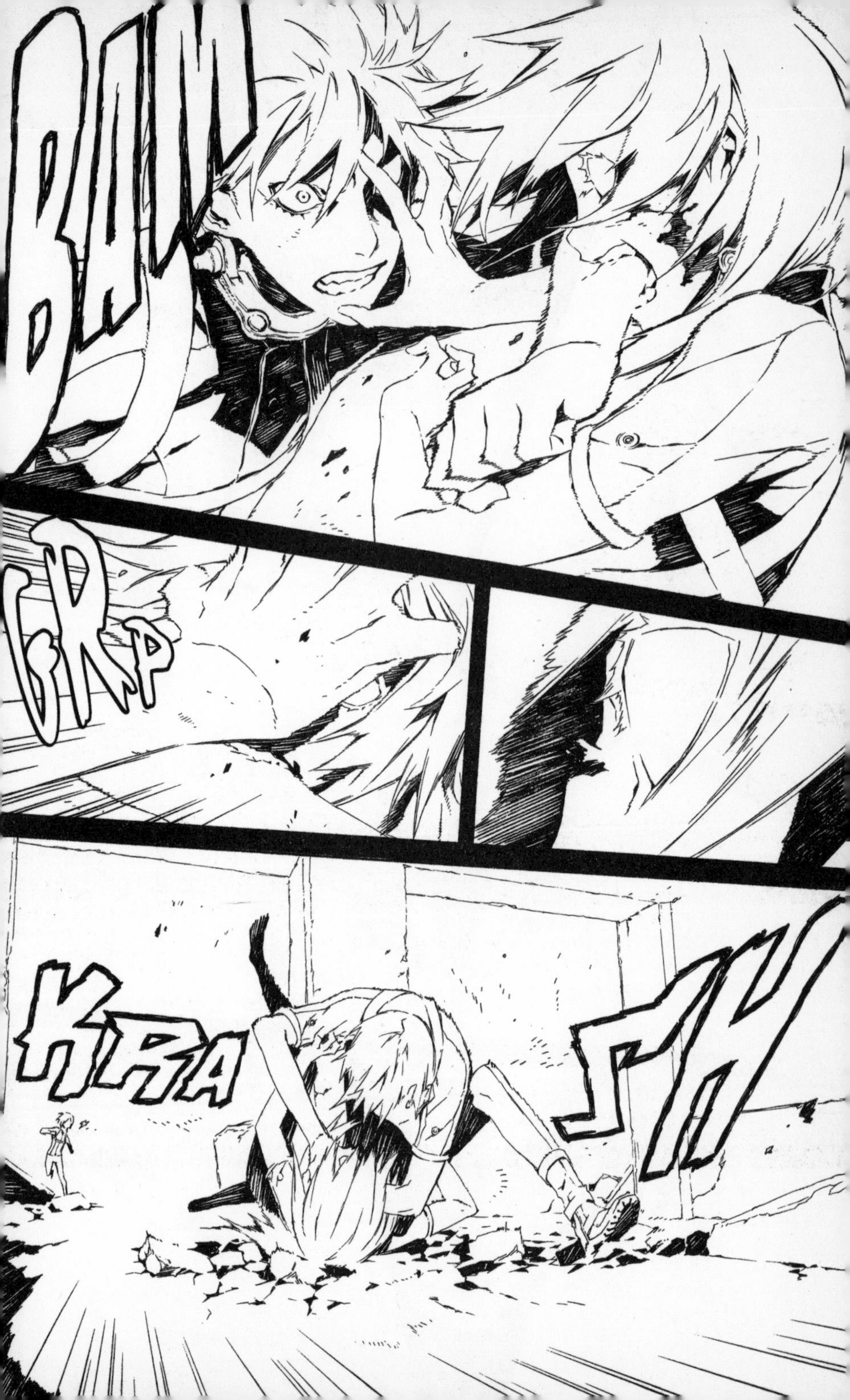
BAM
GRIP
KRASH

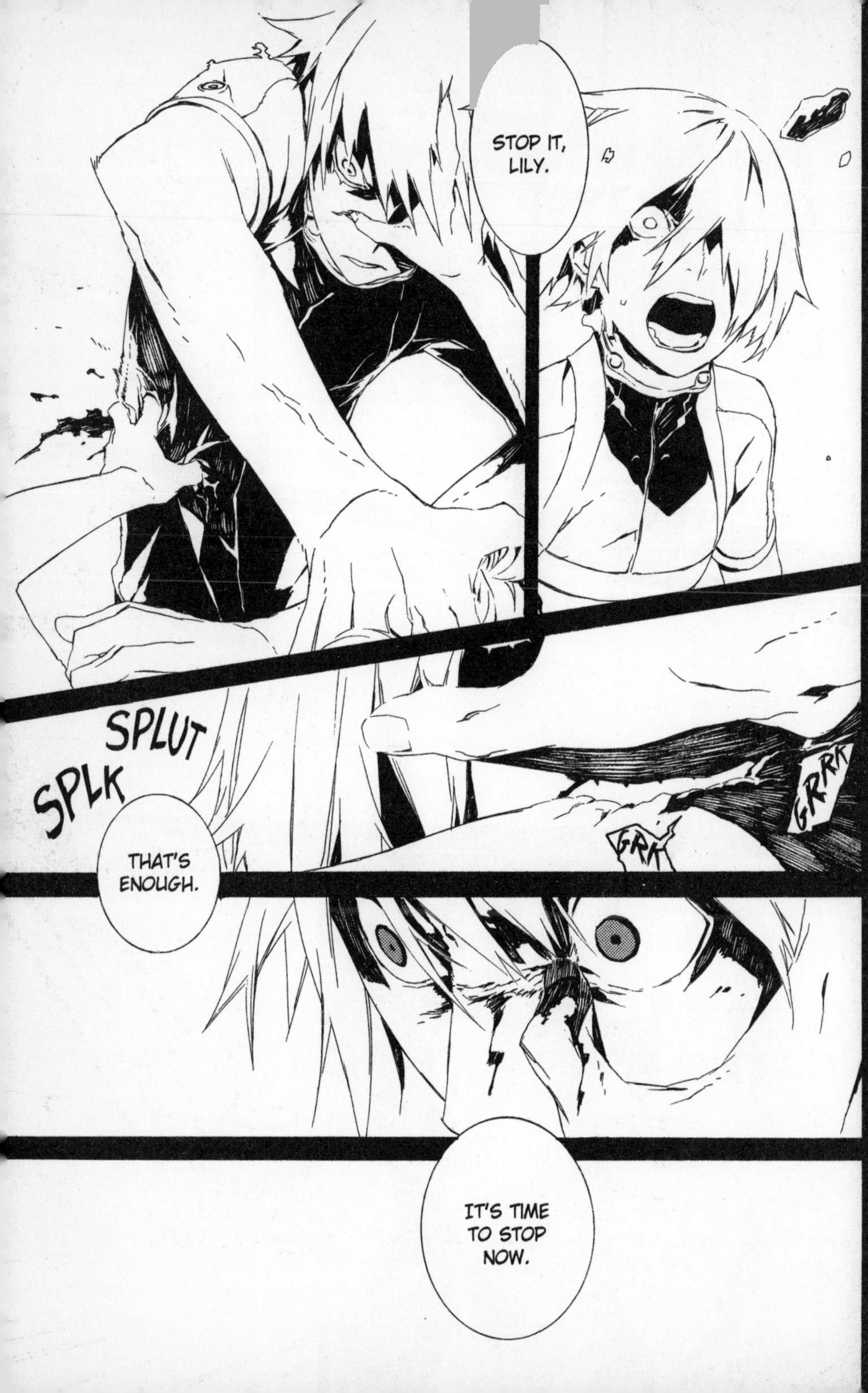
STOP IT, LILY.
GRRK
GRK
SPLUT
SPLK
THAT'S ENOUGH.
IT'S TIME TO STOP NOW.

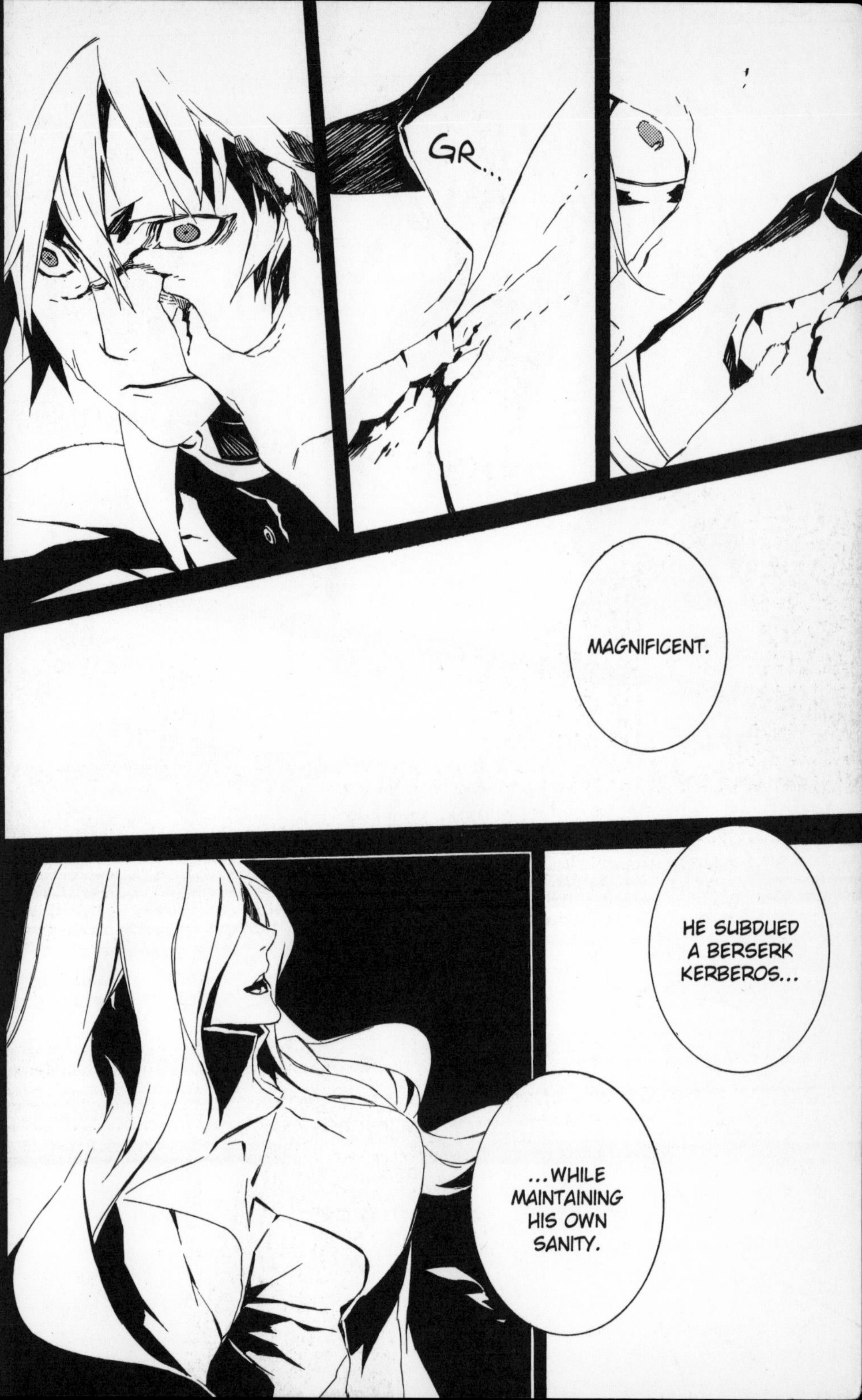
GR...
MAGNIFICENT.
HE SUBDUED A BERSERK KERBEROS...
...WHILE MAINTAINING HIS OWN SANITY.

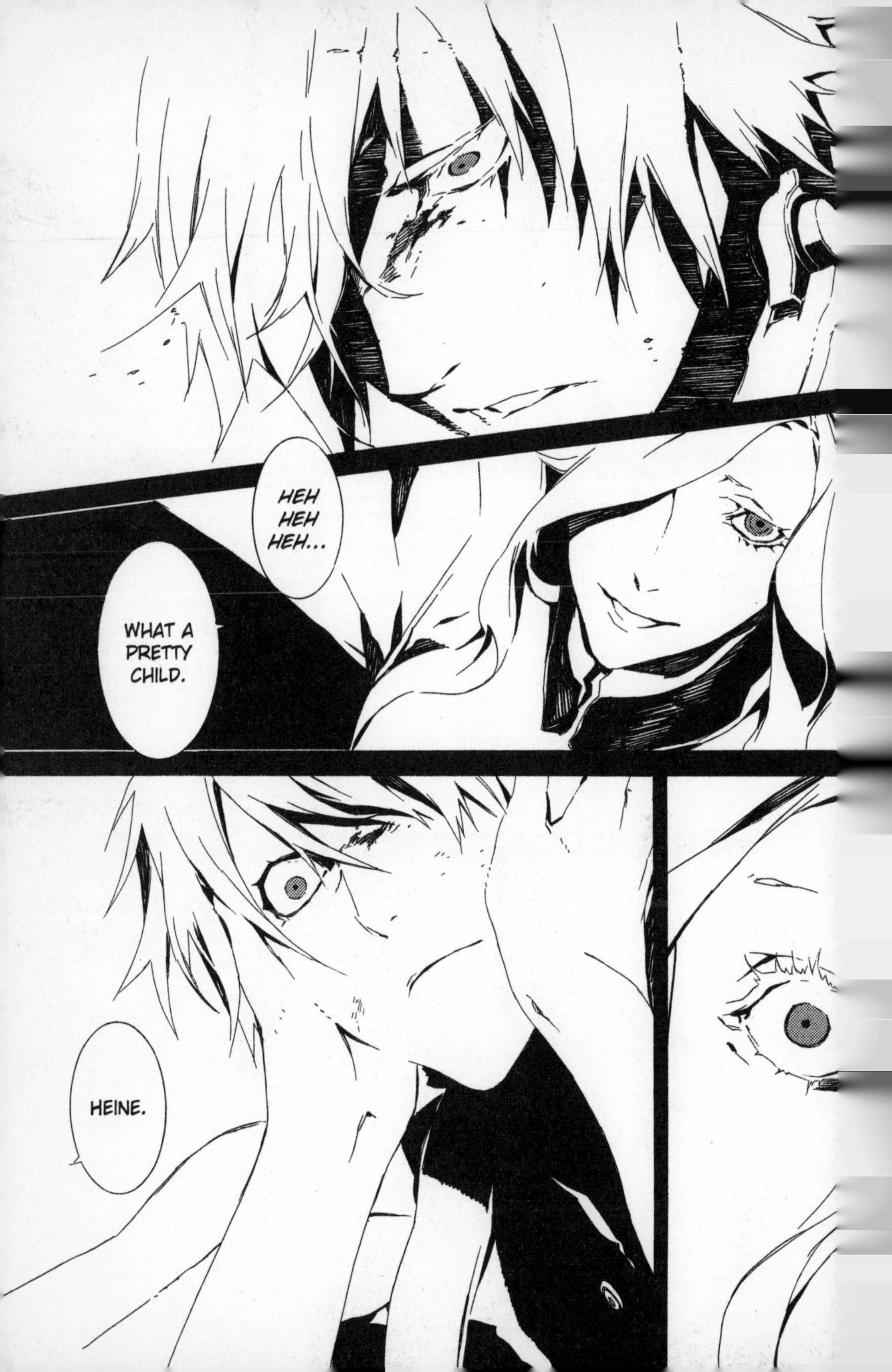
HEH HEH HEH...
WHAT A PRETTY CHILD.
HEINE.

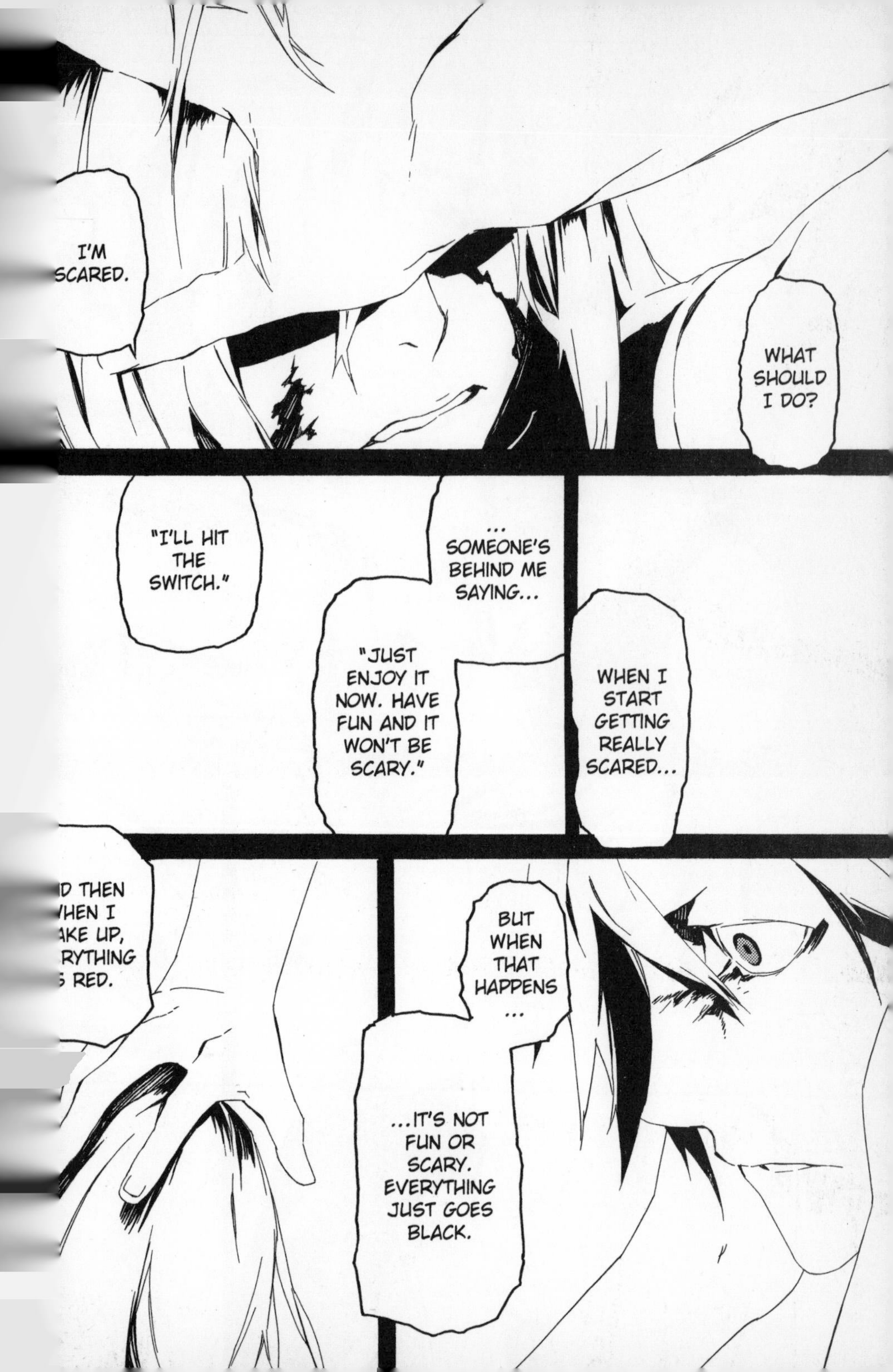
WHAT SHOULD I DO?
I'M SCARED.
WHEN I START GETTING REALLY SCARED...
... SOMEONE'S BEHIND ME SAYING...
"JUST ENJOY IT NOW. HAVE FUN AND IT WON'T BE SCARY."
"I'LL HIT THE SWITCH."
BUT WHEN THAT HAPPENS ...
...IT'S NOT FUN OR SCARY. EVERYTHING JUST GOES BLACK.
D THEN HEN I AKE UP, RYTHING S RED.

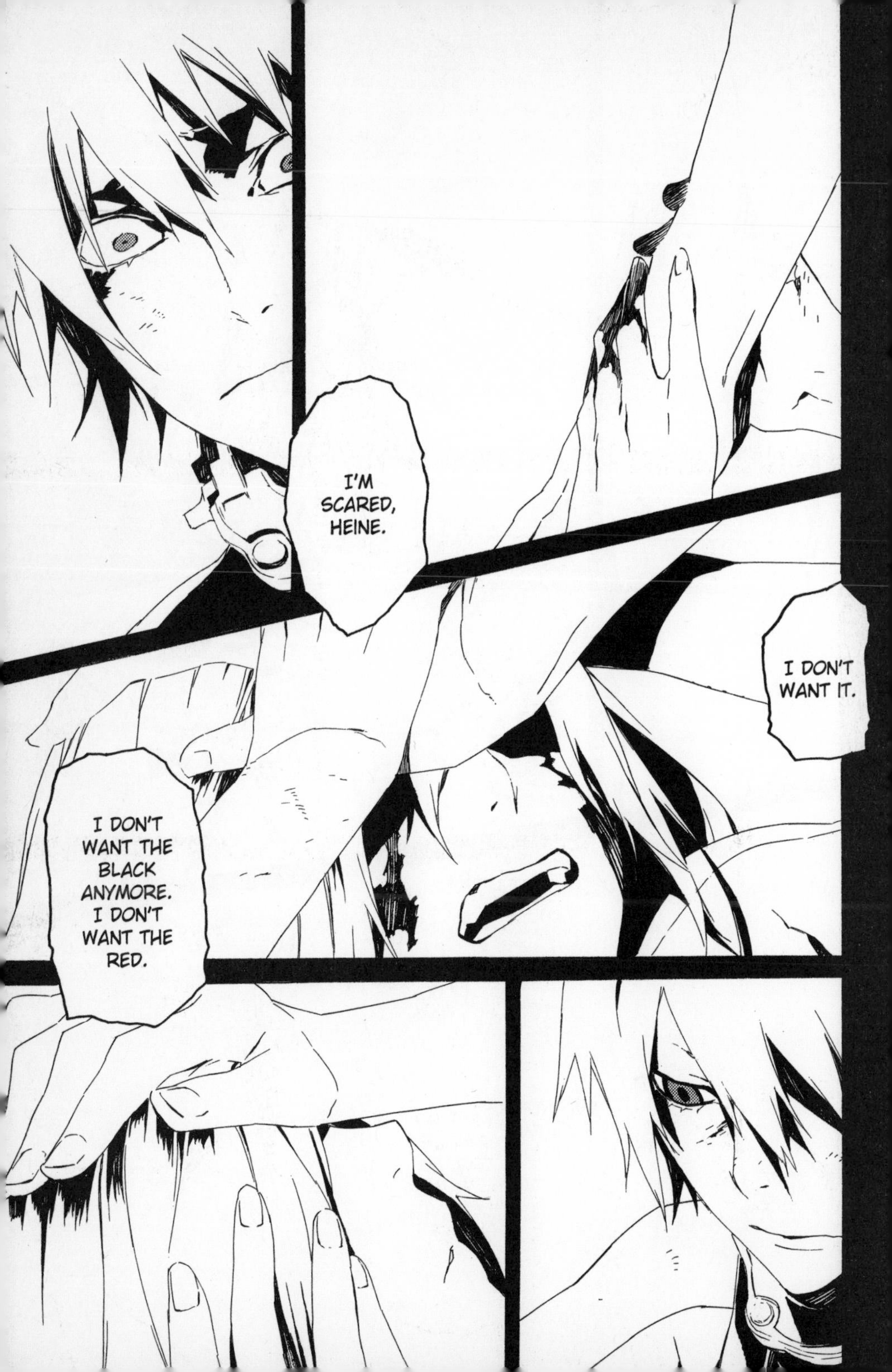
I'M SCARED, HEINE.
I DON'T WANT IT.
I DON'T WANT THE BLACK ANYMORE. I DON'T WANT THE RED.

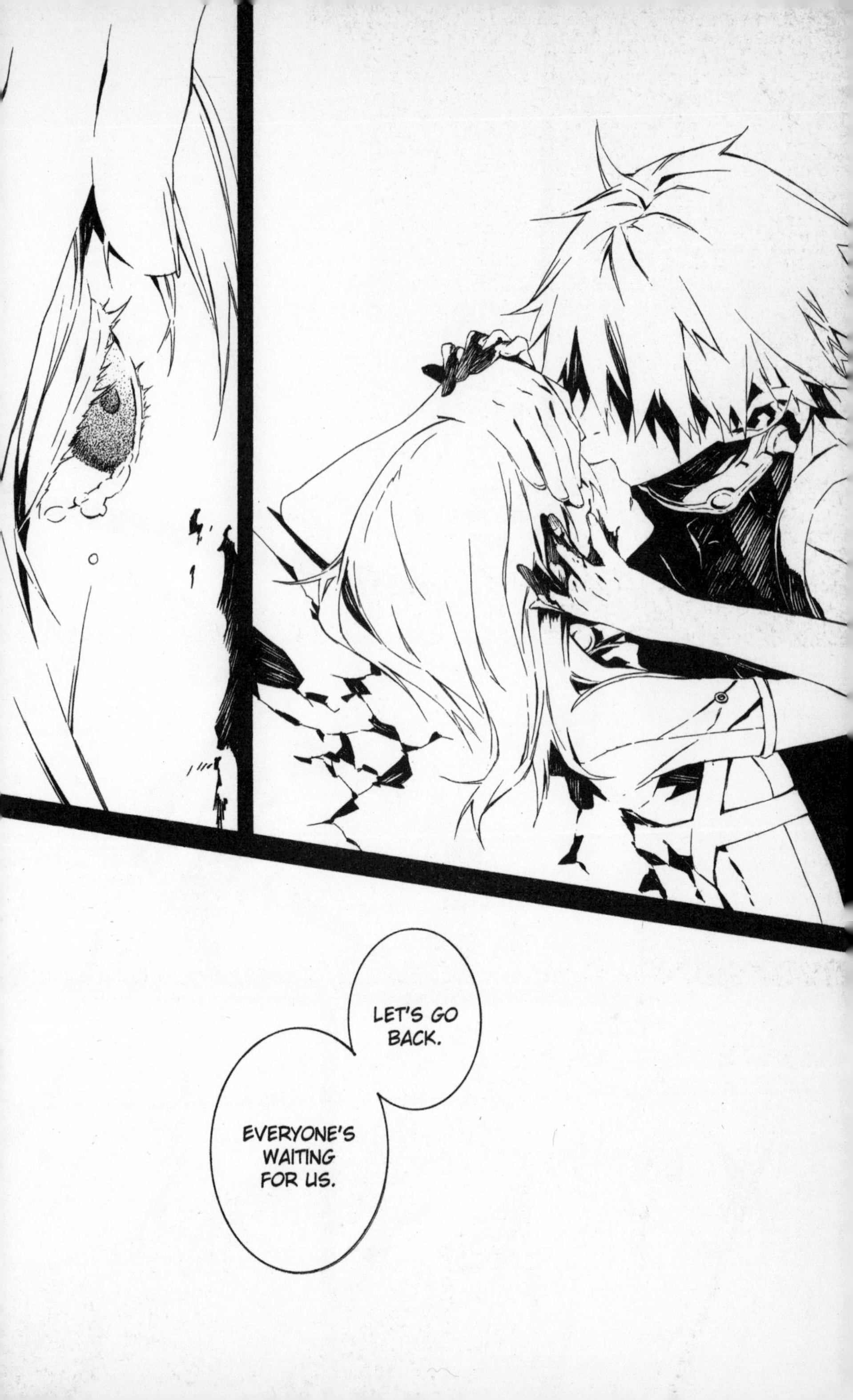
LET'S GO BACK.
EVERYONE'S WAITING FOR US.

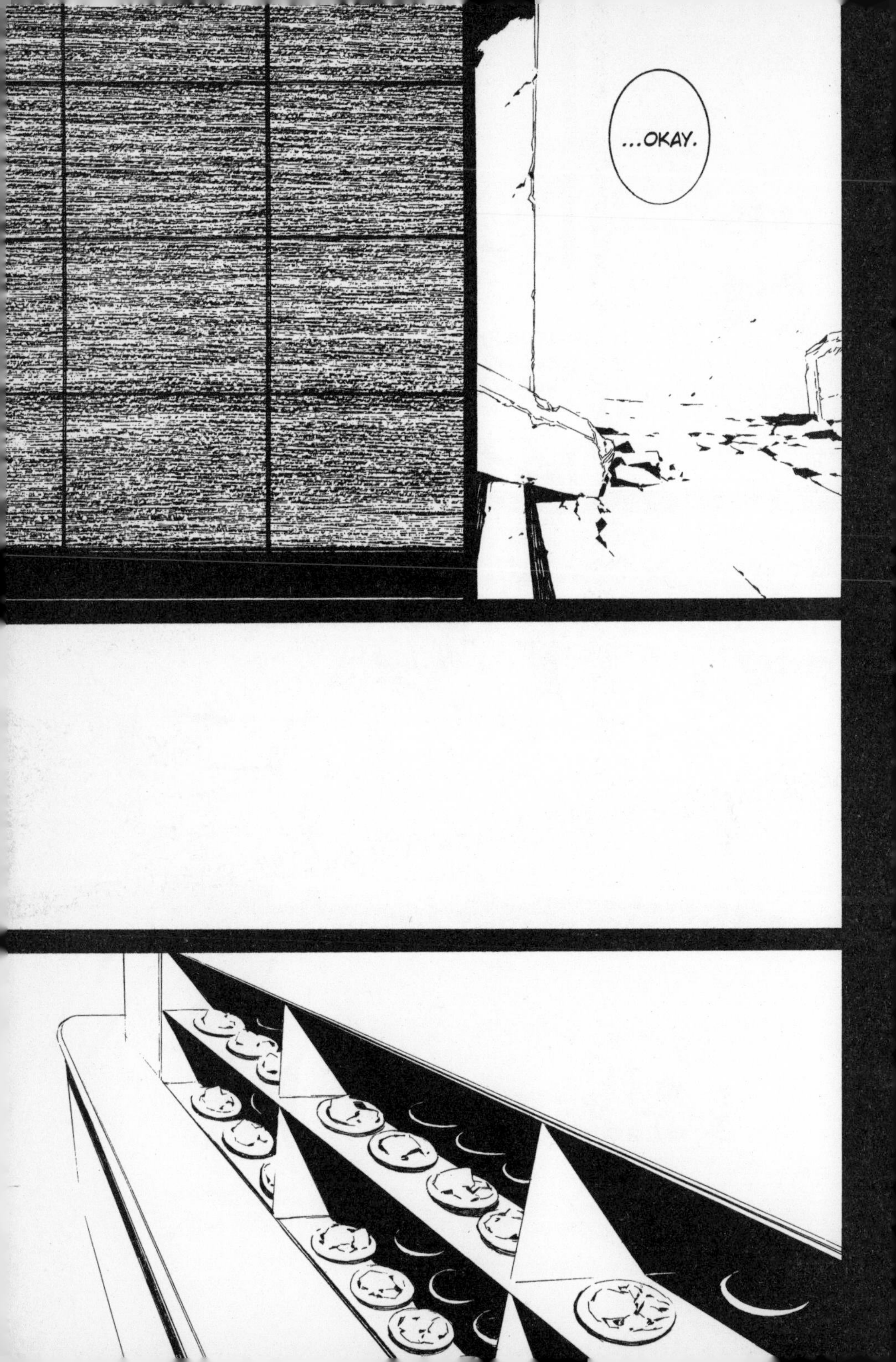
...OKAY.

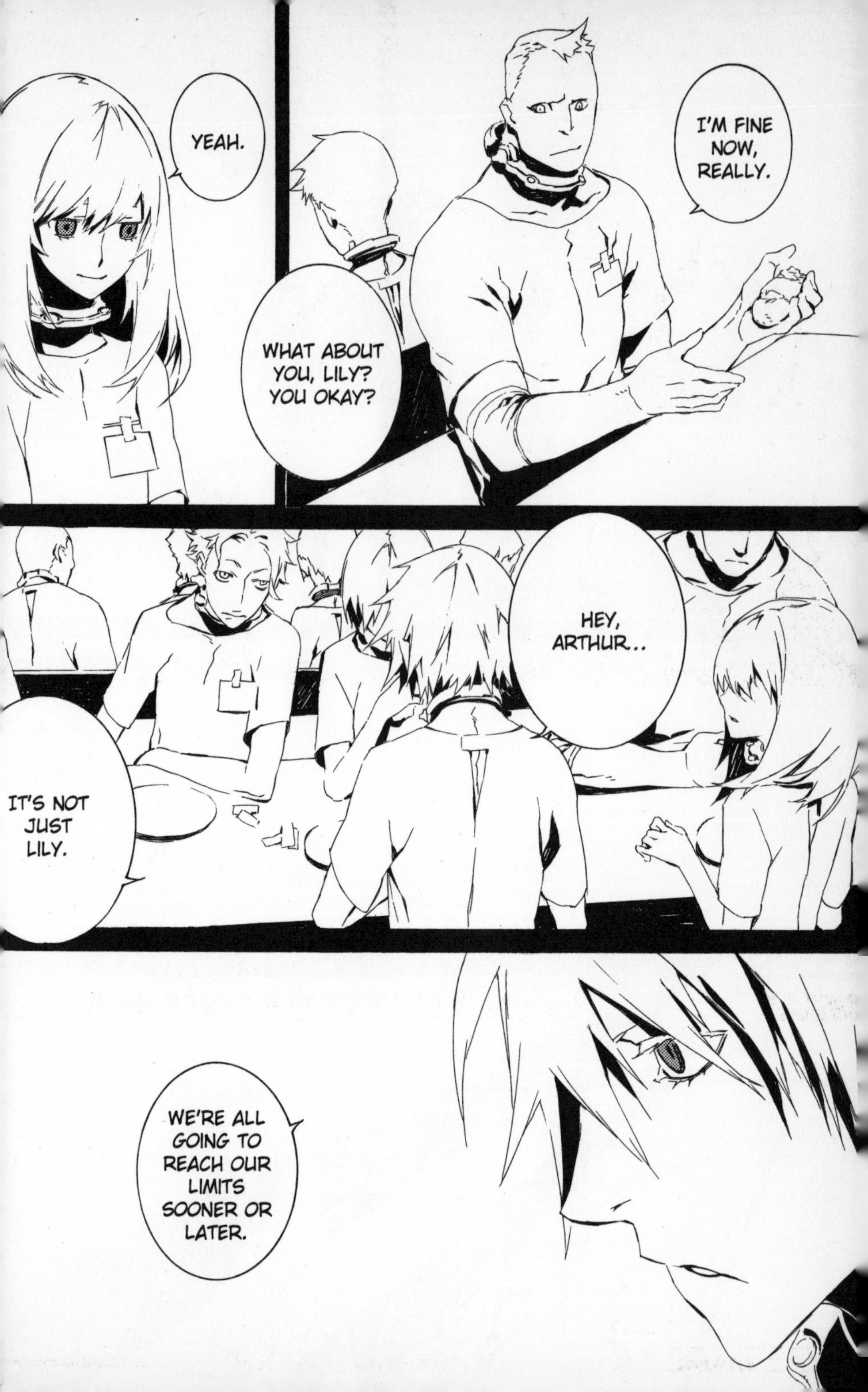
I'M FINE NOW, REALLY.
WHAT ABOUT YOU, LILY? YOU OKAY?
YEAH.
HEY, ARTHUR...
IT'S NOT JUST LILY.
WE'RE ALL GOING TO REACH OUR LIMITS SOONER OR LATER.

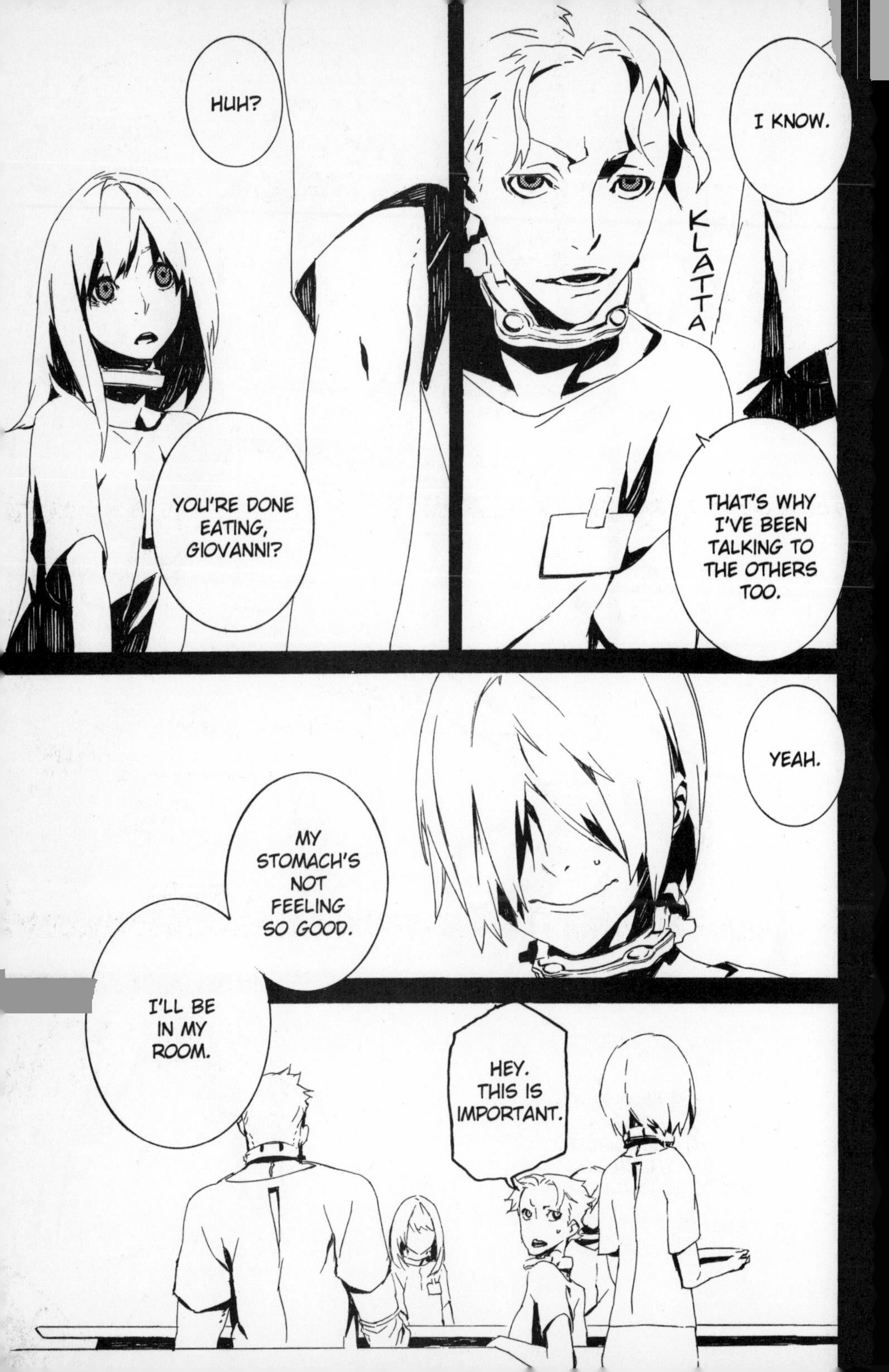
I KNOW.
KLATTA
THAT'S WHY I'VE BEEN TALKING TO THE OTHERS TOO.
HUH?
YOU'RE DONE EATING, GIOVANNI?
YEAH.
MY STOMACH'S NOT FEELING SO GOOD.
I'LL BE IN MY ROOM.
HEY. THIS IS IMPORTANT.

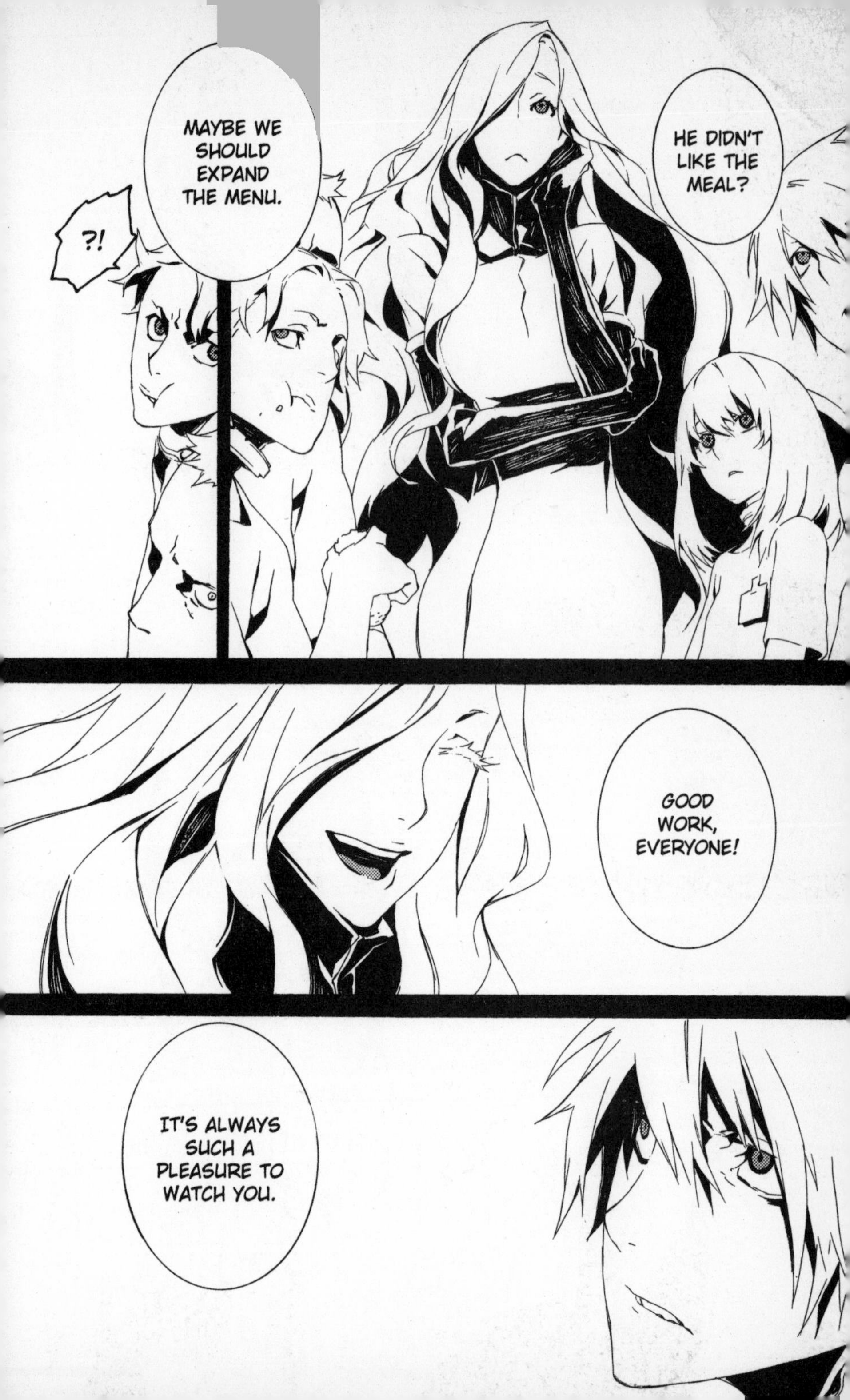
HE DIDN'T LIKE THE MEAL?
MAYBE WE SHOULD EXPAND THE MENU.
?!
GOOD WORK, EVERYONE!
IT'S ALWAYS SUCH A PLEASURE TO WATCH YOU.

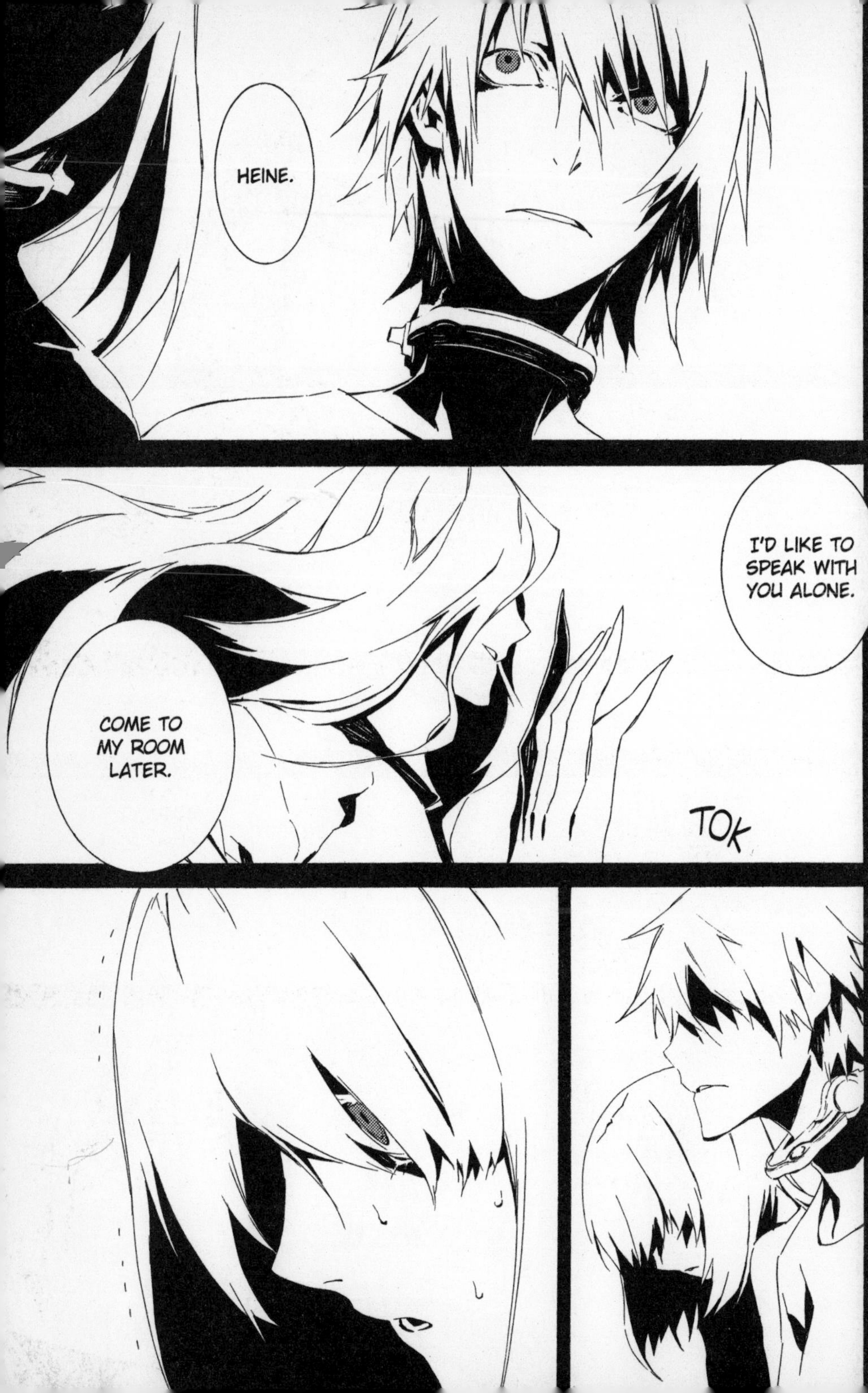
HEINE.
I'D LIKE TO SPEAK WITH YOU ALONE.
COME TO MY ROOM LATER.
TOK

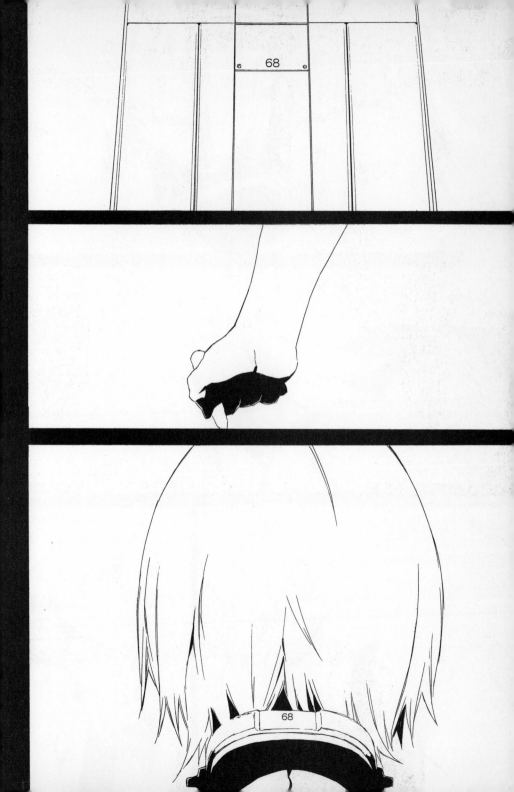

# #54 Cage & Puppies III

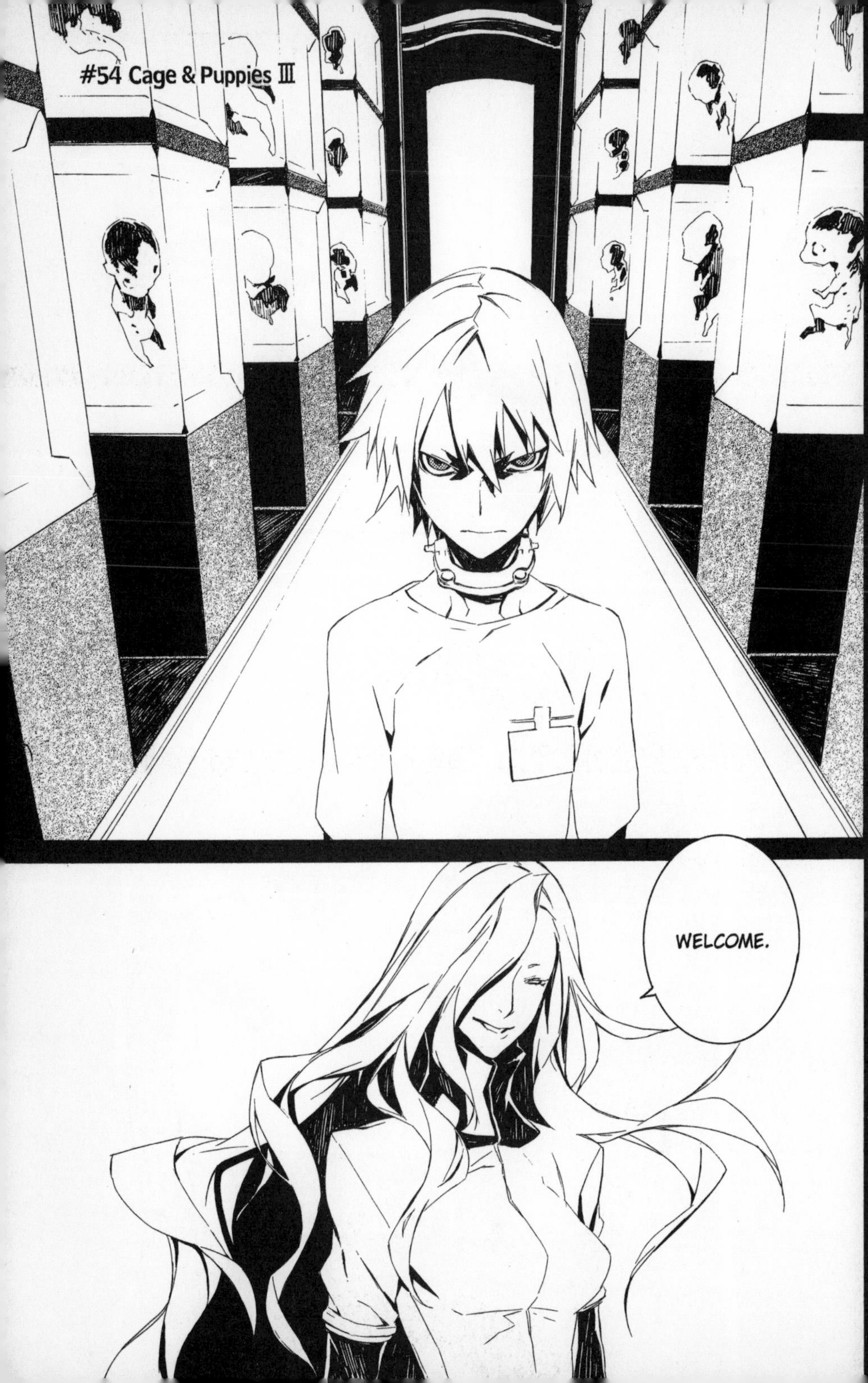
WELCOME.

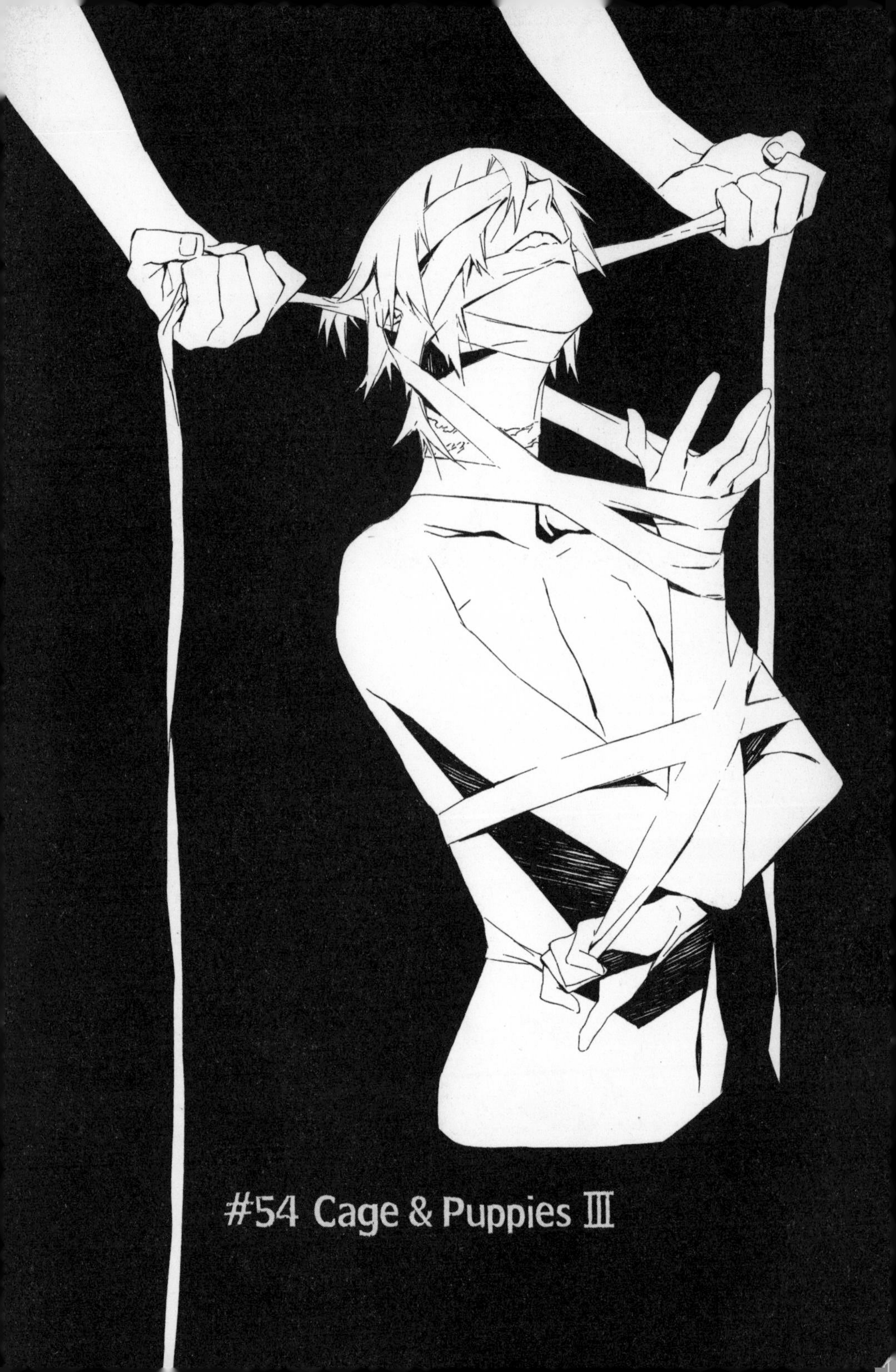

# #54 Cage & Puppies Ⅲ

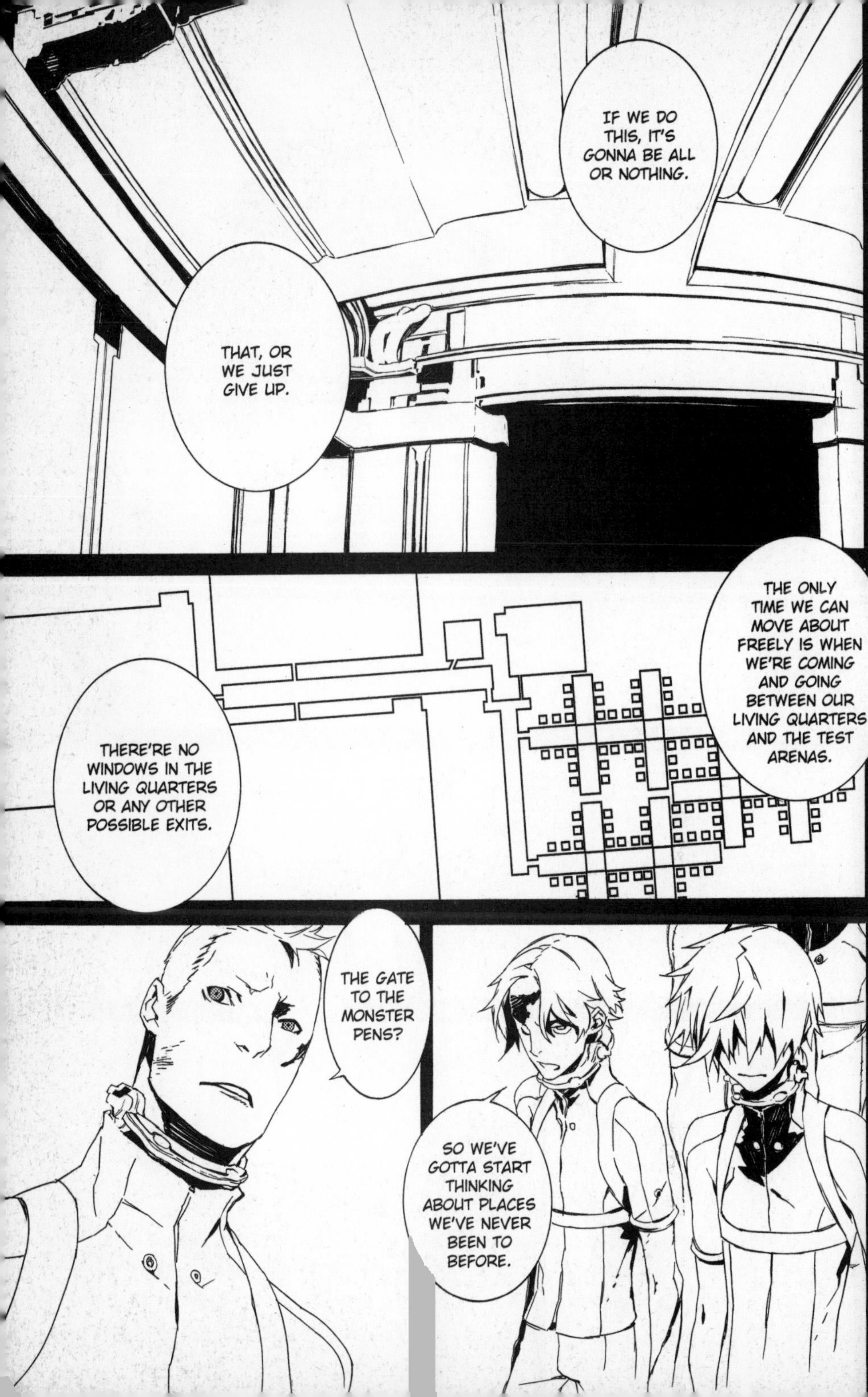
IF WE DO THIS, IT'S GONNA BE ALL OR NOTHING.
THAT, OR WE JUST GIVE UP.
THE ONLY TIME WE CAN MOVE ABOUT FREELY IS WHEN WE'RE COMING AND GOING BETWEEN OUR LIVING QUARTERS AND THE TEST ARENAS.
THERE'RE NO WINDOWS IN THE LIVING QUARTERS OR ANY OTHER POSSIBLE EXITS.
SO WE'VE GOTTA START THINKING ABOUT PLACES WE'VE NEVER BEEN TO BEFORE.
THE GATE TO THE MONSTER PENS?

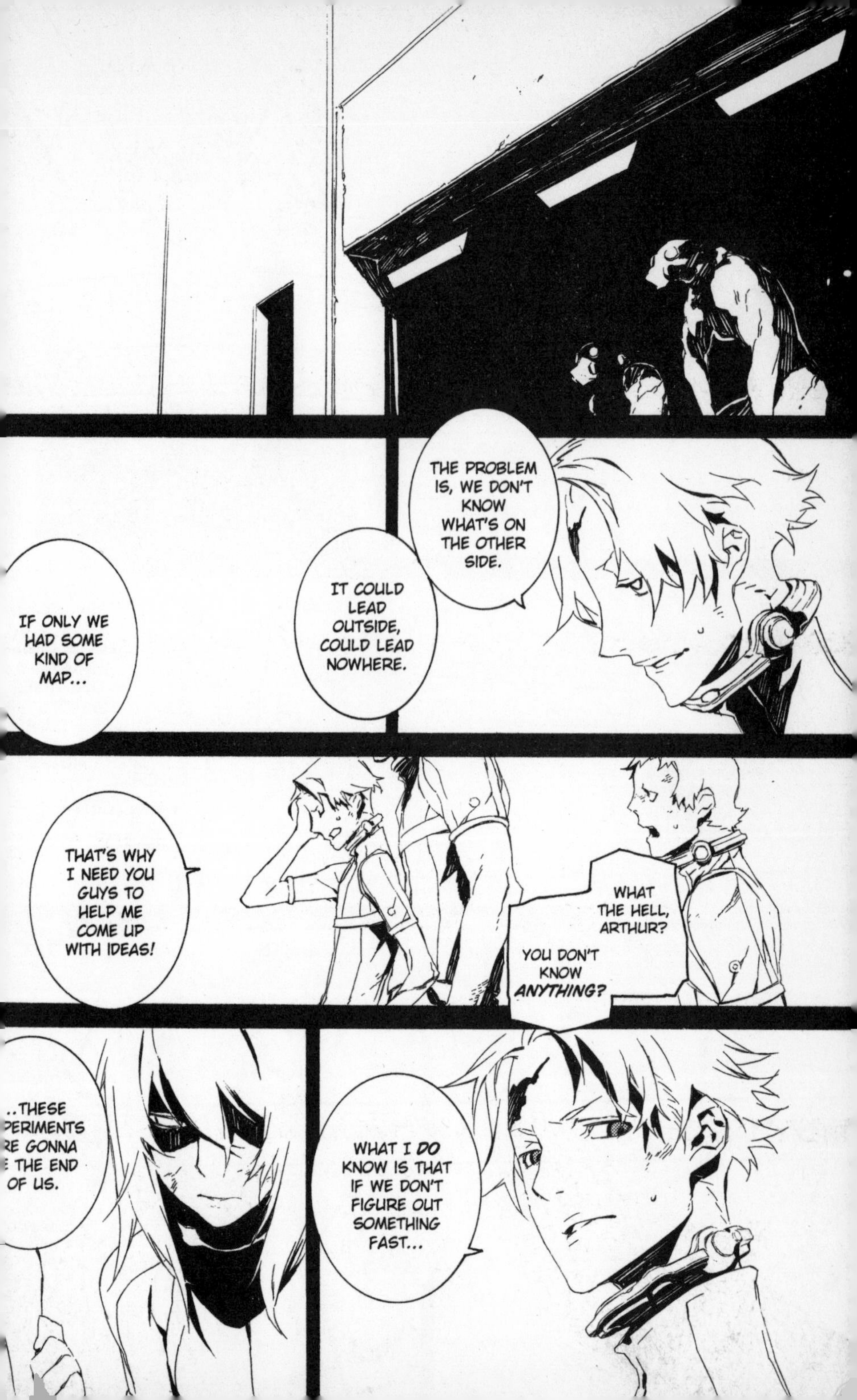
THE PROBLEM IS, WE DON'T KNOW WHAT'S ON THE OTHER SIDE.
IT COULD LEAD OUTSIDE, COULD LEAD NOWHERE.
IF ONLY WE HAD SOME KIND OF MAP...
WHAT THE HELL, ARTHUR?
YOU DON'T KNOW *ANYTHING?*
THAT'S WHY I NEED YOU GUYS TO HELP ME COME UP WITH IDEAS!
WHAT I *DO* KNOW IS THAT IF WE DON'T FIGURE OUT SOMETHING FAST...
..THESE PERIMENTS RE GONNA E THE END OF US.

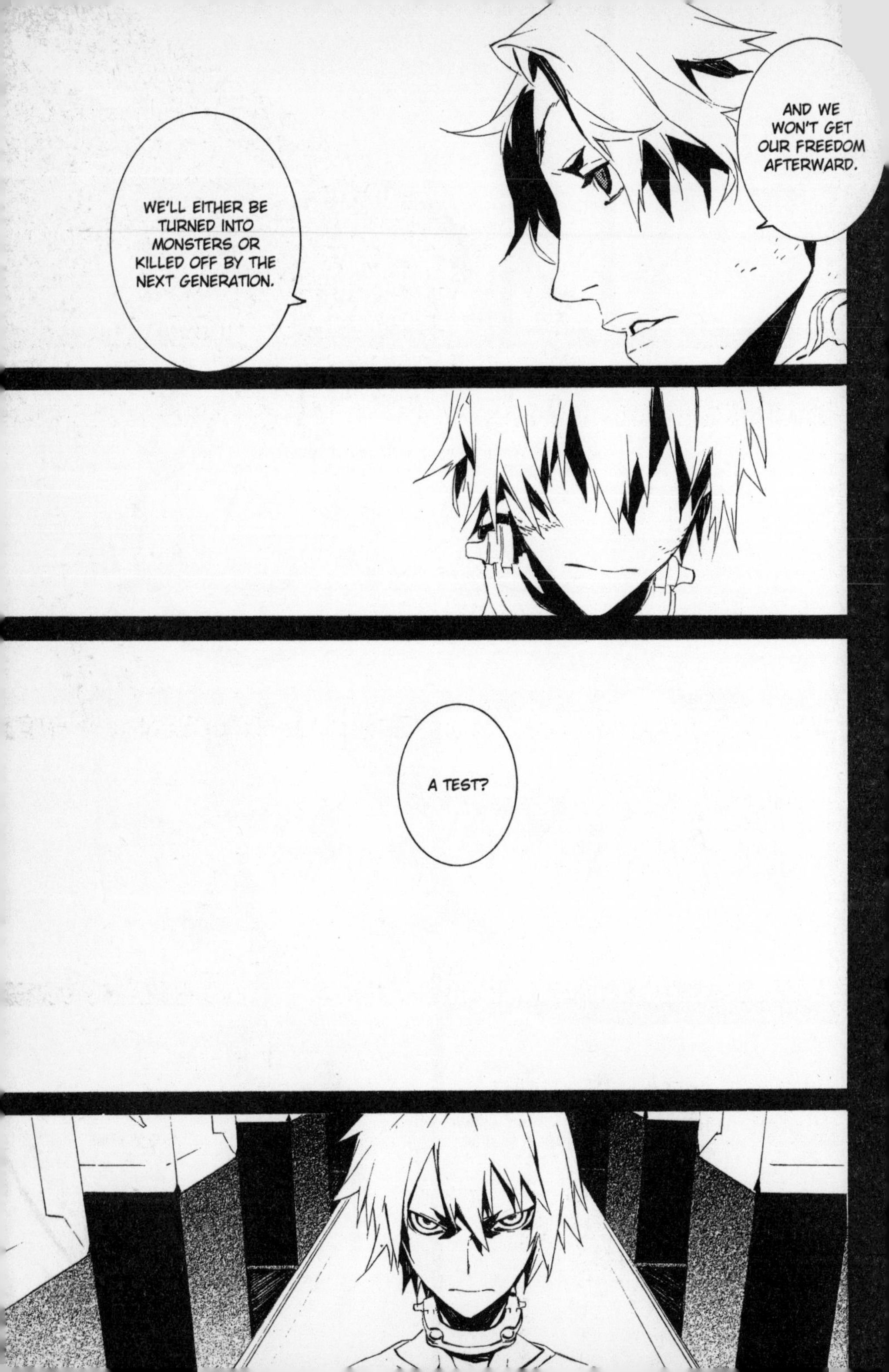
AND WE WON'T GET OUR FREEDOM AFTERWARD.
WE'LL EITHER BE TURNED INTO MONSTERS OR KILLED OFF BY THE NEXT GENERATION.
A TEST?

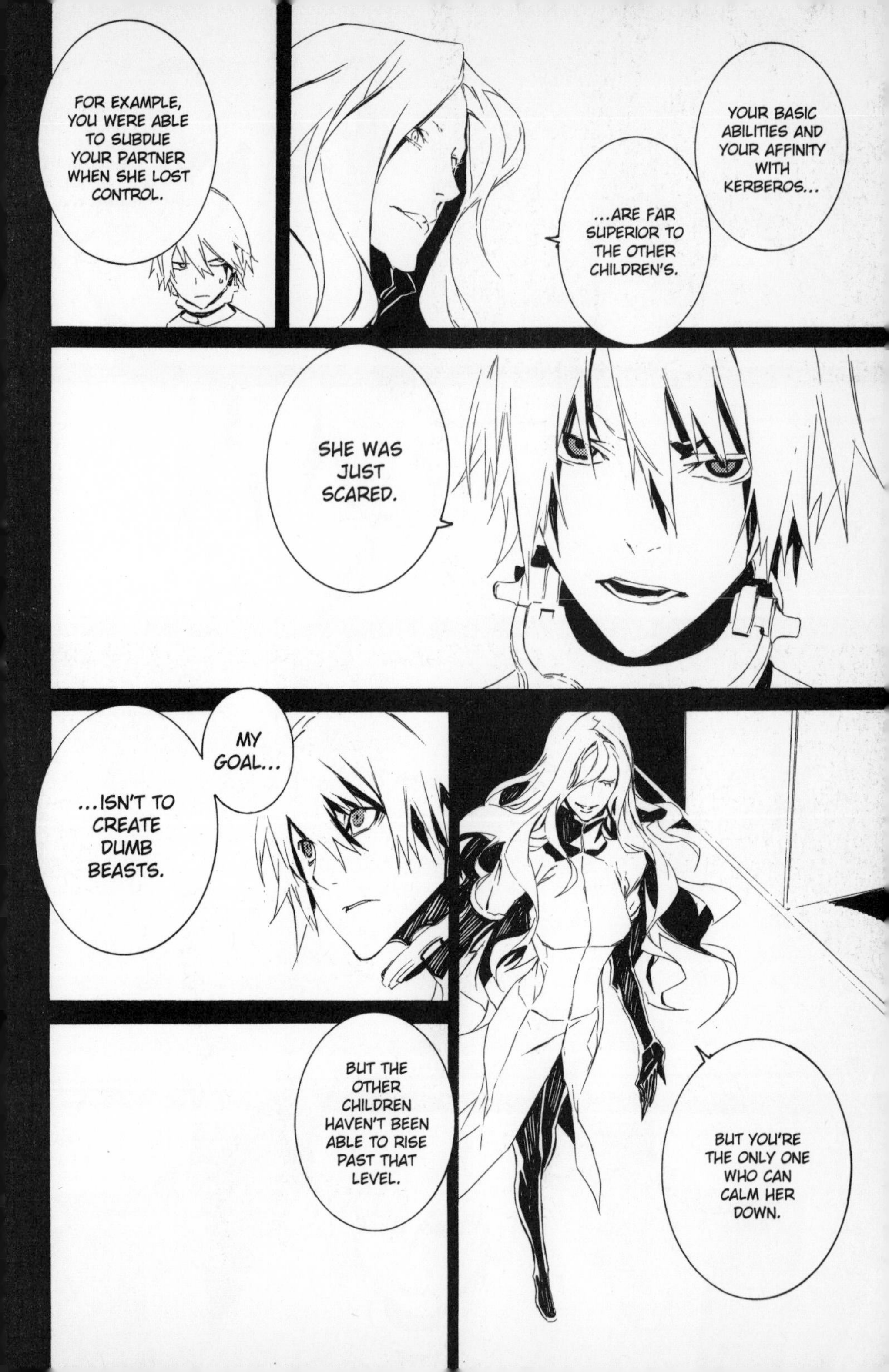
YOUR BASIC ABILITIES AND YOUR AFFINITY WITH KERBEROS...
...ARE FAR SUPERIOR TO THE OTHER CHILDREN'S.
FOR EXAMPLE, YOU WERE ABLE TO SUBDUE YOUR PARTNER WHEN SHE LOST CONTROL.
SHE WAS JUST SCARED.
MY GOAL...
...ISN'T TO CREATE DUMB BEASTS.
BUT THE OTHER CHILDREN HAVEN'T BEEN ABLE TO RISE PAST THAT LEVEL.
BUT YOU'RE THE ONLY ONE WHO CAN CALM HER DOWN.

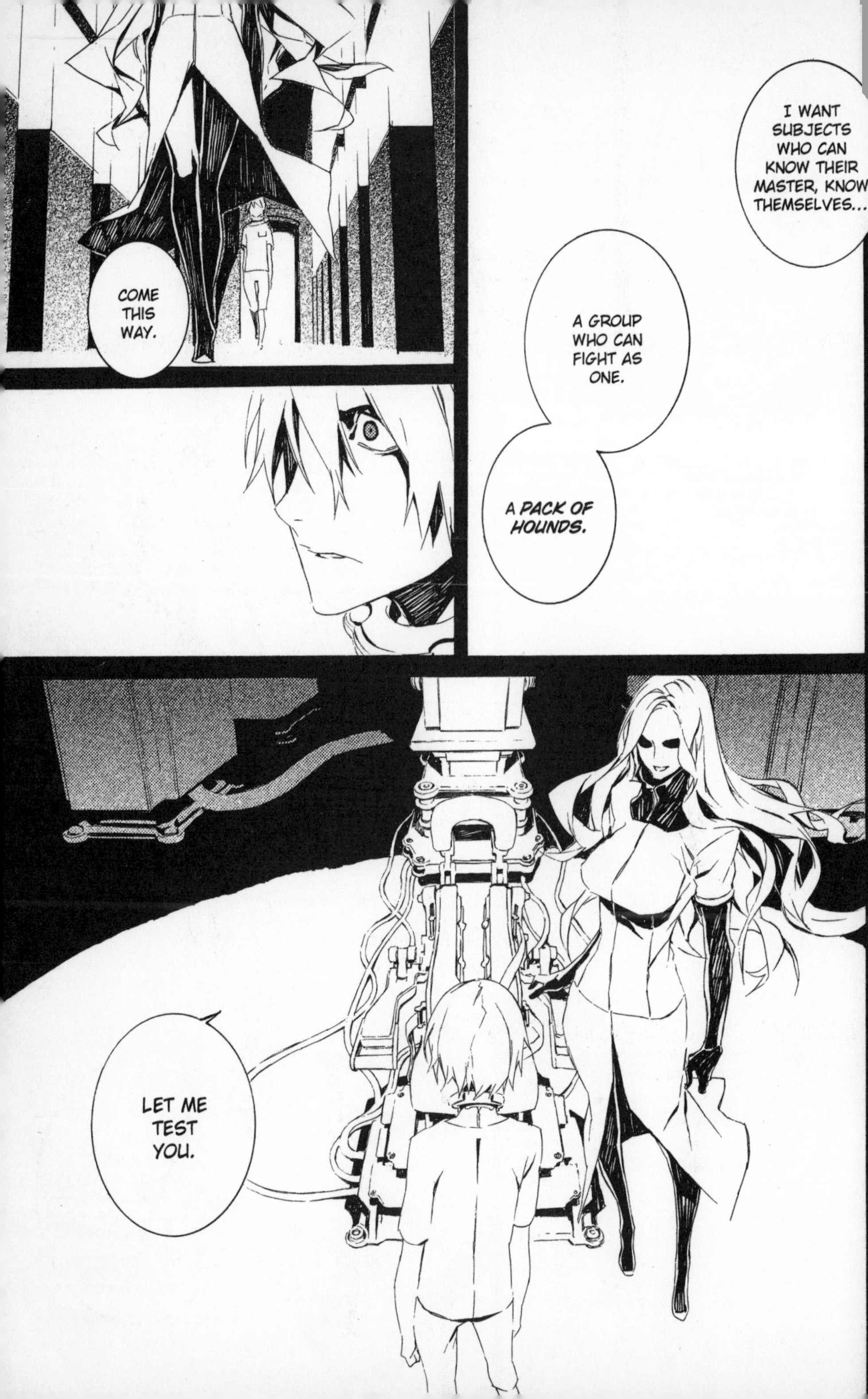
I WANT SUBJECTS WHO CAN KNOW THEIR MASTER, KNOW THEMSELVES...
A GROUP WHO CAN FIGHT AS ONE.
A PACK OF HOUNDS.
COME THIS WAY.
LET ME TEST YOU.

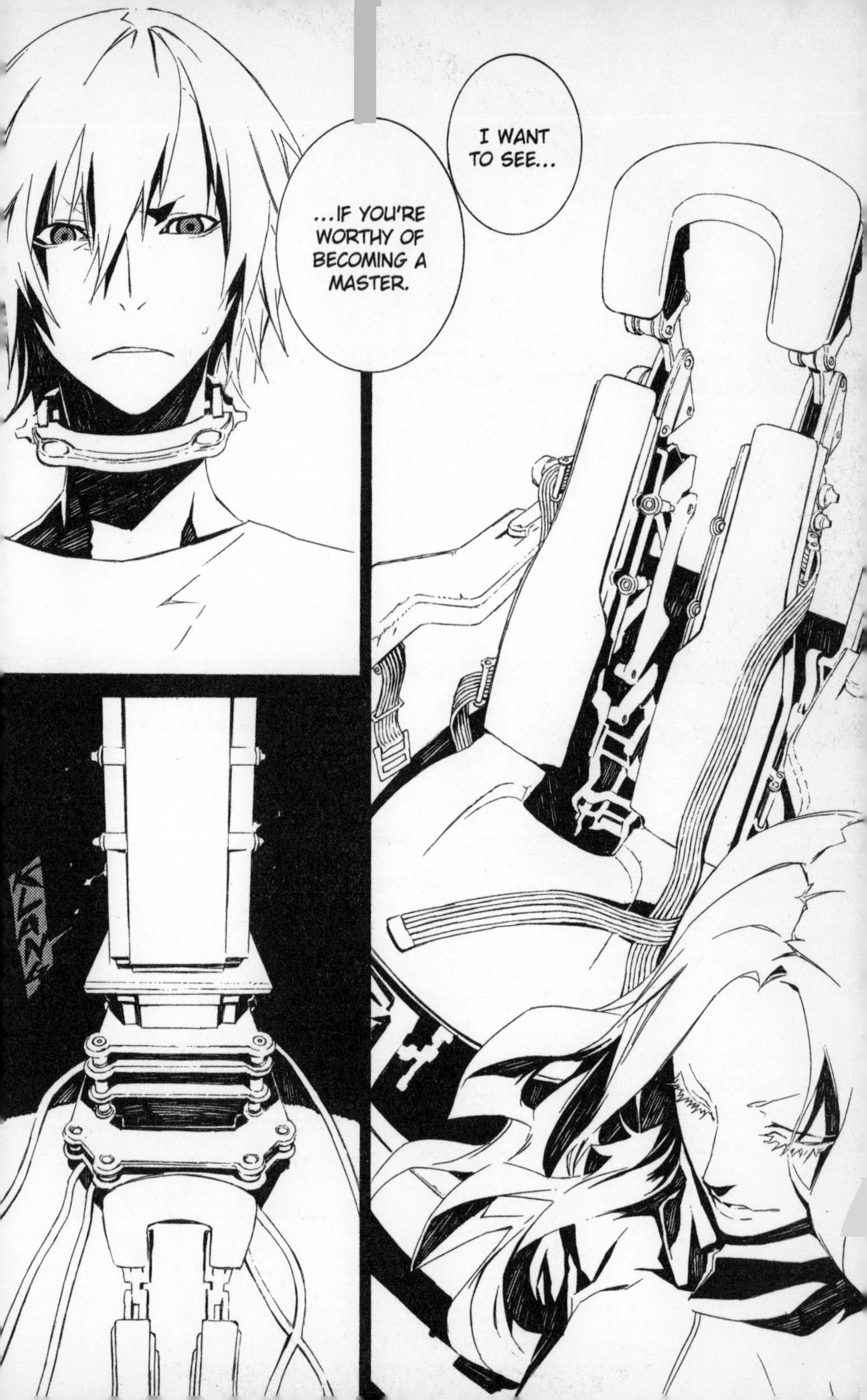
I WANT TO SEE...
...IF YOU'RE WORTHY OF BECOMING A MASTER.

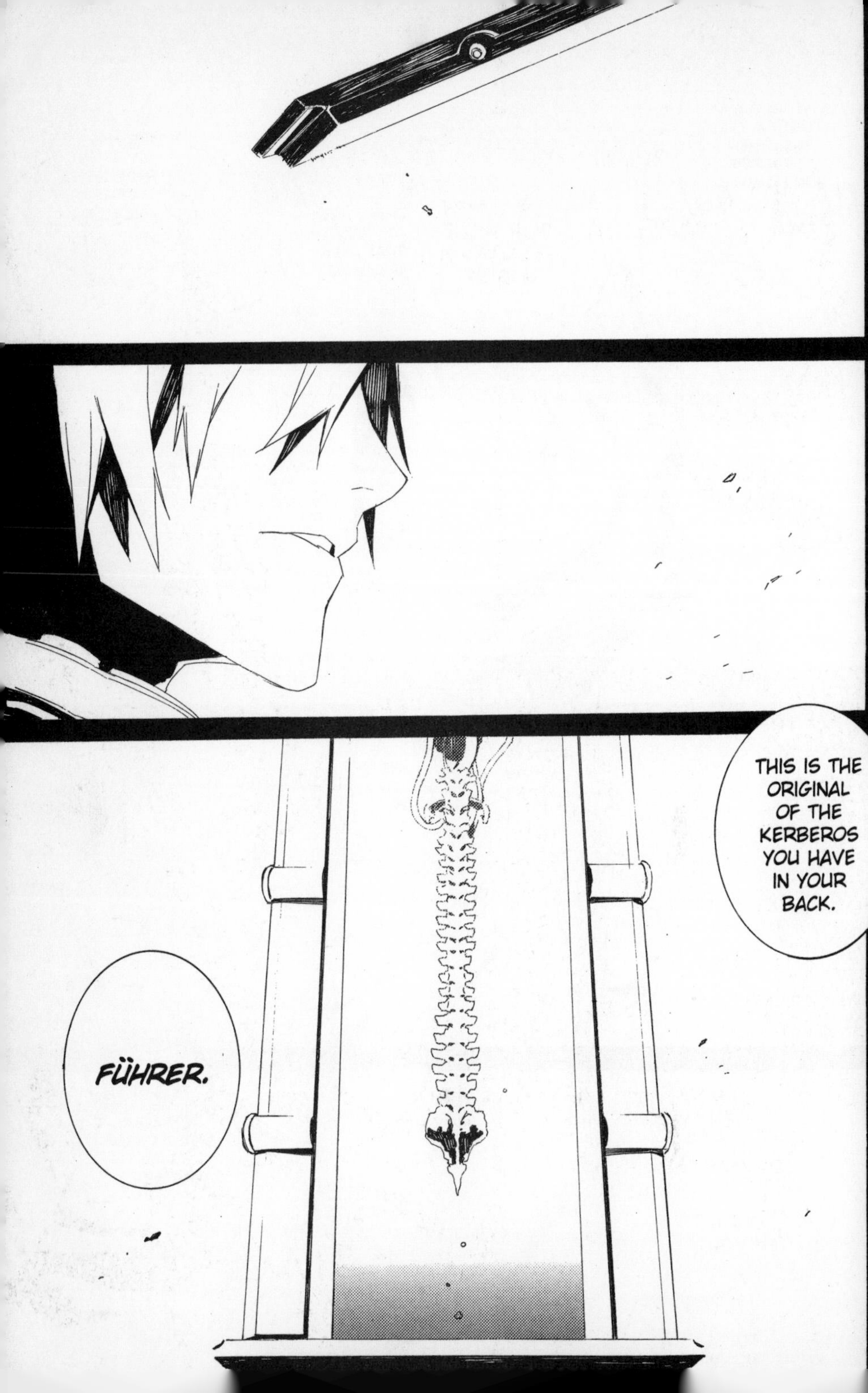
THIS IS THE ORIGINAL OF THE KERBEROS YOU HAVE IN YOUR BACK.
FÜHRER.

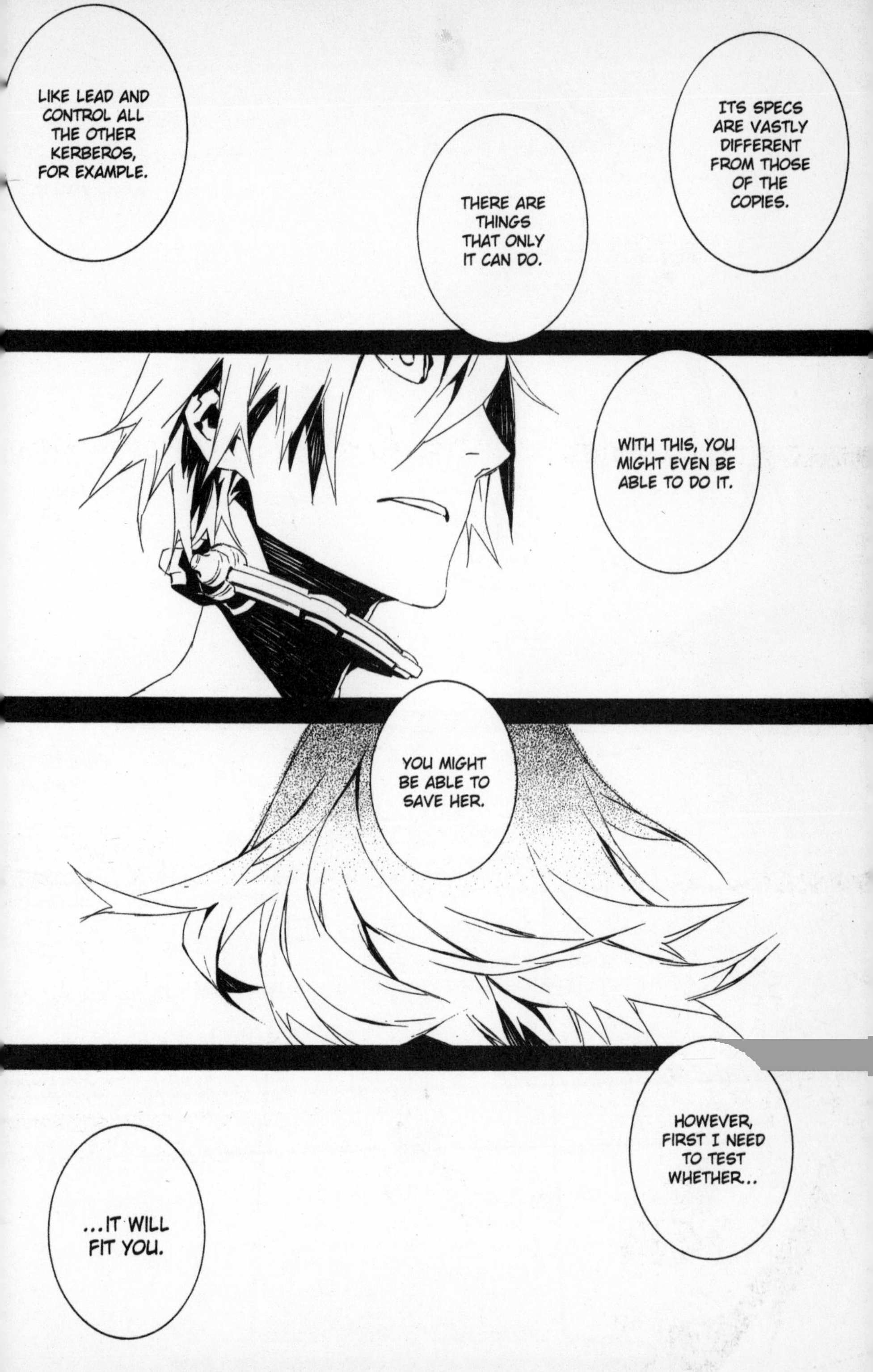
ITS SPECS ARE VASTLY DIFFERENT FROM THOSE OF THE COPIES.
THERE ARE THINGS THAT ONLY IT CAN DO.
LIKE LEAD AND CONTROL ALL THE OTHER KERBEROS, FOR EXAMPLE.
WITH THIS, YOU MIGHT EVEN BE ABLE TO DO IT.
YOU MIGHT BE ABLE TO SAVE HER.
HOWEVER, FIRST I NEED TO TEST WHETHER...
...IT WILL FIT YOU.

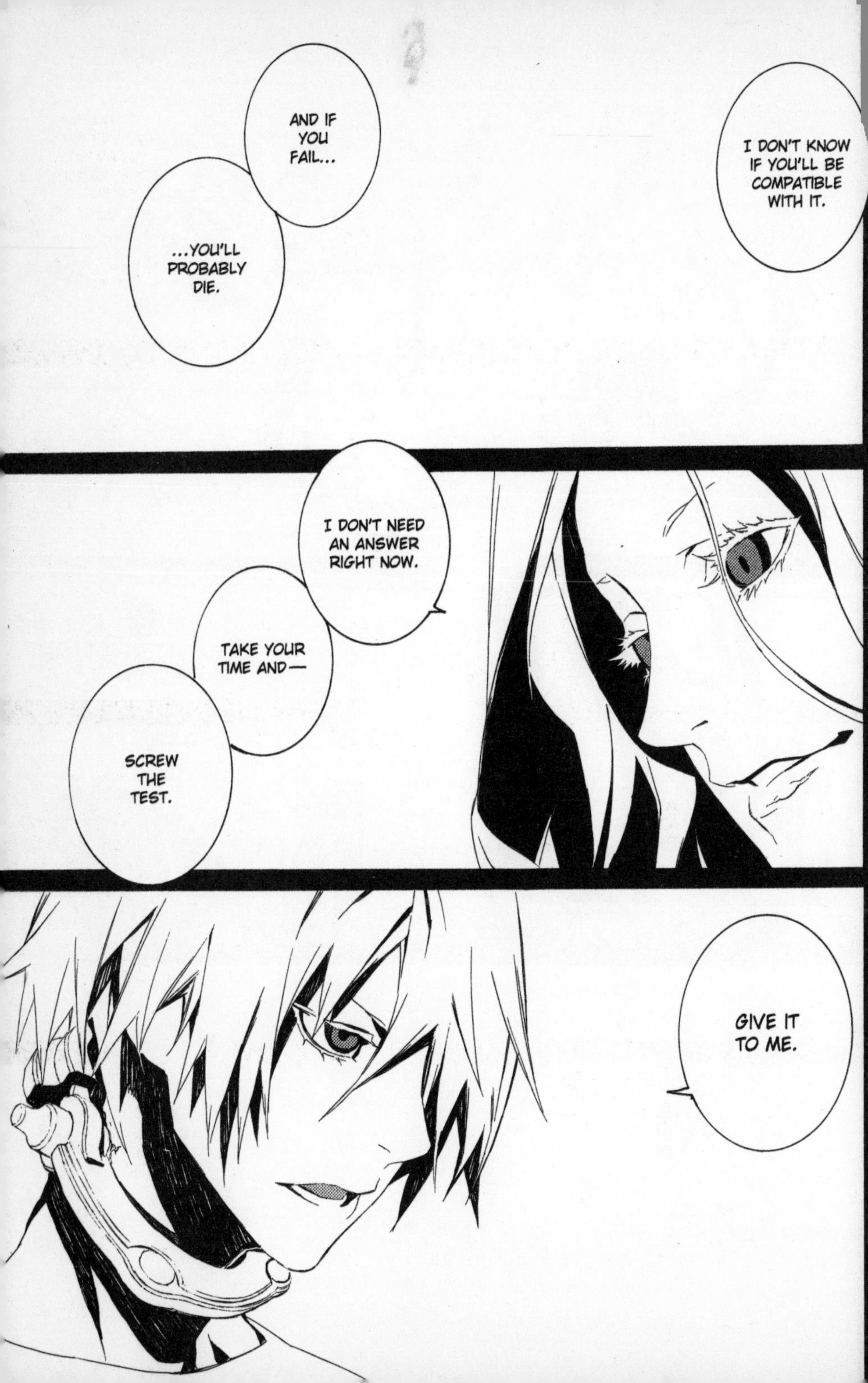
I DON'T KNOW IF YOU'LL BE COMPATIBLE WITH IT.
AND IF YOU FAIL...
...YOU'LL PROBABLY DIE.
I DON'T NEED AN ANSWER RIGHT NOW.
TAKE YOUR TIME AND—
SCREW THE TEST.
GIVE IT TO ME.

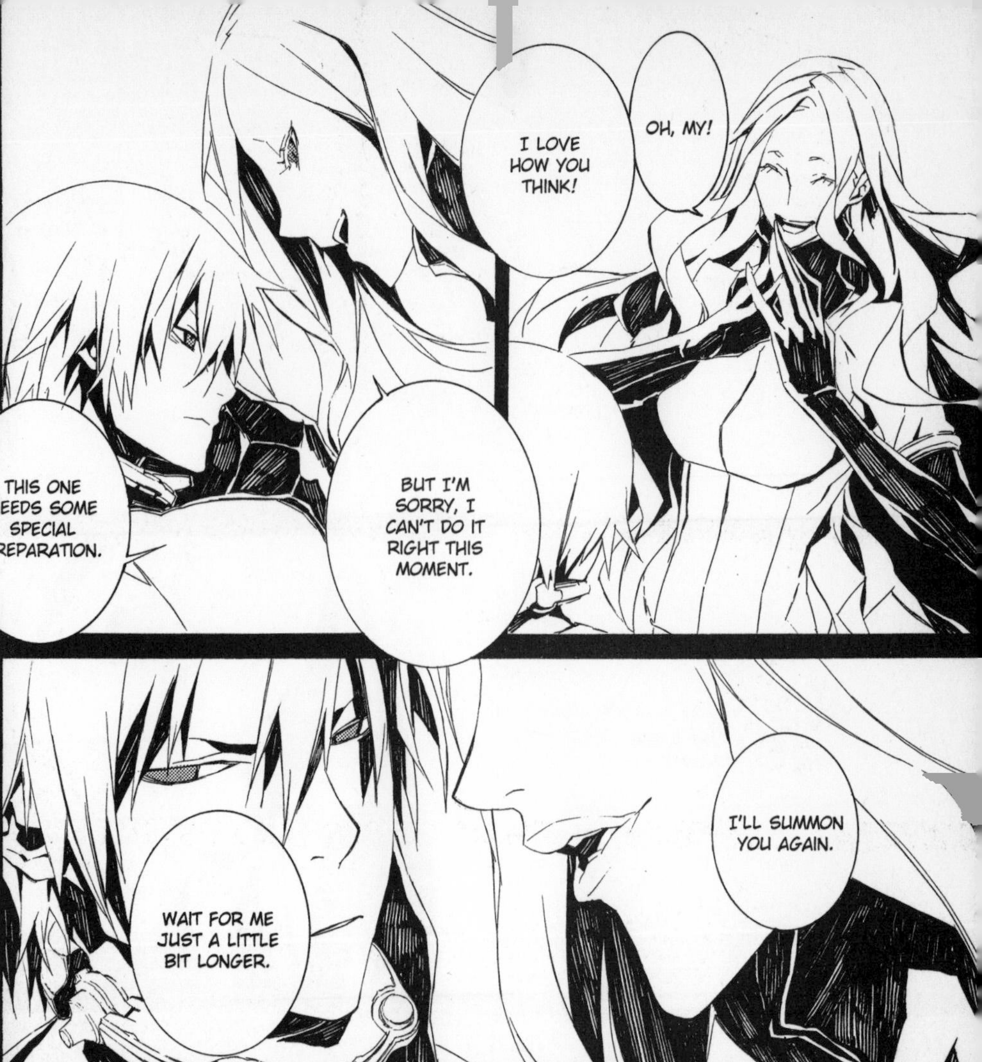
OH, MY!
I LOVE HOW YOU THINK!
BUT I'M SORRY, I CAN'T DO IT RIGHT THIS MOMENT.
THIS ONE NEEDS SOME SPECIAL PREPARATION.
I'LL SUMMON YOU AGAIN.
WAIT FOR ME JUST A LITTLE BIT LONGER.

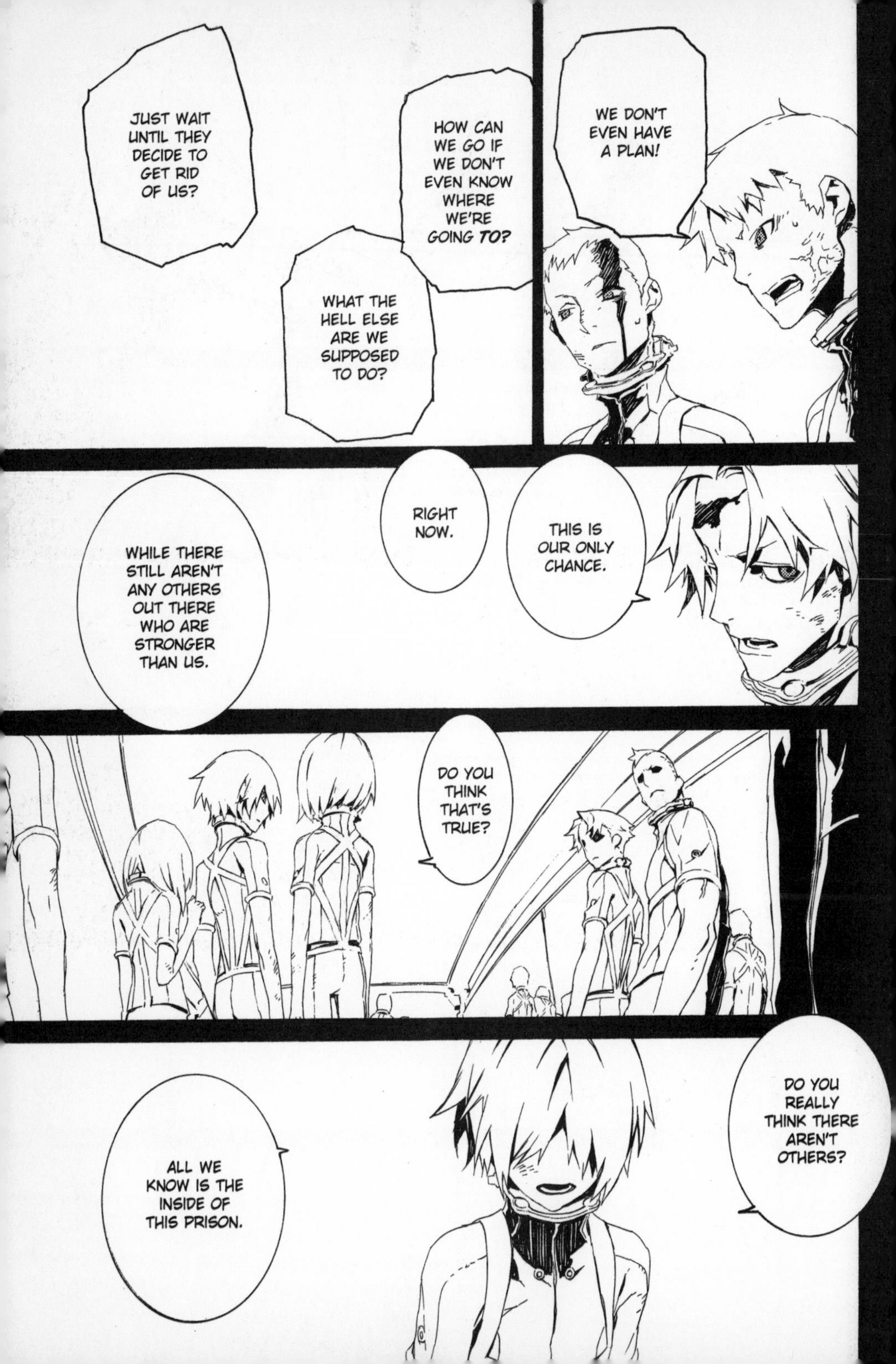
WE DON'T EVEN HAVE A PLAN!
HOW CAN WE GO IF WE DON'T EVEN KNOW WHERE WE'RE GOING *TO*?
WHAT THE HELL ELSE ARE WE SUPPOSED TO DO?
JUST WAIT UNTIL THEY DECIDE TO GET RID OF US?
THIS IS OUR ONLY CHANCE.
RIGHT NOW.
WHILE THERE STILL AREN'T ANY OTHERS OUT THERE WHO ARE STRONGER THAN US.
DO YOU THINK THAT'S TRUE?
DO YOU REALLY THINK THERE AREN'T OTHERS?
ALL WE KNOW IS THE INSIDE OF THIS PRISON.

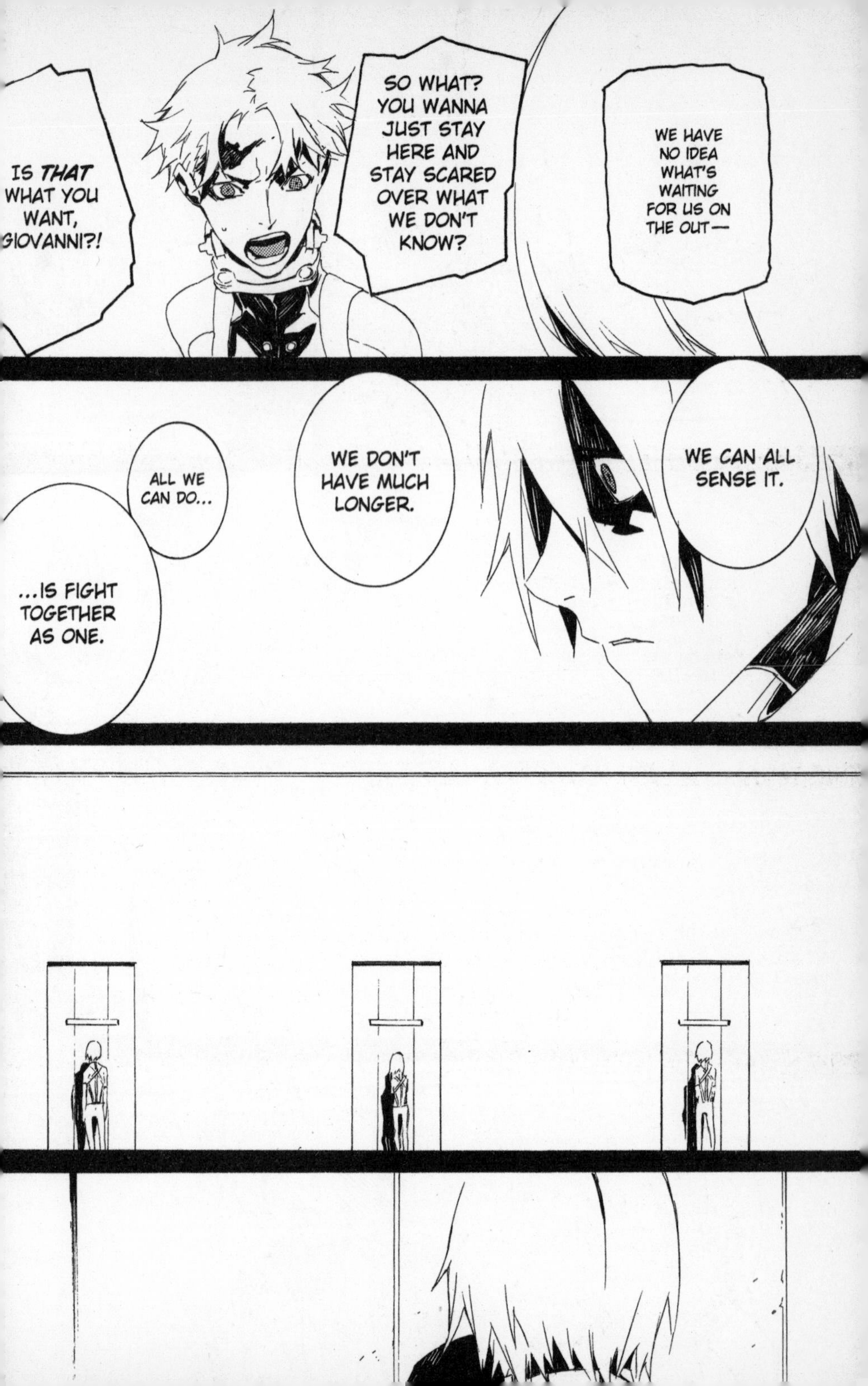
WE HAVE NO IDEA WHAT'S WAITING FOR US ON THE OUT—
SO WHAT? YOU WANNA JUST STAY HERE AND STAY SCARED OVER WHAT WE DON'T KNOW?
IS *THAT* WHAT YOU WANT, GIOVANNI?!
WE CAN ALL SENSE IT.
WE DON'T HAVE MUCH LONGER.
ALL WE CAN DO...
...IS FIGHT TOGETHER AS ONE.

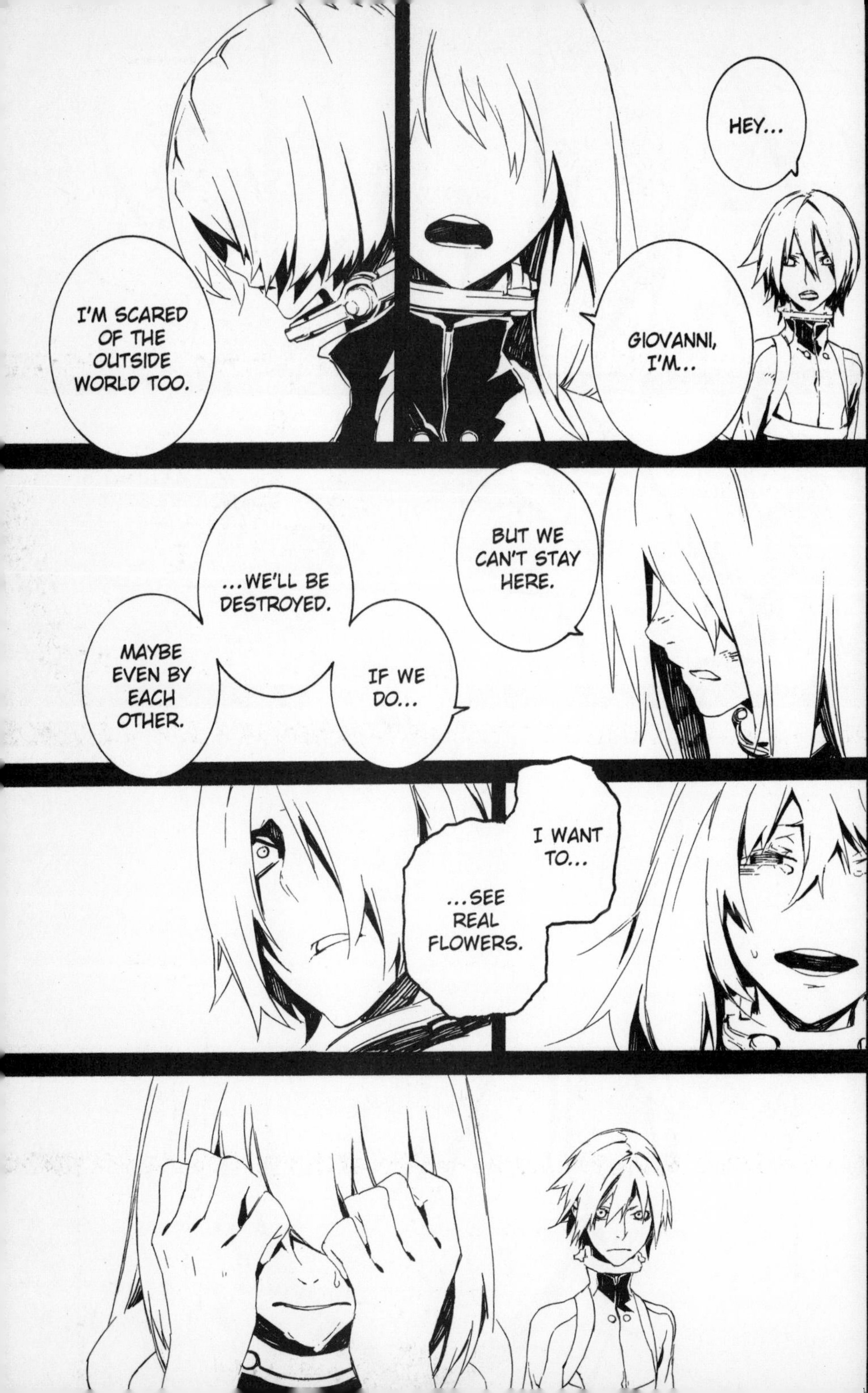
HEY...
GIOVANNI, I'M...
I'M SCARED OF THE OUTSIDE WORLD TOO.
BUT WE CAN'T STAY HERE.
IF WE DO...
...WE'LL BE DESTROYED.
MAYBE EVEN BY EACH OTHER.
I WANT TO...
...SEE REAL FLOWERS.

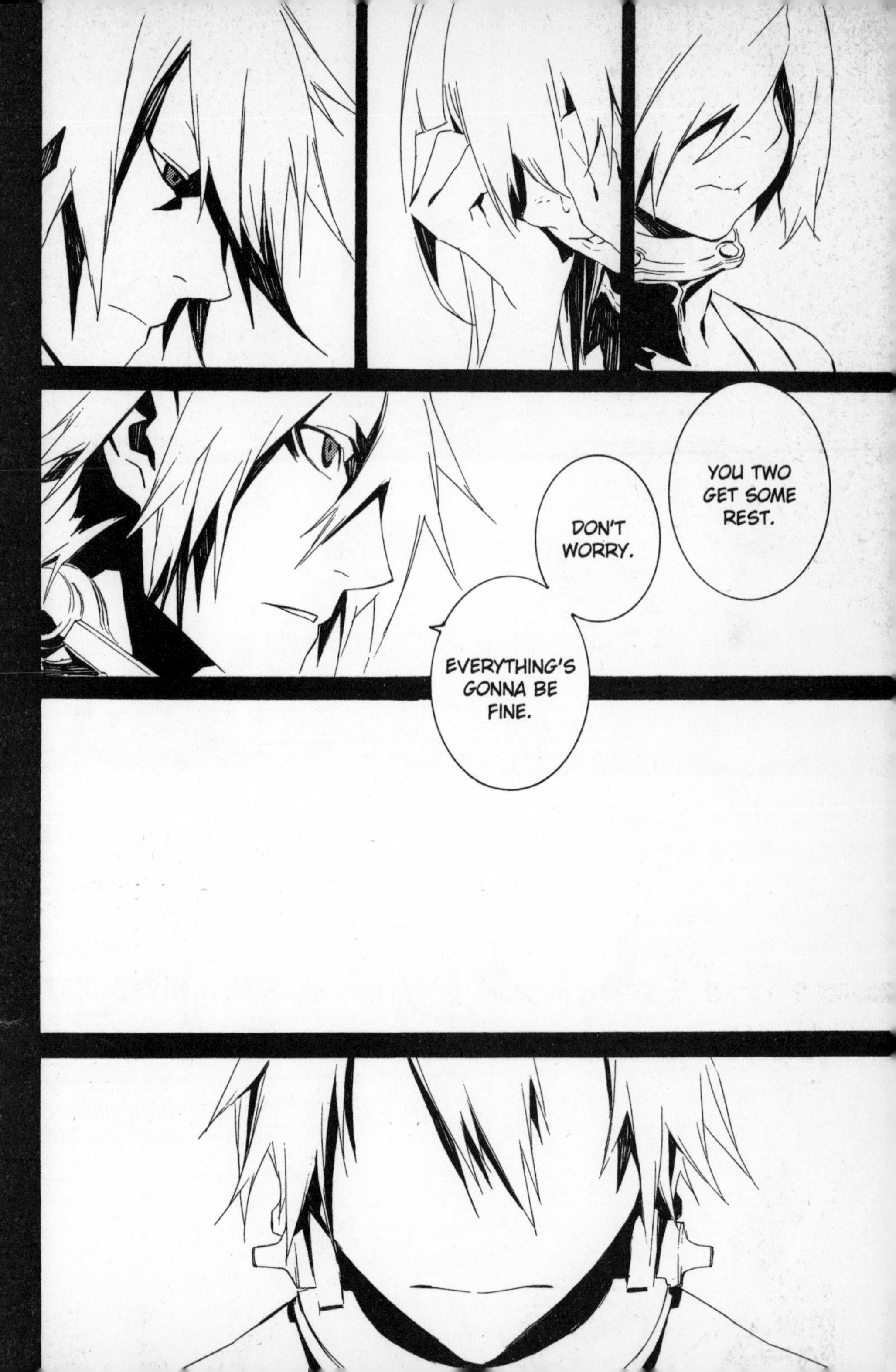
YOU TWO GET SOME REST.
DON'T WORRY.
EVERYTHING'S GONNA BE FINE.

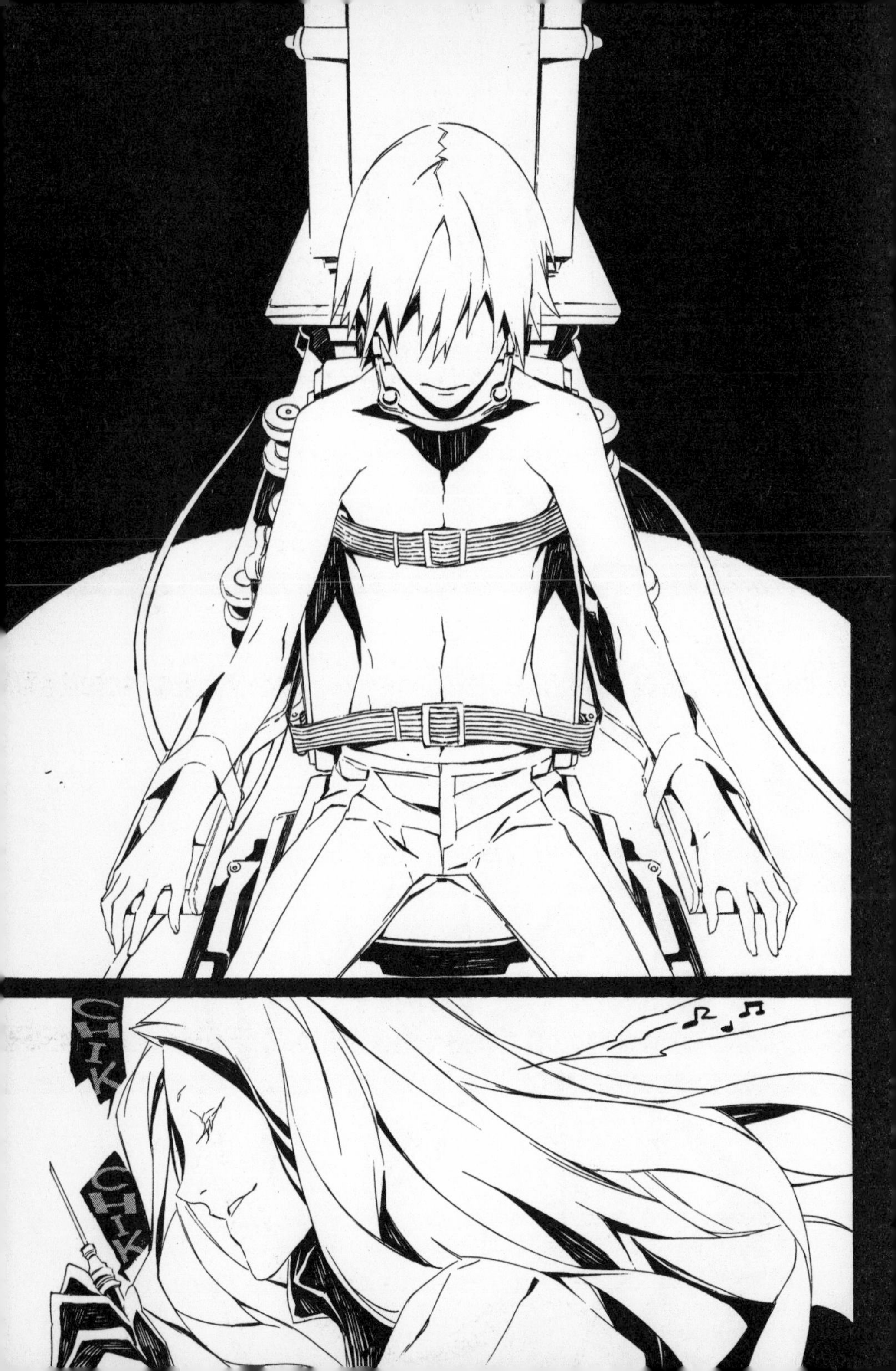
CHIK
CHIK

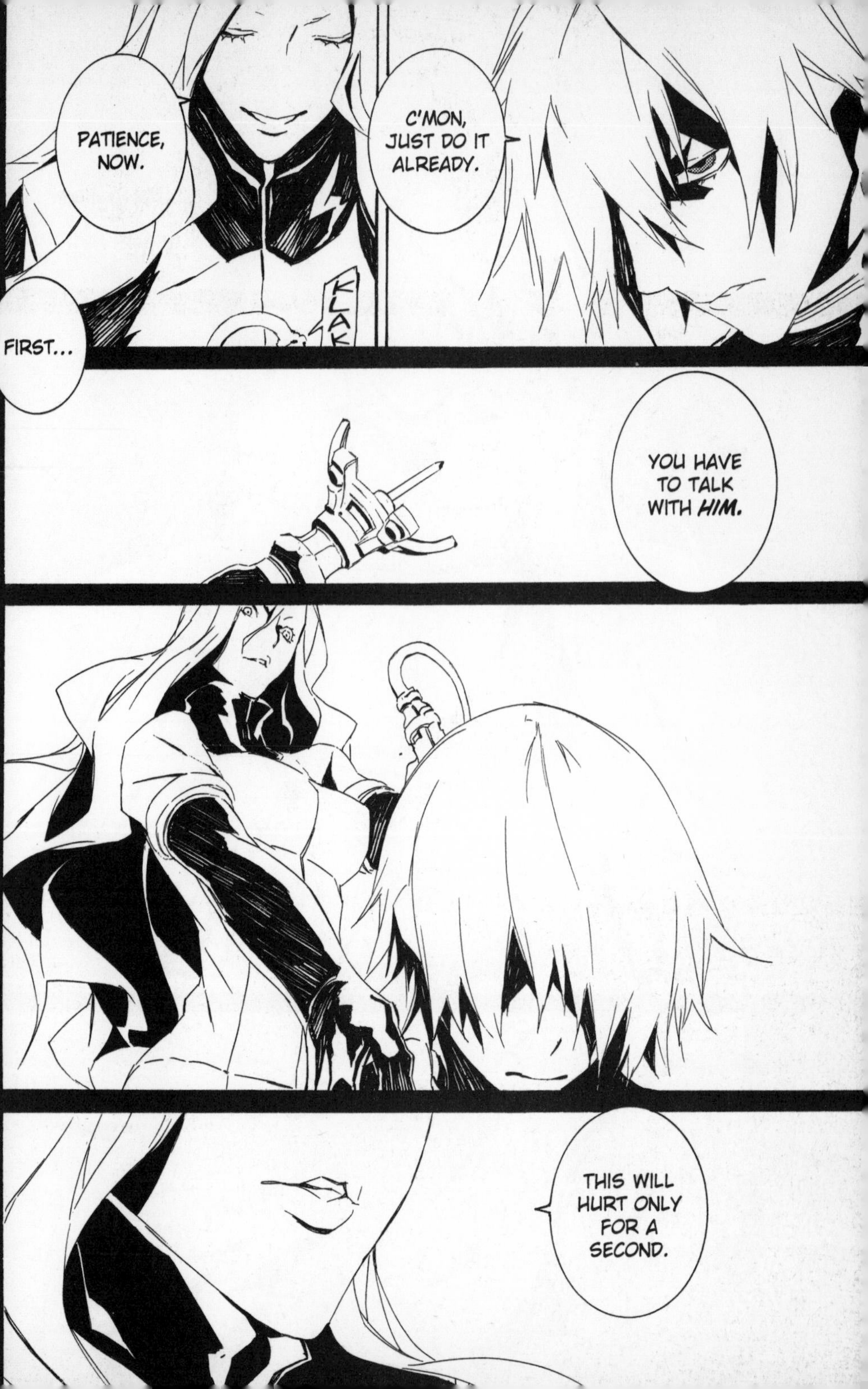
C'MON, JUST DO IT ALREADY.
PATIENCE, NOW.
KLAK
FIRST...
YOU HAVE TO TALK WITH *HIM.*
THIS WILL HURT ONLY FOR A SECOND.

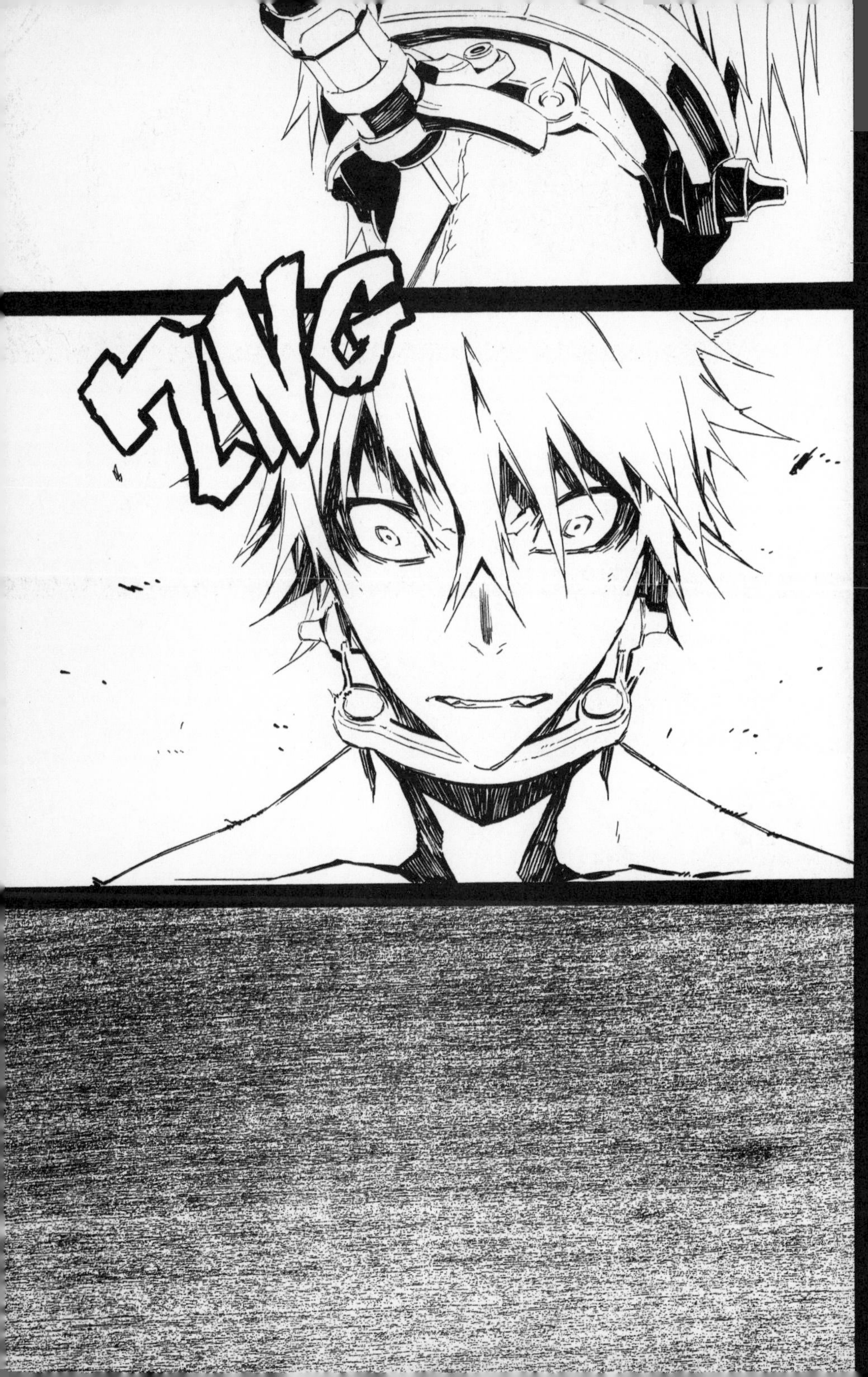
ZING

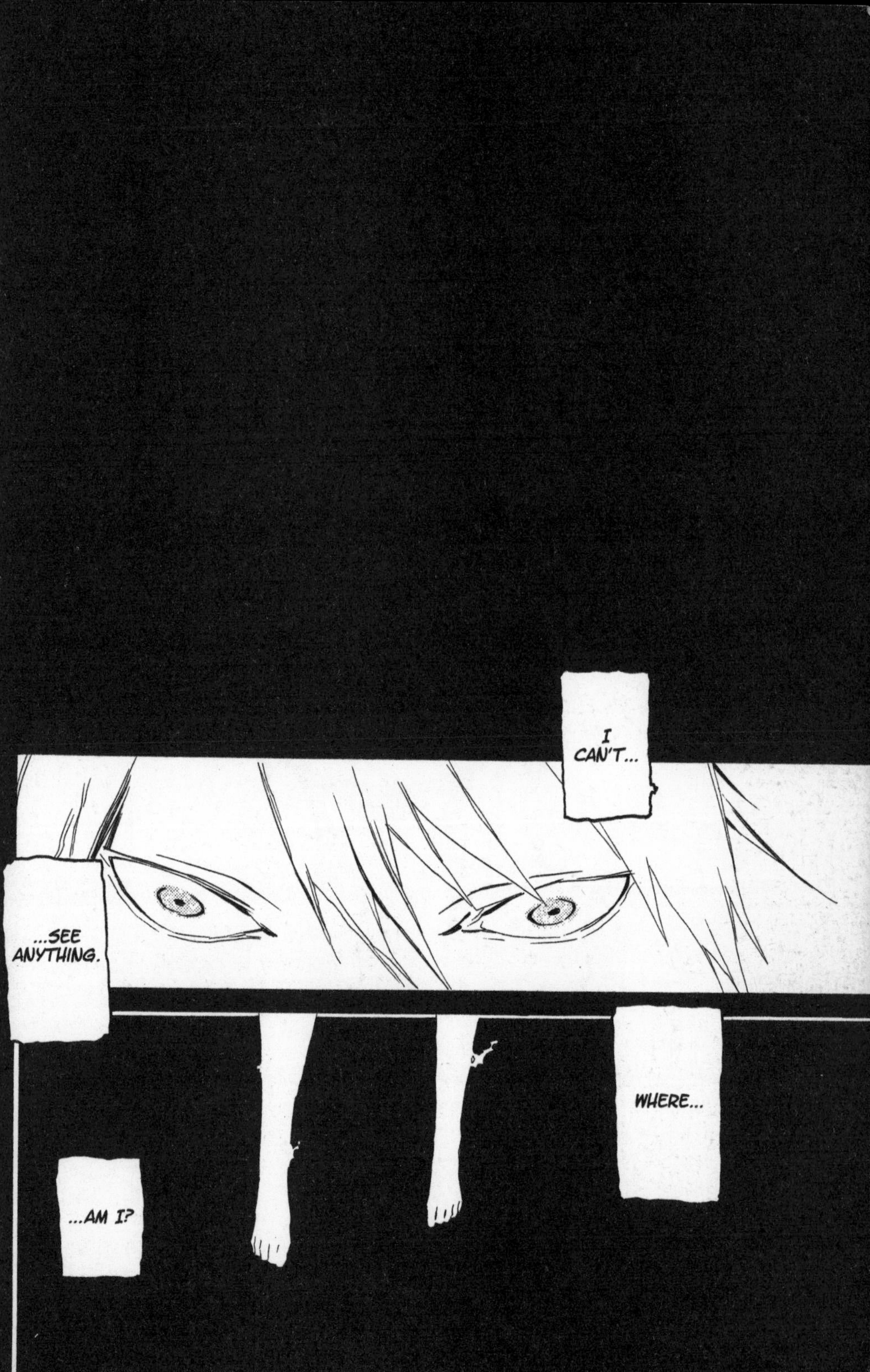
I CAN'T...
...SEE ANYTHING.
WHERE...
...AM I?

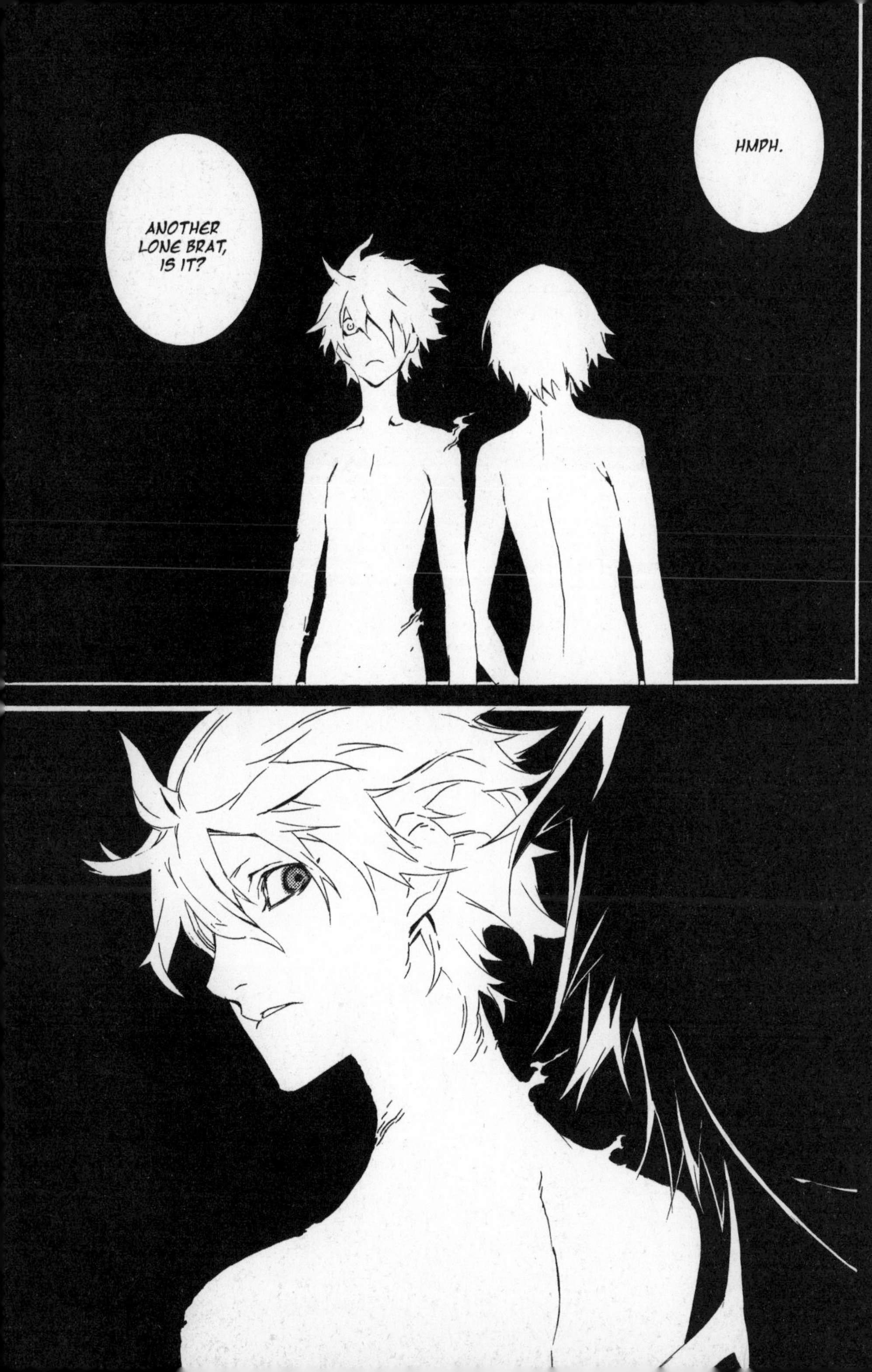
HMPH.
ANOTHER LONE BRAT, IS IT?

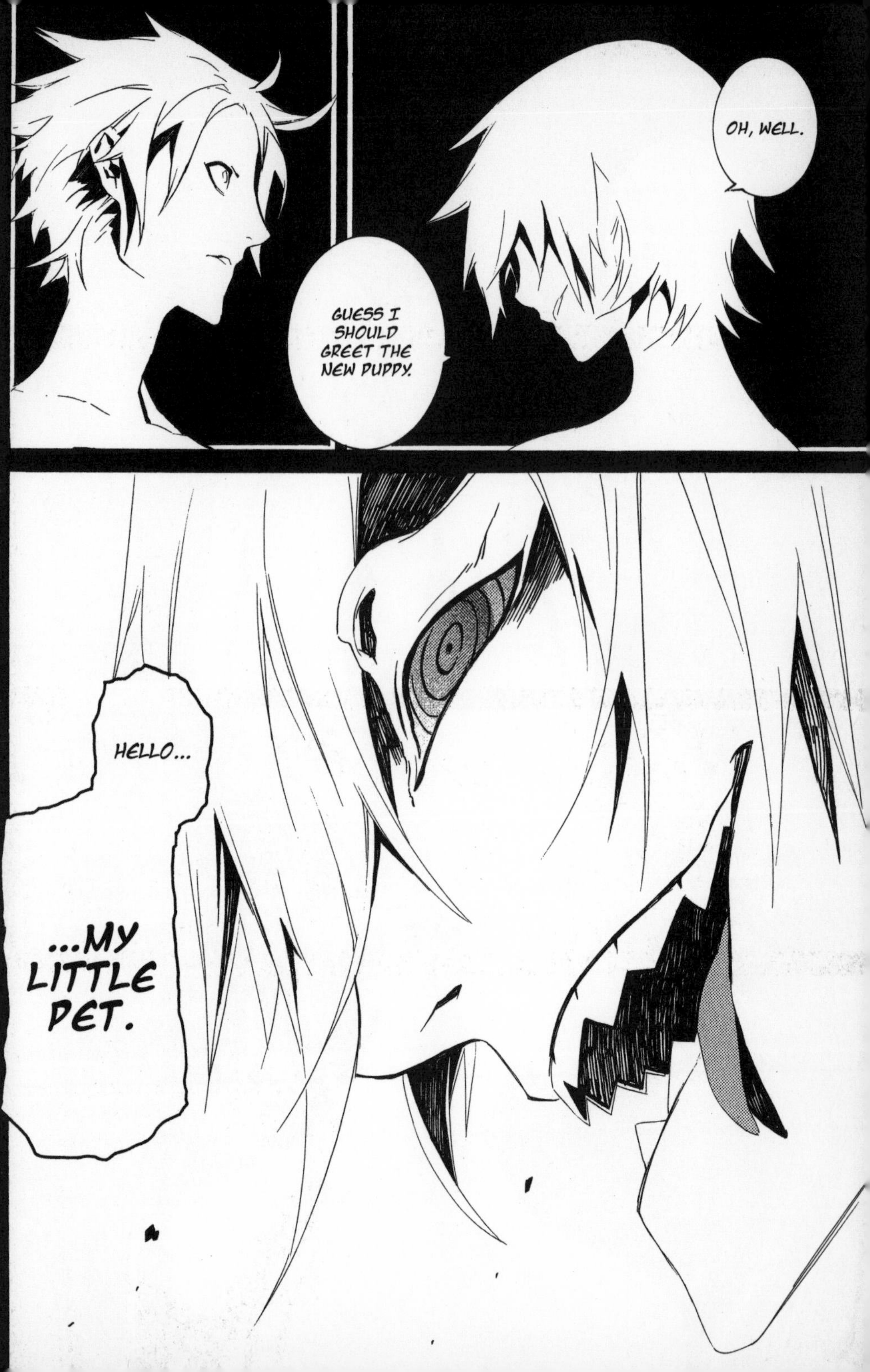
OH, WELL.
GUESS I SHOULD GREET THE NEW PUPPY.
HELLO...
...MY LITTLE PET.

# #55 Cage & Puppies Ⅳ

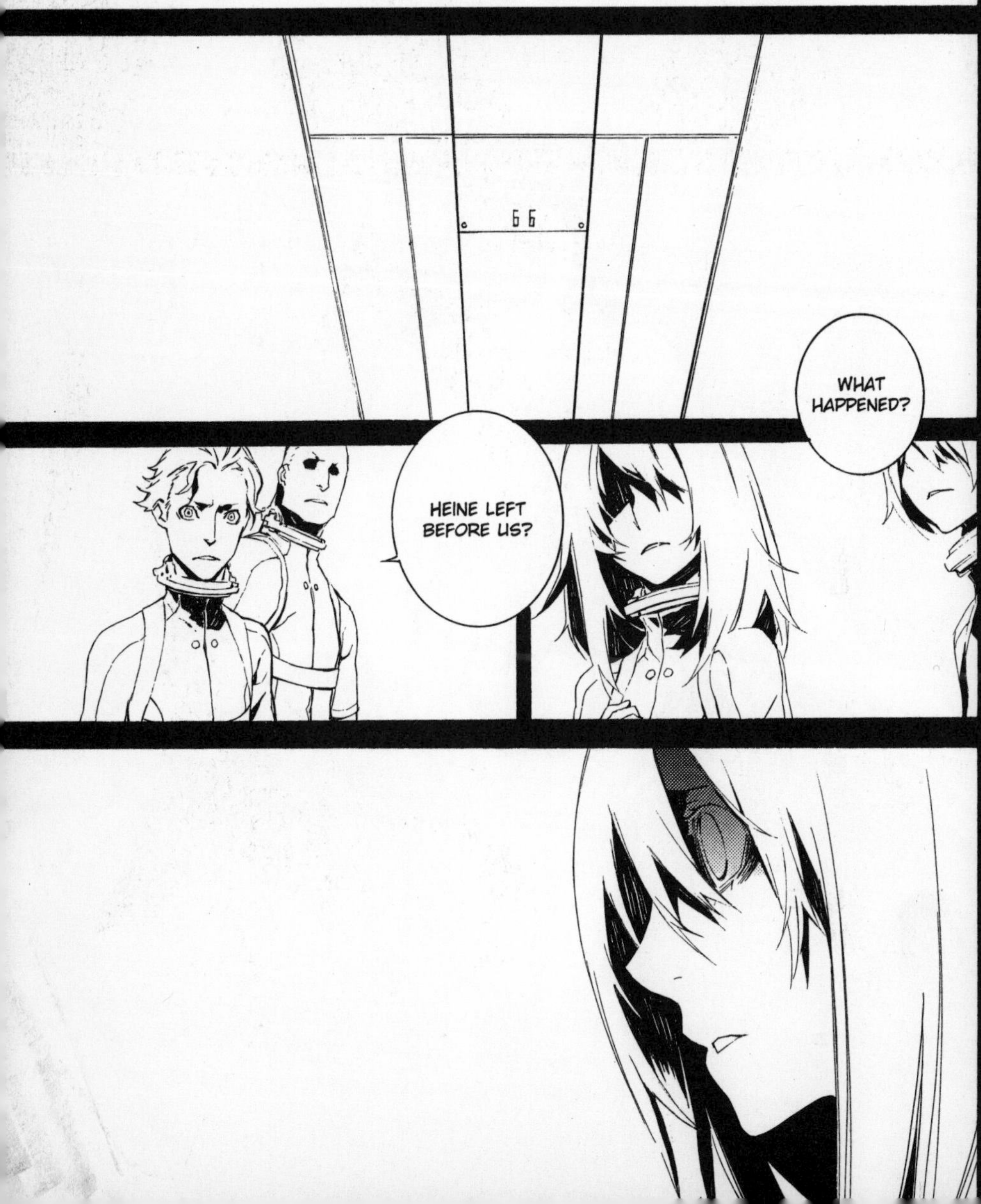
WHAT HAPPENED?
HEINE LEFT BEFORE US?

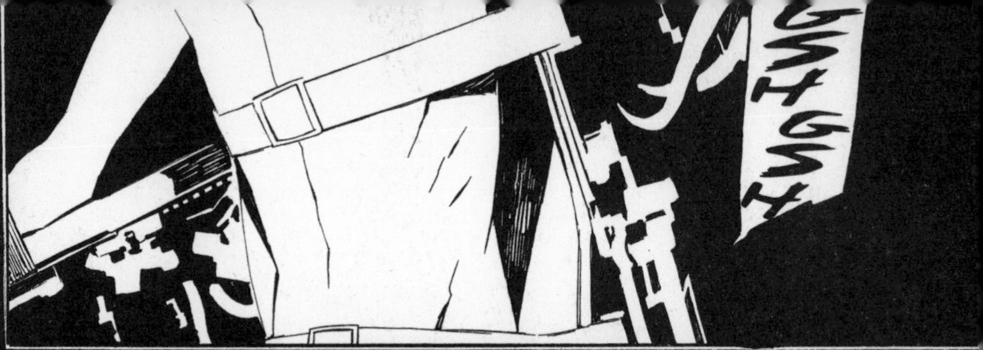

# #55 Cage & Puppies Ⅳ

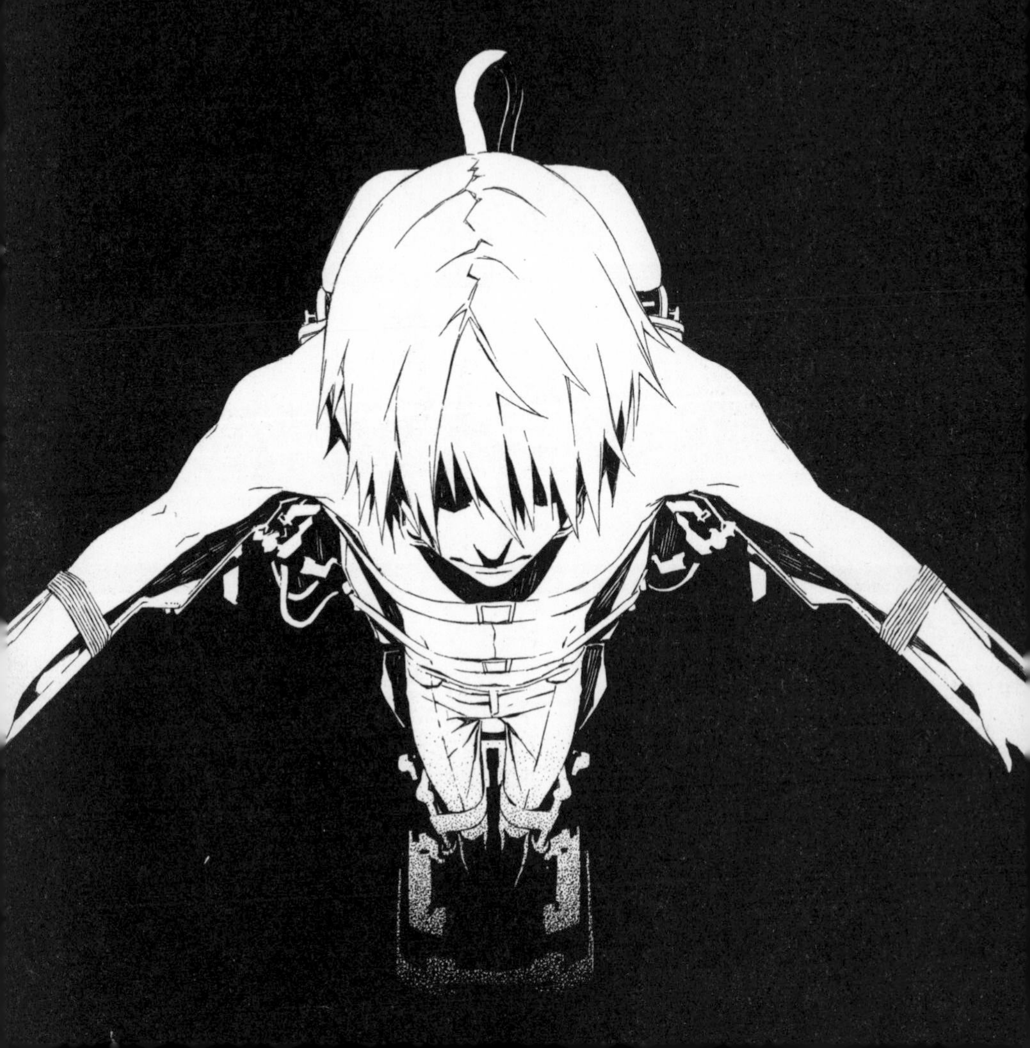

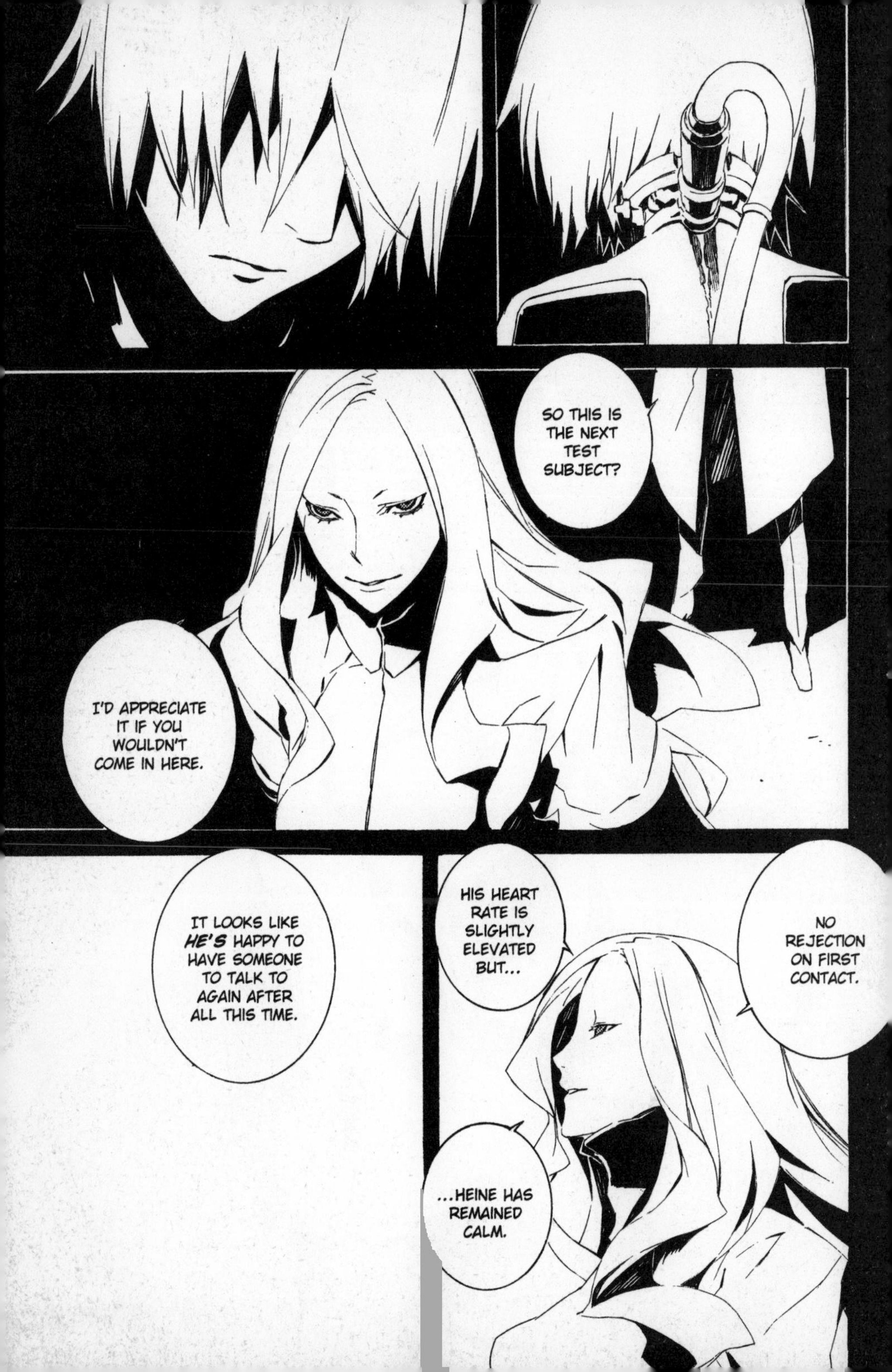
SO THIS IS THE NEXT TEST SUBJECT?
I'D APPRECIATE IT IF YOU WOULDN'T COME IN HERE.
NO REJECTION ON FIRST CONTACT.
HIS HEART RATE IS SLIGHTLY ELEVATED BUT...
...HEINE HAS REMAINED CALM.
IT LOOKS LIKE *HE'S* HAPPY TO HAVE SOMEONE TO TALK TO AGAIN AFTER ALL THIS TIME.

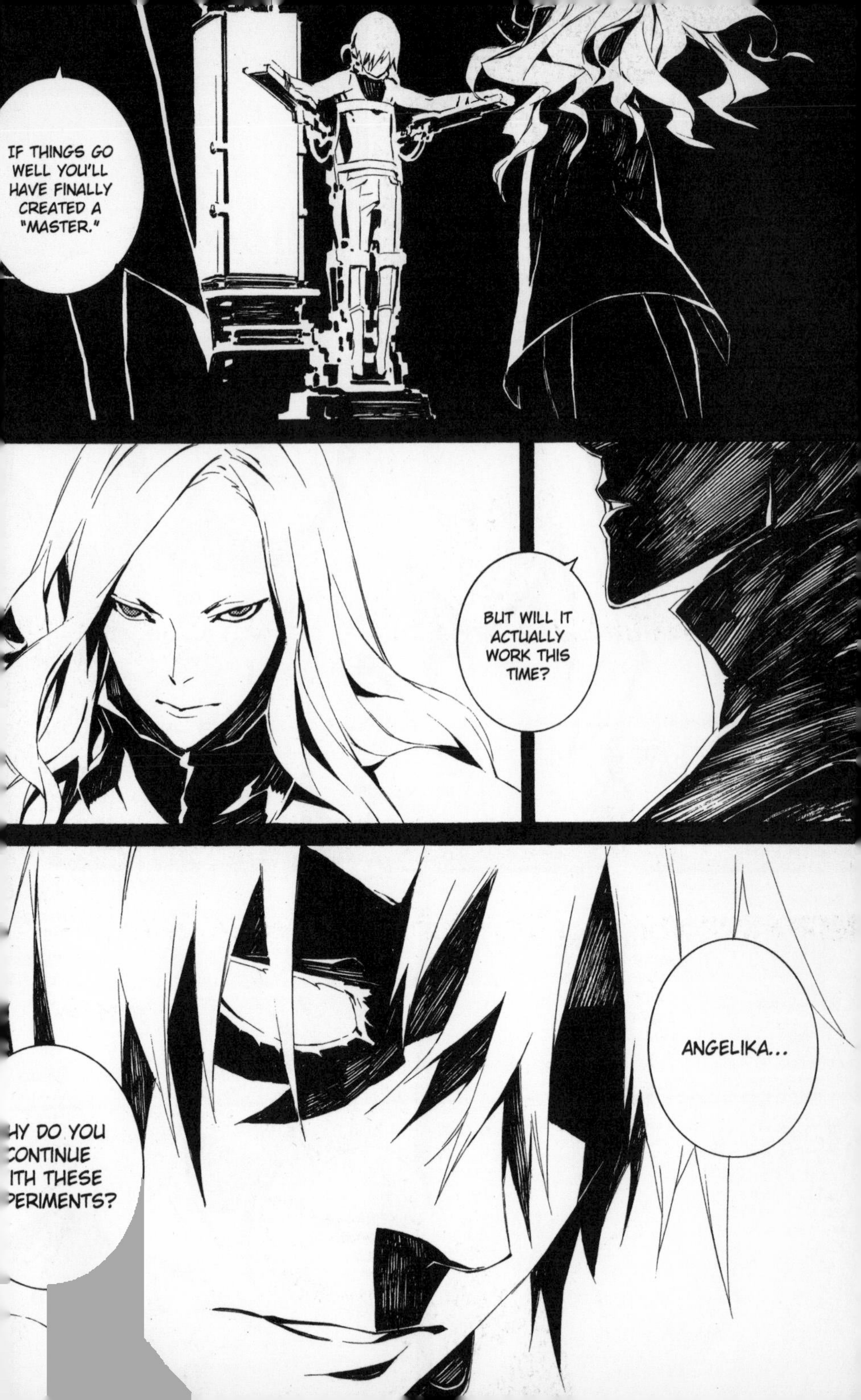
IF THINGS GO WELL YOU'LL HAVE FINALLY CREATED A "MASTER."
BUT WILL IT ACTUALLY WORK THIS TIME?
ANGELIKA...
HY DO YOU CONTINUE ITH THESE PERIMENTS?

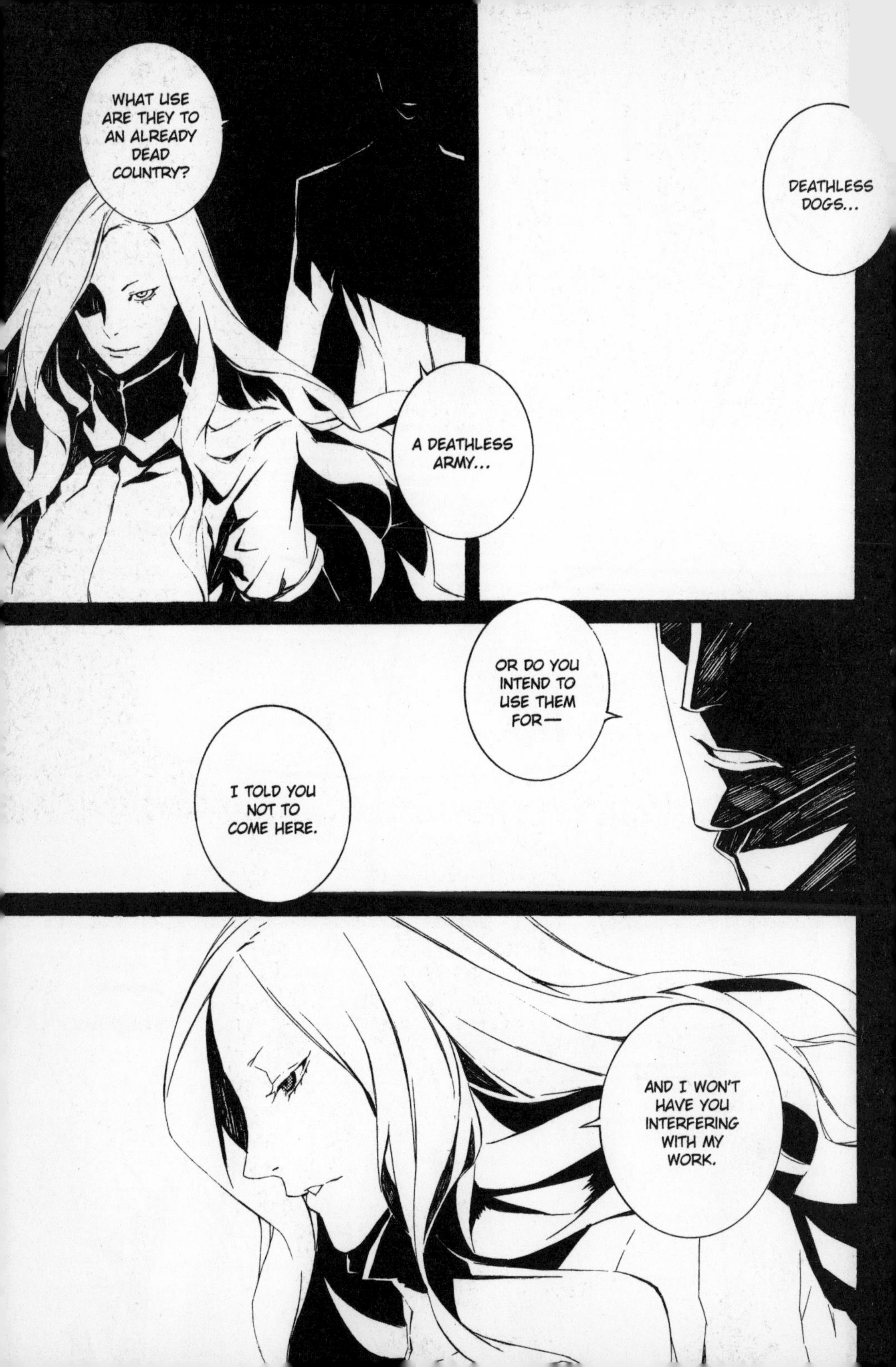
DEATHLESS DOGS...
A DEATHLESS ARMY...
WHAT USE ARE THEY TO AN ALREADY DEAD COUNTRY?
OR DO YOU INTEND TO USE THEM FOR—
I TOLD YOU NOT TO COME HERE.
AND I WON'T HAVE YOU INTERFERING WITH MY WORK.

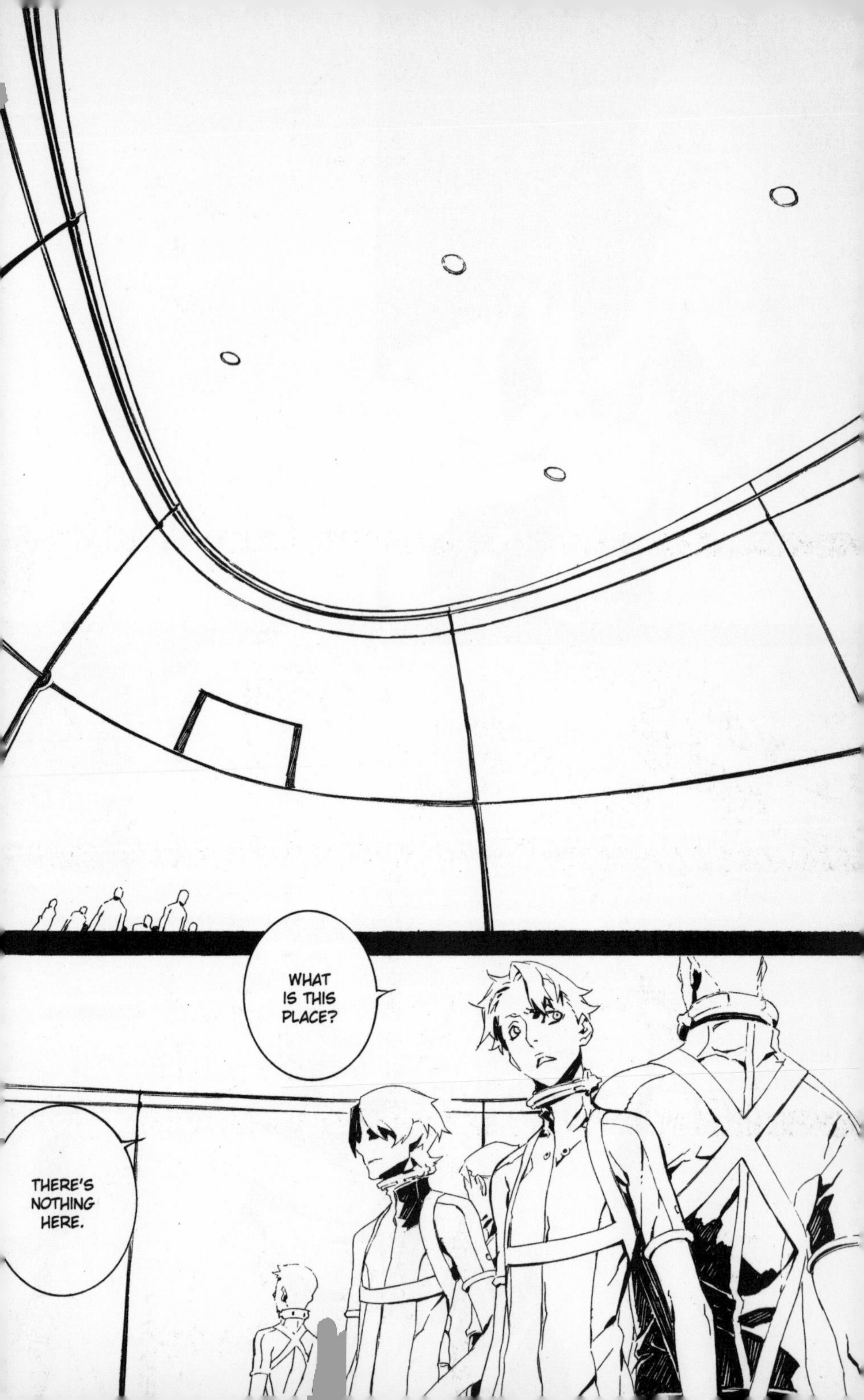
WHAT IS THIS PLACE?
THERE'S NOTHING HERE.

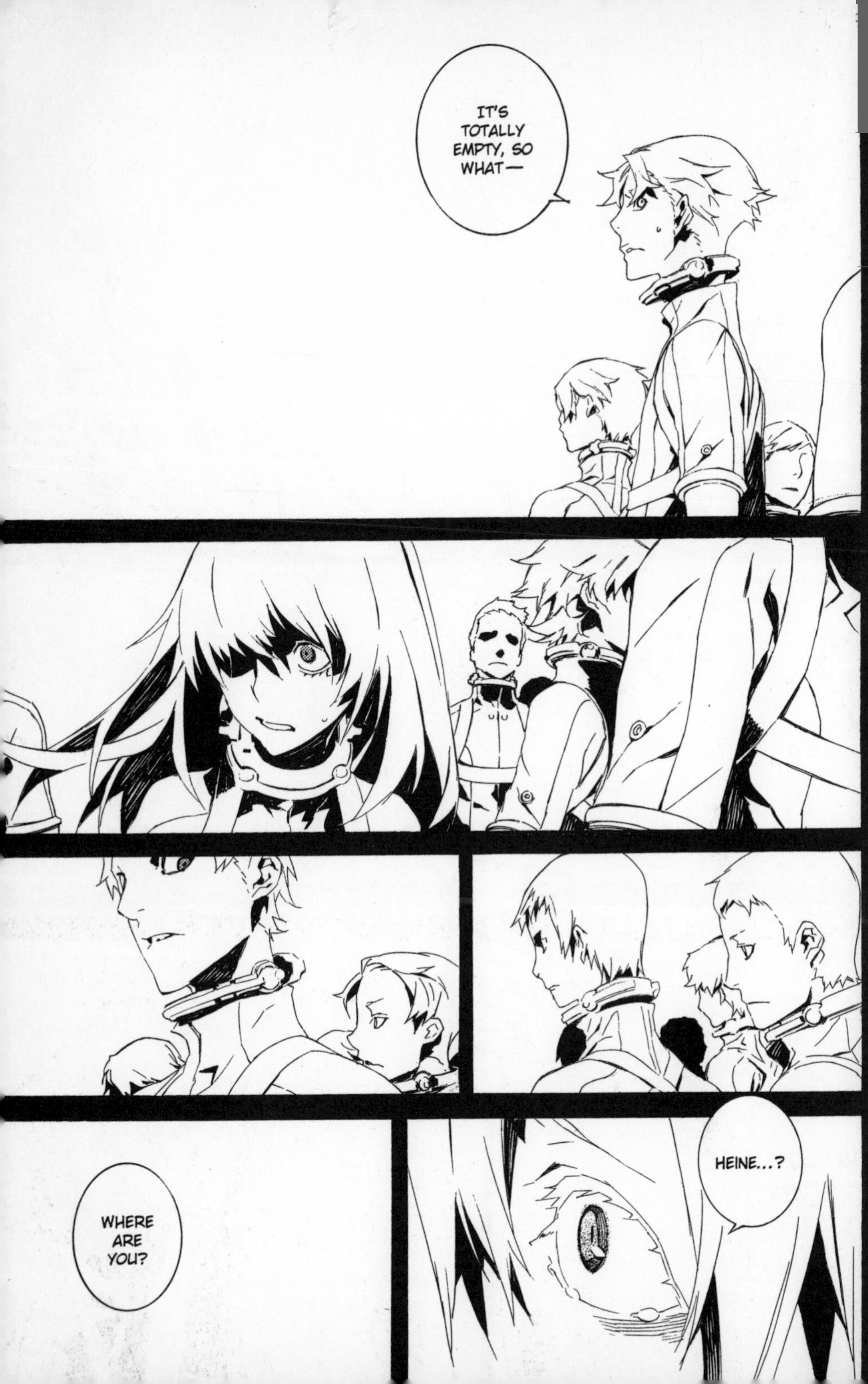
IT'S TOTALLY EMPTY, SO WHAT—
HEINE...?
WHERE ARE YOU?

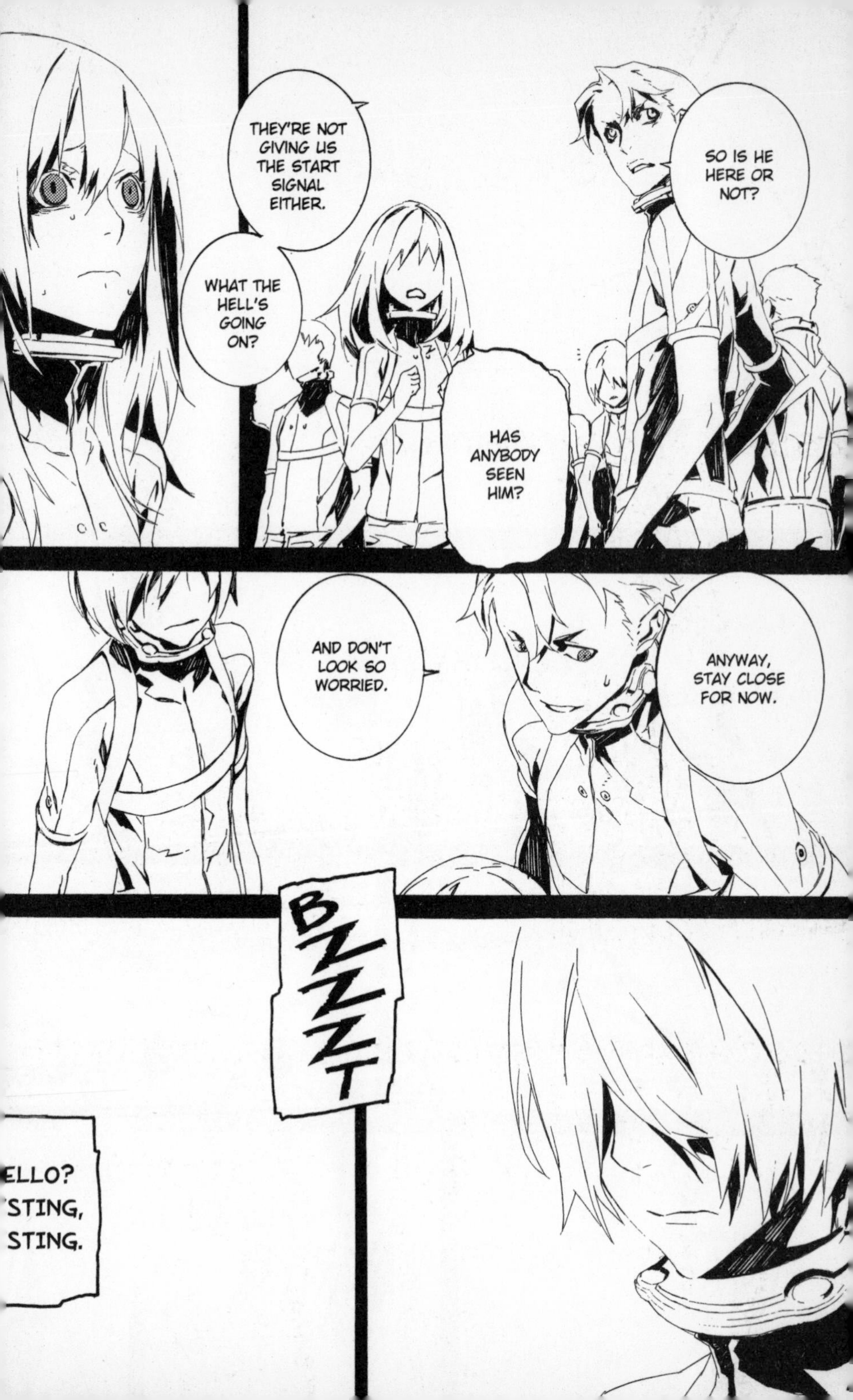
SO IS HE HERE OR NOT?
THEY'RE NOT GIVING US THE START SIGNAL EITHER.
WHAT THE HELL'S GOING ON?
HAS ANYBODY SEEN HIM?
ANYWAY, STAY CLOSE FOR NOW.
AND DON'T LOOK SO WORRIED.
BZZZT
ELLO?
STING,
STING.

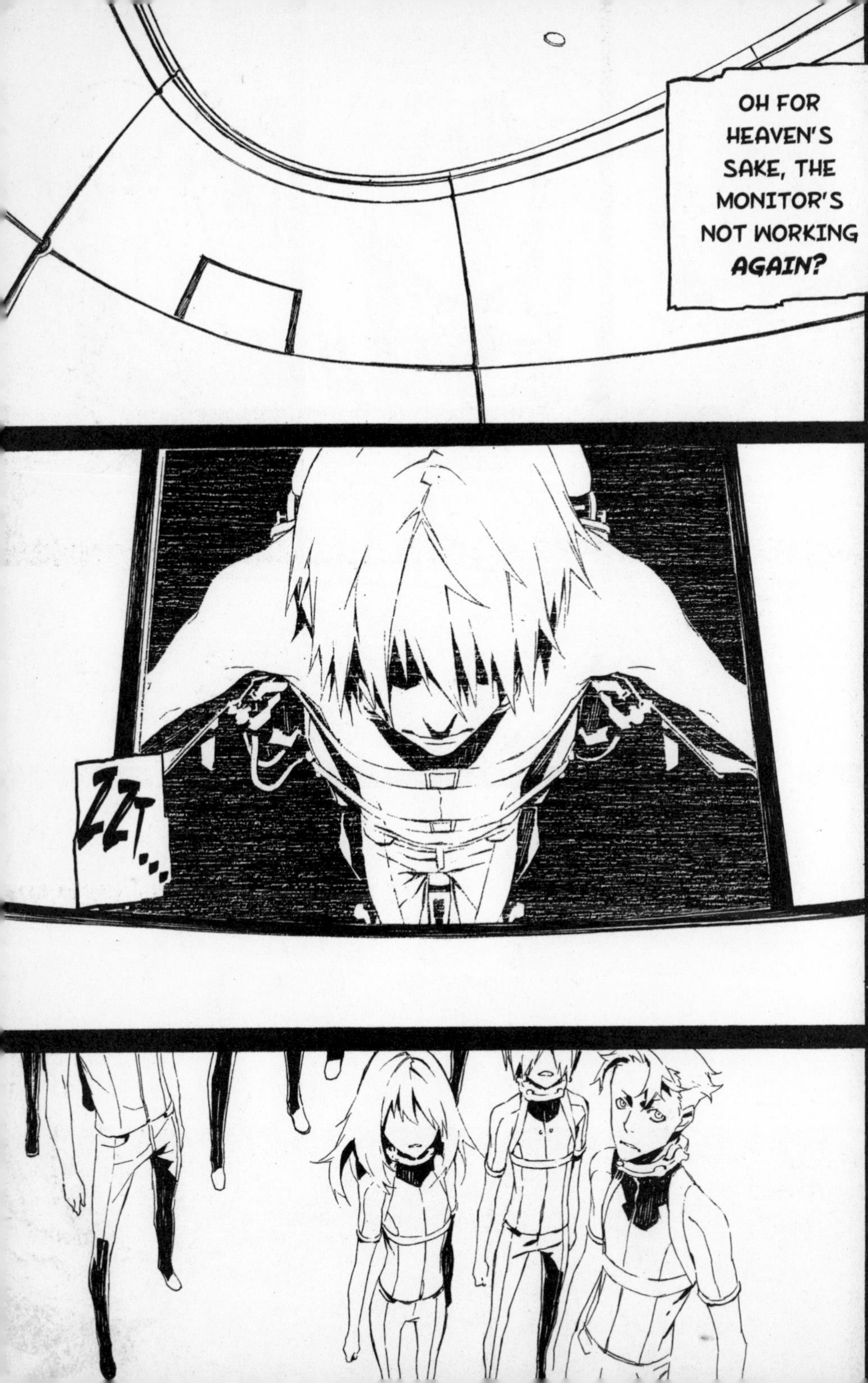
OH FOR HEAVEN'S SAKE, THE MONITOR'S NOT WORKING AGAIN?
ZZT...

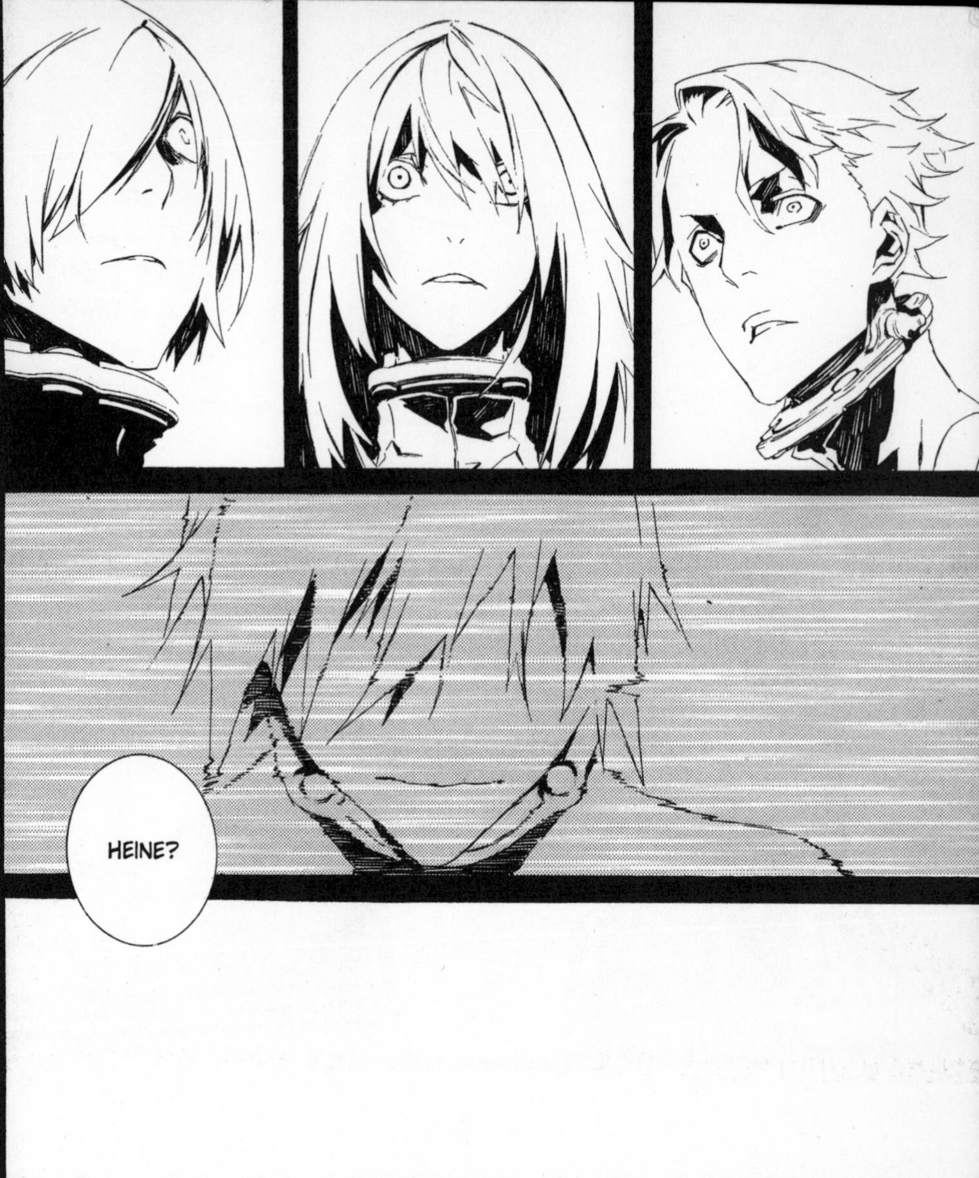
HEINE?

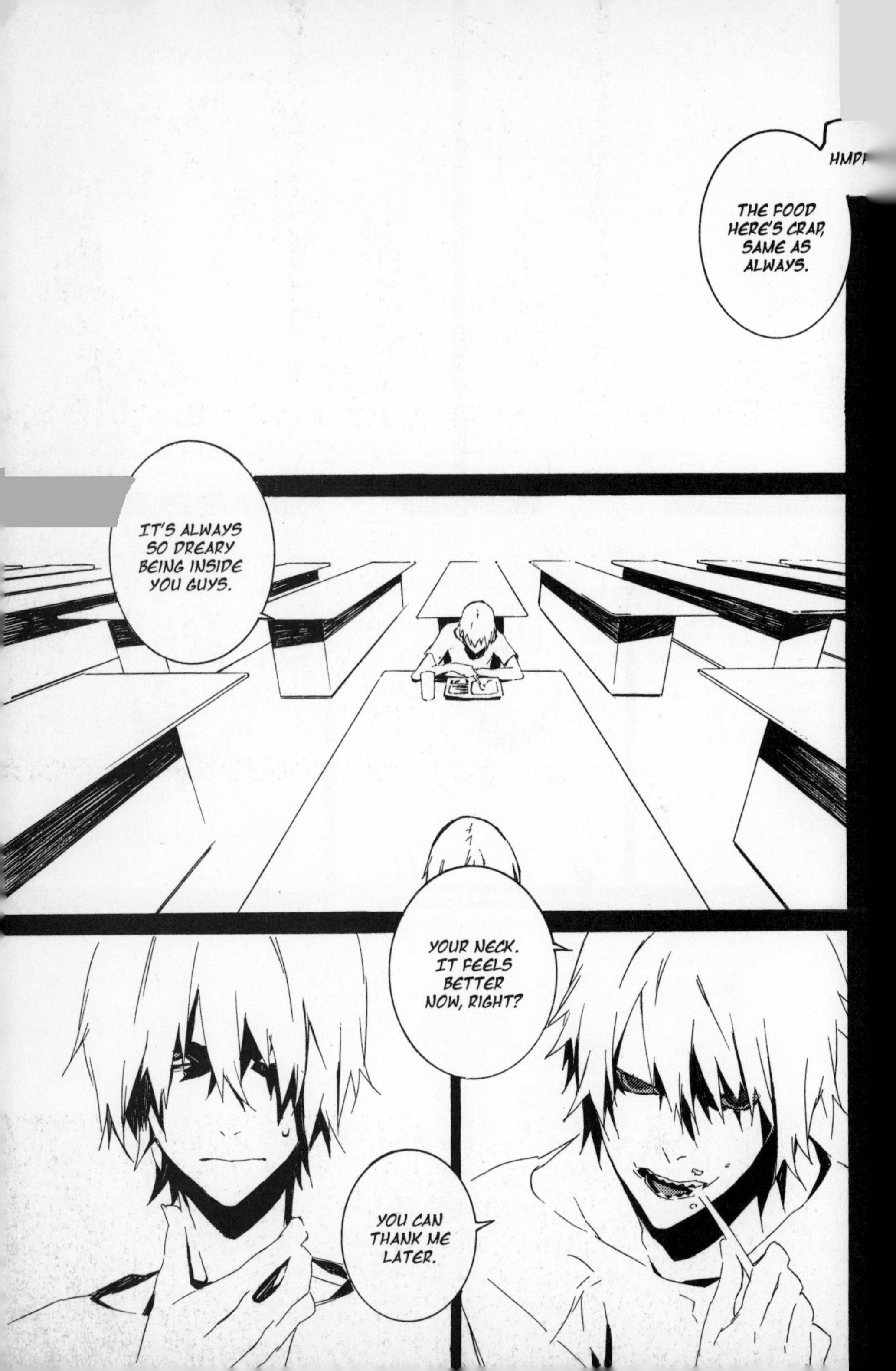
HMPH
THE FOOD HERE'S CRAP, SAME AS ALWAYS.
IT'S ALWAYS SO DREARY BEING INSIDE YOU GUYS.
YOUR NECK. IT FEELS BETTER NOW, RIGHT?
YOU CAN THANK ME LATER.

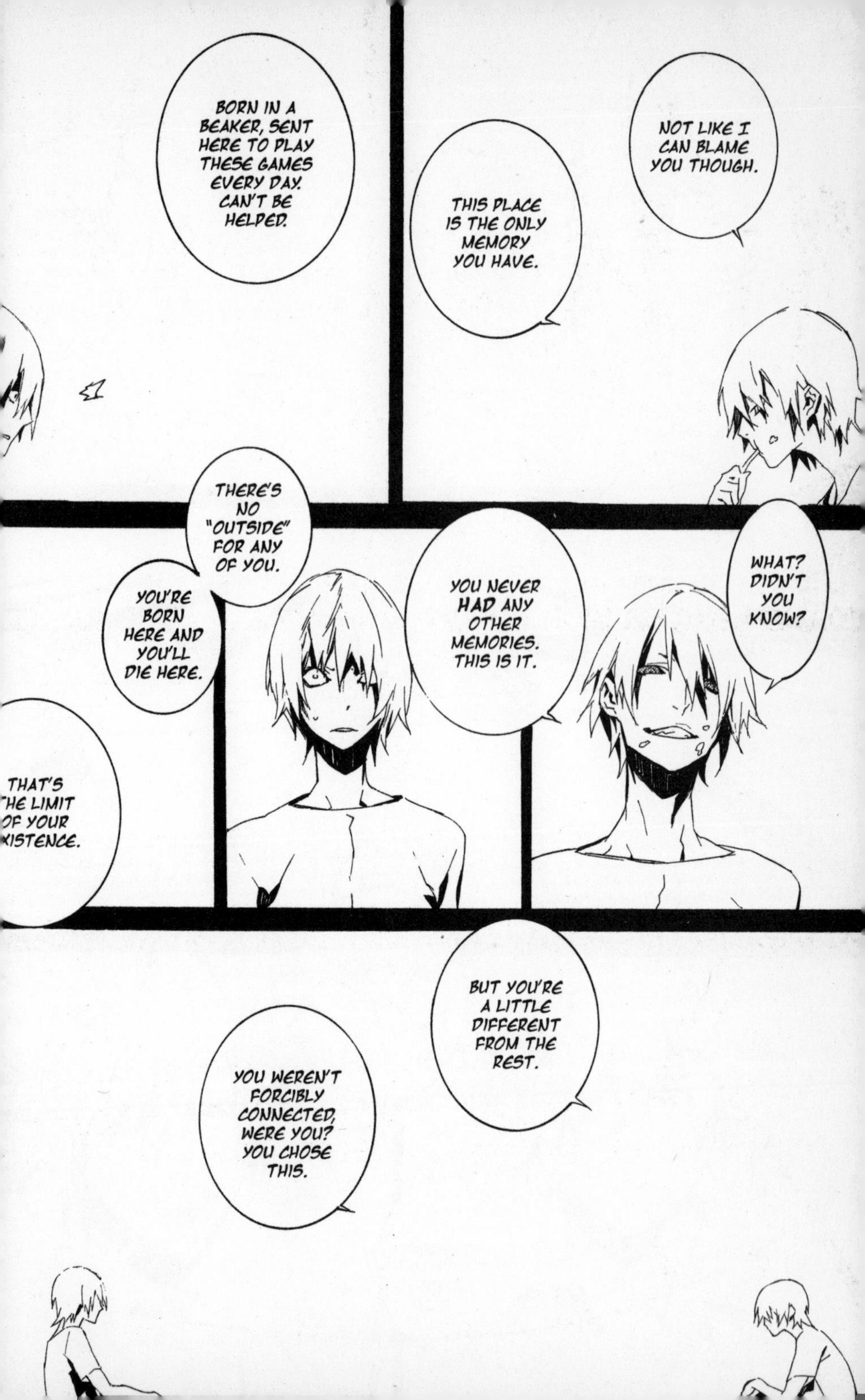
NOT LIKE I CAN BLAME YOU THOUGH.
THIS PLACE IS THE ONLY MEMORY YOU HAVE.
BORN IN A BEAKER, SENT HERE TO PLAY THESE GAMES EVERY DAY. CAN'T BE HELPED.
WHAT? DIDN'T YOU KNOW?
YOU NEVER HAD ANY OTHER MEMORIES. THIS IS IT.
THERE'S NO "OUTSIDE" FOR ANY OF YOU.
YOU'RE BORN HERE AND YOU'LL DIE HERE.
THAT'S THE LIMIT OF YOUR EXISTENCE.
BUT YOU'RE A LITTLE DIFFERENT FROM THE REST.
YOU WEREN'T FORCIBLY CONNECTED, WERE YOU? YOU CHOSE THIS.

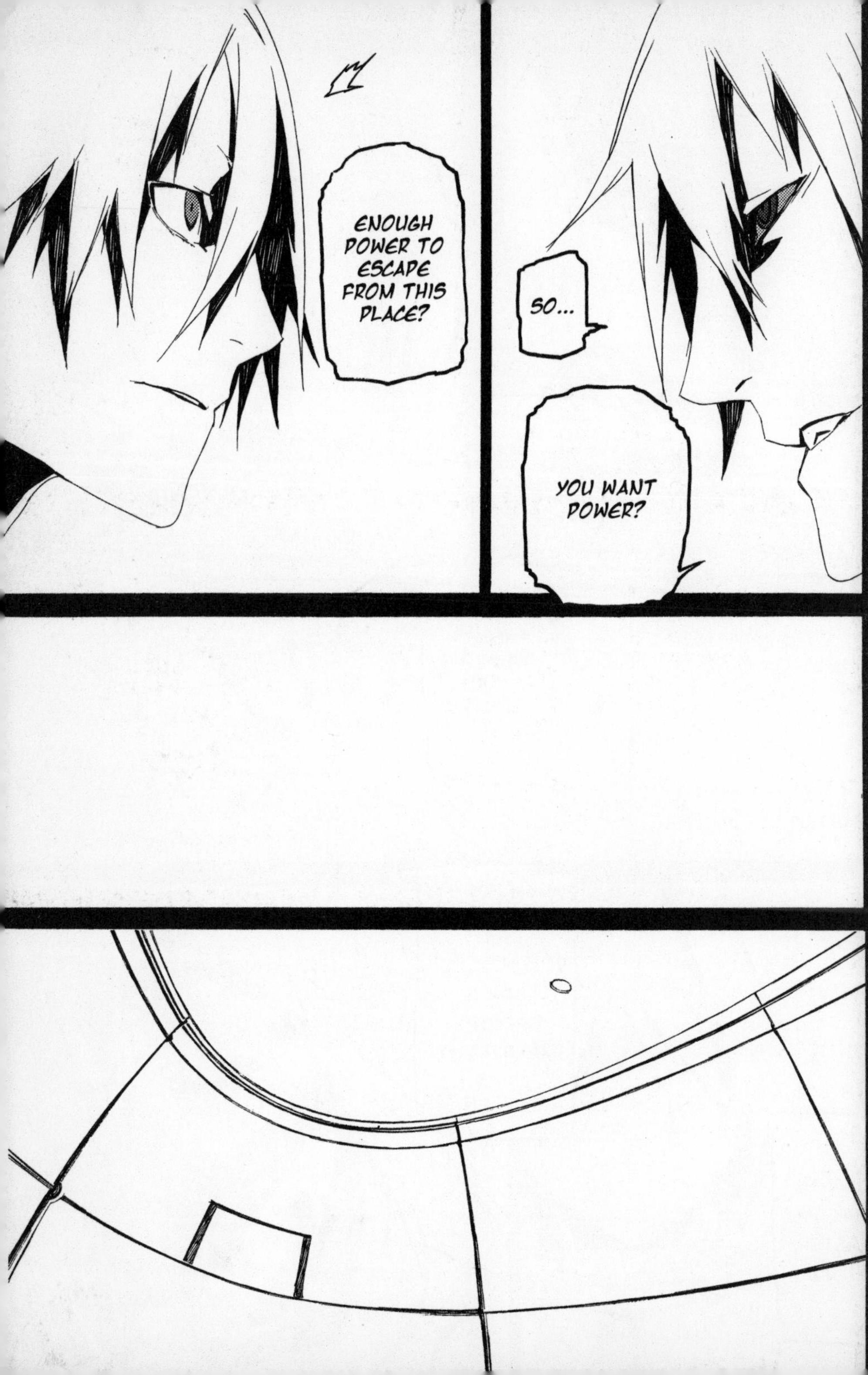
SO...
YOU WANT POWER?
ENOUGH POWER TO ESCAPE FROM THIS PLACE?

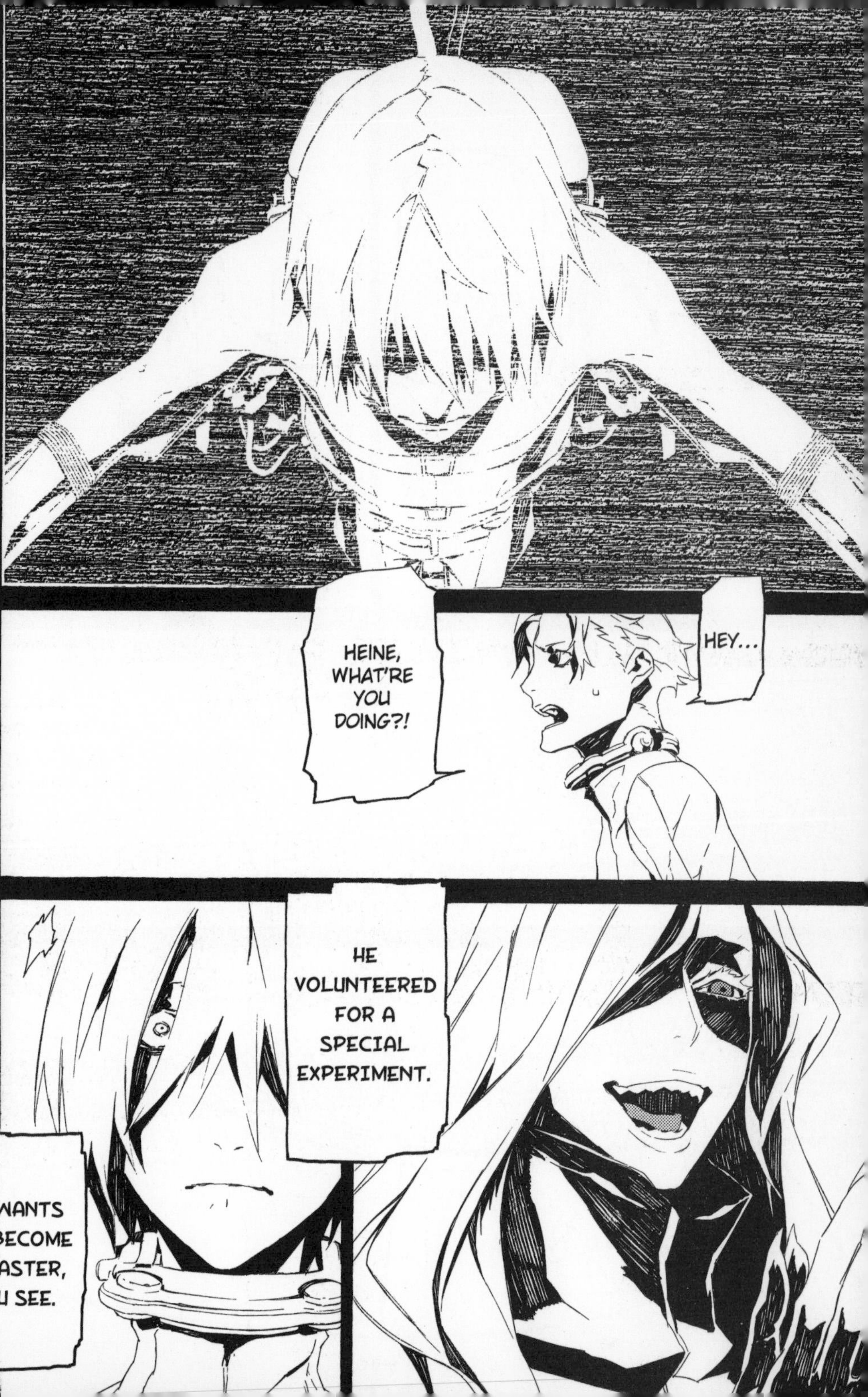
HEY...
HEINE, WHAT'RE YOU DOING?!
HE VOLUNTEERED FOR A SPECIAL EXPERIMENT.
WANTS BECOME MASTER, OU SEE.

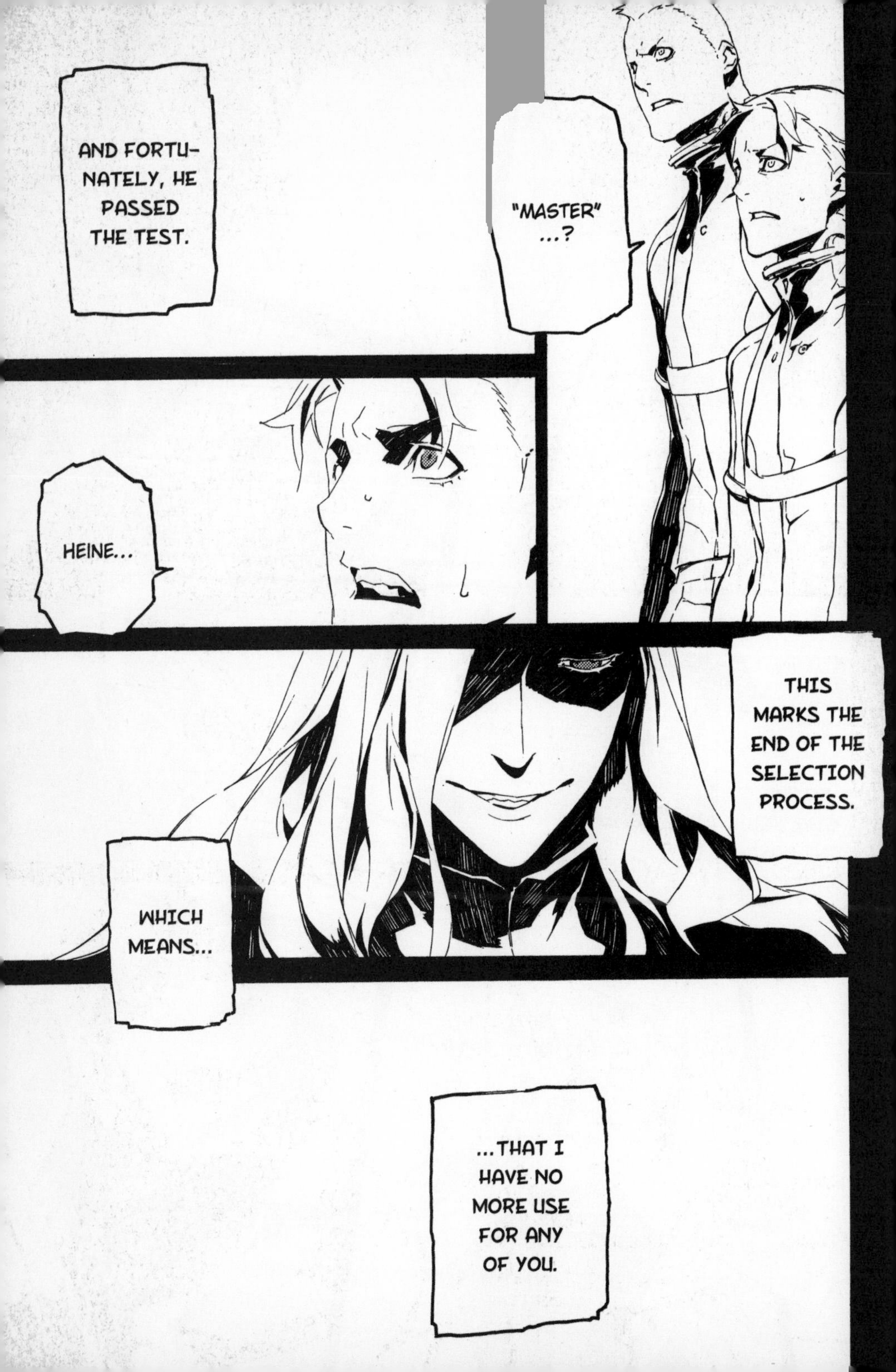
"MASTER" ...?
AND FORTUNATELY, HE PASSED THE TEST.
HEINE...
THIS MARKS THE END OF THE SELECTION PROCESS.
WHICH MEANS...
...THAT I HAVE NO MORE USE FOR ANY OF YOU.

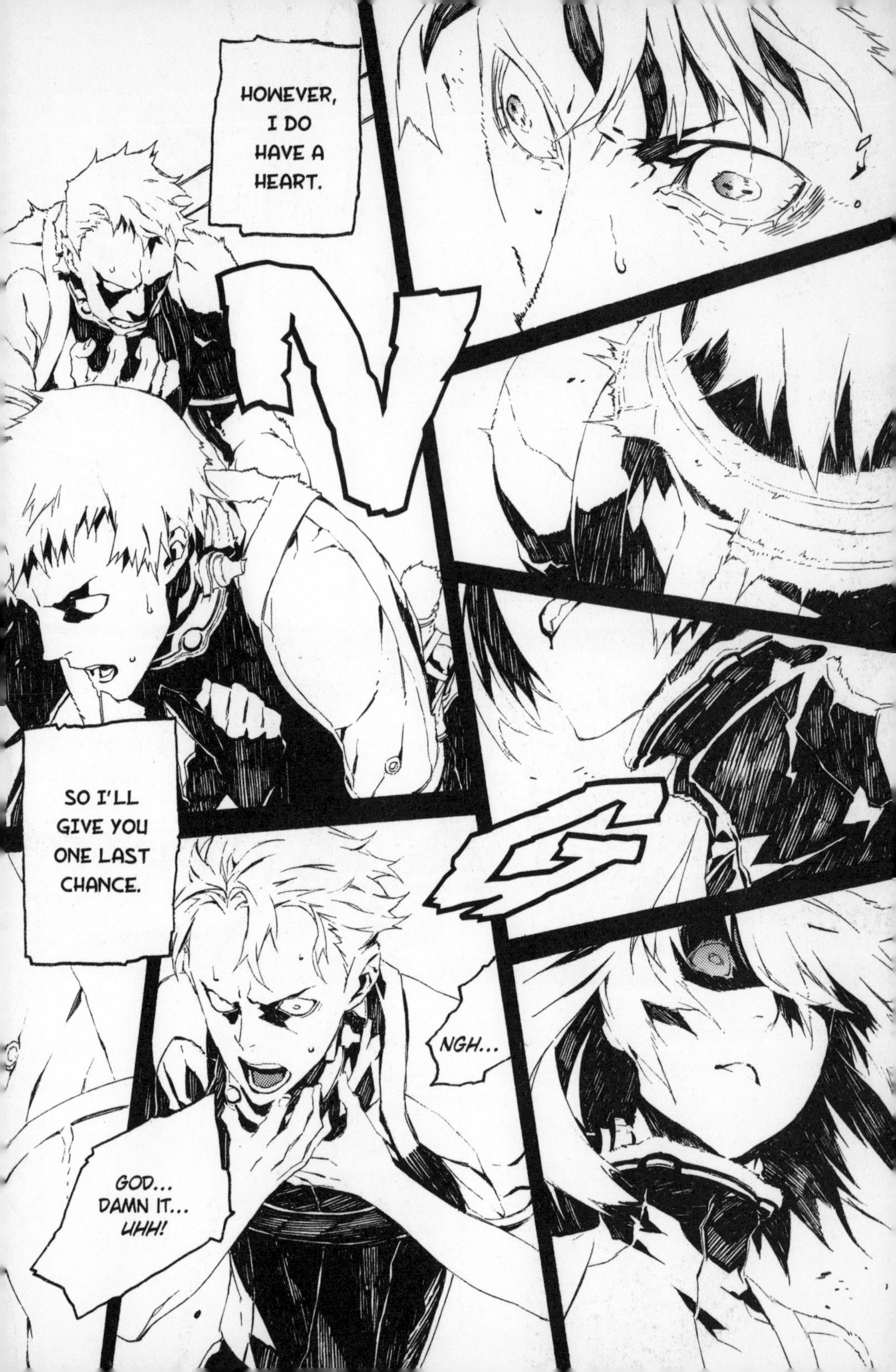
HOWEVER, I DO HAVE A HEART.
SO I'LL GIVE YOU ONE LAST CHANCE.
NGH...
GOD... DAMN IT... UHH!

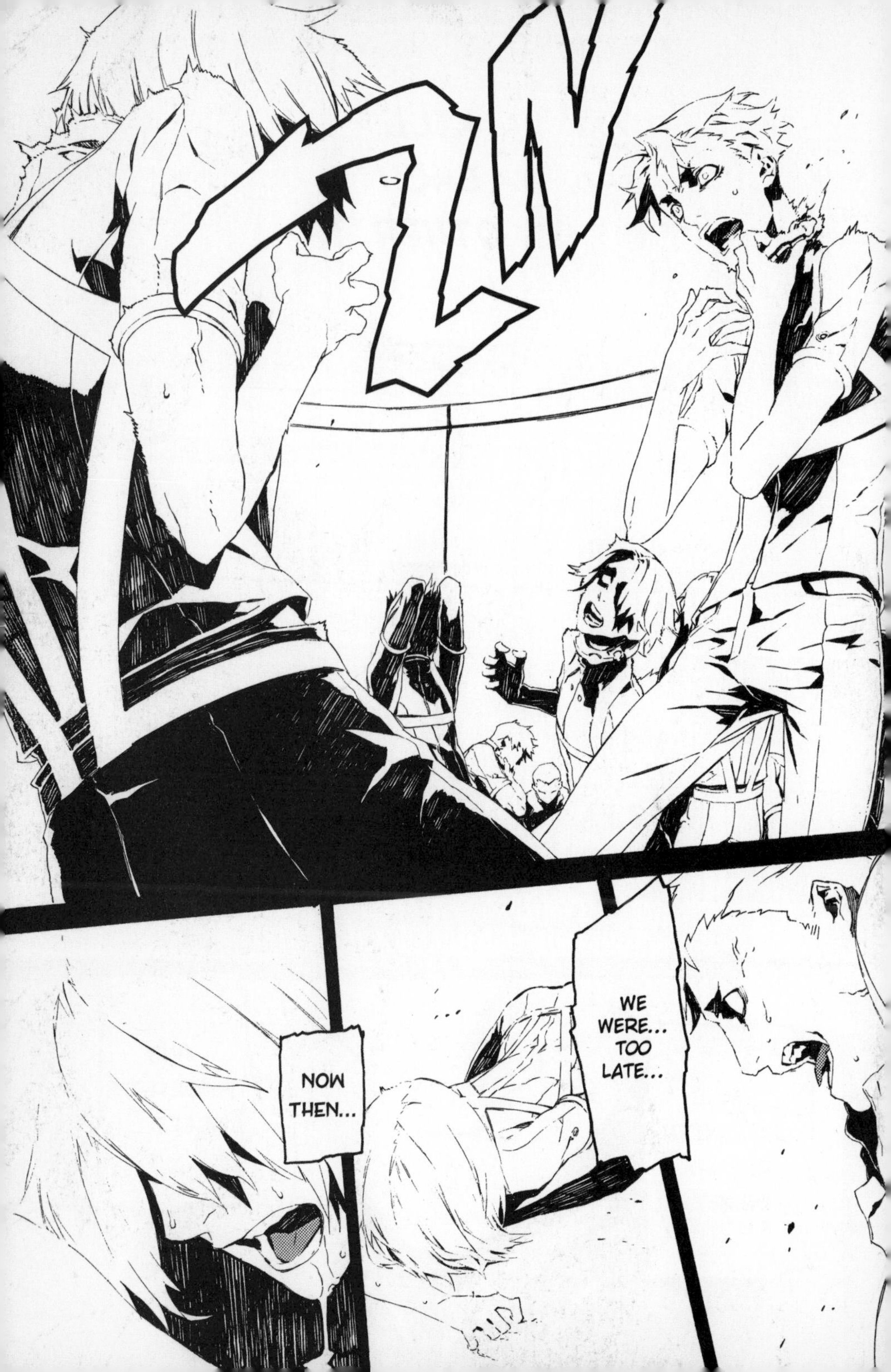
ZN
WE WERE... TOO LATE...
...
NOW THEN...

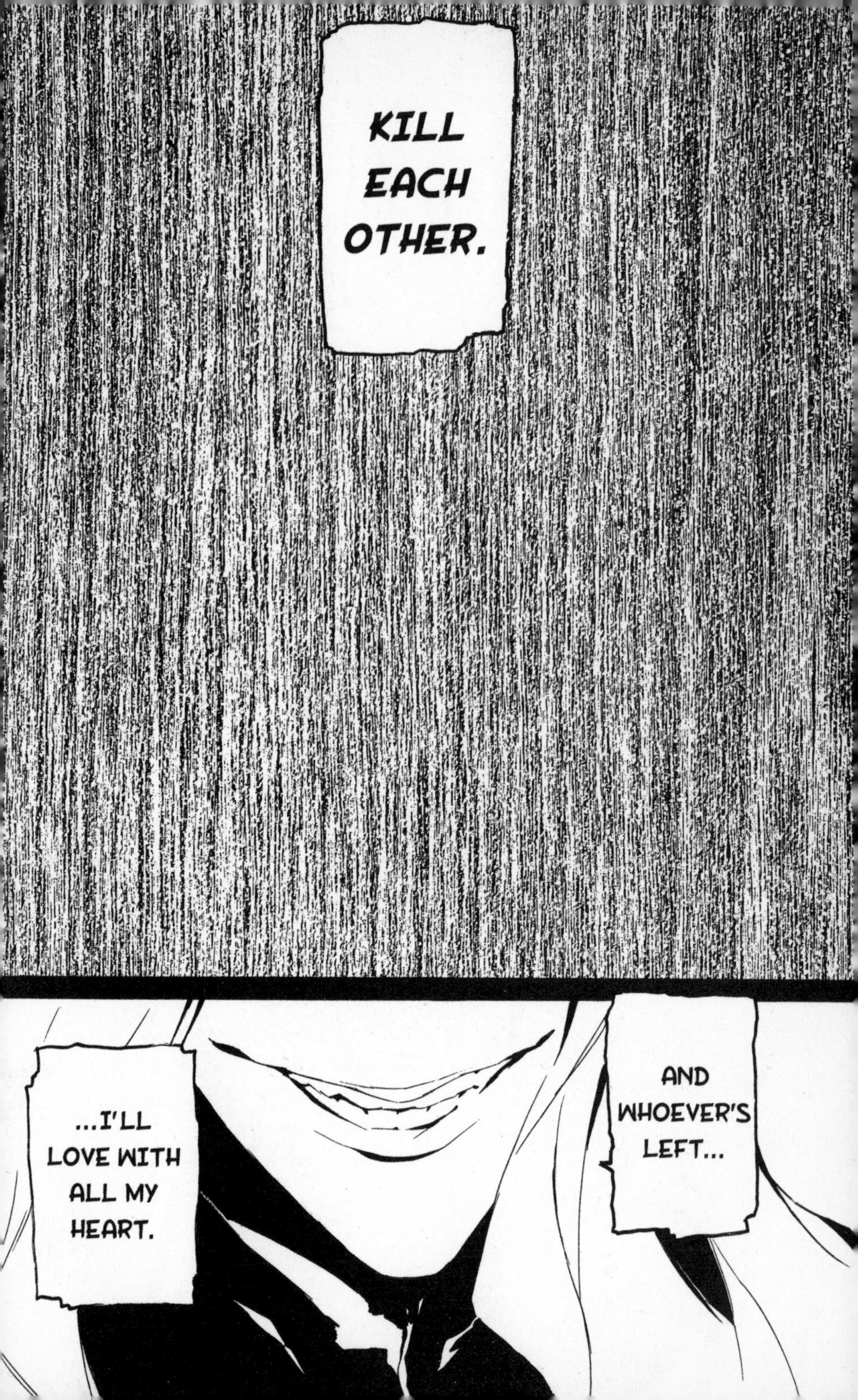
KILL EACH OTHER.
AND WHOEVER'S LEFT...
...I'LL LOVE WITH ALL MY HEART.

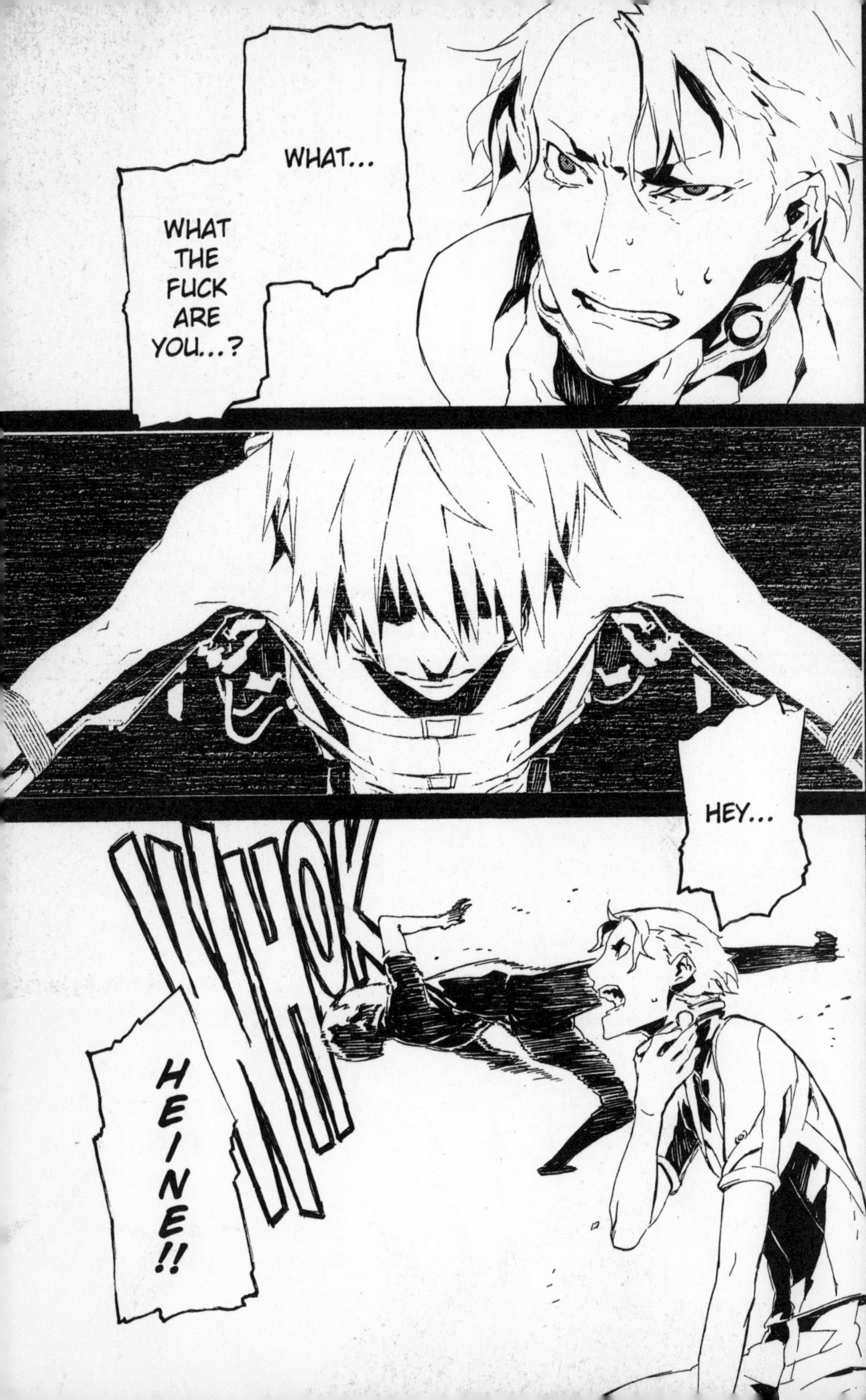
WHAT...
WHAT THE FUCK ARE YOU...?
HEY...
HEINE!!

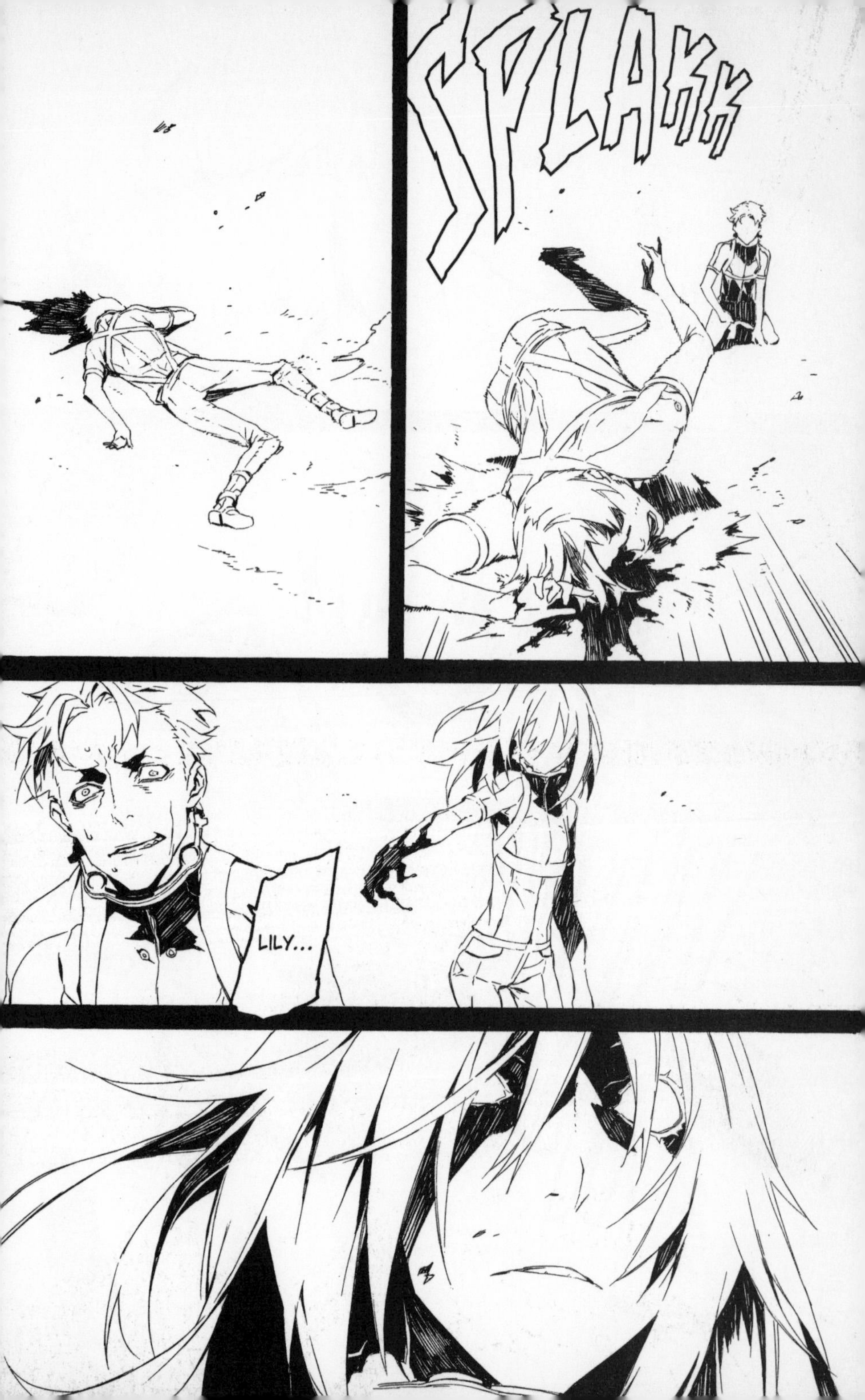
SPLAKK
LILY...

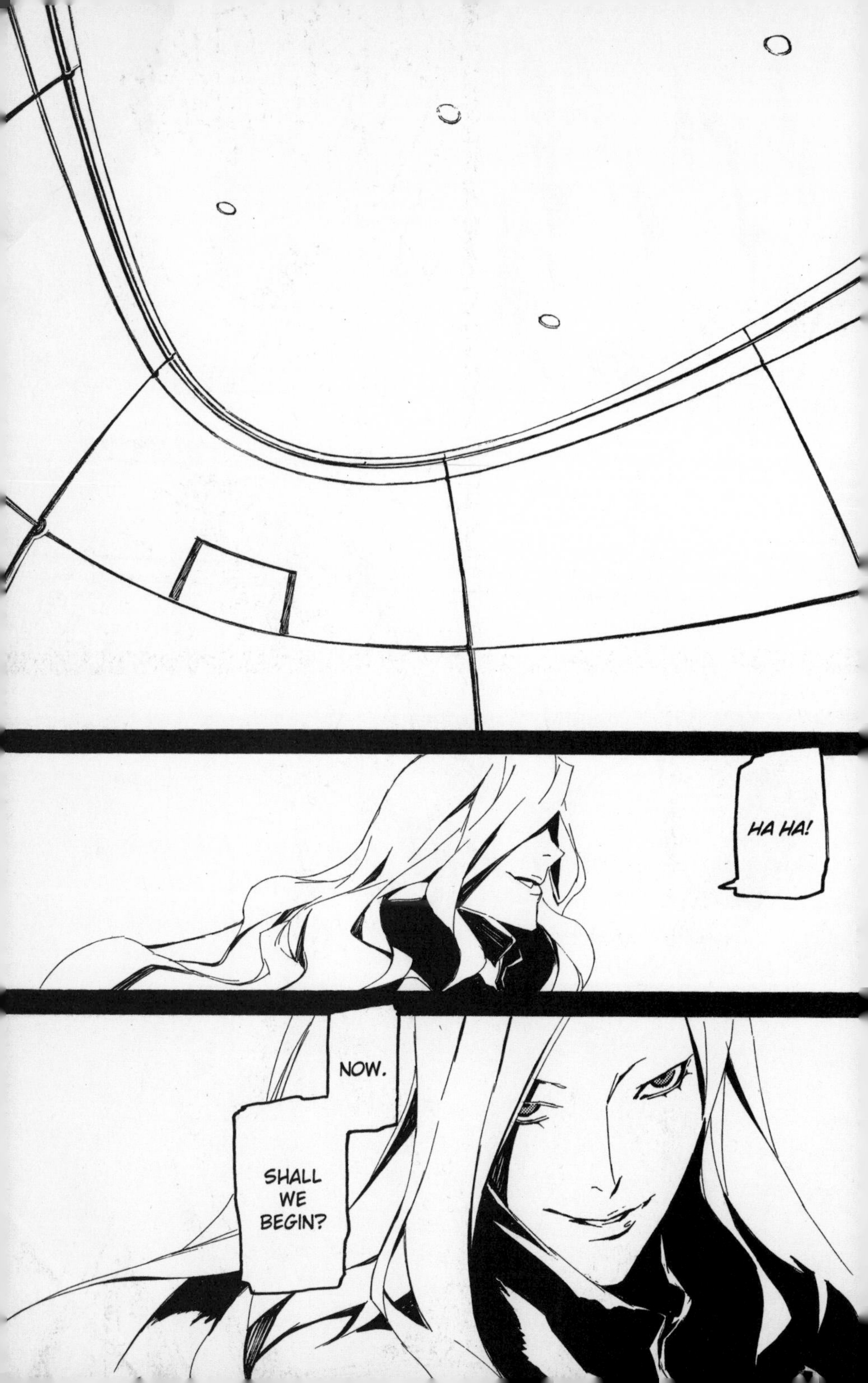
HA HA!
NOW.
SHALL WE BEGIN?

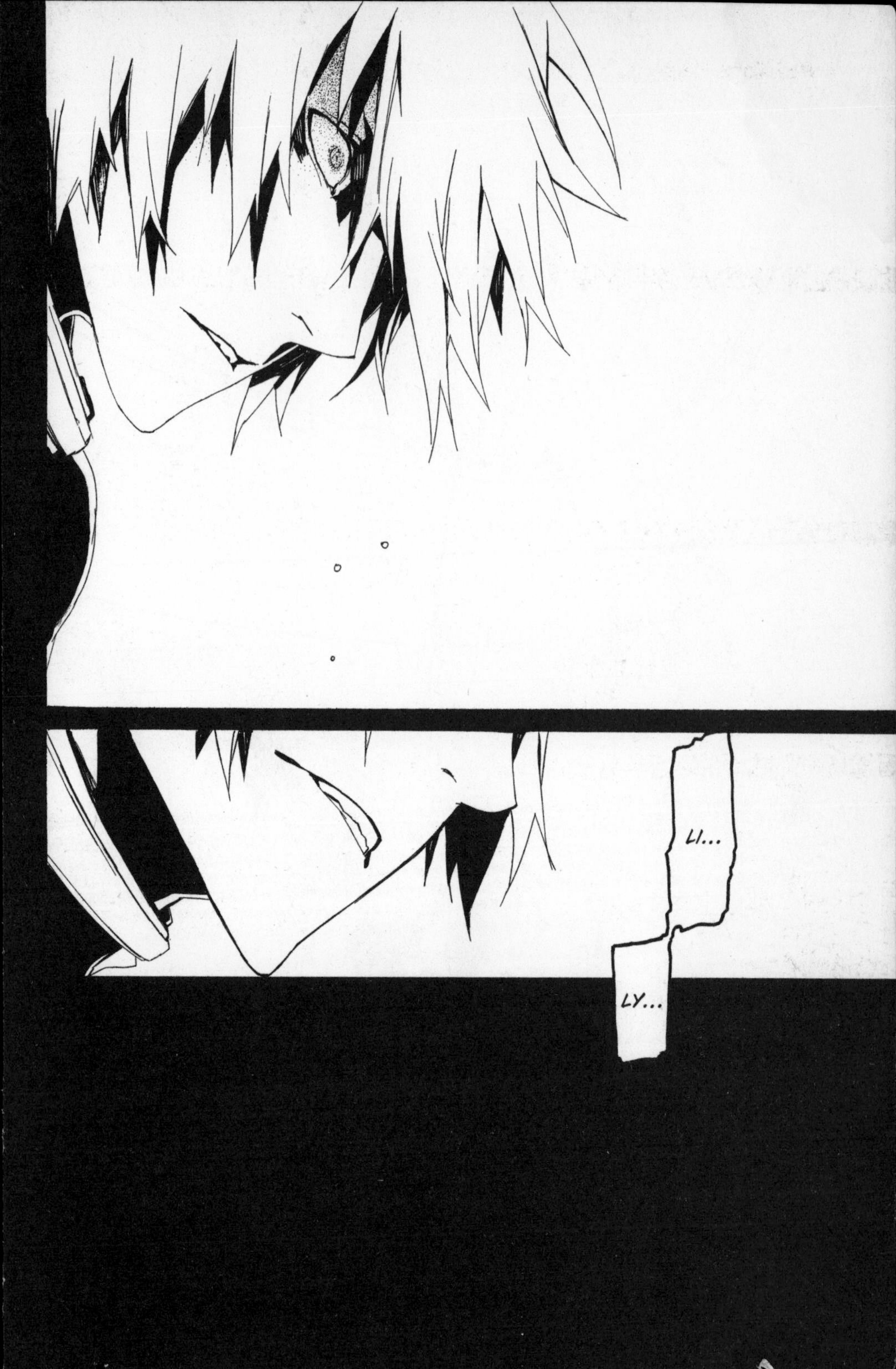
LI...
LY...

# #56 Cage & Puppies V

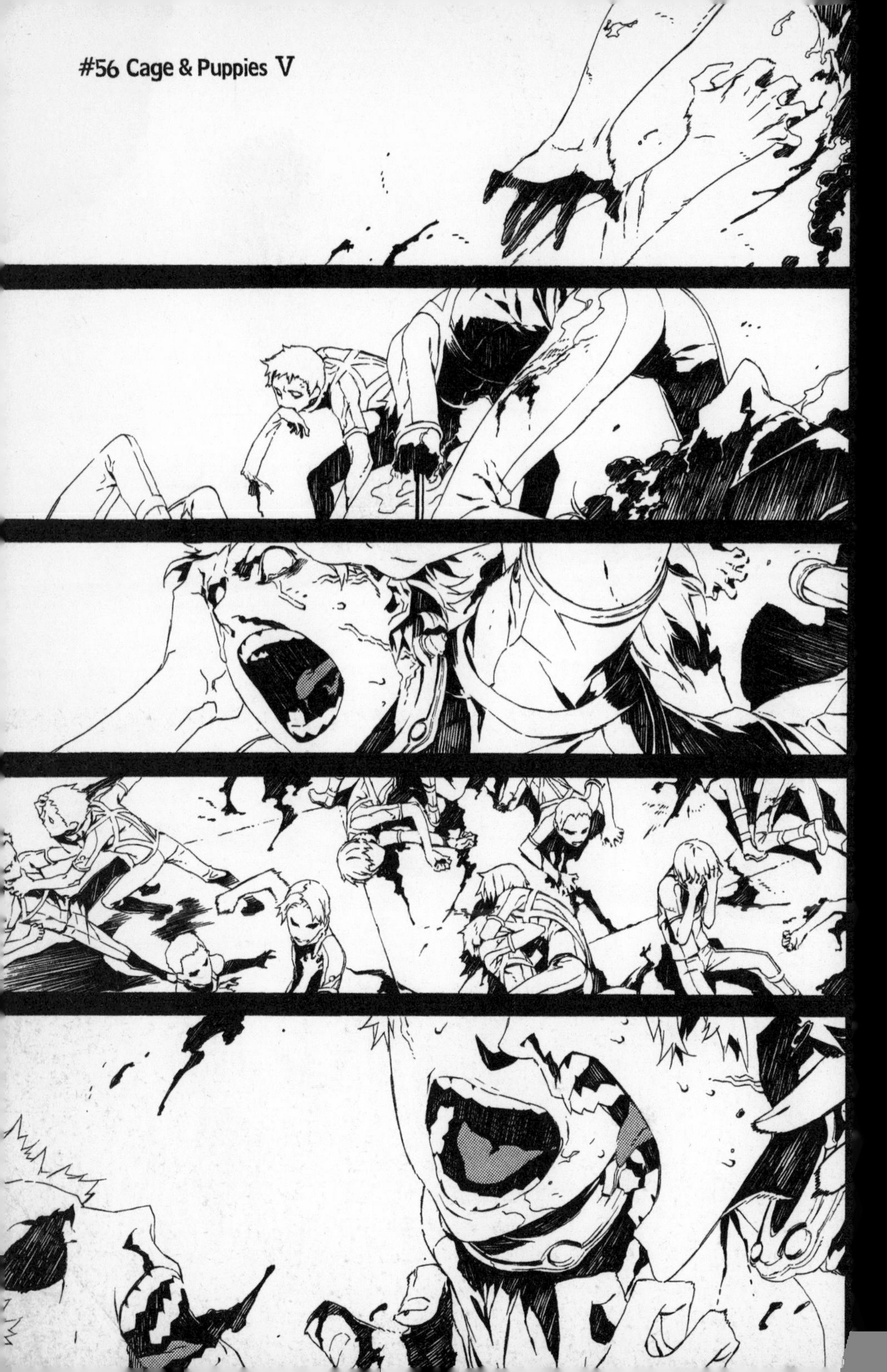

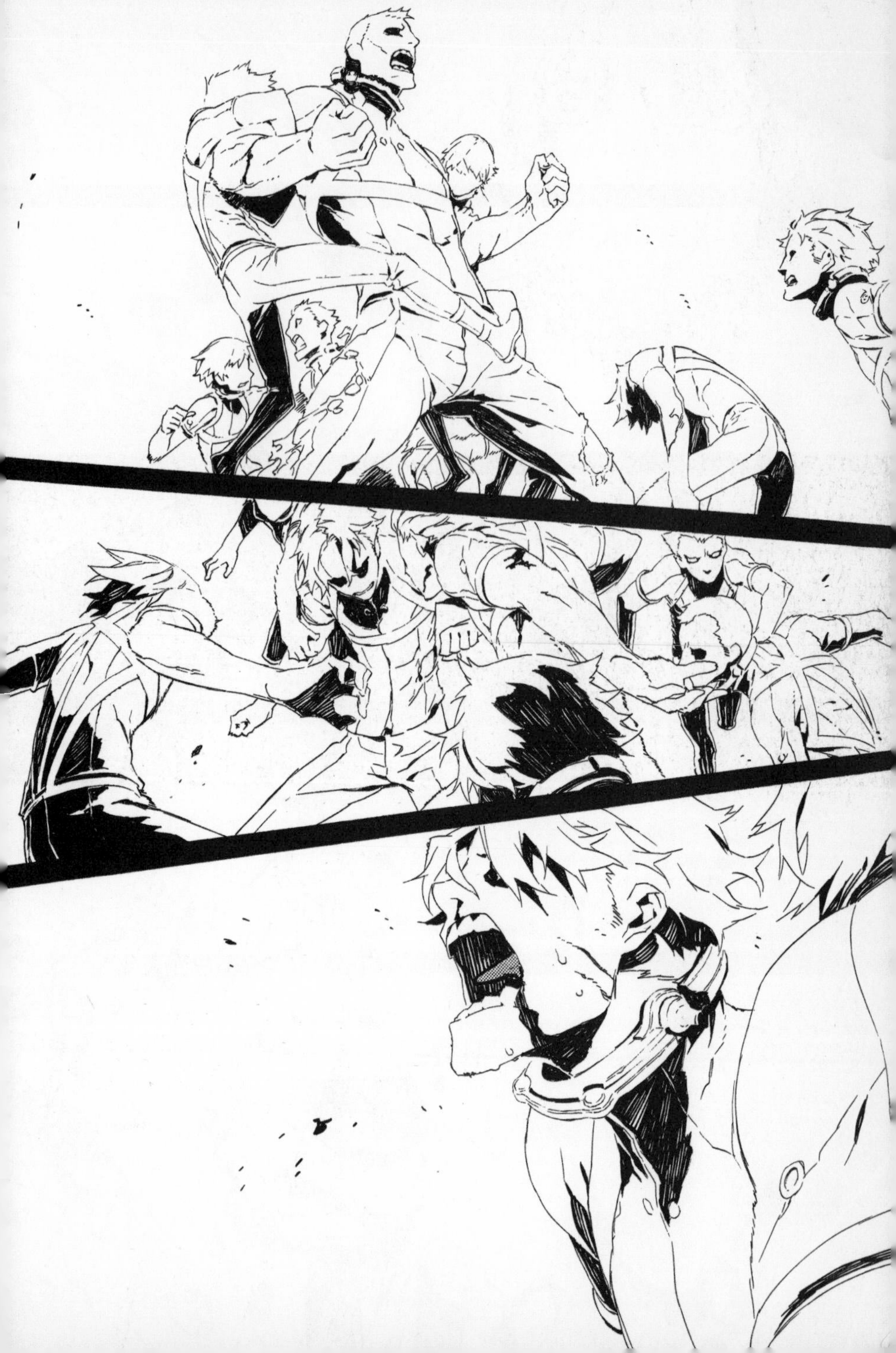

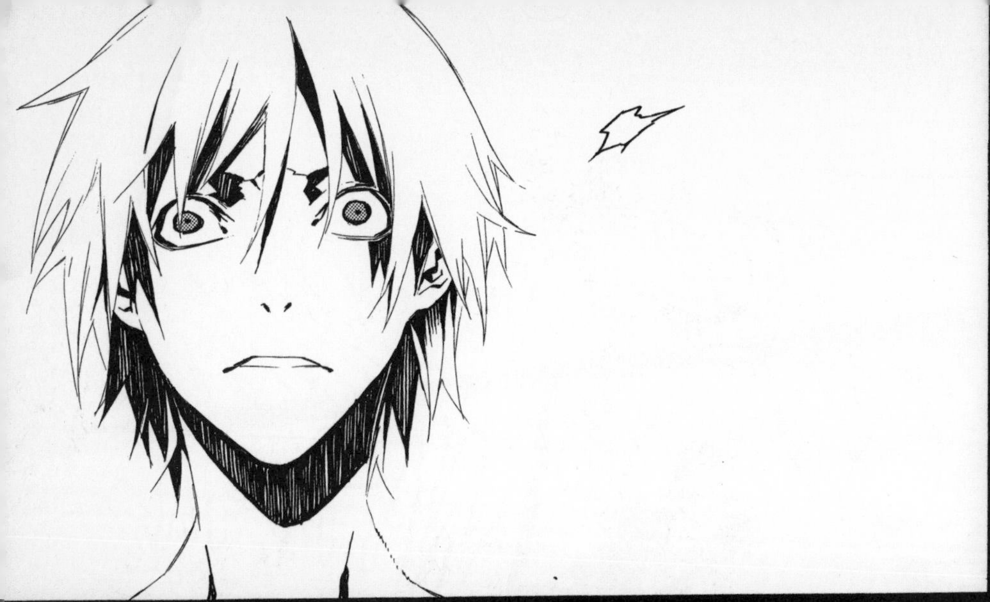

# #56 Cage & Puppies V

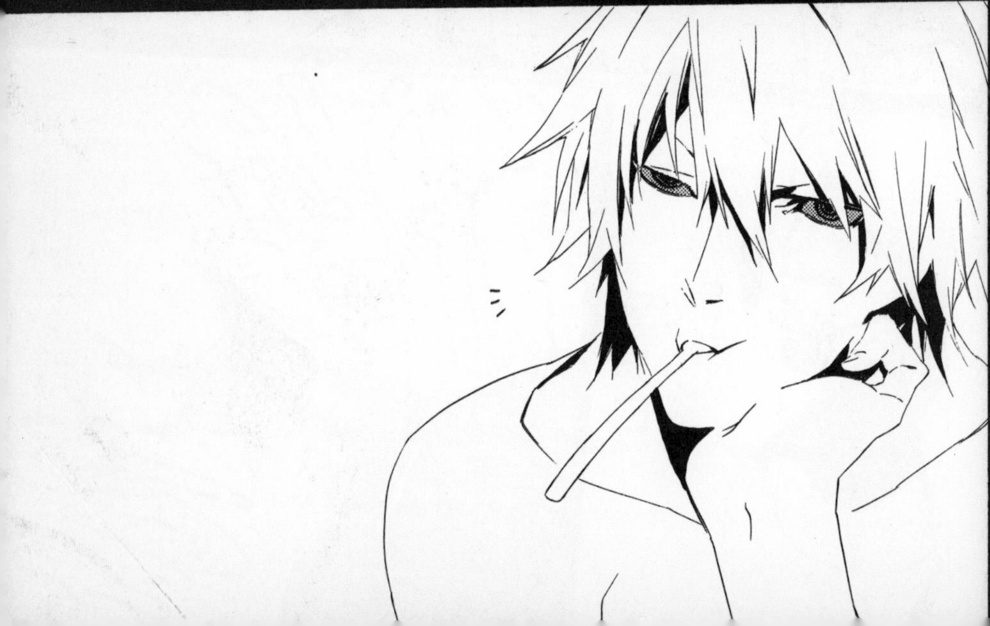

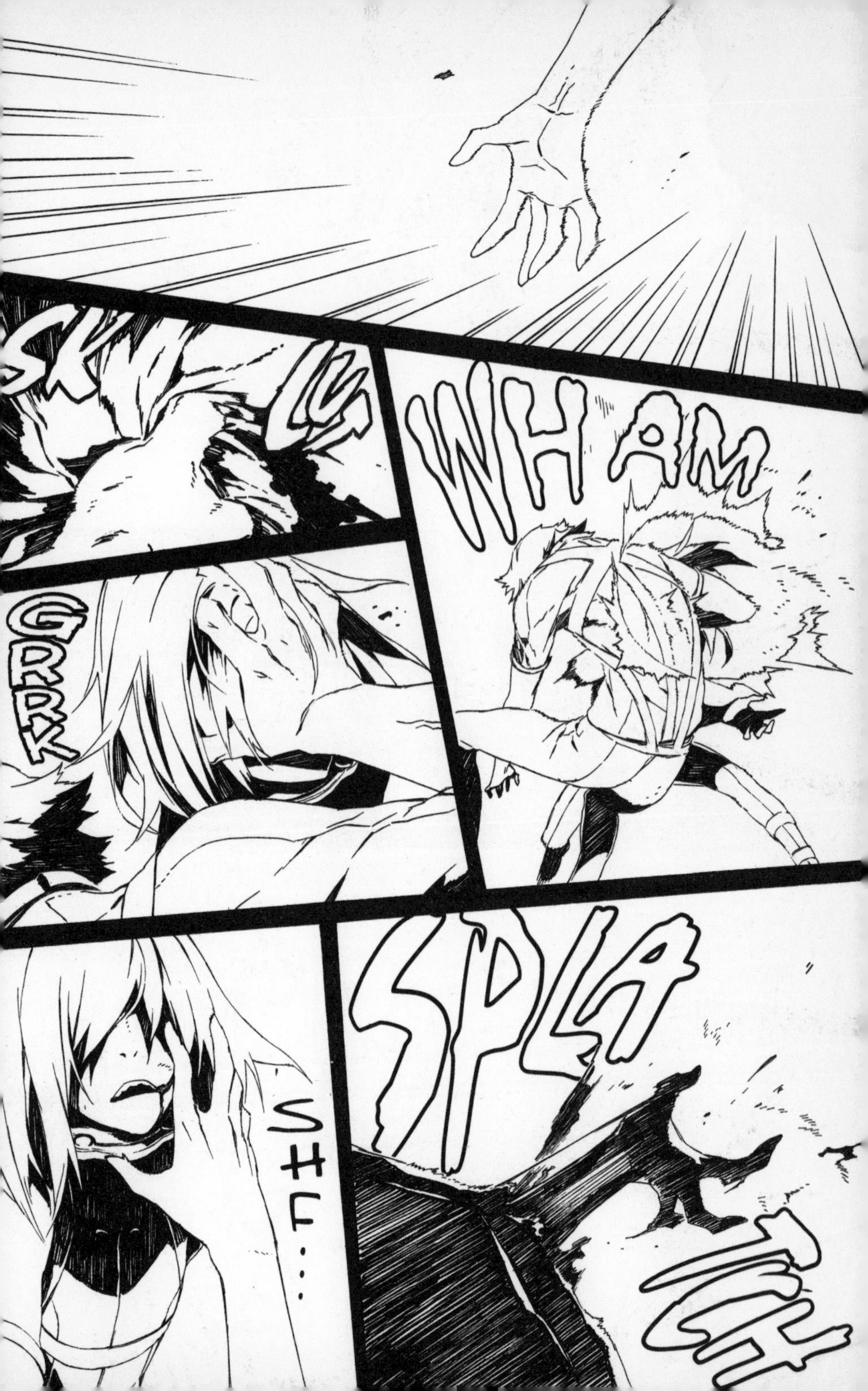
WHAM
GRRRK
SPLATCH
SHF...

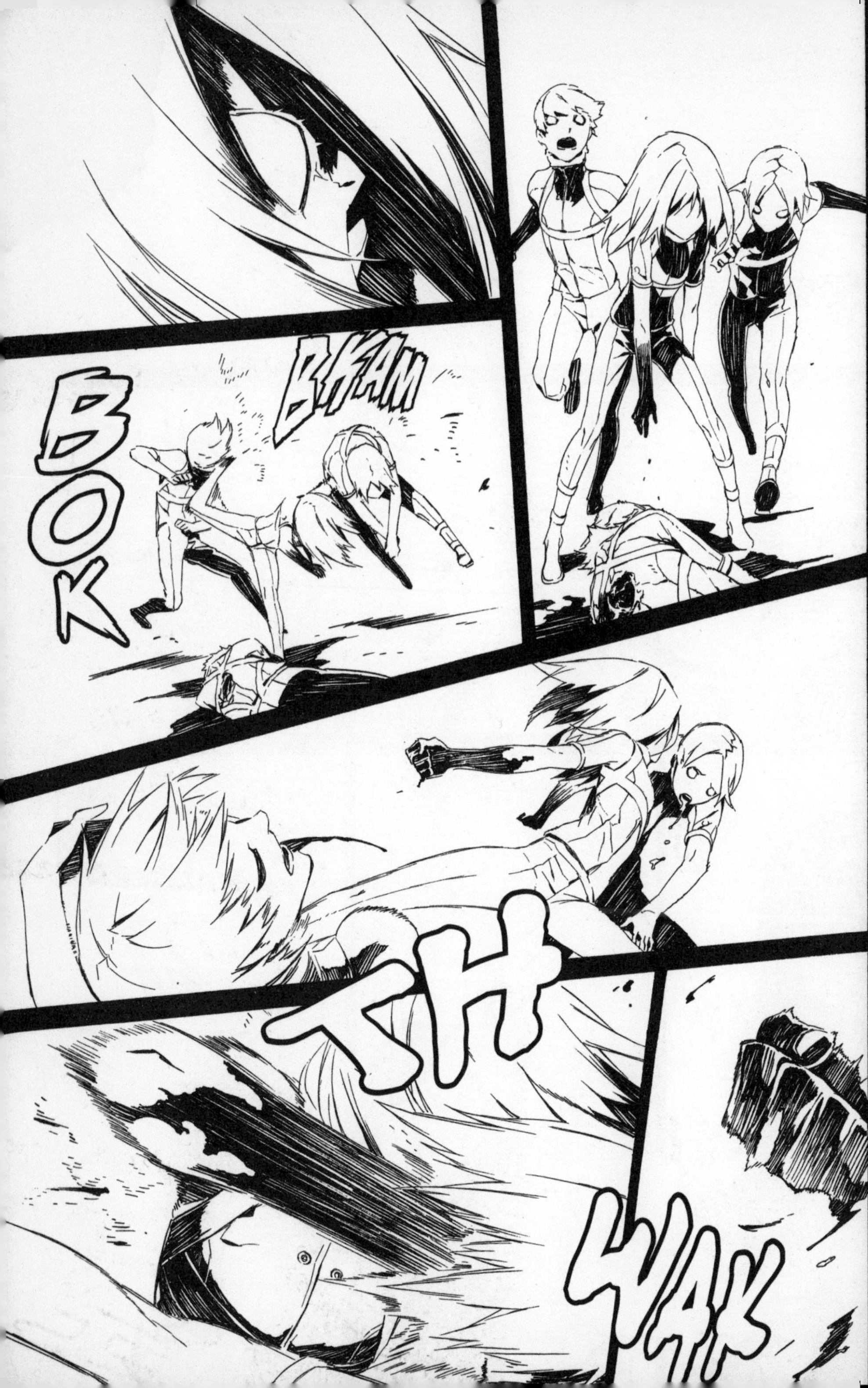
BKAM
BOK
TH
WAK

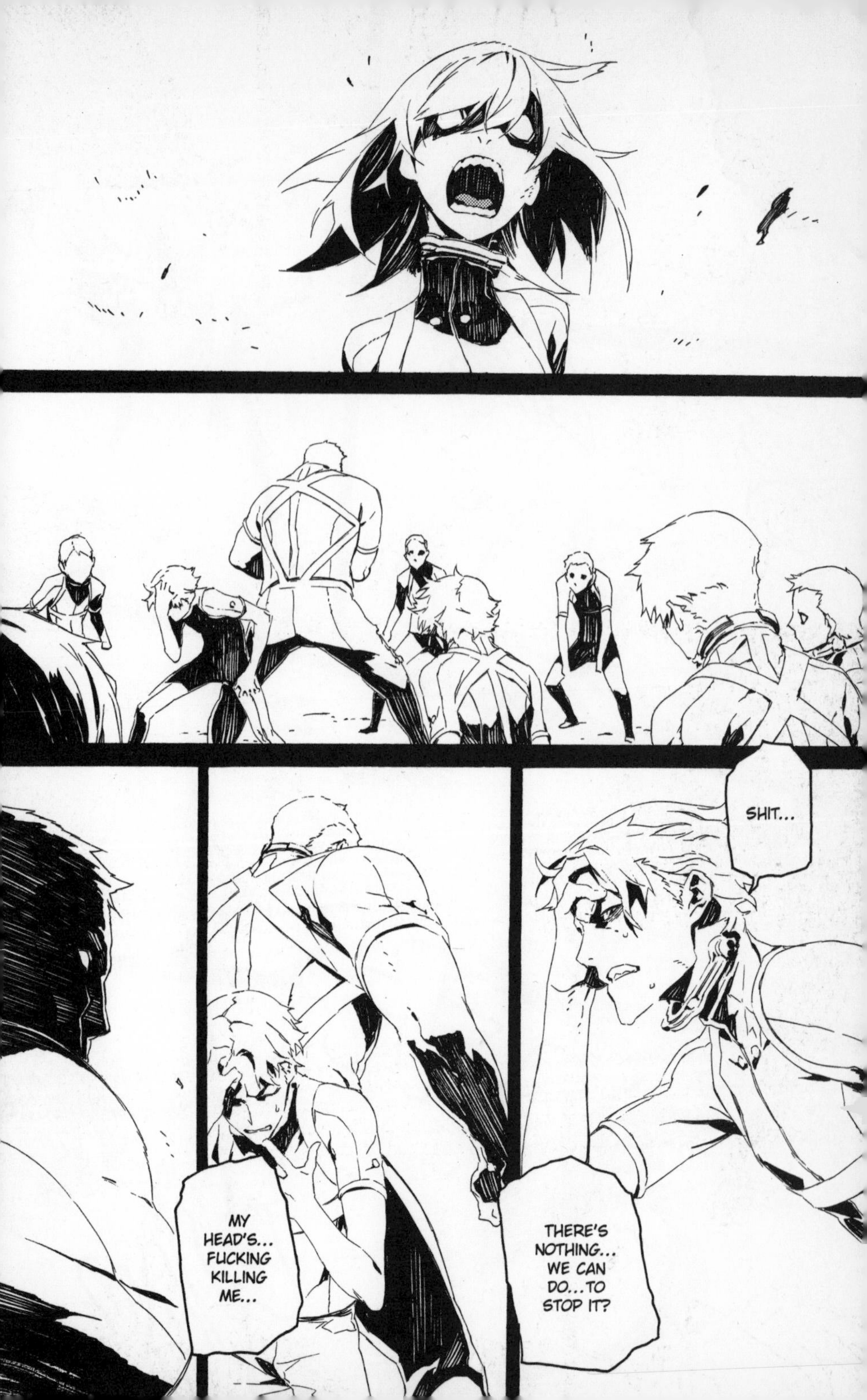
SHIT...
THERE'S NOTHING... WE CAN DO...TO STOP IT?
MY HEAD'S... FUCKING KILLING ME...

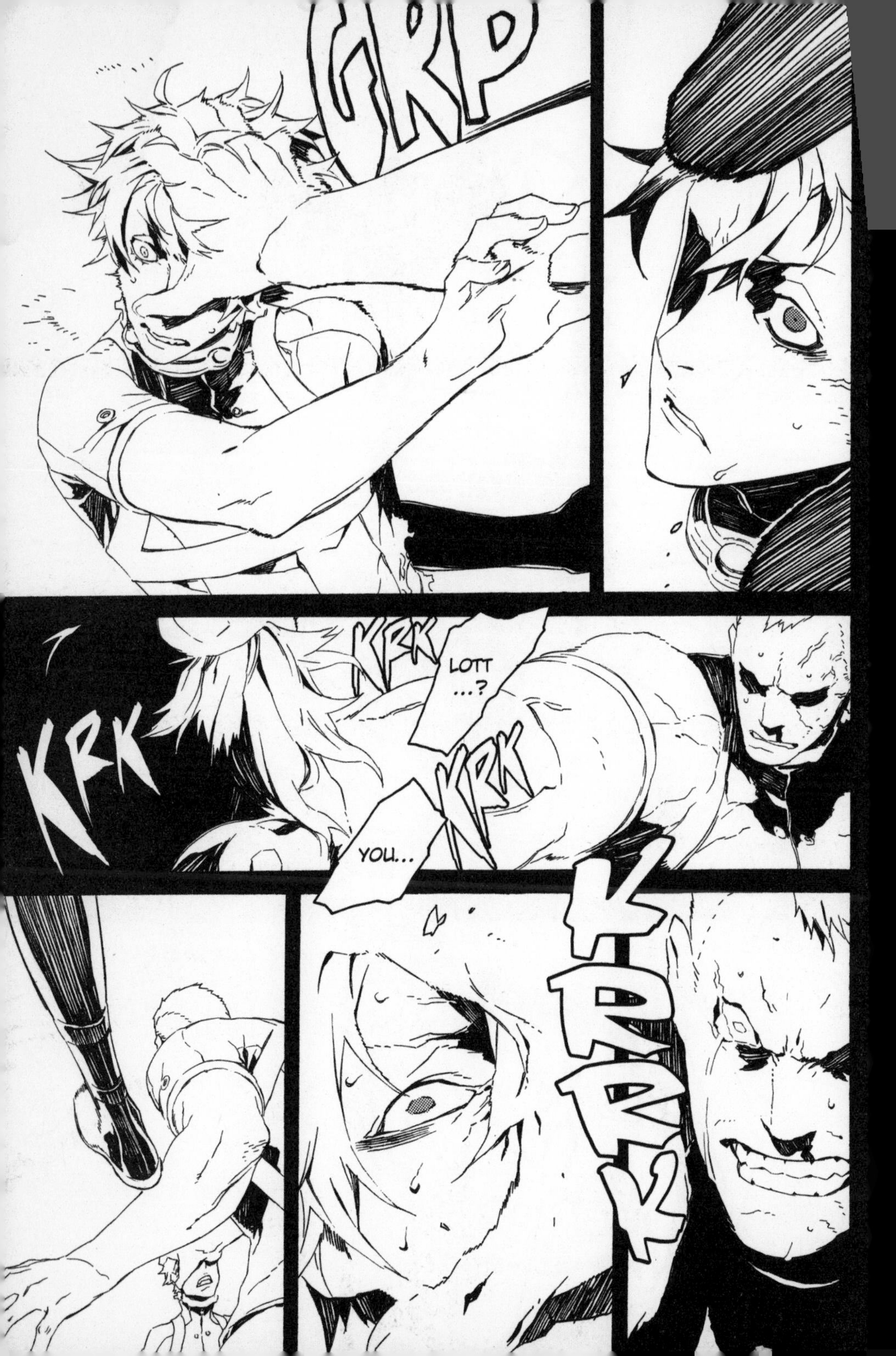
GRP
LOTT ...?
KRK
KRK
YOU...
KRK
KRRK

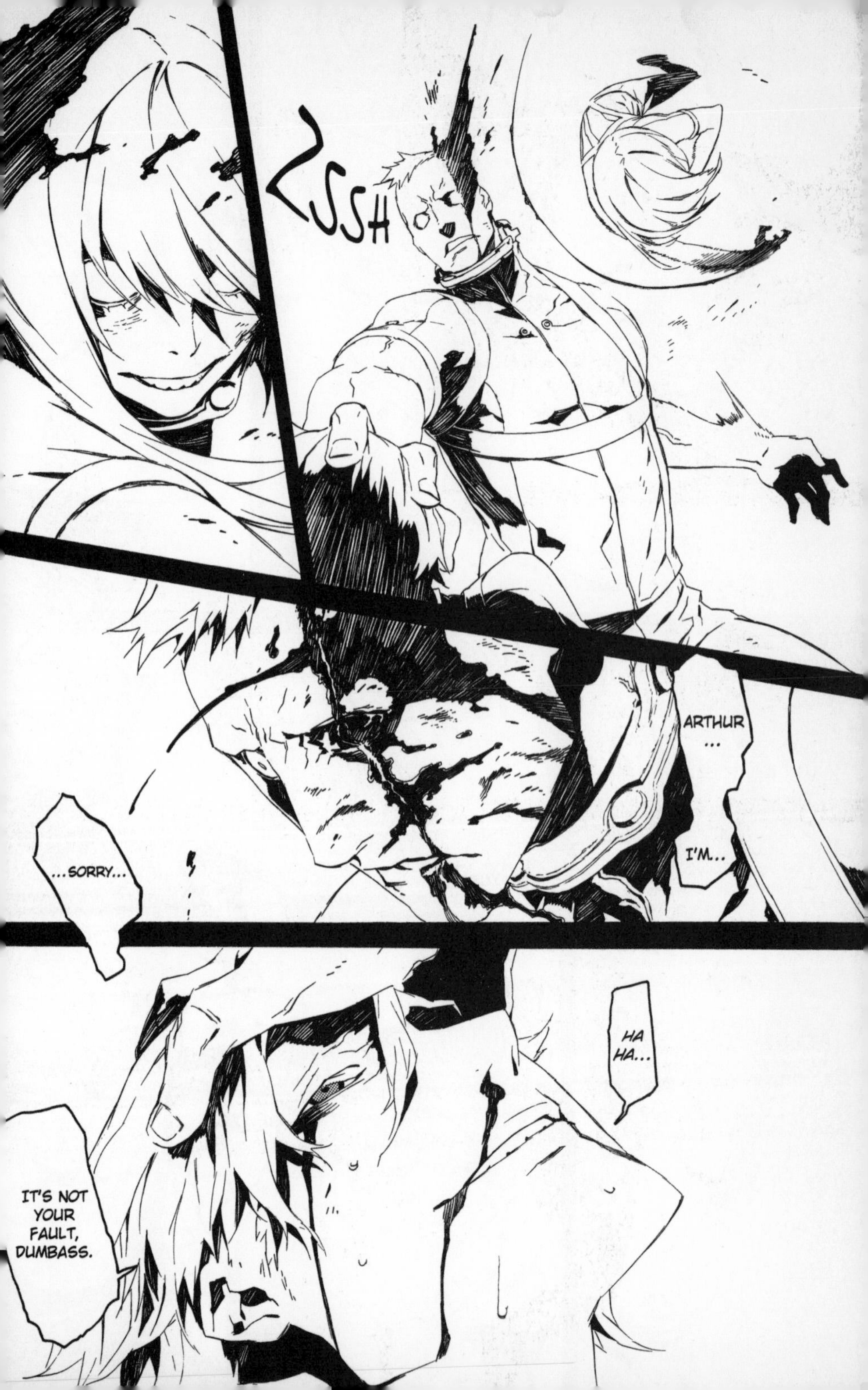
ZSSH
ARTHUR ...
I'M...
...SORRY...
HA HA...
IT'S NOT YOUR FAULT, DUMBASS.

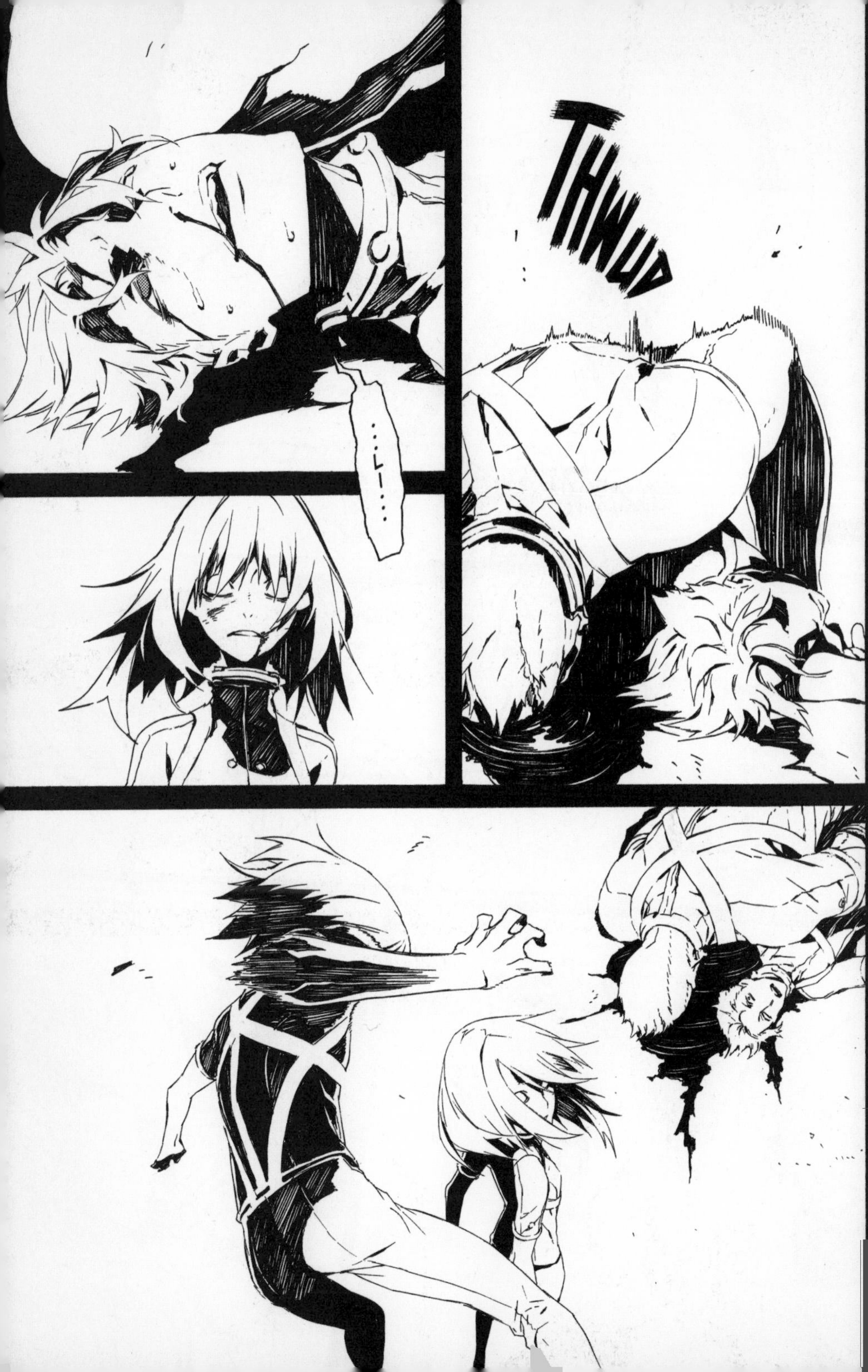
THWUD
...LI...

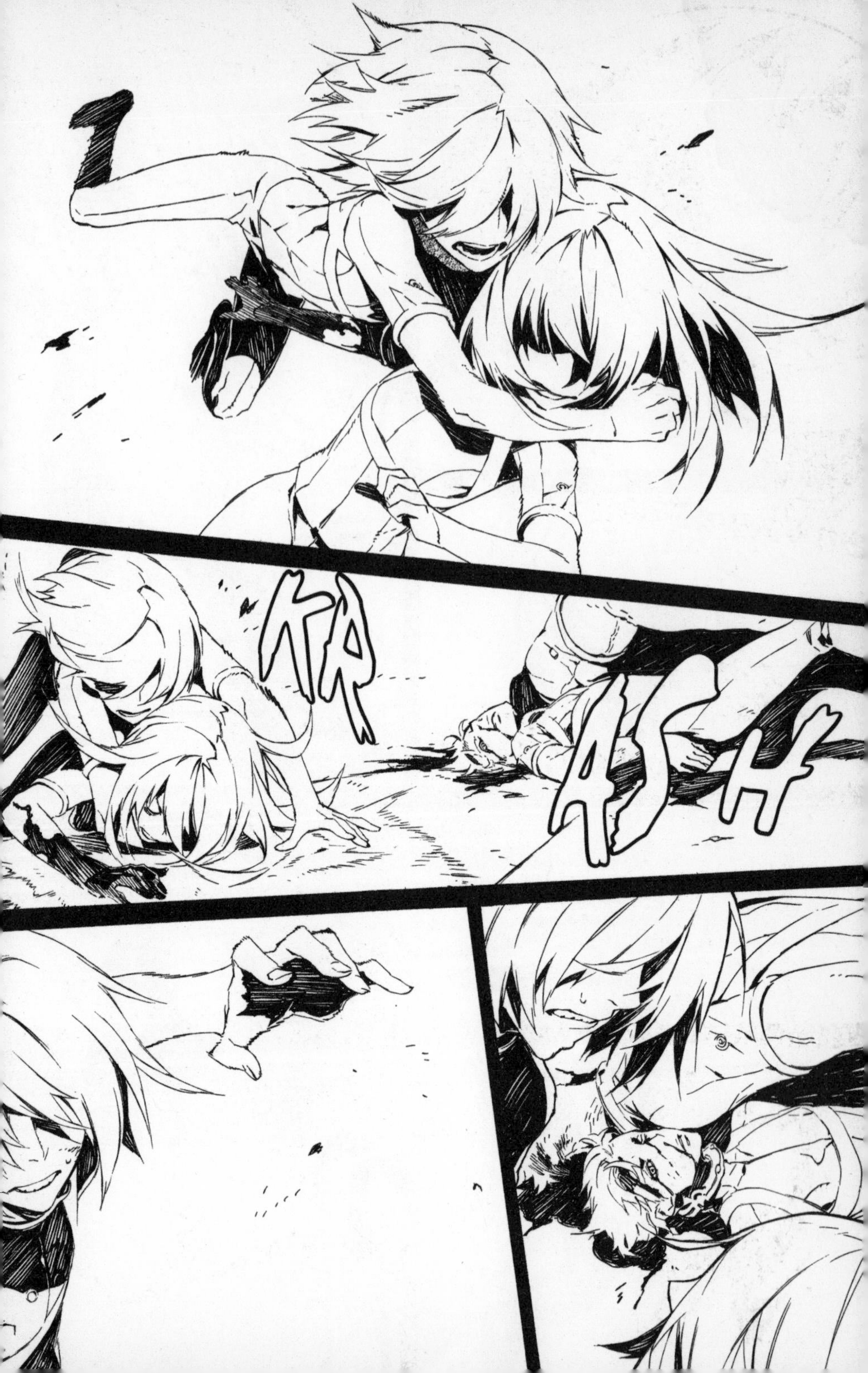
KR
ASH

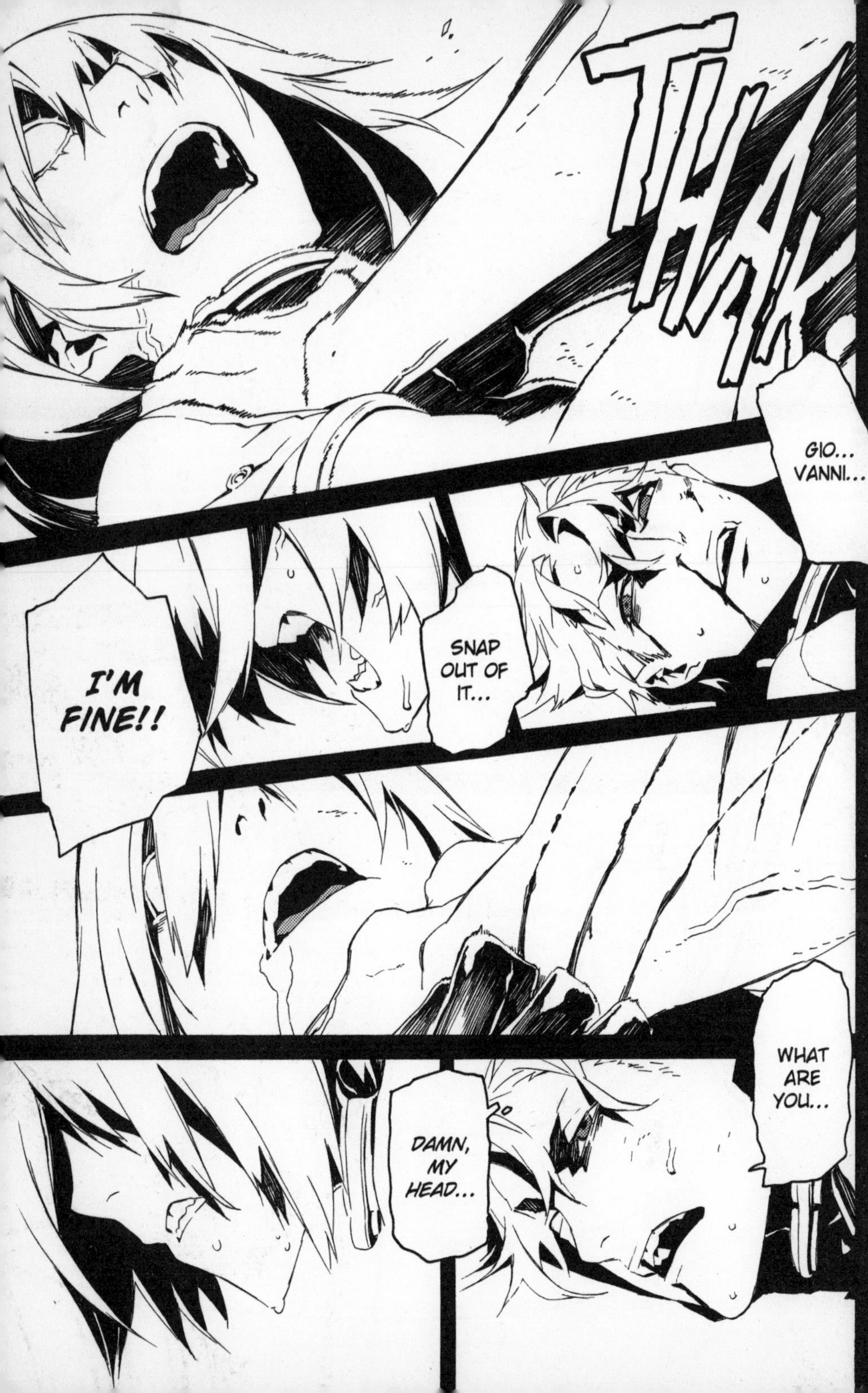
THAK
GIO... VANNI...
SNAP OUT OF IT...
I'M FINE!!
WHAT ARE YOU...
DAMN, MY HEAD...

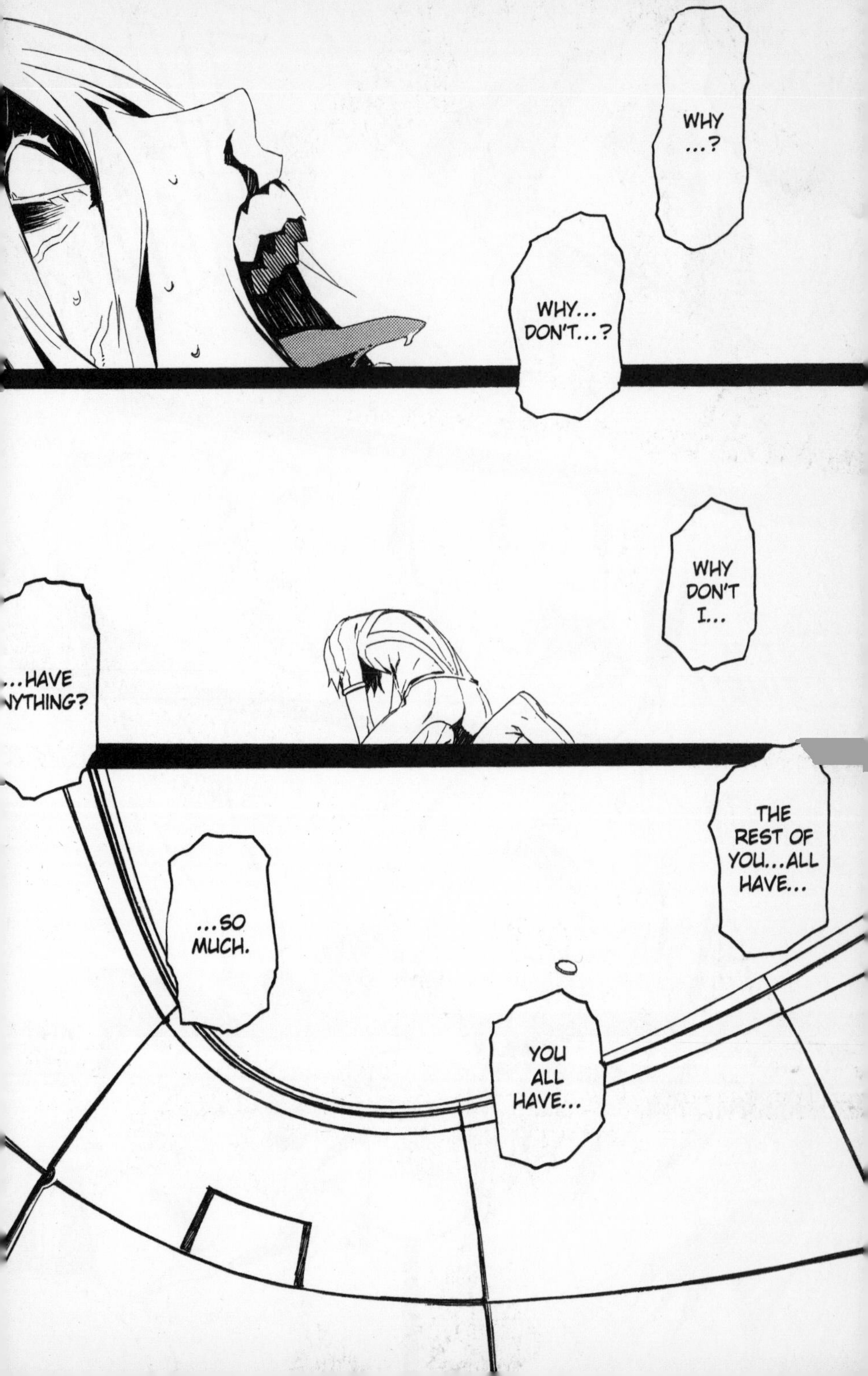
WHY ...?
WHY... DON'T...?
WHY DON'T I...
...HAVE NYTHING?
THE REST OF YOU...ALL HAVE...
YOU ALL HAVE...
...SO MUCH.

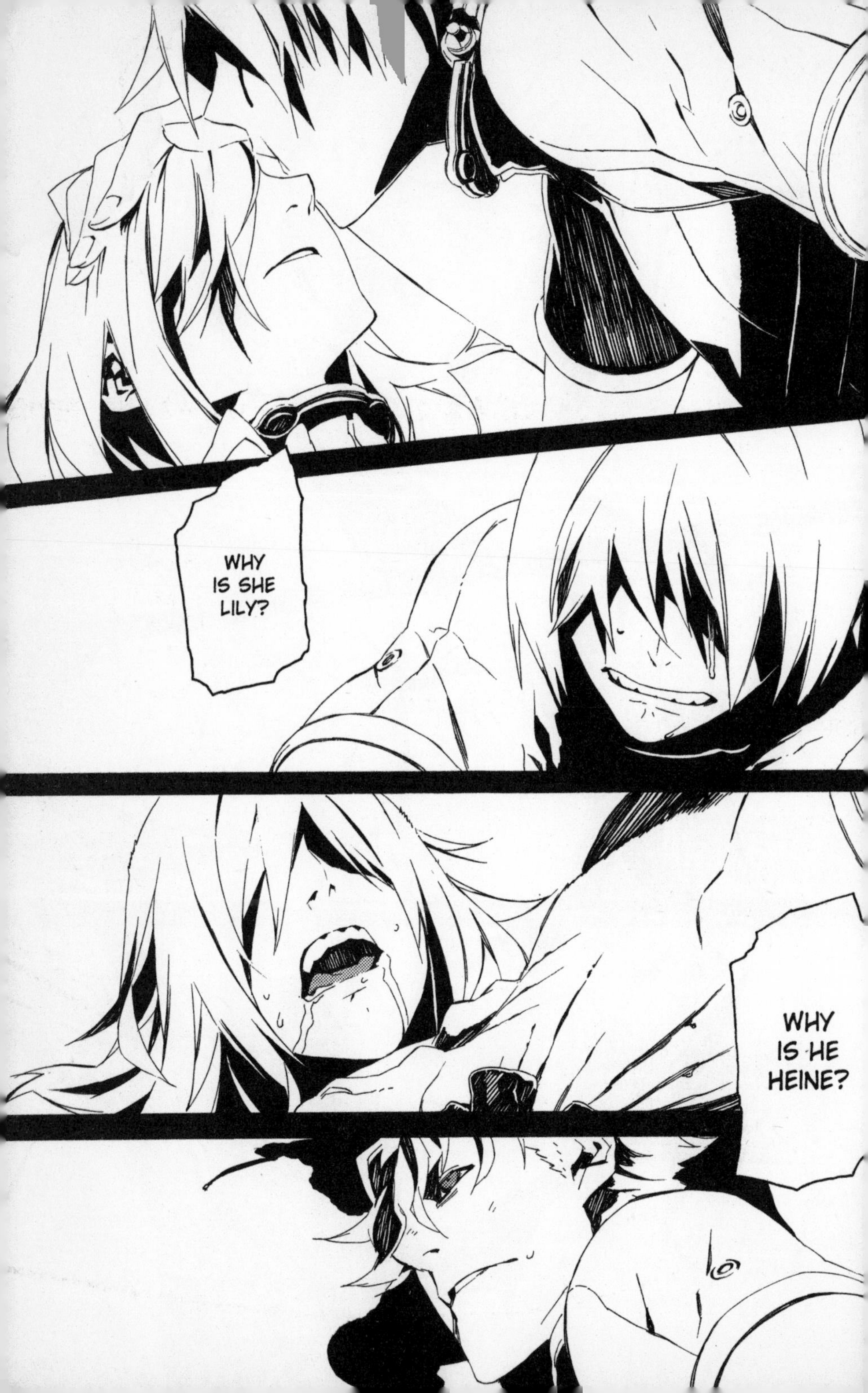
WHY IS SHE LILY?
WHY IS HE HEINE?

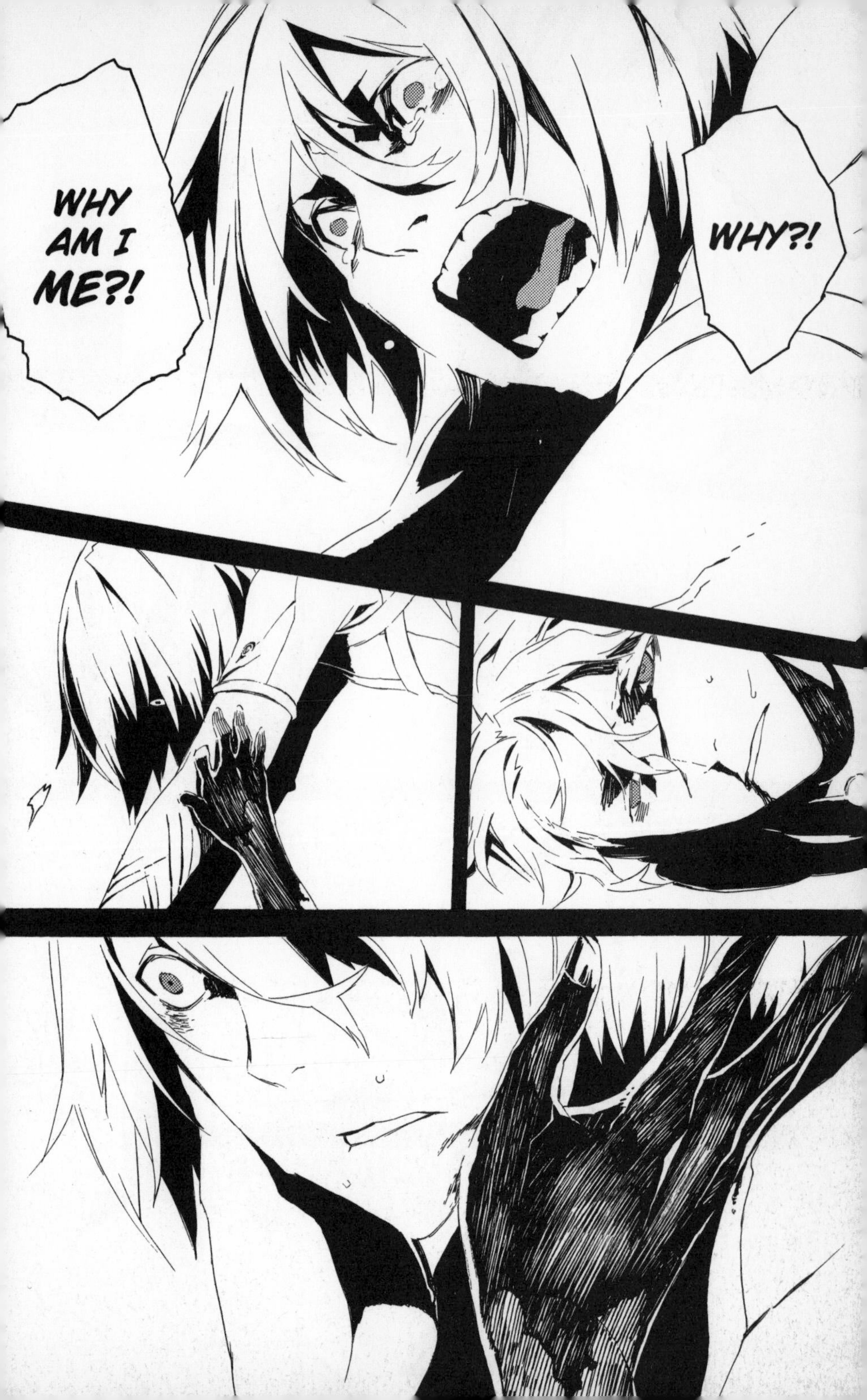
WHY?!
WHY AM I ME?!

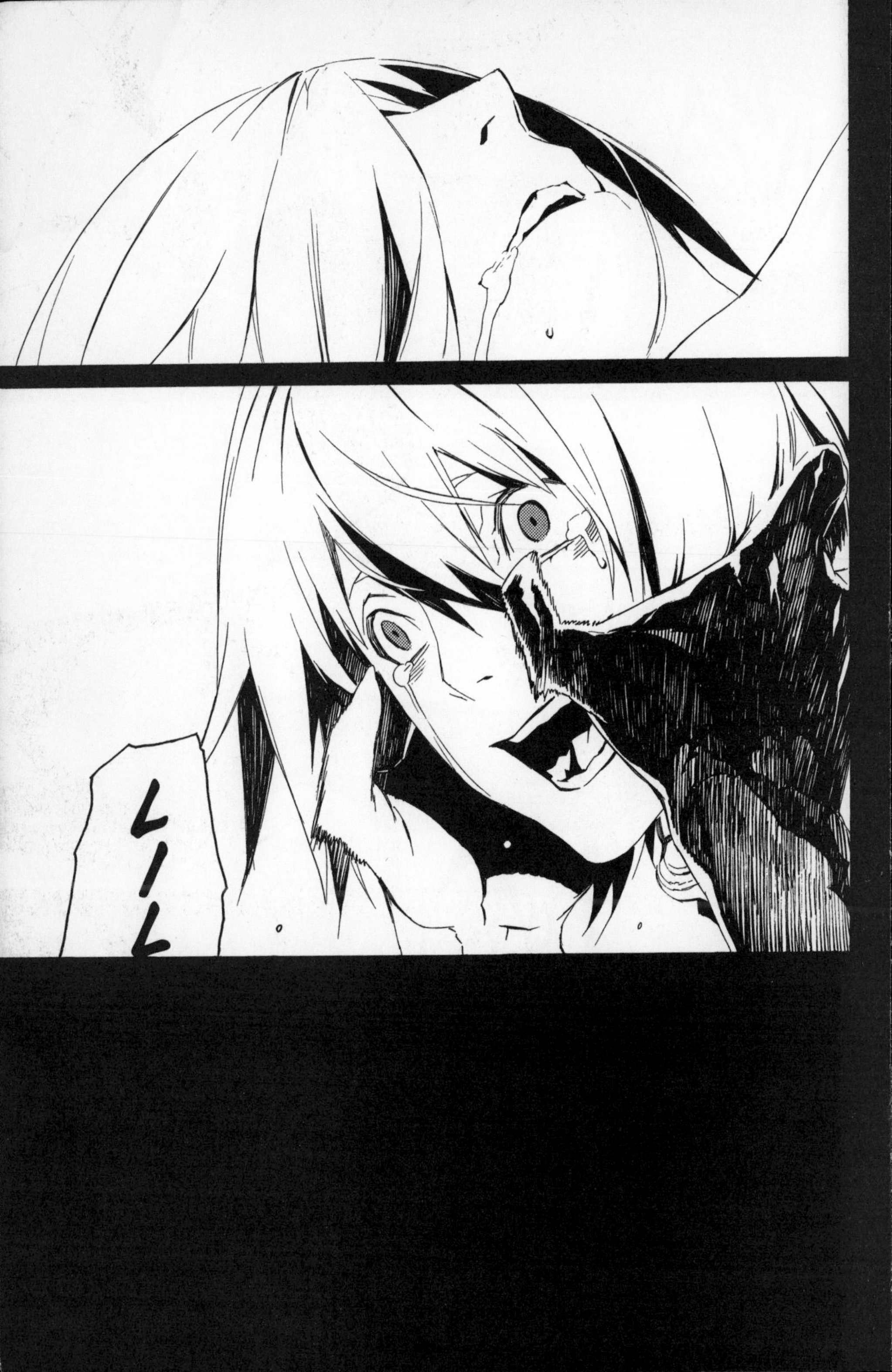

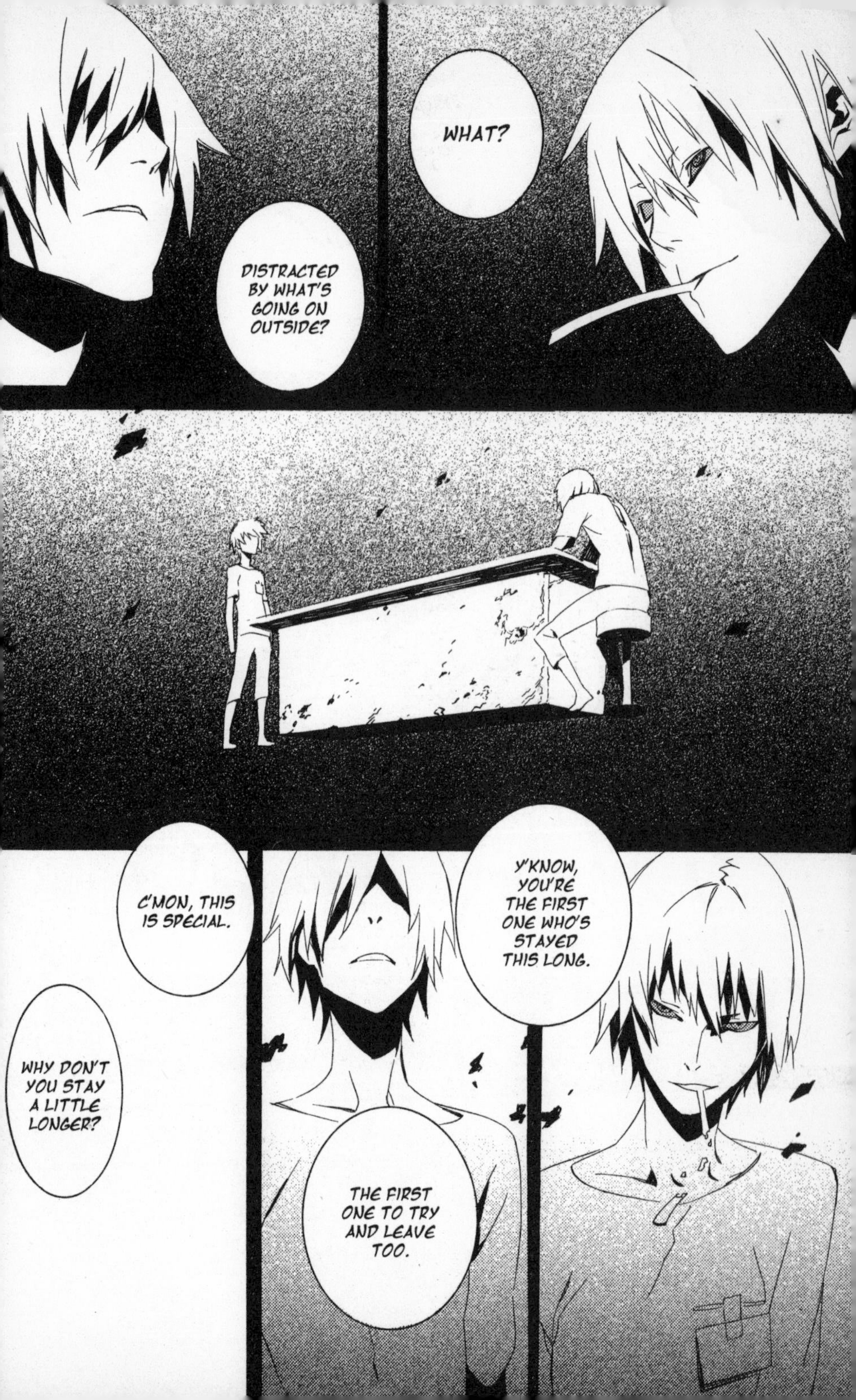
WHAT?
DISTRACTED BY WHAT'S GOING ON OUTSIDE?
Y'KNOW, YOU'RE THE FIRST ONE WHO'S STAYED THIS LONG.
THE FIRST ONE TO TRY AND LEAVE TOO.
C'MON, THIS IS SPECIAL.
WHY DON'T YOU STAY A LITTLE LONGER?

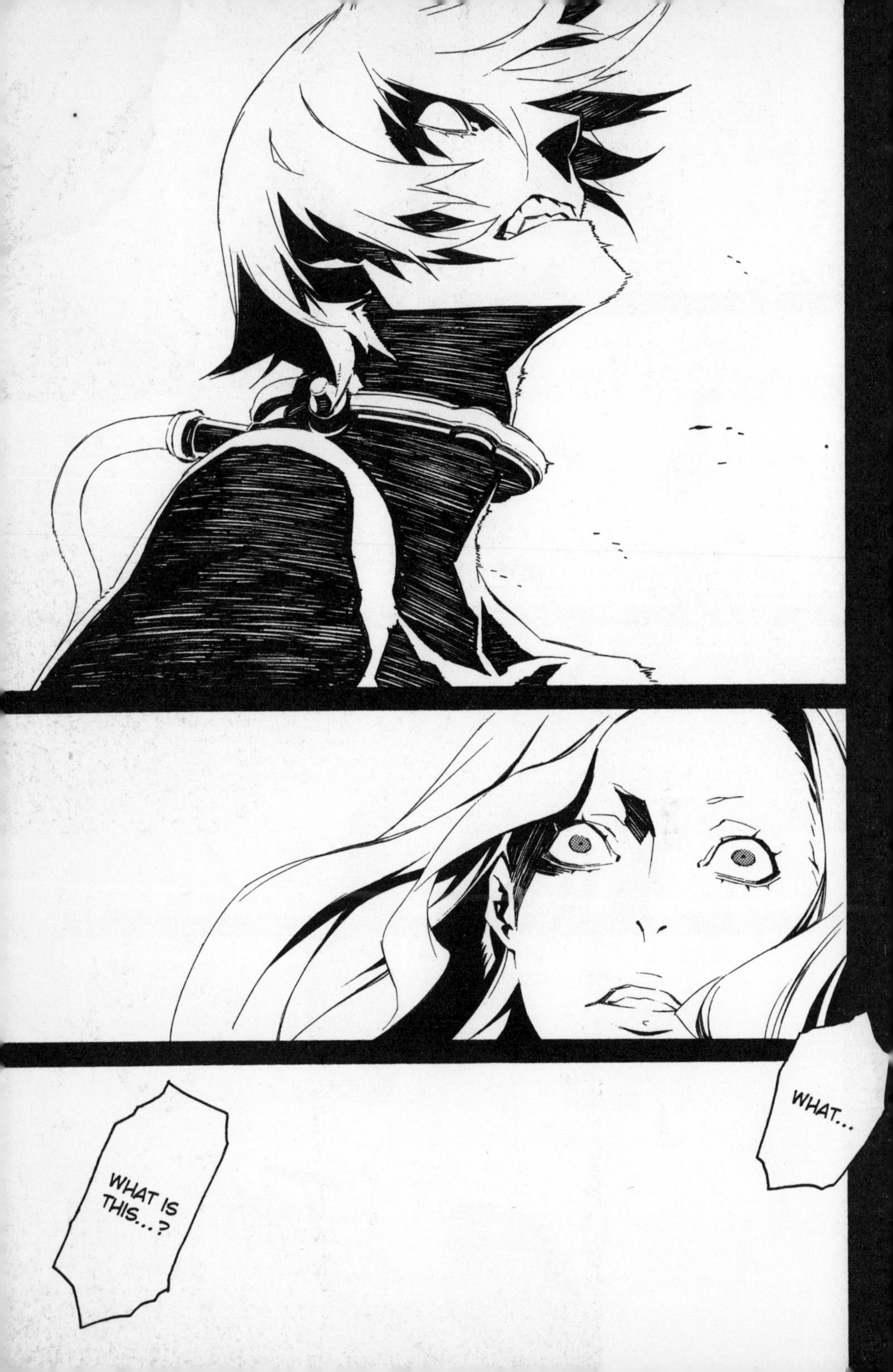
WHAT...
WHAT IS THIS...?

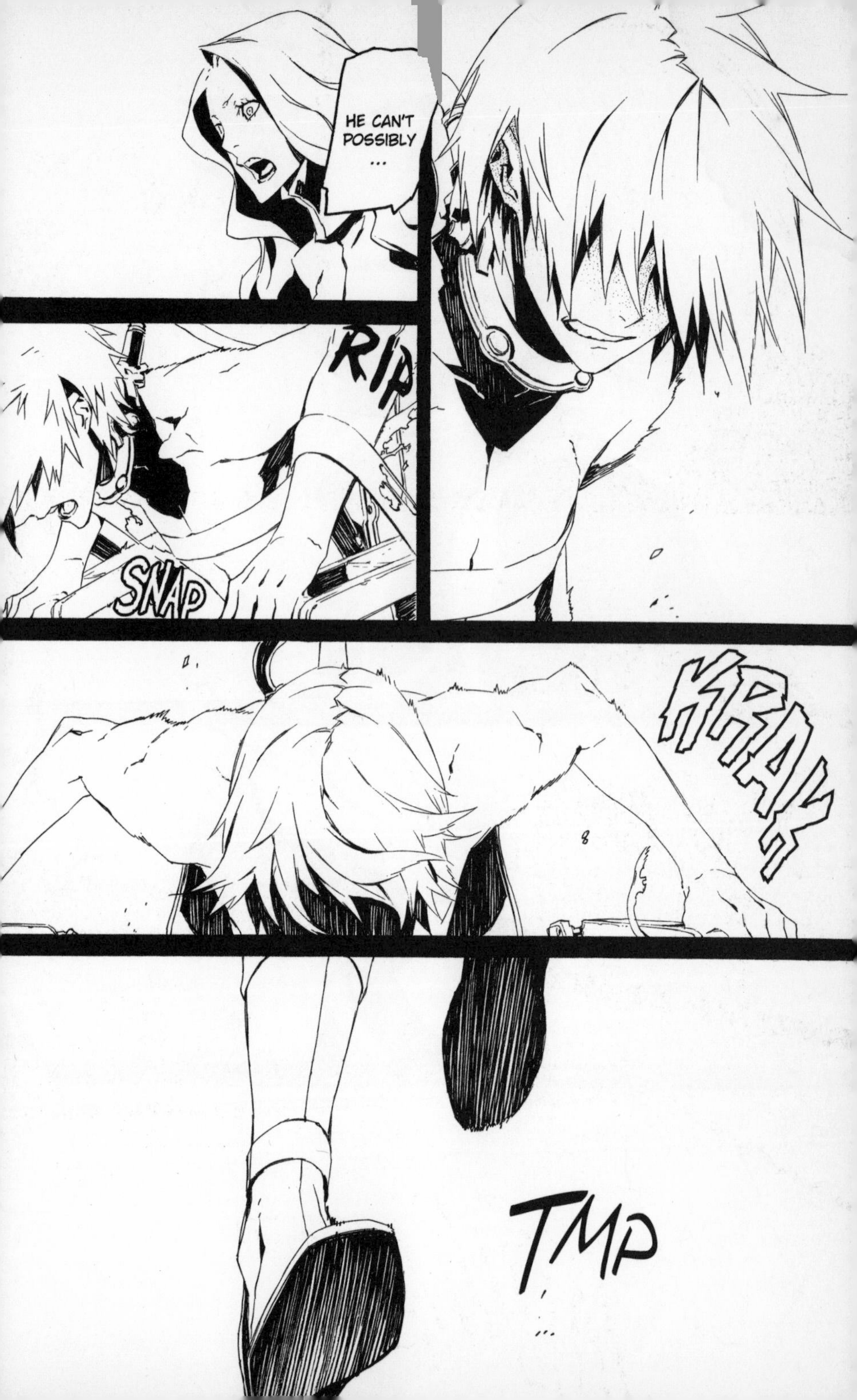
HE CAN'T POSSIBLY ...
RIP
SNAP
KRAK
TMP
...

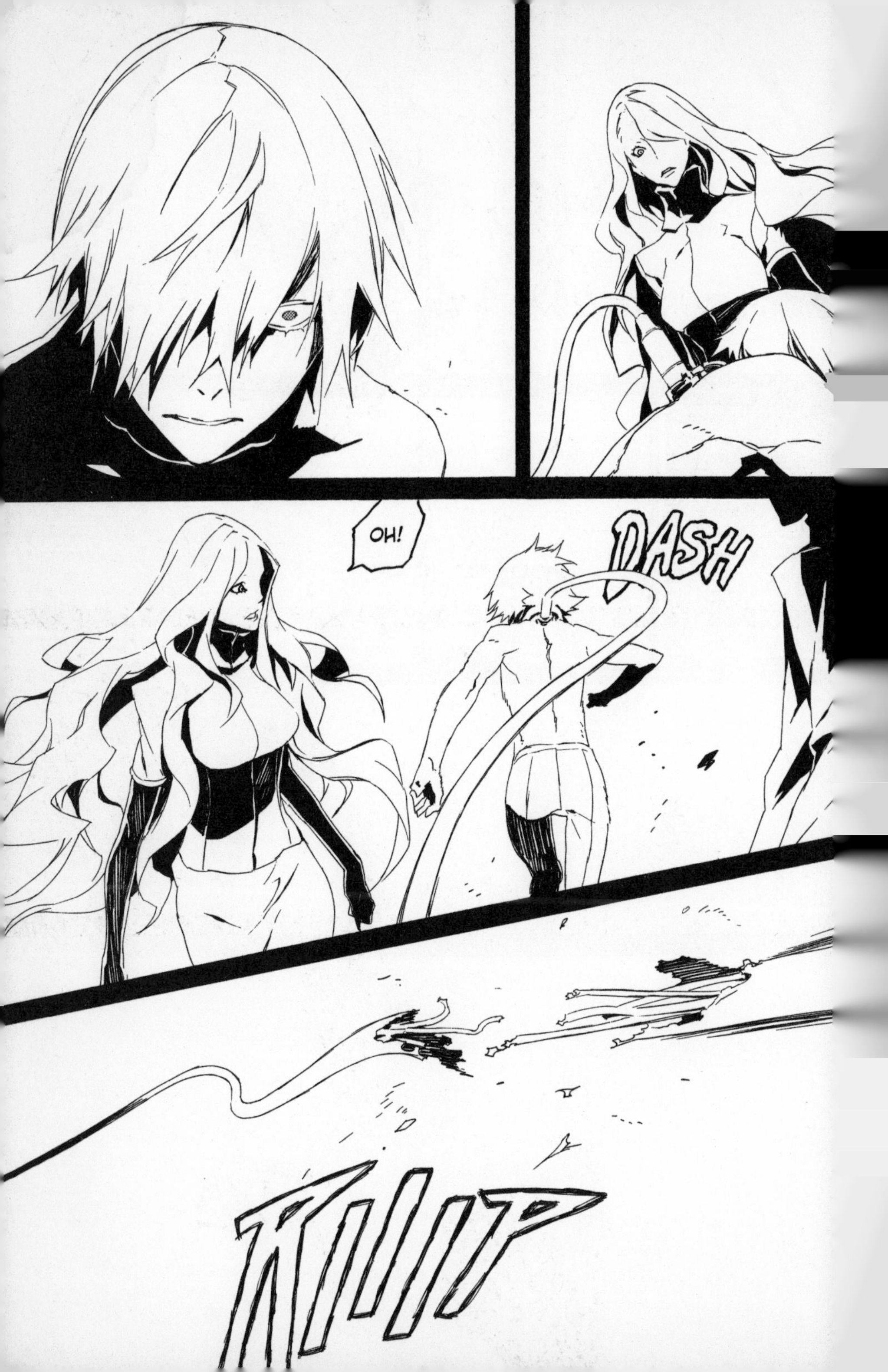
OH!
DASH
RIIIP

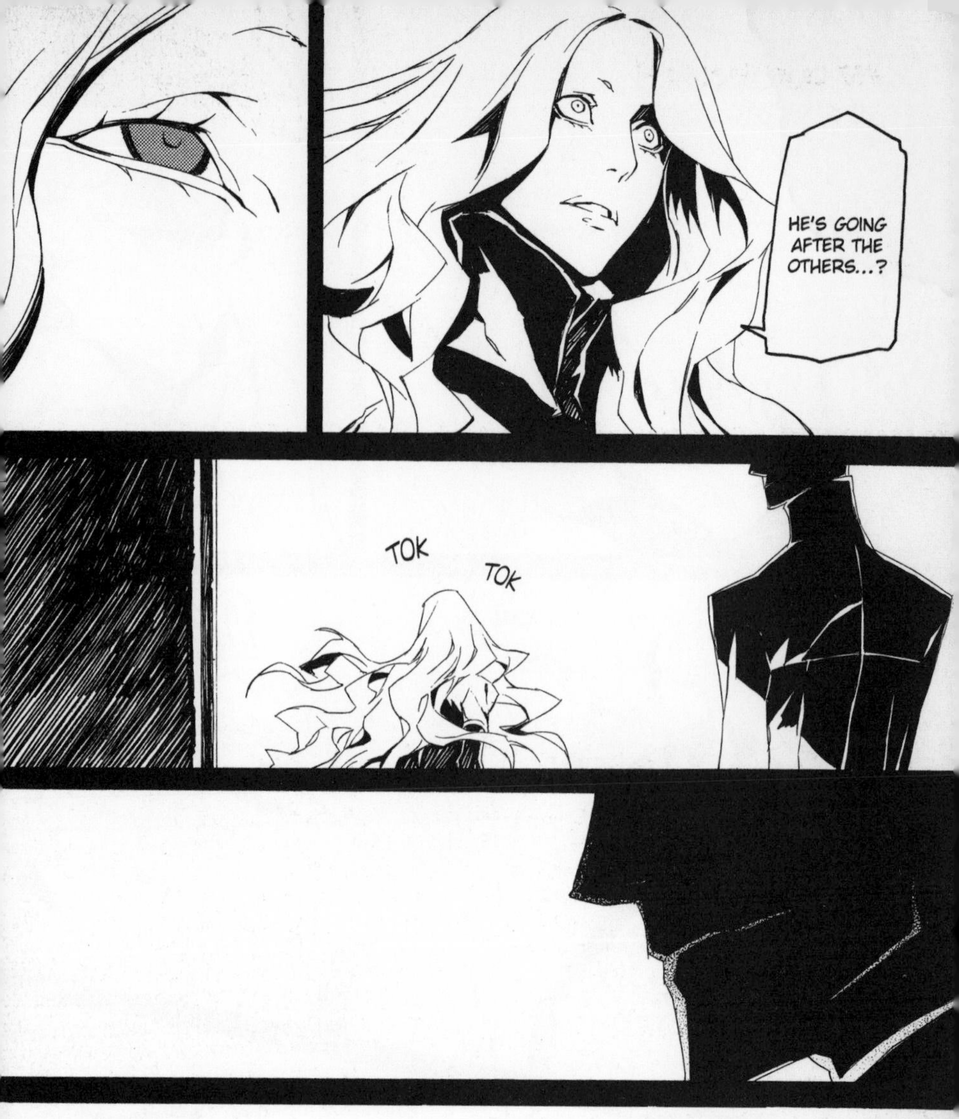
HE'S GOING AFTER THE OTHERS...?
TOK
TOK

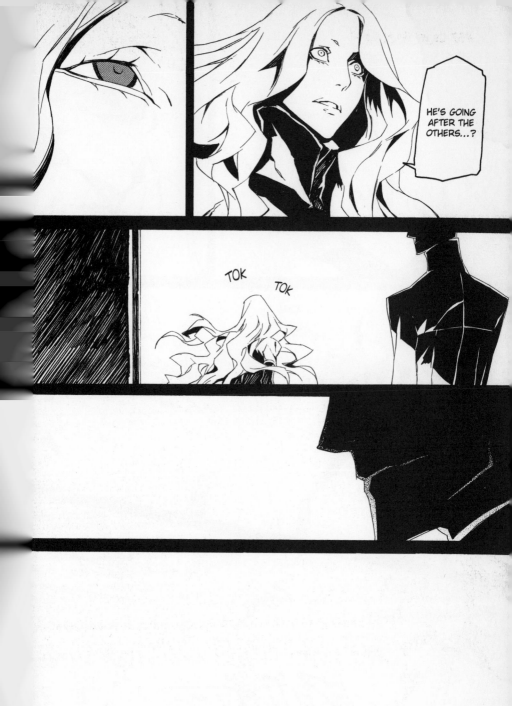

# #57 Cage & Puppies VI

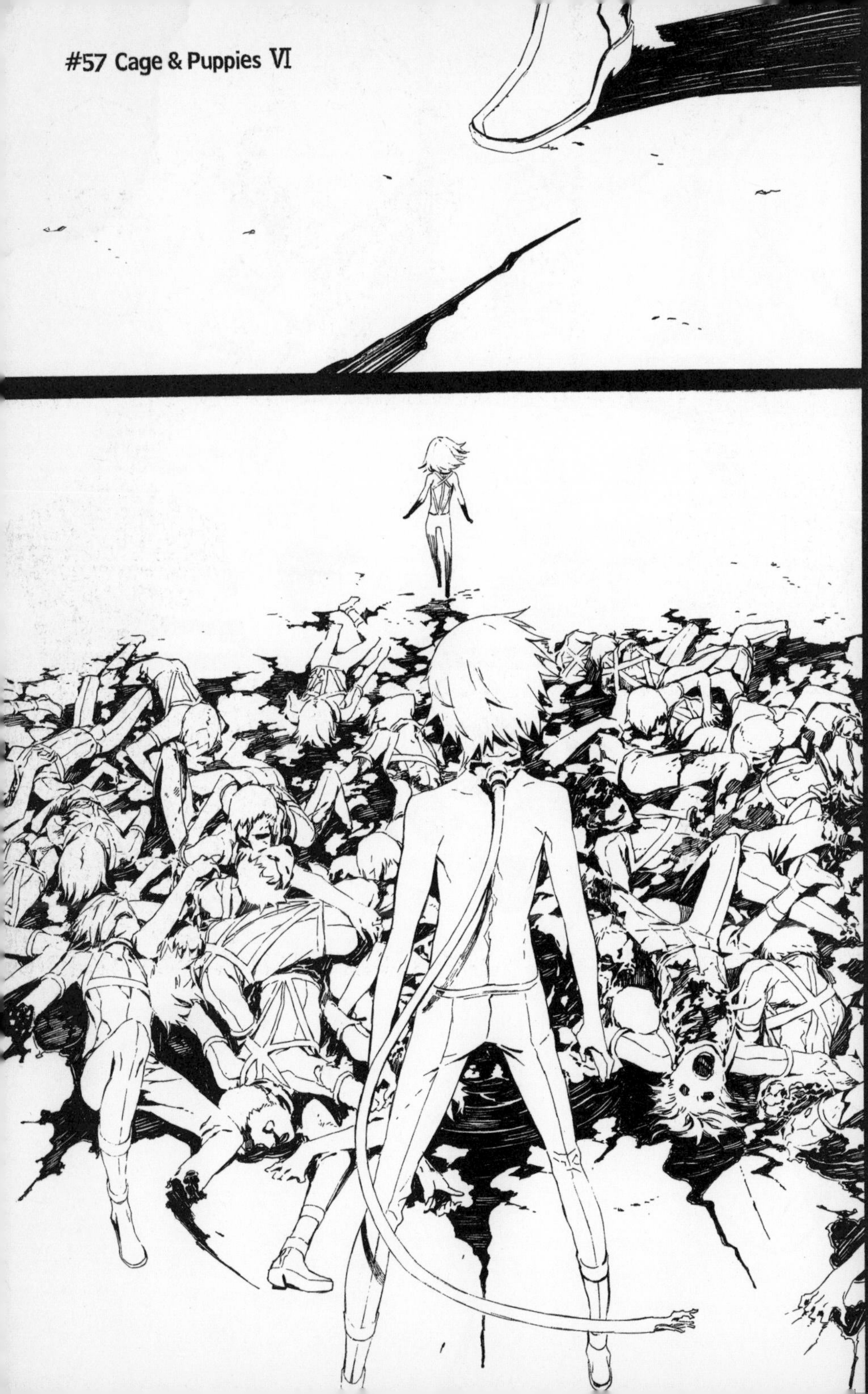

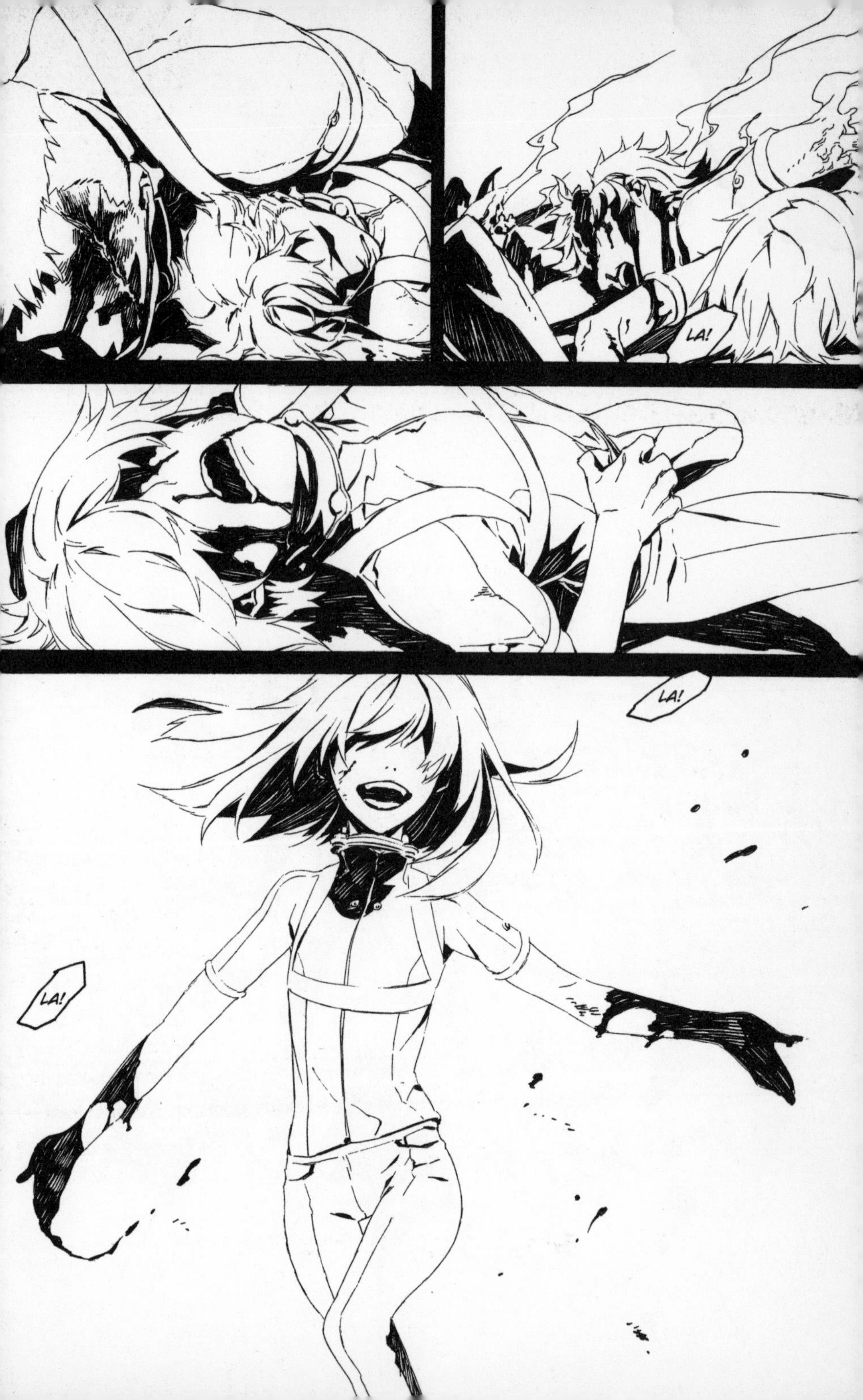
LA!
LA!
LA!

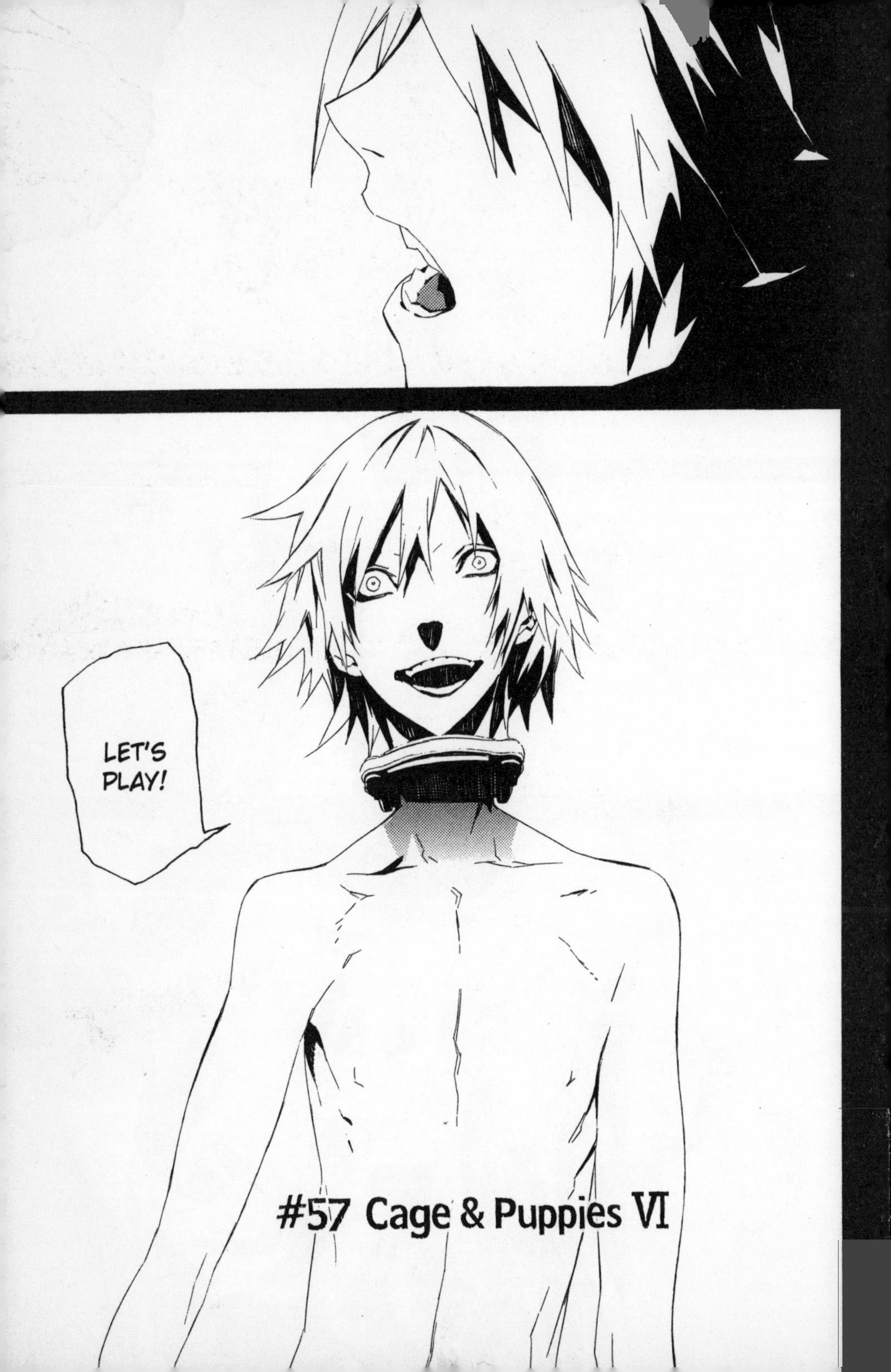
LET'S PLAY!
#57 Cage & Puppies VI

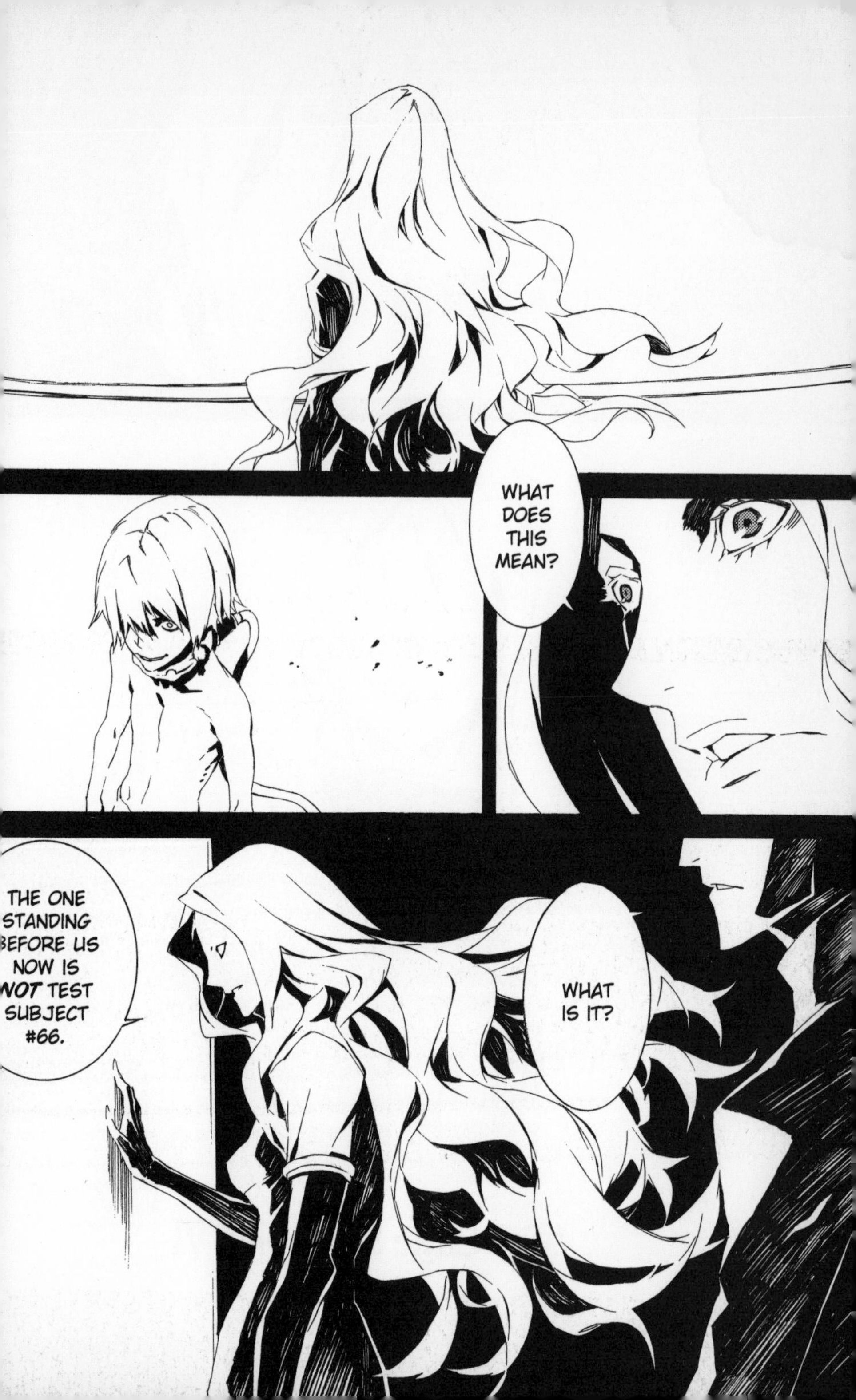
WHAT DOES THIS MEAN?
WHAT IS IT?
THE ONE STANDING BEFORE US NOW IS *NOT* TEST SUBJECT #66.

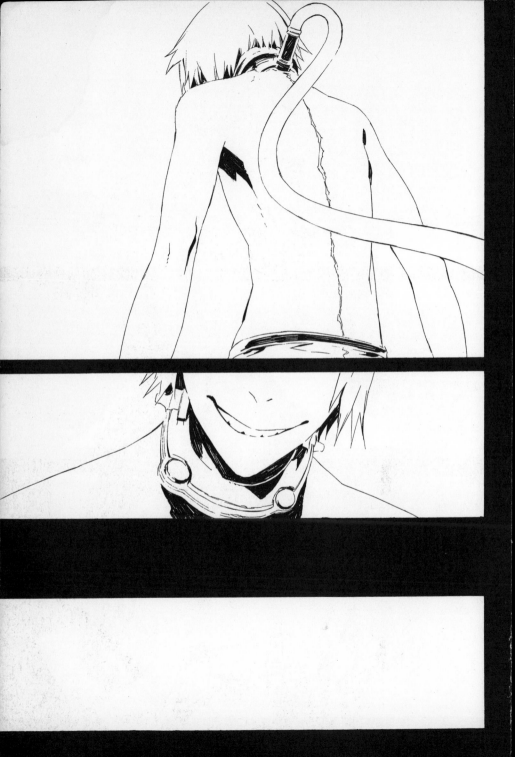

AGAIN...

I CAN'T
SEE
ANYTHING.

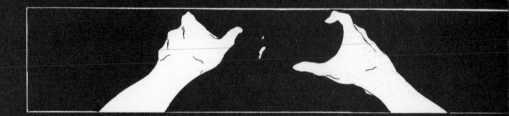

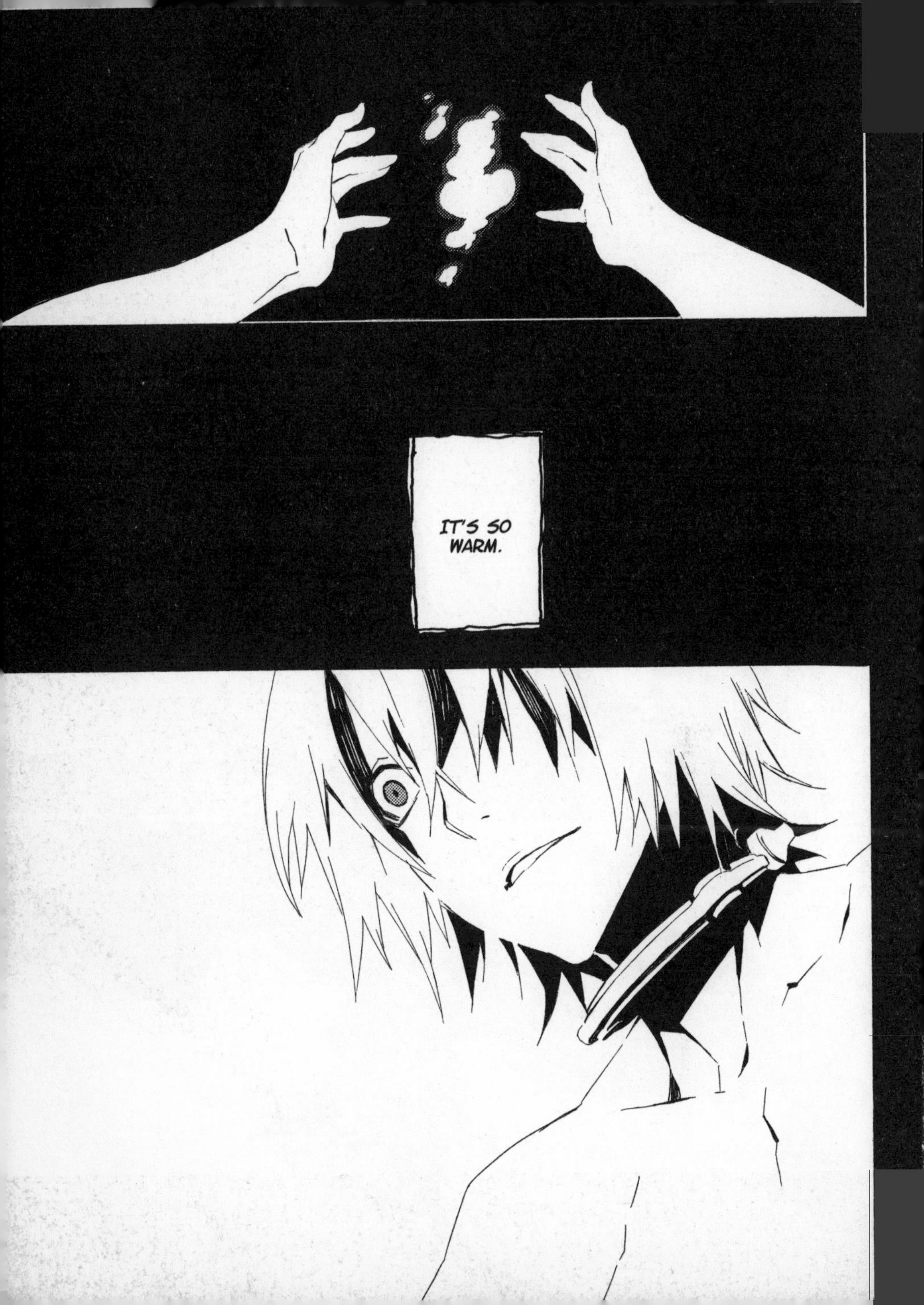
IT'S SO WARM.

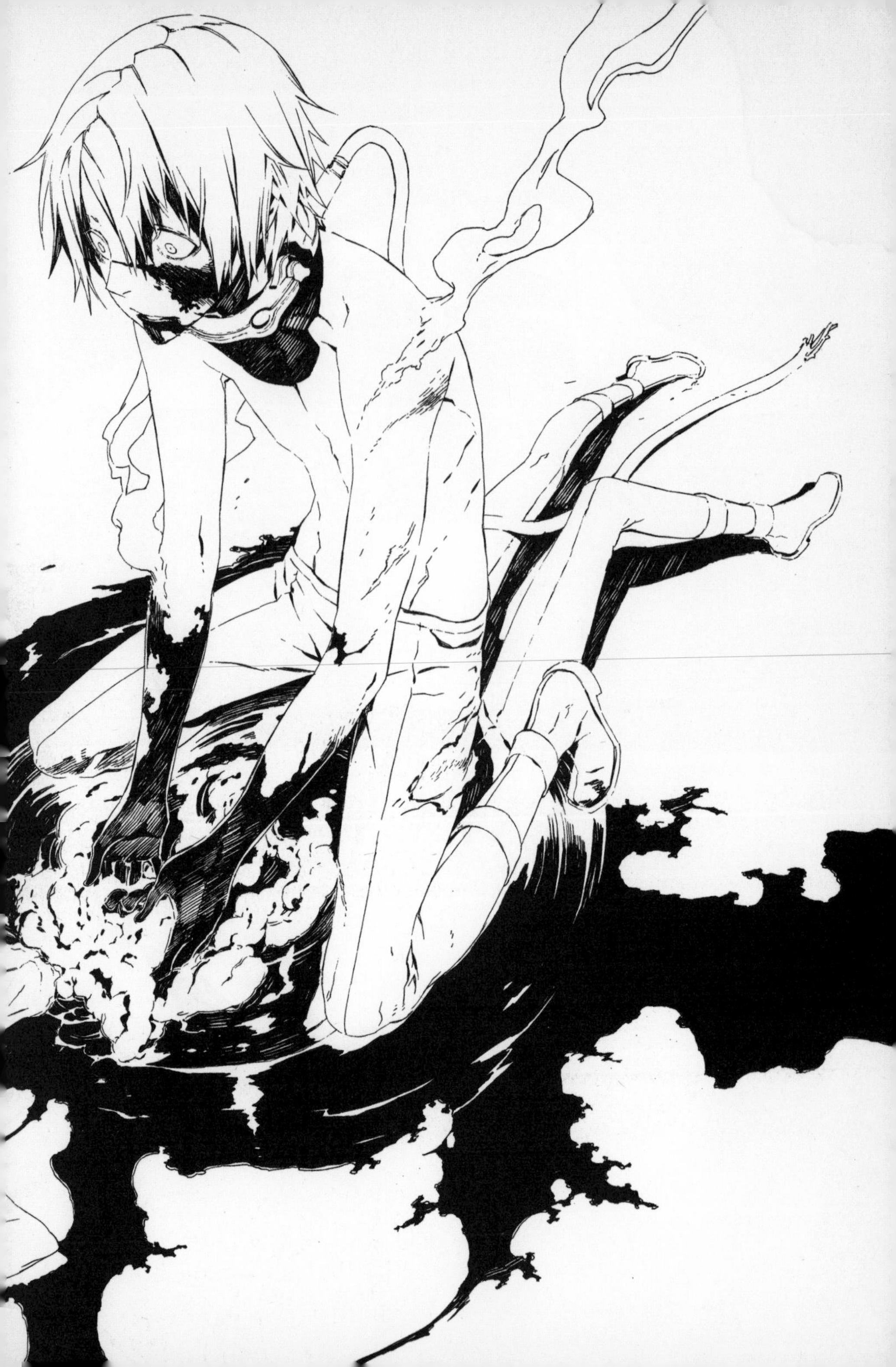

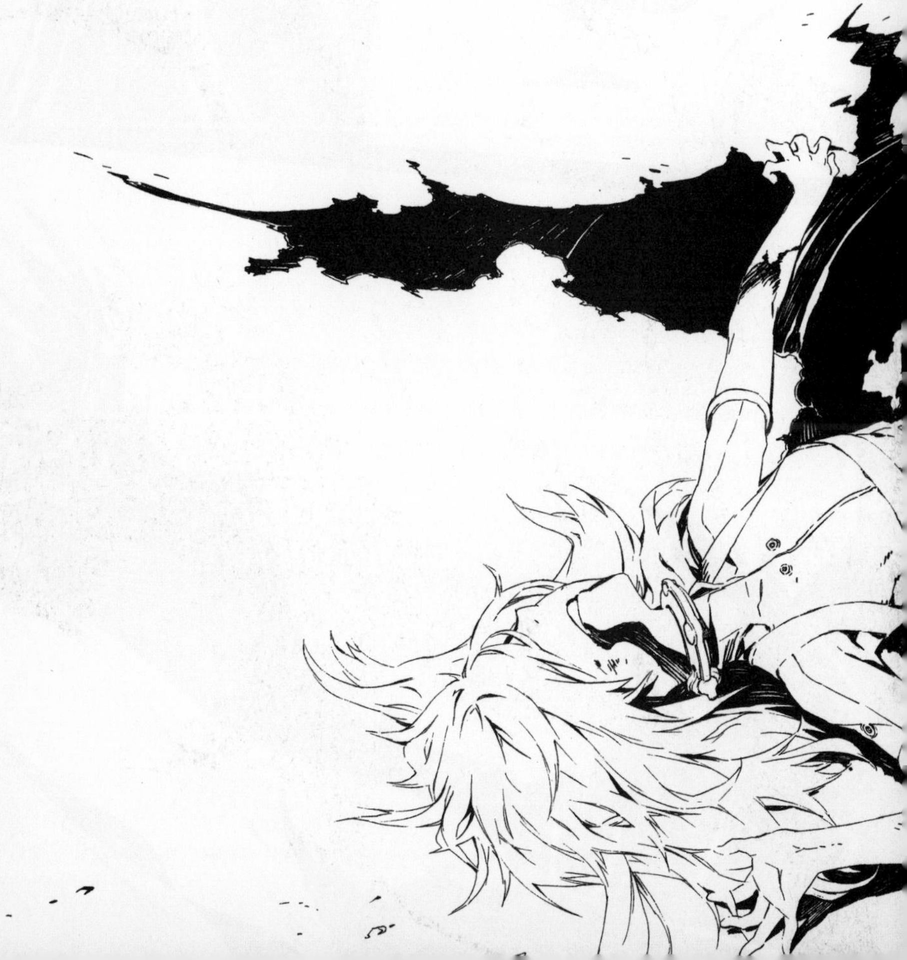

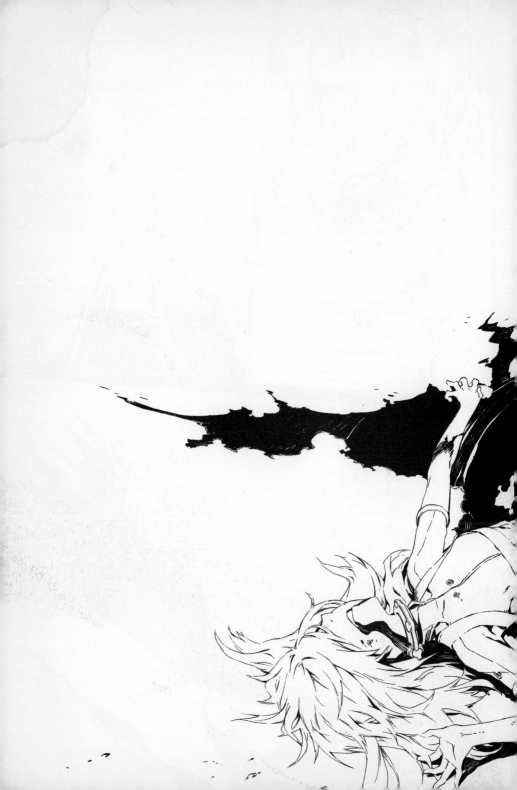

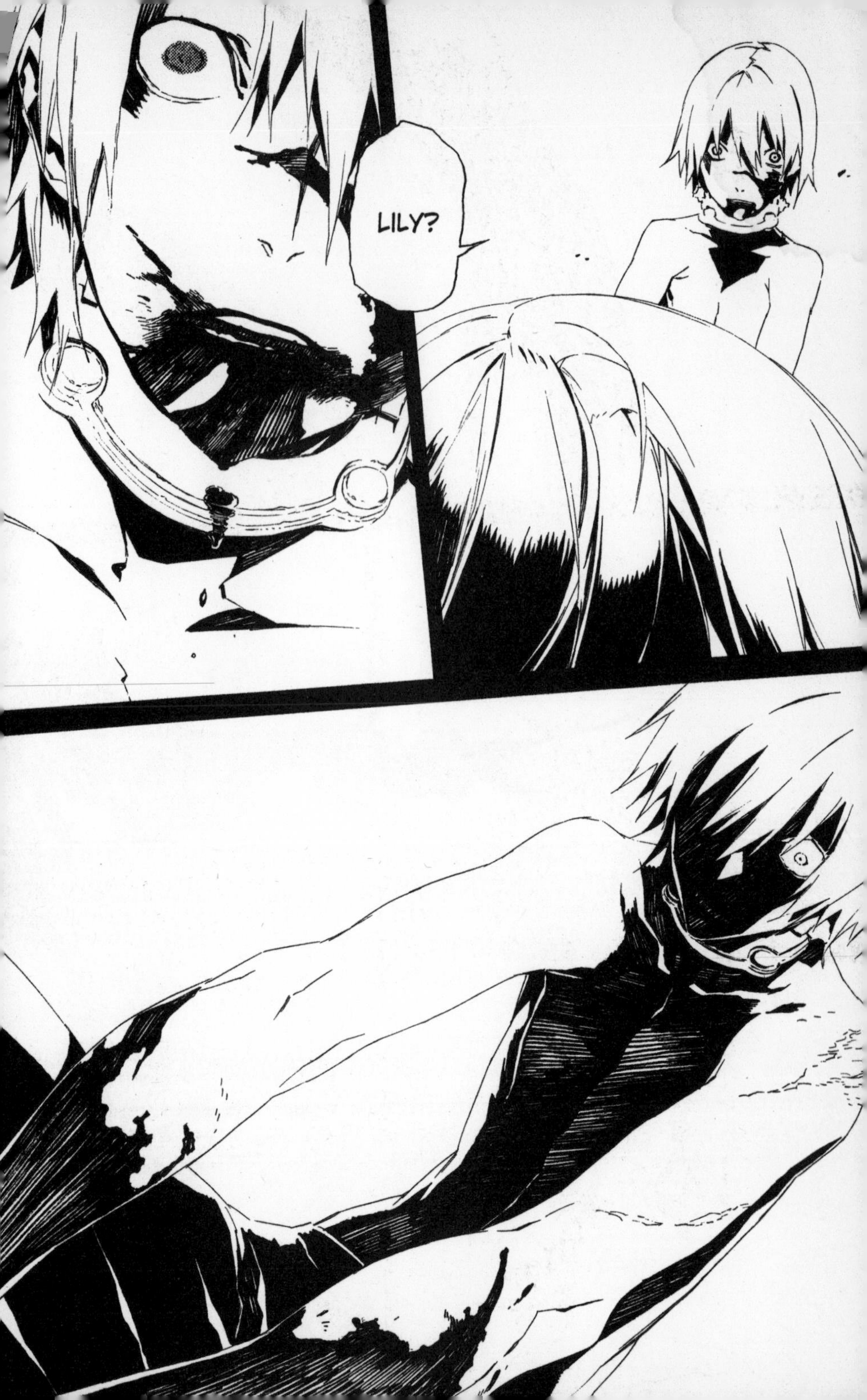
LILY?

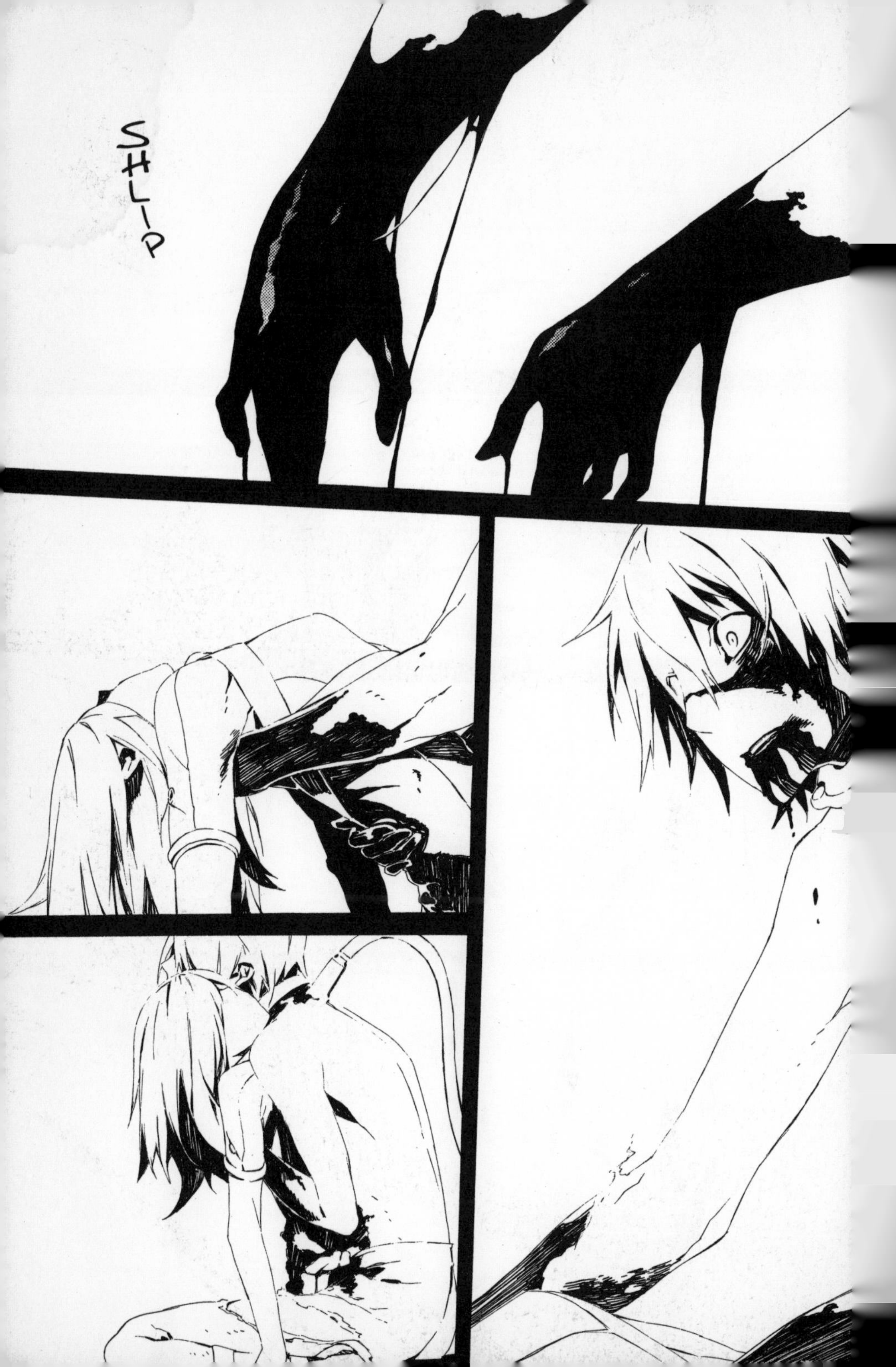
SHLIP

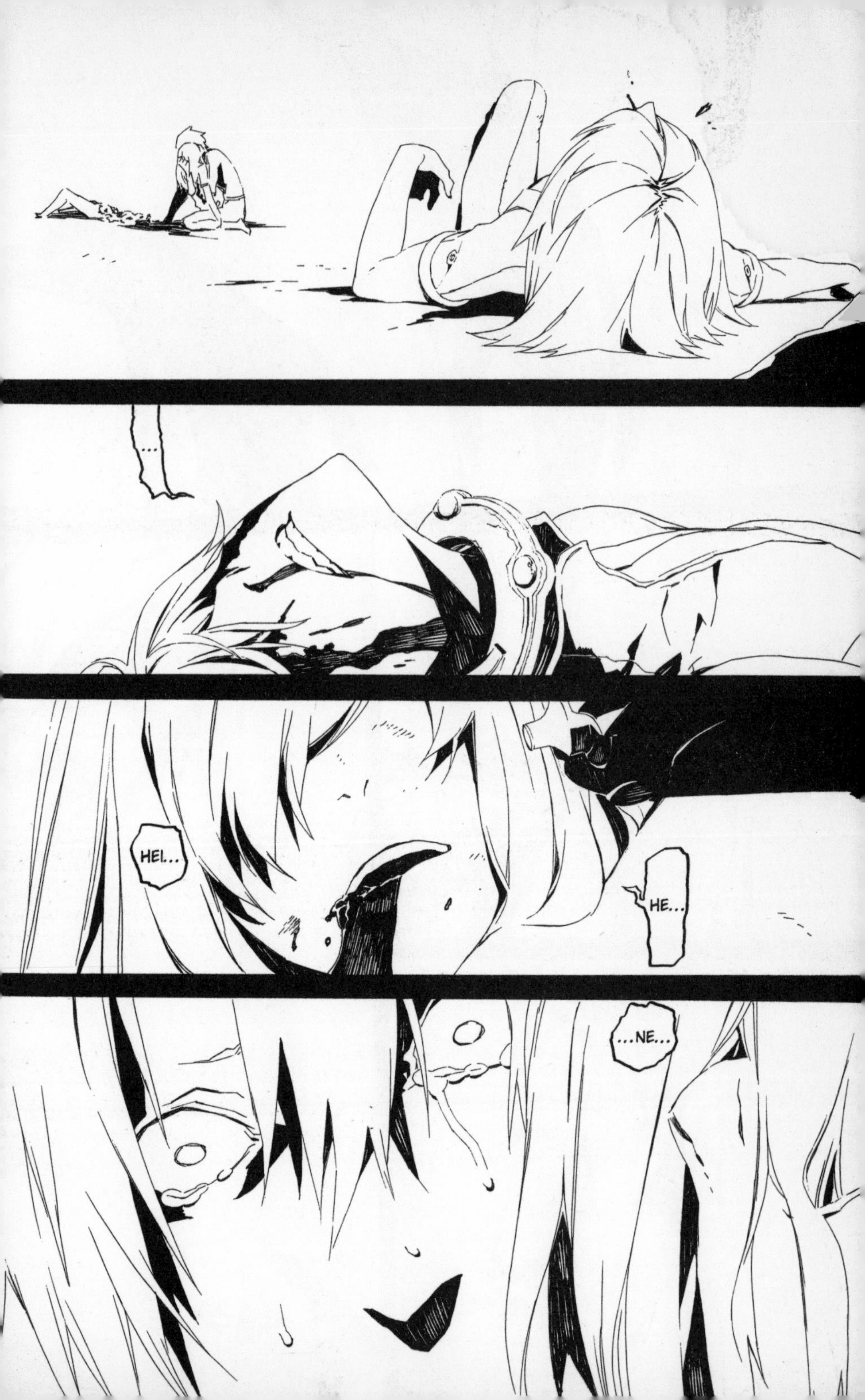
...
HE...
HEI...
...NE...

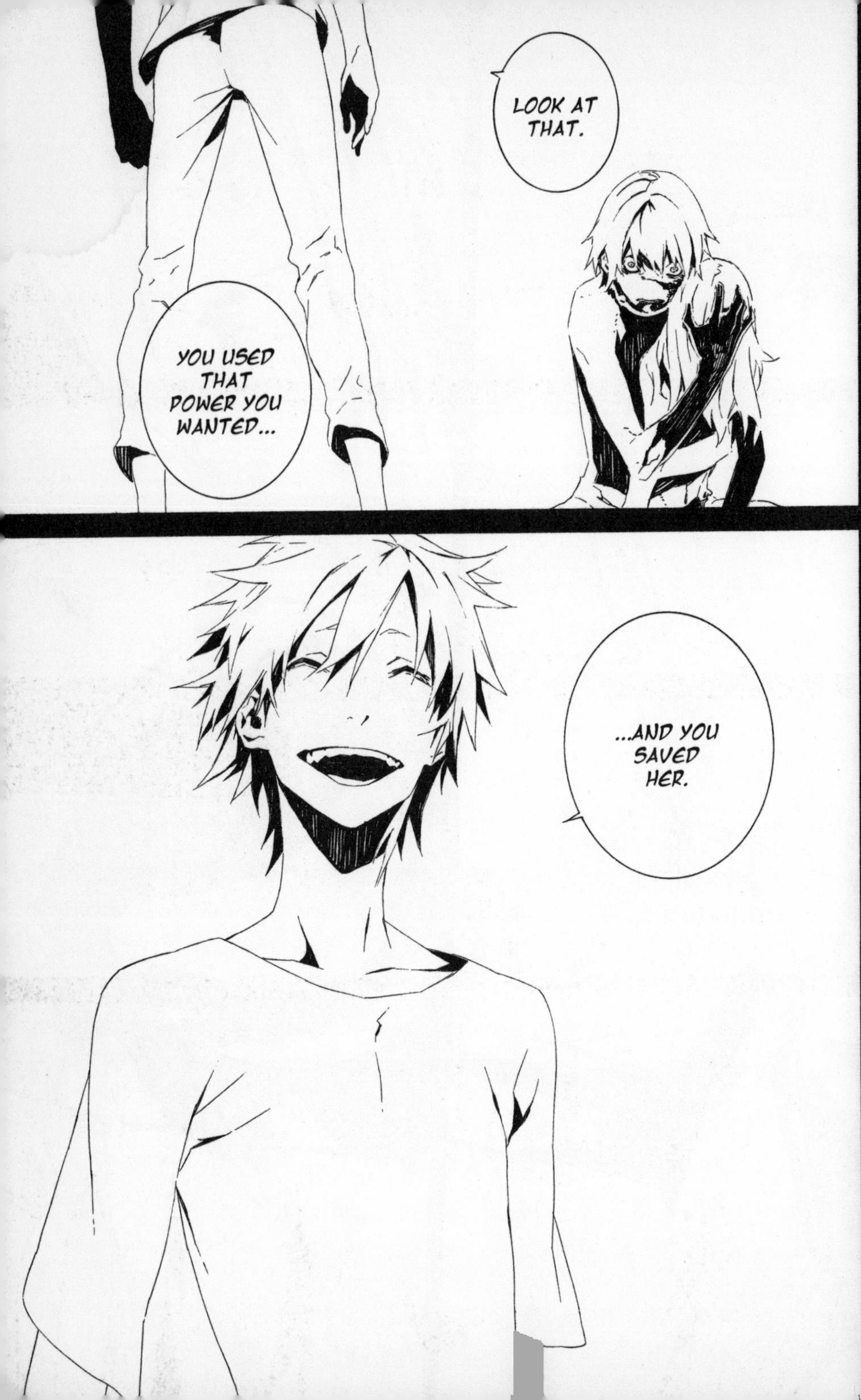
LOOK AT THAT.
YOU USED THAT POWER YOU WANTED...
...AND YOU SAVED HER.

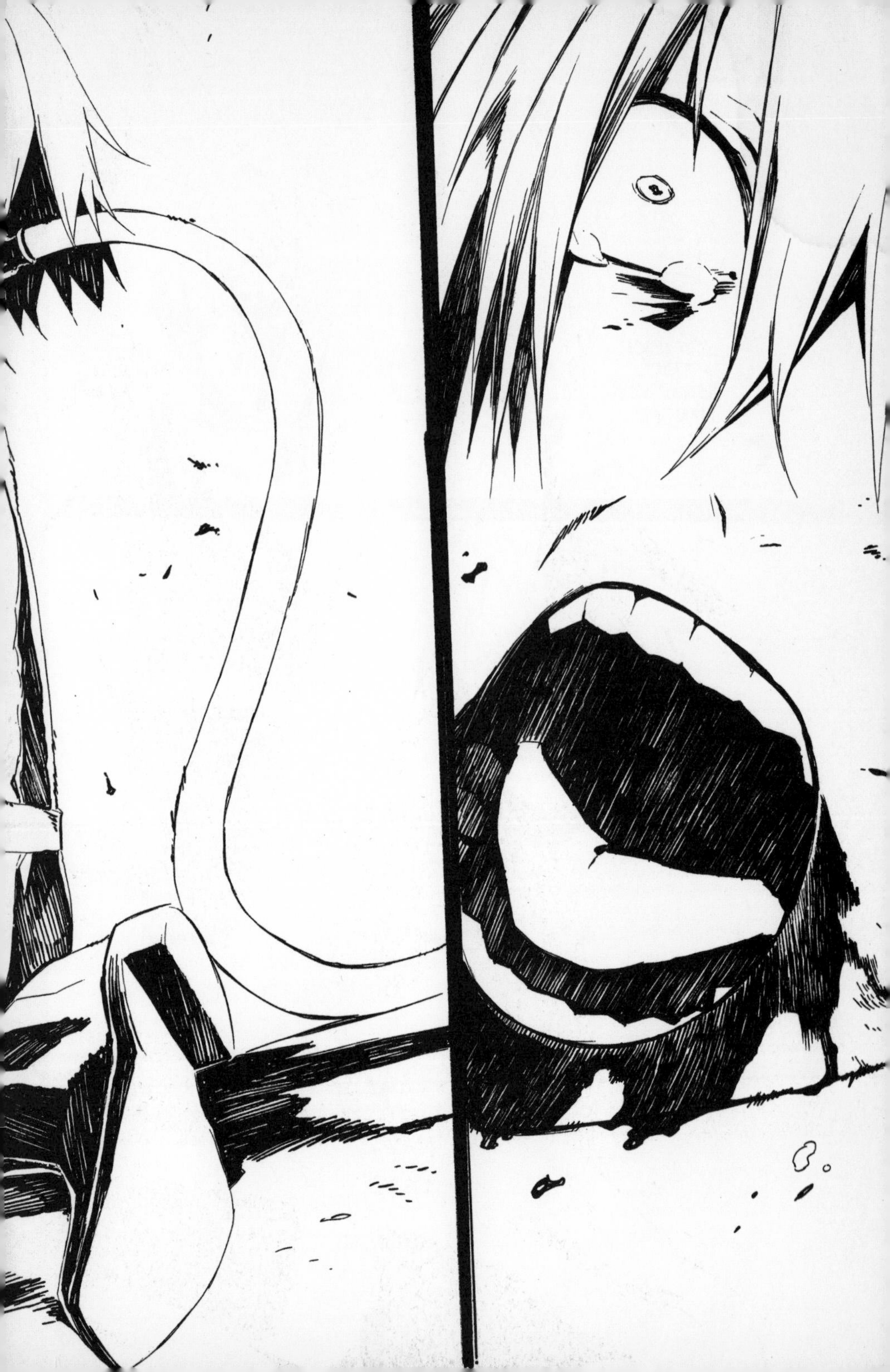

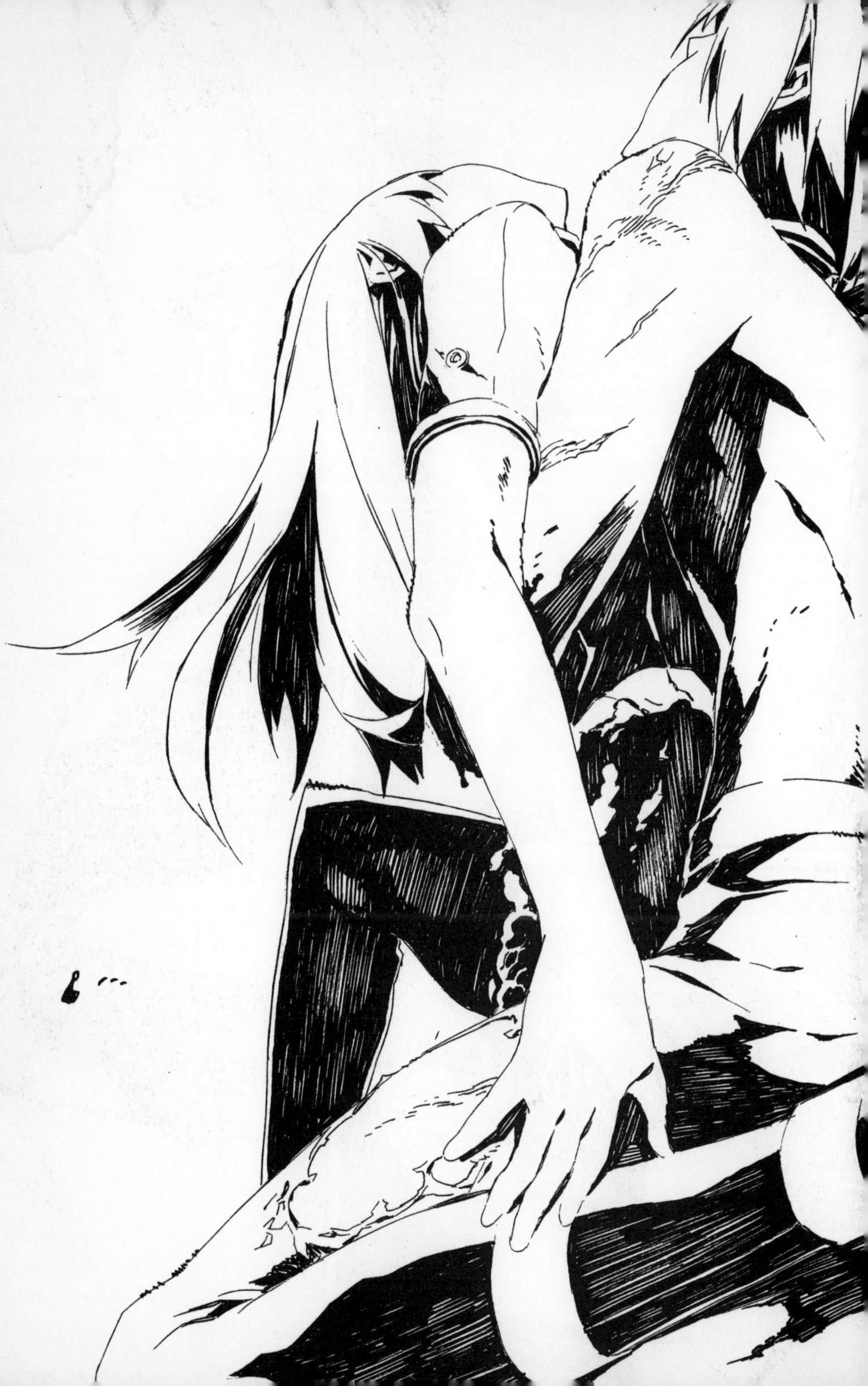

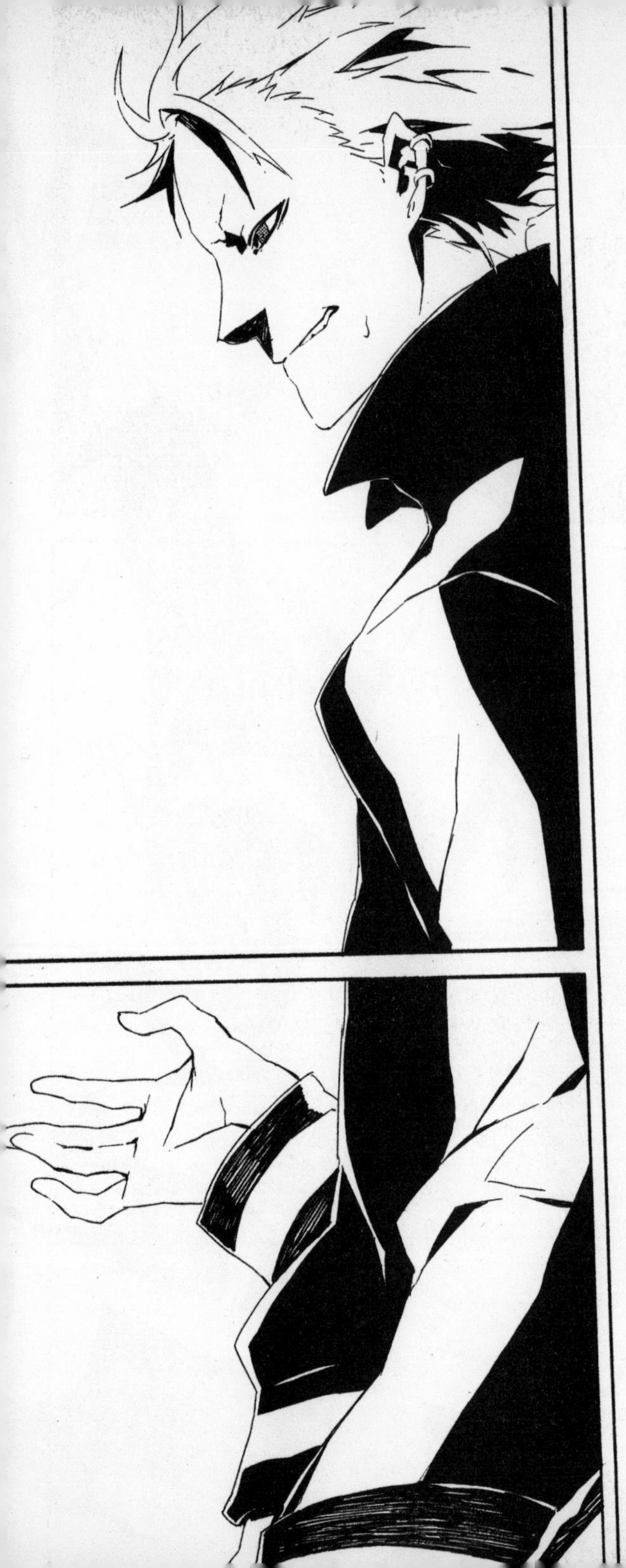

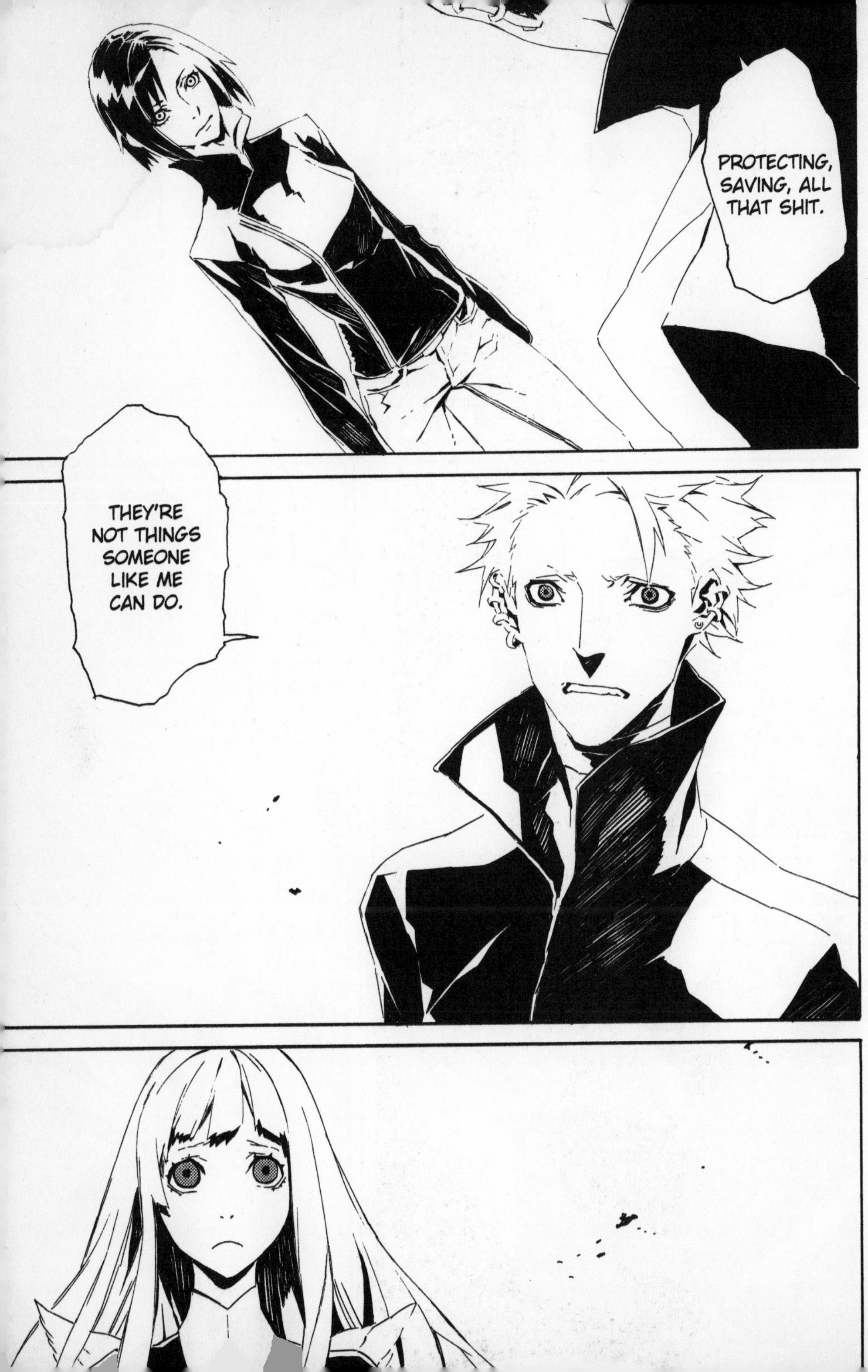
PROTECTING, SAVING, ALL THAT SHIT.
THEY'RE NOT THINGS SOMEONE LIKE ME CAN DO.

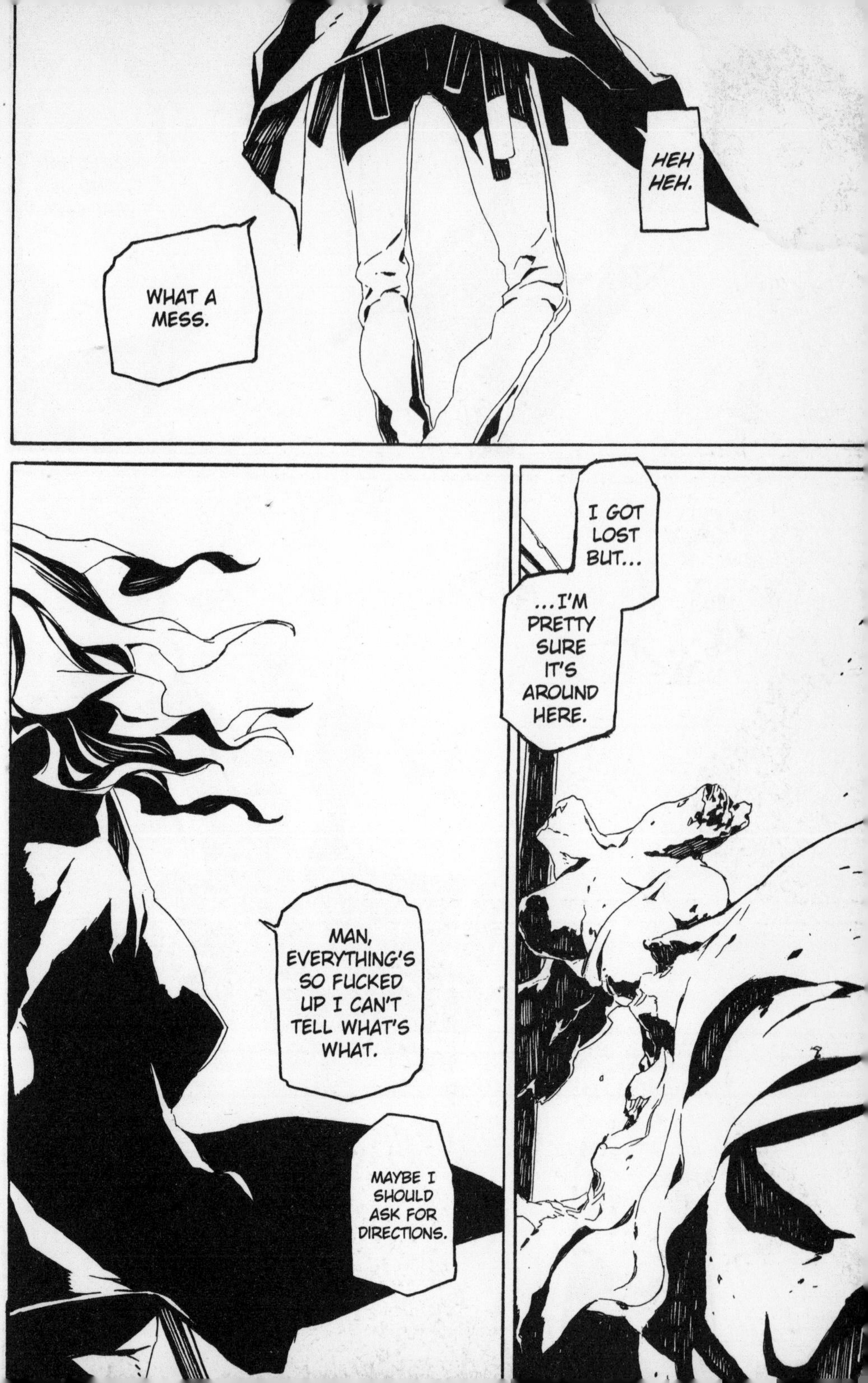
HEH HEH.
WHAT A MESS.
I GOT LOST BUT...
...I'M PRETTY SURE IT'S AROUND HERE.
MAN, EVERYTHING'S SO FUCKED UP I CAN'T TELL WHAT'S WHAT.
MAYBE I SHOULD ASK FOR DIRECTIONS.

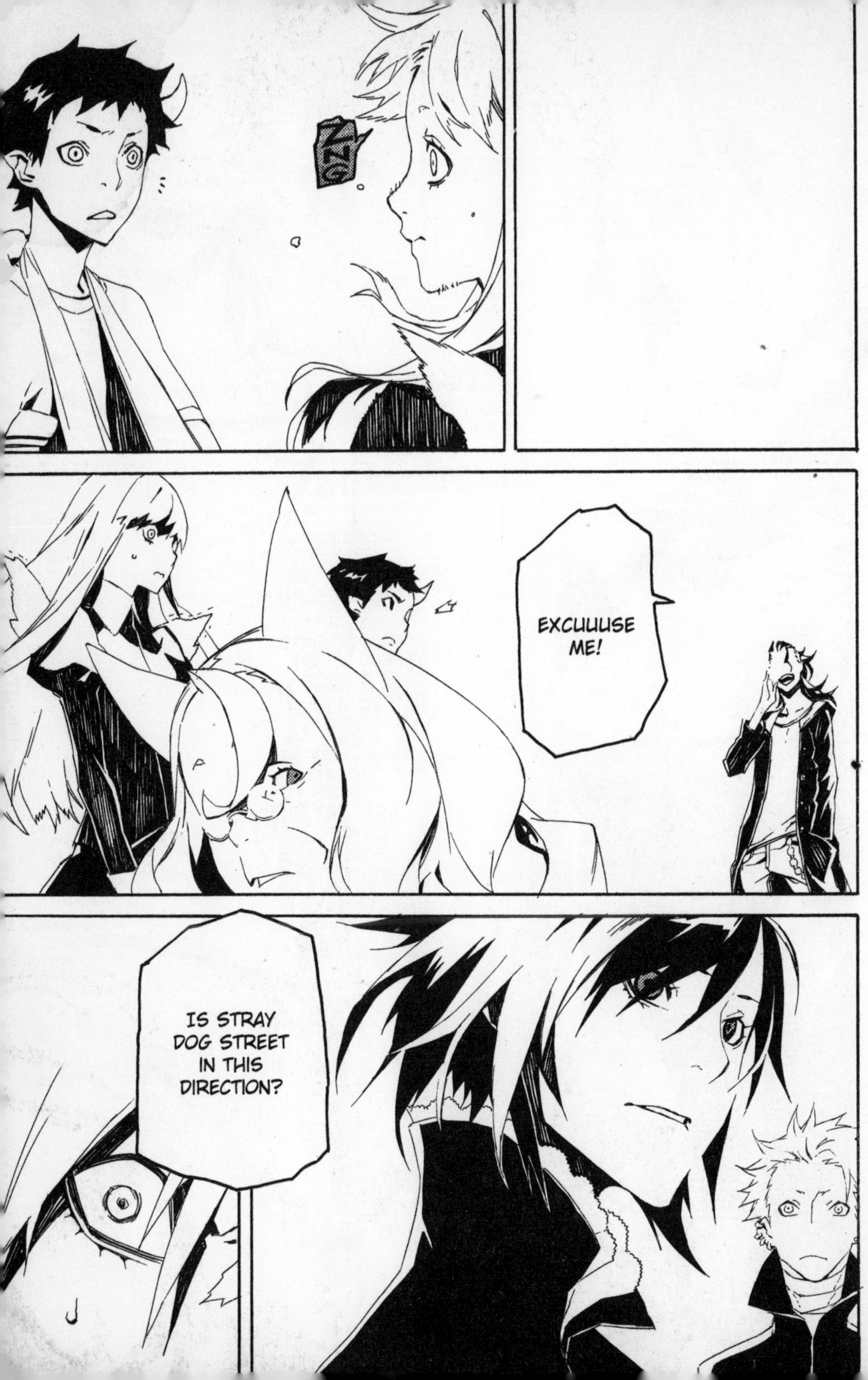
ZNG
EXCUUUSE ME!
IS STRAY DOG STREET IN THIS DIRECTION?

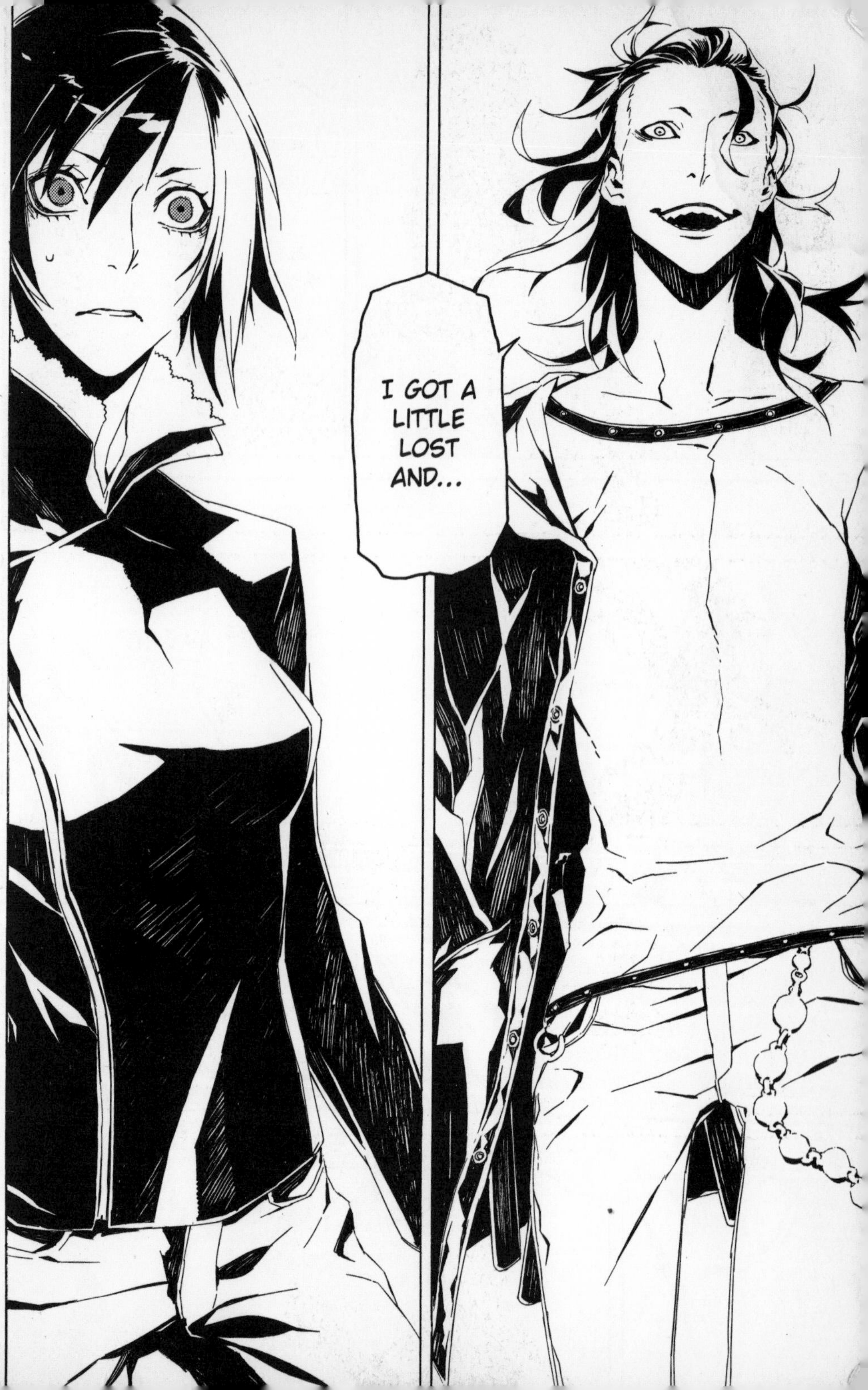
I GOT A LITTLE LOST AND...

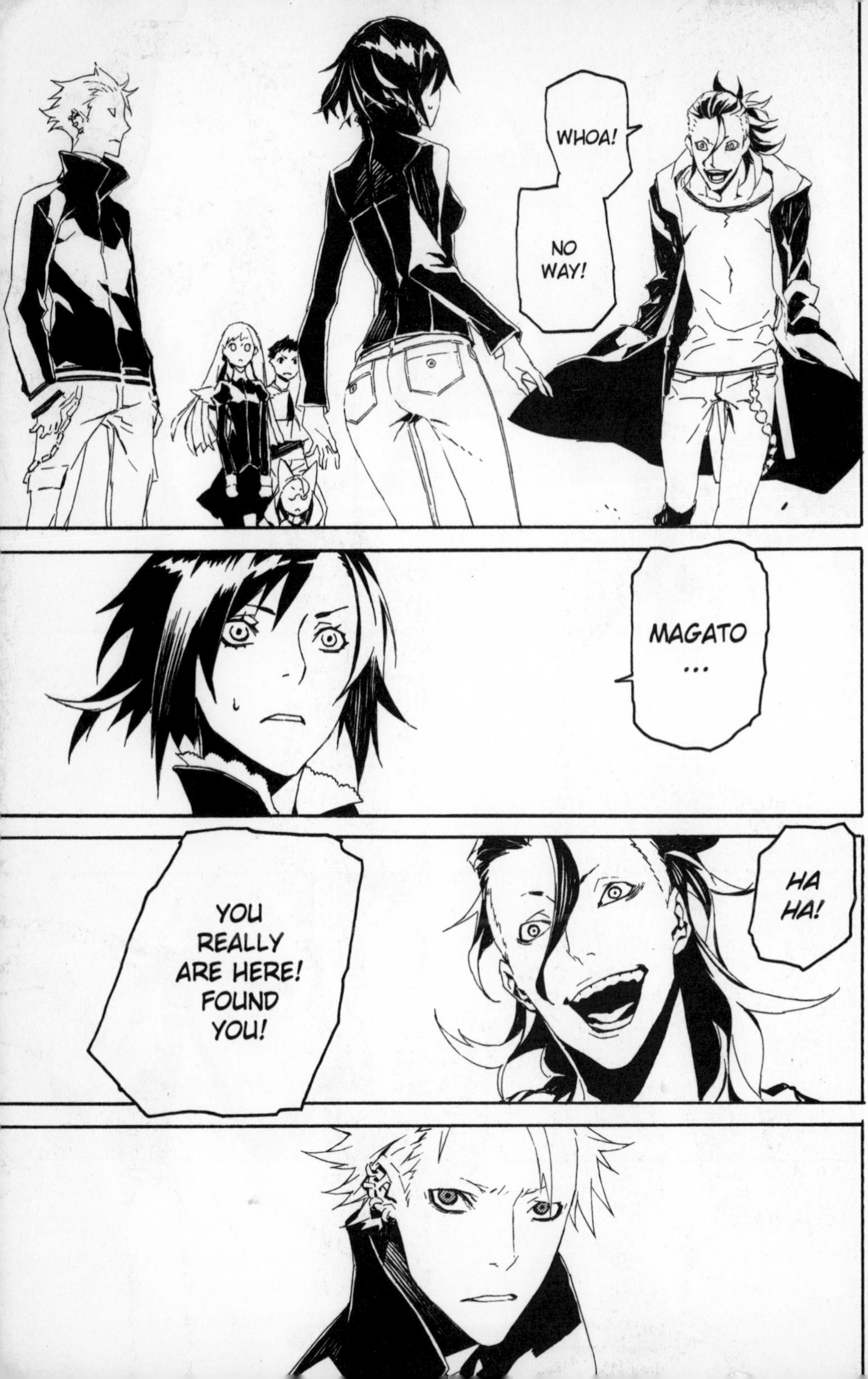
WHOA!
NO WAY!
MAGATO ...
HA HA!
YOU REALLY ARE HERE! FOUND YOU!

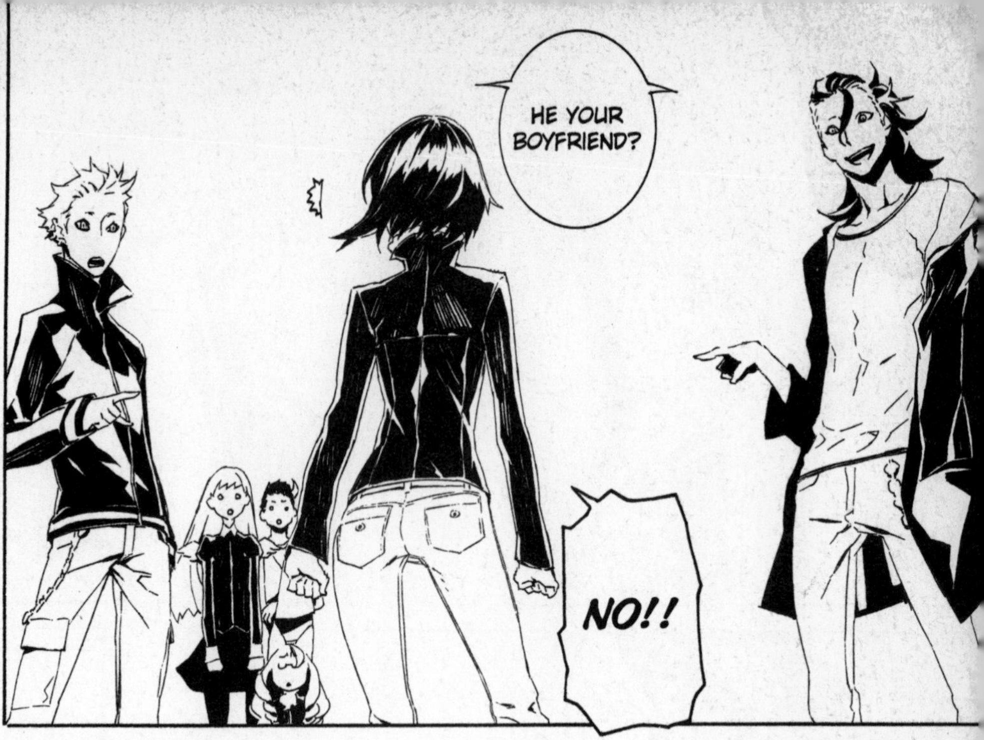
HE YOUR BOYFRIEND?
NO!!

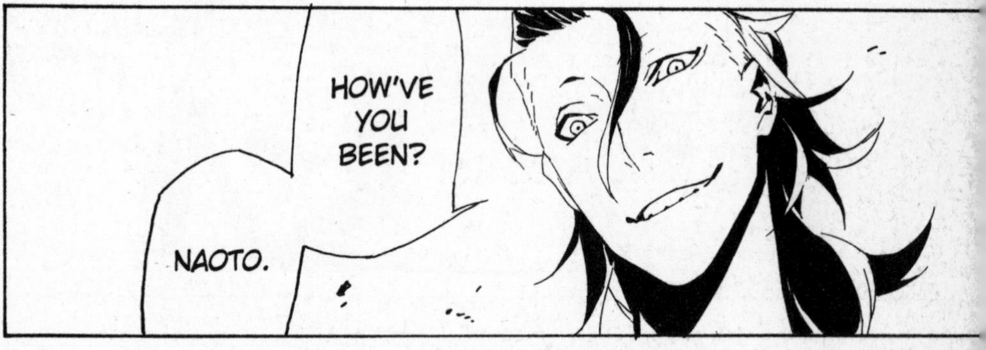
HOW'VE YOU BEEN?
NAOTO.

DOGS BULLETS & CARNAGE 6 / END

TO
BE
CONTINUED

SPECIAL THANKS
Iko Sasagawa
U
Suga

SERIES EDITOR
Satoshi Yamauchi

BOOK EDITOR
Jun Kobayashi

ORIGINAL DESIGN
LIGHTNING

 # ABOUT THE AUTHOR

Shirow Miwa debuted in *UltraJump* magazine in 1999 with the short series *Black Mind*. His next series, *Dogs*, published in the magazine from 2000 to 2001, instantly became a popular success. He returned in 2005 with *Dogs: Bullets & Carnage*, which is currently running in *UltraJump*. Miwa also creates illustrations for books, music videos and magazines, and produces doujinshi (independent comics) under the circle name m.m.m.WORKS. His website is http://mmm-gee.net.

# DOGS: BULLETS & CARNAGE
# Volume 6

VIZ Signature Edition

Story & Art by
SHIROW MIWA

Translation & Adaptation/Katherine Schilling
Touch-up Art & Lettering/Eric Erbes
Cover & Graphic Design/Sam Elzway
Editor/Leyla Aker

Printed in the U.S.A.

Published by VIZ Media, LLC
P.O. Box 77010
San Francisco, CA 94107

10 9 8 7 6 5 4 3 2 1
First printing, November 2011

 **VIZ SIGNATURE**

www.viz.com

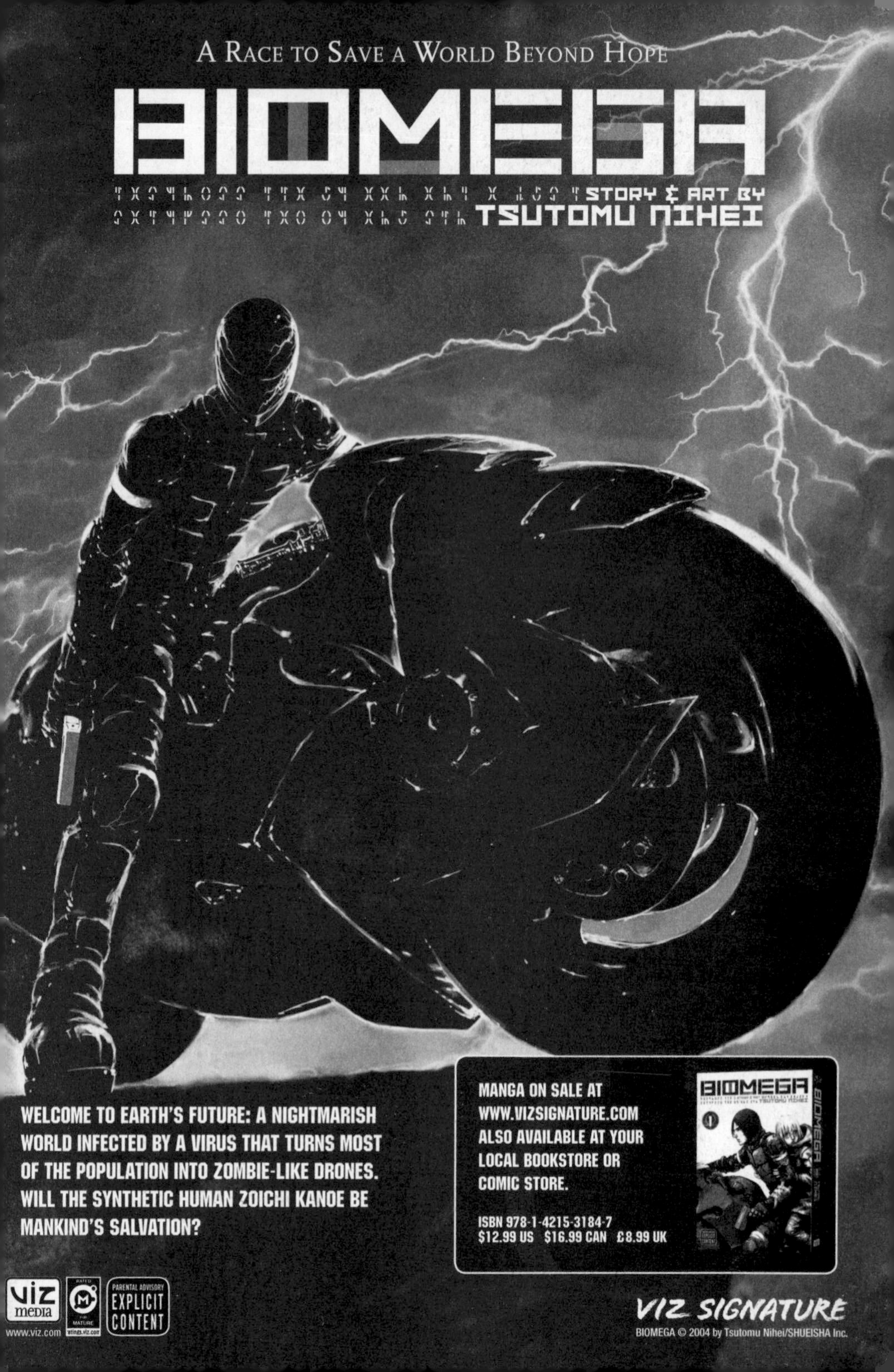
A Race to Save a World Beyond Hope
BIOMEGA
STORY & ART BY
TSUTOMU NIHEI
WELCOME TO EARTH'S FUTURE: A NIGHTMARISH WORLD INFECTED BY A VIRUS THAT TURNS MOST OF THE POPULATION INTO ZOMBIE-LIKE DRONES. WILL THE SYNTHETIC HUMAN ZOICHI KANOE BE MANKIND'S SALVATION?
MANGA ON SALE AT WWW.VIZSIGNATURE.COM
ALSO AVAILABLE AT YOUR LOCAL BOOKSTORE OR COMIC STORE.
ISBN 978-1-4215-3184-7
$12.99 US $16.99 CAN £8.99 UK
BIOMEGA
viz media
www.viz.com
PARENTAL ADVISORY
EXPLICIT CONTENT
VIZ SIGNATURE
BIOMEGA © 2004 by Tsutomu Nihei/SHUEISHA Inc.

Hey, you're reading the wrong way.

**Badou's right—this is actually the end of the book.**

**To properly enjoy this VIZ graphic novel, please turn it over and begin reading the pages from right to left, starting at the upper right corner of each page and ending at the lower left.**

**This book has been printed in the Japanese format (right to left) instead of the English format (left to right) in order to preserve the original orientation of the artwork and stay true to the artist's intent. So please flip it over—and have fun.**